Religions in Asian America

Critical Perspectives on Asian Pacific Americans Series

Books in the series will educate and inform readers in the academy, in Asian American communities, and the general public regarding Asian Pacific American experiences. They examine key social, economic, psychological, cultural, and political issues. Theoretically innovative, engaging, comparative, and multidisciplinary, these books reflect the contemporary issues that are of critical importance to understanding and empowering Asian Pacific Americans.

Series Titles Include

Diana Ting Liu Wu, *Asian Pacific Americans in the Workplace* (1997)

Juanita Tamayo Lott, *Asian Americans: From Racial Category to Multiple Identities* (1997)

Jun Xing, *Asian America through the Lens: History, Representations, and Identity* (1998)

Pyong Gap Min and Rose Kim, editors, *Struggle for Ethnic Identity: Narratives by Asian American Professionals* (1999)

Wendy Ho, *In Her Mother's House: The Politics of Asian American Mother Daughter Writing* (2000)

Deborah Woo, *Glass Ceilings and Asian Americans: The New Face of Workplace Barriers* (2000)

Patricia Wong Hall and Victor M. Hwang, editors, *Anti-Asian Violence in North America: Asian American and Asian Canadian Reflections on Hate, Healing, and Resistance* (2001)

Pyong Gap Min and Jung Ha Kim, editors, *Religions in Asian America: Building Faith Communities* (2002)

Pyong Gap Min, editor, *The Second Generation: Ethnic Identity among Asian Americans* (2002)

Submission Guidelines

Prospective authors of single or co-authored books and editors of anthologies should submit a letter of introduction, the manuscript or a four- to ten-page proposal, a book outline, and a curriculum vitae to:

Critical Perspectives on Asian Pacific Americans Series
AltaMira Press
1630 North Main Street, #367
Walnut Creek, CA 94596

May. 8.07

Religions in Asian America

Building Faith Communities

EDITED BY

PYONG GAP MIN AND JUNG HA KIM

ALTAMIRA
PRESS

A Division of Rowman & Littlefield Publishers, Inc.
Walnut Creek • Lanham • New York • Oxford

ALTAMIRA PRESS

A Division of Rowman & Littlefield Publishers, Inc.
1630 North Main Street, #367
Walnut Creek, CA 94596
www.altamirapress.com

Rowman & Littlefield Publishers, Inc.
4720 Boston Way
Lanham, MD 20706

12 Hid's Copse Road
Cumnor Hill, Oxford OX2 9JJ, England

British Library Cataloguing in Publication Information Available

Library of Congress Cataloging-in-Publication Data

Min, Pyong Gap, 1942-
    Religions in Asian America : building faith communities / Pyong Gap Min and Jung Ha Kim.
        p. cm.
    Includes bibliographical references and index.
    ISBN 0-7591-0082-9 (alk. paper)—ISBN 0-7591-0083-7 (pbk. : alk. paper)
    1. Asian Americans—Religion. 2. United States—Religion—20th century. I. Kim, Jung
Ha. II. Title.

BL2525 .M56 2002
200'.89'95073—dc21   2001022788

Printed in the United States of America

CONTENTS

CONTENTS

INTRODUCTION

Pyong Gap Min

The permanent settlement of Europeans in the United States started in 1620 when 102 English Pilgrims from Holland arrived at Plymouth. Successive Protestant immigrant groups, mostly from northwestern European countries, followed the pilgrims in settling in the American colonies and subsequently in the independent republic until the mid-nineteenth century. These Protestant immigrant groups represented a wide range of denominations: Presbyterian, Methodist, Baptist, Congregational, Lutheran, the Church of God, the Assembly of God, and so forth. Yet the various Protestant denominations shared many similarities in religious faith and rituals, enough similarities to make them the Protestant mainstream.

Irish Catholics, who began to move in large numbers in the 1840s, composed the first major non-Protestant immigrant group in the United States. During the mass migration period between 1880 and 1930, large numbers of Catholic, Jewish, and Eastern Orthodox Christian immigrants joined Irish Catholics in crossing the Atlantic for permanent or temporary settlement in the United States. They originated largely from southern and eastern European countries. This influx of nearly twenty million Irish and southeastern, non-Protestant immigrants between 1840 and 1930 contributed greatly to religious and ethnic diversity in the United States.[1] By 1920, Catholics accounted for 21 percent of the white population in the United States and Jews composed nearly 2 percent.[2]

The number of Asian immigrants who moved to the United States before the 1924 Asian Exclusion Act was insignificant, compared to the numbers of Catholic, Jewish, and Eastern Orthodox Christian immigrants. According to Immigration and Naturalization Service data, only about 676,000 people from Asian and Middle Eastern countries immigrated to the United States between 1820 and 1924.[3] Most of them were Chinese and Japanese, with the vast majority settled in the West Coast, especially in Hawaii and California.

However, the transpacific migration of Asians in the nineteenth and early twentieth centuries contributed to religious diversity in the United

States, as Asian countries are homes to several major "Oriental religions," fundamentally different from Judeo-Christian religions. Thailand, China, Vietnam, Korea, and Japan were and still are largely Buddhist countries. The nineteenth-century Chinese immigrants and turn-of-the-century Japanese immigrants transplanted their versions of Buddhism to California, Hawaii, and other western states.[4] Japanese immigrants established the Young Men's Buddhist Association of San Francisco in 1898, which was the first Jodo Shinshu organization in the continental United States.[5]

While Hinduism is the dominant religion in India, Islam, Sikhism, Catholicism, and other religions each have millions of worshippers in various south Asian countries. Minority members in any country have greater proclivity to use the path of international migration than members of the dominant group, whether to improve their economic conditions or to avoid discrimination and/or persecution. Thus, the majority of Indian immigrants to California at the turn of the century were Sikh farmers from the Punjab. To demonstrate their religious commitment, the Sikh farmers wore turbans and did not cut their hair. The first Sikh temple in the United States was established in Stockton, California, in 1912.[6] The white Americans who encountered Sikh farmers in California in the early twentieth century referred to them as "Hindoo," assuming that all Indians were Hindus.[7]

Beginning with the Chinese Exclusion Act of 1882, the U.S. government took various measures to restrict Asian immigration formally.[8] The anti-Asian immigration measures culminated in the Asiatic Exclusion of 1924, which barred Asian immigration for almost sixty years. The Immigration and Nationality Act of 1952 ended the absolute exclusion of Asians and made Asian immigrants eligible for citizenship through naturalization.[9] Yet it still severely restricted Asians' immigration to the United States. Most Asian immigrants admitted between 1945 and 1964 were Asian women who married U.S. servicemen in various Asian countries and who were subsequently admitted as nonquota immigrants. The restrictive measures had kept the Asian American population insignificant until the 1960s; the 1970 census count of the Asian and Pacific Islander population was approximately 1.4 million.

However, the abolition of the national origin quota system in the Harte-Celler Act of 1965, along with several other factors, has resulted in a mass influx of Asian immigrants to the United States. These other factors include close political, military, and economic connections between the United States and several Asian countries (especially the Philippines and Korea), the fall of South Vietnam in 1975, and population explosions in many Asian countries. More than 7 million Asians crossed the Pacific to live in the United States as permanent residents between 1965 and 2000, comprising approximately 25 percent of the immigrants admitted to the

United States during the period.[10] The Philippines has been the second largest source country of post-1965 immigrants, following Mexico. South Korea, China, India, and Vietnam were among the ten largest source countries of immigrants in the 1980s and/or the 1990s. In addition, large numbers of overseas Chinese and Indians who were settled in other Asian countries and/or the Caribbean Islands have remigrated to the United States. As a result of the massive immigration of Asians, the Asian American population increased from 1.5 million in 1970 to 10.5 million in 2000, thus far exceeding the 6 million Jewish people in the United States. Even contemporary Asian immigrants are heavily concentrated on the West Coast with approximately 40 percent , but there are also large Asian populations in such non-Western cities as New York, Chicago, Washington, D.C., Philadelphia, Houston, and Atlanta.

In the post-1965 era, more immigrants have originated from Latin American countries than from Asian countries. Yet new Asian immigrants have made a greater contribution to religious diversity than Latinos. While Latin American countries are predominantly Catholic and partly Protestant, Asian countries are homes to several non-Judeo-Christian religions. The immigrants from India, Pakistan, and other south Asian countries account for a significant proportion of post-1965 Asian immigrants. They, along with Caribbean Indians, have transplanted three major non-Christian religions: Hinduism, Sikhism, and Islam. In the New York–New Jersey metropolitan area alone, nearly fifty Hindu and Sikh temples have mushroomed over the past thirty years. Moreover, approximately 1.5 million Muslims have immigrated from Pakistan and other south Asian countries over the past thirty years. They account for approximately 25 percent of the 6 million Muslim people in the United States in 1999.

The majority of Indo-Chinese refugees and Thai immigrants are Buddhists.[11] Buddhism is the most important religion for Chinese immigrants from various Asian countries as well, although Confucianism has had a greater influence on their family lives and social norms.[12] In this connection, it is important to note that Chinese and Southeast Asian (Indo-Chinese) Americans combined compose 40 percent of the Asian American population. In addition, large numbers of immigrants from other Asian countries, such as South Korea and Japan, practiced their own versions of Buddhism prior to their migration. As a result, the influx of Asian immigrants to the United States over the past thirty years has led to a phenomenal increase in the Buddhist population. In his 1972 revised edition (originally published in 1958) of *Separated Brethren*, William Whalen commented: "The religion [Buddhism] which dominates the religious life of Asia, except for India, has attracted only about 10,000 followers in the United States. Most of the Buddhists in this country are Japanese Americans."[13] In 1994 on *ABC Nightline News*,

Peter Jennings said that his researchers estimated the American Buddhist population to be between 4 million and 6 million people. However, Jennings's research team may have overestimated the Buddhist population in the United States in 1994.[14] But, given an influx of immigrants from Asian Buddhist countries since that time, it may not be an exaggeration to estimate the U.S. Buddhist population as of January 2000 to be over 3 million.

Contemporary Asian immigrants have contributed to religious pluralism in the United States not only by transplanting several "Oriental" religions, but also by introducing Asianized Protestant and Catholic religions. Of course, Asian immigrants' participation in Christian ethnic congregations did not start with contemporary immigrants. Many Chinese, Japanese, and Korean immigrants at the turn of the twentieth century, Christianized by American missionaries prior to or after migration, participated in Christian congregations.[15] As a result of nearly four hundred years of colonization by Spain, the Philippines has been a predominantly Catholic country.[16] Naturally, the vast majority of the early Filipino immigrants were Catholics. In the early twentieth century, three parishes were established specifically to serve Filipino Catholics on the West Coast.[17] Yet the mass migration of Asian immigrants since 1965 has led to the phenomenal increase in the number of Asian immigrant congregations, which are significantly different from mainstream Christian congregations.

Two major Asian immigrant groups—Filipinos and Koreans—have heavily Christian backgrounds. The mass migration of Filipino immigrants in the post-1965 era has contributed greatly to diversity within Catholicism in the United States. Filipinos, with the vast majority of them being Catholics, represent the largest Asian immigrant group. They have emerged as the second largest ethnic group, following Mexicans, in Los Angeles' Catholic Archdiocese.[18] While Filipino immigrants are mostly Catholic, Korean immigrants are predominantly Protestant. Although Protestantism is a growing religion in Korea, it remains a minority religion, with about 25 percent of the Korean population affiliated with Protestant churches in 1990. Contemporary Korean immigrants, however, are drawn largely from the Christian population, especially from the Protestant population. Approximately 75 percent of the immigrants are affiliated with Korean churches.[19] Korean immigrants are probably more active participants in ethnic congregations than any other contemporary immigrant group.[20] Korean immigrants' congregation-oriented religious activities have attracted a great deal of attention from the mainstream media.[21]

Only a small proportion of Chinese immigrants are Christian when they enter the United States. Yet many Chinese immigrants have become born-again Christians since immigration;[22] thus, one out of five Chinese immigrants is affiliated with a Christian church.[23] Given that about 25

percent of total Asian immigrants are ethnic Chinese from several different Asian countries, the number of Chinese Christian immigrants is significant.[24] There are more than one hundred Chinese Christian congregations in the New York–New Jersey metropolitan area alone. Chinese
students, along with Korean students, compose a significant proportion
of Evangelical Christians on college campuses.[25]

Despite French missionary activities and colonization since the seventeenth century, Catholics compose a tiny fraction of the population of
Vietnam. However, due to their fear of communism, Catholics were overrepresented among refugees from Vietnam (one-third to two-fifths of the
Vietnamese refugees in the United States were Catholic, as noted in chapter 2). In many Vietnamese communities across the United States, a
Catholic parish is the single most important ethnic institution, serving
various social functions.[26] Although Christians are a small minority in India, they make up a significant proportion of the population (about 20
percent) in several southern Indian states, particularly in the state of Kerala.[27] As a result of a selective migration, the majority of immigrants from
Kerala are Christians. The Keralites have transplanted several different
Christian denominations, each of which has been imbued with Indian traditional culture. Members of the Orthodox Syrian Christian Church of India are probably the most popular denomination among Indian immigrants from Kerala.[28]

Lack of Research on Asian Immigrants' Religions

Asian Buddhist and Hindu temples, Muslim mosques, and Catholic and
Protestant churches have mushroomed in Los Angeles, New York, and other
major cities over the past thirty years. This reflects Asian immigrants' active
participation in religious congregations. As will be documented in the following chapters, contemporary Asian immigrants have used their religious
congregations to provide social services for new arrivals, to maintain fellowship with co-ethnic members, and to pass on their cultural traditions to
their children. In short, for Asian immigrants as well as for other immigrant
groups, religion and immigrant life are inseparably tied.[29] Given this fact,
studying the religious experiences and religious institutions of Asian immigrants is essential to understanding the everyday experiences as well as the
social and cultural adjustments made by these groups.

However, the topic of Asian immigrants' religious experiences has
not received the level of scholarly attention it deserves. Several whole
books and dozens of journal articles and book chapters focusing on the religious experiences of Asian immigrants have been published thus far.[30]
However, many of these book chapters and journal articles were included

in the following three edited books published over the past three years: *New Spiritual Homes: Religion and Asian Americans,* edited by David Yoo (University of Hawaii Press, 1998); *Gatherings in Diaspora: Religious Communities and the New Immigration,* edited by Stephen Warner and Judith Wittner (Temple University Press, 1998); and *Religion and the New Immigrants: Continuities and Adaptations in Immigrant Congregations,* edited by Helen Rose Ebaugh and Janet Saltzman Chafetz (AltaMira Press, 2000). *New Spiritual Homes* is a collection of articles published in the 1996 special issue of *Amerasia Journal* and includes a few new entries. *Gatherings in Diaspora* is an outcome of the New Ethnic and Immigrant Congregation Project headed by Stephen Warner, the first editor of the book. *Religion and the New Immigrants* is an outcome of a major study of immigrant congregations in Houston funded by the Pew Charitable Trusts; it is the first of several studies funded by the same foundation. In stark contrast, several dozen books and numerous journal articles and book chapters have been written about Asian immigrants' economic adjustments.

Three major factors seem to have led researchers to neglect research on Asian and other immigrants' religious practices. First, as indicated by Warner, U.S. government agencies cannot ask people about their religion, and thus census data and other government documents do not include information about immigrants' religious affiliation.[31] The General Social Survey provides statistical data on immigrants' religious participation. But the Asian American population—needless to say, each Asian group— is still too small to be included in the survey in significant numbers. Individual researchers interested in Asian immigrants' religious activities are usually ethnographers, and thus are not in a position to tap numerical information about immigrants' religious affiliations and their frequency of participation in congregations. All the books and most of the articles and book chapters that have examined Asian immigrants' religious experiences are based on ethnographic research. As a result, we do not have quantitative data about Asian immigrants' religious participation, with the exception of Korean immigrants.[32]

Another major reason for the lack of research on Asian immigrants' religions has something to do with the direction of Asian American studies. There has been an emphasis on Marxist, postcolonial, postmodernist, and feminist theories in Asian American studies. Asian American scholars seem to have neglected to examine Asian Americans' religious experiences, as David Yoo has pointed out, partly because of the scholars' bias against religion as an opiate of the masses and their postcolonial association of Asian Christianity with Western missionary activities.[33] Five of the previously cited books were written by White American scholars.[34] Two other books, written by Korean American women scholars, examine from two different feminist perspectives the patriarchal practices of Korean immigrant churches.[35]

Asian American scholars specializing in Asian American studies are beginning to pay more attention to Asian immigrants' religious experiences. Establishment of the Asian and Pacific American Research on Religions Initiatives (APARRI), which has had an annual meeting for three consecutive years, is a testimony to the increasing interest on the part of Asian American scholars in Asian Americans' religions. In 1999, Paul Spickard, Jane Naomi Iwamura, and their associates on the West Coast established APARRI as a study group focusing on Asian Americans' religions. The group, consisting of about fifty Asian American social scientists, religious study people, and theologians, held two meetings at the University of California at Santa Barbara in 1999 and 2000, with a third meeting scheduled for August 2001. The members of APARRI exchange information about research and conferences on Asian American religions over the Internet. Based on papers presented at the annual meetings, Jane Noami Iwamura and Paul Spickard are editing a book, tentatively titled *Revealing the Sacred in Asian and Pacific America*, which is to be published in 2002.

Finally, a third major reason for the paucity of research on Asian immigrants' religious experiences has much to do with the dominant pattern of immigrant research in the United States in general. Research on contemporary immigrants has largely focused on their economic adjustment, with little attention paid to their cultural lives. As indicated by Pew Charitable Trusts representatives, major immigrant scholars have not considered religion a major variable that may have significant effects on immigrants' adjustment to American society. Following the general trend in research on immigrants, few books covering Asian immigrants' overall adjustment have devoted even a chapter to the role of religion in their new lives.[36]

Mostly as a result of the initiative of the Pew Charitable Trusts, researchers are now paying more attention to immigrants' religious experiences. To encourage research on the role of religion in immigrants' adjustment, the Pew Charitable Trusts has recently supported major grants to several university research institutes in gateway cities and the Social Science Research Council. Each of these Pew-funded projects is studying the role of religion in immigrants' adjustment. Currently, *Religion and the New Immigrants*, edited by Ebaugh and Chafetz, is the only book published based on a Pew project (the Houston project), but more such books are expected to be published in the next several years. Since every Pew gateway project includes several Asian immigrant groups, we will see the expansion of the literature on Asian immigrants' religions—both individual and institutional religions—in the next several years.

Of course, there are intergroup differentials in the level of scholarly investigation of immigrants' religious experiences. Korean immigrants' participation in Korean immigrant churches has been relatively well documented from different theoretical angles by both survey researchers and ethnographers.[37] Thus, we have detailed information not only about Korean immigrants' frequency of participation in ethnic congregations but also about the structure and hierarchy of Korean immigrant churches. Furthermore, several pieces of work focusing on second-generation Korean evangelical Christians have been published recently, and this subject is popular among doctoral students of religious studies, the social sciences, and theology as a dissertation topic.[38]

By contrast, Filipino immigrants' religious experiences have been least studied. Filipino immigrants compose the largest Asian national origin group, and they are probably more active in religious participation than any other Asian immigrant group, with the exception of Korean immigrants. Yet there is only piecemeal information about Filipino immigrants' religious experiences.[39] Curiously enough, none of the recently published books on Filipino immigrants or Filipino Americans devotes even one page to discussion of the role of religion in Filipino immigrant or Filipino Americans' adjustment to American society.[40]

The Focus and Coverage of This Book

This book intends to bridge the gap in information about Asian immigrants' religious experiences. Its main objective is to provide comprehensive and systematic information about the religious experiences of six major Asian immigrant groups: the Chinese, Filipinos, Indians, Koreans, Japanese, and Southeast Asians. Following the traditional sociological approach to immigrant and ethnic congregations, each chapter examines the roles that an immigrant congregation plays in preserving ethnic culture and identity, facilitating fellowship with co-ethnic members, and providing services for church members.[41]

However, this book goes beyond the traditional approach to immigrant congregations, which was largely based on the religious experiences of turn-of-the-century European immigrant groups. It tries to incorporate newly emerging theoretical perspectives useful for understanding the religious experiences of contemporary, Third World immigrants. In particular, this book pays special attention to gender, race, and transnationalism—the themes that have received increasing scholarly attention during recent years. Chapter 1 discusses each of these themes in detail, citing the relevant literature. It is impossible for each chapter to discuss each of these themes in relation to the religious experiences of a particular group. Yet each chapter discusses one or more of these themes as far as they are useful in interpreting the religious experiences of members of the group(s) under consideration. While two recently published books on immigrant congregations—*Gatherings in Diaspora* and *Religion and the New Immigrants*—have devoted space to gender and transnationalism, neither book has paid attention to race. By contrast, several chapters of this book, especially chapters 3, 5, 6, 7, and 8, examine the role of race in Asian immigrants' religious experiences.

Although this book focuses on the religious practices of contemporary Asian immigrants, it also covers the earlier Asian immigrants' religious practices. Depending on a group's immigration history, some chapters devote more space to examining the religious experiences of the earlier immigrants. For instance, the Japanese were the largest Asian ethnic group in the pre-1965 era, with a sizable American-born population, but only a relatively small number of Japanese immigrants have entered the United States annually since 1965. Therefore, the chapter on the Japanese group, written by a historian, devotes more time to examining the religious experiences of the Nisei before World War II than to those of contemporary Japanese immigrants. While Filipinos compose the largest Asian immigrant group in the post-1965 era, they have a long immigration history, especially in Hawaii and California. Thus, the chapter on the Filipino group can be both historical and sociological. However, due to the author's background as a historian, the Filipino chapter devotes far more space to historical analyses of Filipinos' religious experiences at the expense of sociological analyses. Chinese, Indian, and Korean groups, too, had sizable populations on the West Coast in the first half of the twentieth century. As such, the chapters on each of these groups also devote space to examining the religious experiences of the earlier immigrants.

In their effort to adjust to American society, Asian immigrants have transformed their religious traditions as well as their other cultural traditions. The children of contemporary Asian immigrants will further transform the various religions that their parents brought from their home countries. A separate volume is needed to systematically examine the religious experiences of second-generation Asian Americans. But a volume on Asian immigrants' religious experiences may be incomplete without touching on the issue of the intergenerational transmission and transformation of religions. Thus, we have included a chapter by Russell Jeung that examines evangelical and mainline pan-Asian congregations among U.S-born Chinese and Japanese Americans in San Francisco.

Data Sources

All contributors did research on ethnic congregations for their chosen groups, mostly using ethnographic research. Four contributors are members of the ethnic groups on whose religious experiences they write. They have written their chapters based largely on their own ethnographic research and their insider's knowledge of ethnic congregations. Yet they have also used one or more of three other data sources in completing their chapters: secondary sources; survey data, including public documents; and historical data. The chapter on the Japanese group is largely based on historical data. The chapter on Filipino Americans also uses historical data extensively.

Each substantive chapter covers not only immigrant congregations, but also other useful pieces of information about each group, such as immigration history, settlement patterns, economic adjustments, and cultural and religious customs in the home country. Each author has used secondary sources available at the time of this writing (1999 and 2000). A comprehensive reference list included at the end of the book, as well as chapter end notes, will be of great help to those who want to conduct research on Asian immigrants' religious participation.

We may not be able to understand Asian immigrants' religious practices adequately without understanding the religious background of their home country. Thus, I have asked the contributors to devote a few paragraphs to this matter. Not all contributors followed this instruction, but most chapters provide enough information—using statistical and/or historical data—about the religious customs of the home countries. In particular, chapter 6 offers detailed information about the colonial and religious history of the Philippines.

Notes

1. See Pyong Gap Min, "A Comparison of Post-1965 and Turn-of-the-Century Immigrants in Intergeneration Mobility and Cultural Transmission," *Journal of American Ethnic History* 18 (1999): 65–94.

2. Gerald Shaunessy, *Religion in America: Has the Immigrant Kept the Faith?* (New York: Arno Press and the New York Times, 1969), 182.

3. Fred Arnold, Urmil Minocha, and James Fawcett, "The Changing Face of Asian Immigration to the United States," in *Pacific Bridges: The New Immigration from Asia and the Pacific Islands*, ed. James Fawcett and Benjamin Carino (Staten Island: Center for Migration Studies, 1987), 122–27: table 61.

4. Stephen Batchelor, *The Awakening of the West: The Encounter of Buddhism and Western Culture* (Berkeley: Parallax Press, 1994); Tetsuden Kashima, *Buddhism in America: The Social Organization of an Ethnic Religious Institution* (Westport, Conn.: Greenwood, 1977).

5. Kashima, *Buddhism in America*, 13.

6. J. M. Jensen, *Passage from India: Asian Indian Immigrants in North America* (New Haven, Conn.: Yale University Press, 1988), 41.

7. Ronald Takaki, *Strangers from a Different Shore: A History of Asian Americans* (Boston: Little, Brown, 1989), 296.

8. For detailed information about various measures the U.S. government took to restrict immigration from Asian countries between 1850 and 1990, see Bill Ong Hing, *Making and Remaking Asian America through Immigration Policy, 1850 and 1990* (Stanford, Calif.: Stanford University Press, 1993).

9. The 1952 Immigration and Nationality Act allowed each Asian-Pacific country to send one hundred quota immigrants per year, with a maximum of two thousand immigrants from the "Asia-Pacific triangle" area. See Hing, *Making and Remaking Asian America through Immigration Policy*, 38–39.

10. Min, "A Comparison of Post-1965 and Turn-of-the-Century Immigrants."

11. Carl Bankston III and Min Zhou, "The Ethnic Church, Ethnic Identification, and the Social Adjustment of Vietnamese Adolescents," *Review of Religious Research* 38 (1995): 18–37; Paul David Numrich, *Old Wisdom in the New World: Americanization in Two Immigrant Theravada Buddhist Temples* (Knoxville: University of Tennessee Press, 1996); Thanh Van Tran, "The Vietnamese American Family," in *Ethnic Families in America*, ed. Charles Mindel, Robert Habenstein, and Roosevelt Wright Jr. (Upper Saddle River, N.J.: Prentice Hall, 1998), 256. For information about the Buddhist background of Indo-Chinese refugees, see also the chapter by Zhou, Bankston, and Kim included in this book.

12. Fenggang Yang, *Chinese Christians in America: Conversion, Assimilation, and Adhesive Identities* (University Park: Pennsylvania State University Press, 1999), 46, 160. In a survey conducted in 1999 and 1998, 25 percent of Chinese immigrant respondents in Queens, New York, indicated Buddhism as their religion. See Pyong Gap Min, *Asian Ethnic Groups in New York: A Comparative Analysis* (New York: Columbia University Press, forthcoming), ch. 5.

13. William Whalen, *Separated Brethren* (Huntington, Ind.: Our Sunday Visitor, 1972), 283.

14. Charles Prebish, introduction to *The Face of Buddhism in America*, ed. Charles Prebish and Kenneth Tanaka (Berkeley: University of California Press, 1998).

15. Bong Yoon Choy, *Koreans in America* (Chicago: Neilson Hall, 1979), 77; Brian Masaru Hayashi, "The Untold Story of the Nikkei Baptists in Southern California, 1913–1924," *Foundations* 22 (1979): 313–23; Timothy Tseng, "Chinese Protestant Nationalism in the United States, 1870–1927," in *New Spiritual Homes: Religion and Asian Americans*, ed. David Yoo (Honolulu: University of Hawaii Press, 1998), 19–51.

16. Antonio Pido, *The Filipinos in America* (Staten Island: Center for Migration Studies, 1986), 18.

17. Sucheng Chan, *Asian Americans: An Interpretive History* (Boston: Twayne, 1991), 77.

18. John Dart, "Filipino Services Offer Touch of Home," *Los Angeles Times*, December 25, 1993.

19. Won Moo Hurh and Kwang Chung Kim, "Religious Participation of Korean Immigrants in the United States," *Journal of the Scientific Study of Religion* 29 (1990): 19–34; Pyong Gap Min, "The Structure and Social Functions of Korean Immigrants Churches in the United States," *International Migration Review* 26 (1992): 1370–94.

20. According to the Racial Ethnic Presbyterian Panel Study of 1997–1999, 78 percent of Korean Presbyterians participate in the church at least once a week, in comparison to 28 percent of white, 34 percent of black, and 49 percent of Latino Presbyterians. See Kwang Chung Kim and Shin Kim, "The Ethnic Roles of Korean Immigrant Churches in the U.S.," in *Pilgrims and Missionaries from a Different Shore: Korean Americans and Their Religions*, ed. Ho-Youn Kwon, Kwang Chung Kim, and Stephen Warner (University Park: Pennsylvania State University Press, 2001).

21. Joseph Burger, "Koreans Breathe New Life into Queens Church," *New York Times*, July 30, 1986; Stephanie Storm, "Korean Ordained in Baptist Church in Queens," *New York Times*, April 29, 1991; Robert Worth, "Easter Players Rise in Churches and a Transformed Factory," *New York Times*, April 24, 2001.

22. Chinese immigrants tend to turn to Christianity more readily than other Asian immigrants do after immigration because an overwhelming majority of them were not officially affiliated with a religion in their home country.

23. According to a survey conducted in Queens, New York, in 1999 and 1998, 20 percent of Chinese immigrant respondents reported that they were either Protestant (11 percent) or Catholic (9 percent). See Pyong Gap Min, *Asian Ethnic Groups in New York*, ch. 5.

24. U.S. Bureau of the Census, *Asian and Pacific Islander Americans* (Washington, D.C.: U.S. Government Printing Office [GPO], 1993), table 1.

25. Rudy Busto, "The Gospel According to Model Minority?: Hazarding an Interpretation of Asian American Evangelical College Students," *Amerasia Journal* 22 (1996): 133–48.

26. Min Zhou and Carl Bankston III, *Growing Up American: How Vietnamese Children Adapt to Life in the United States* (New York: Russell Sage Foundation, 1998), 98. See also the chapter on Indo-Chinese refugees included in this book.

27. Sheba George, "Caroling with the Keralites: The Negotiation of Gendered Space in an Indian Immigrant Church," in *Gatherings in Diaspora: Religious Communities and the New Immigration,* ed. Stephen Warner and Judith Wittner (Philadelphia: Temple University Press, 1998), 265–94; Raymond Brady Williams, *Religions of Immigrants from India and Pakistan*, 103–4.

28. George, "Caroling with the Keralites."

29. Peter Krivisto, "Religion and the New Immigrants," in *A Future for Religion*, ed. William H. Swatos Jr. (Newbury Park, Calif.: Sage, 1993, 92–108); Stephen Warner, "Immigration and Religious Communities in the United States," in *Gatherings in Diaspora*, ed. Warner and Wittner, 3–34.

30. John Fenton, *Transplanting Religious Traditions: Asian Indians in America* (New York: Praeger, 1988); Ai Ra Kim, *Women Struggling for a New Life: The Role of Religion in the Cultural Passage from Korea to America* (Albany: State University of New York Press, 1996); Jung Ha Kim, *Bridge-Makers and Cross-Bearers: Korean American Women and the Church* (Atlanta, Ga.: Scholar's Press, 1997); Kwon, Kim, and Warner, *Korean Americans and their Religions*; Numrich, *Old Wisdom in the New World*; L. A. Palinkas, *Rhetoric and Religious Experience: The Discourse of Immigrant Chinese Churches* (Fairfax, Va.: George Mason University Press, 1989); Paul Rutledge, *The Role of Religion in Ethnic Self-Identity: A Vietnamese Community* (Lanham, Md.: University Press of America, 1985); Williams, *Religions of Immigrants from India and Pakistan*; Yang, *Chinese Christians in America*.

31. Stephen Warner, "Immigration and Religious Communities," 11.

32. Hurh and Kim, "Religious Participation of Korean Immigrants in the United States"; Min, "The Structure and Social Functions of Korean Immigrant Churches in the United States."

33. David Yoo, "For Those Who Have Eyes to See: Religious Sightings in Asian America," *Amerasia Journal* 22 (1996:1): xiii–xxii.

34. John Fenton, *Transplanting Religious Traditions: Asian Indians in America* (New York; Praeger, 1988); Numrich, *Old Wisdom in the New World*; Rutledge, *Role of Religion in Ethnic Identity*; Williams, *Religions of Immigrants from India and Pakistan.*

35. A. Kim, *Women Struggling for a New Life*; J. Kim, *Bridge-Makers and Cross-Bearers.*

36. The following books on Asian Americans have devoted one chapter or at least several pages to description of religious organizations: Fred Cordova, *Filipinos: Forgotten Americans, A Pictorial Essay, 1963–1963* (Dubuque, Iowa: Kendall/Hunt, 1983); Steven Gold, *Refugee Communities: A Comparative Field Study* (Newbury Park, Calif.: Sage, 1992); Illsoo Kim, *New Urban Immigrants: The Korean Community in New York* (Princeton, N.J.: Princeton University Press, 1981); Pyong Gap Min, *Changes and Conflicts: Korean Immigrant Families in New York* (Boston: Allyn & Bacon, 1998); Kyeyoung Park, *The Korean American Dream: Immigrants and Small Business in New York City* (Ithaca, N.Y.: Cornell University Press, 1998); Zhou and Bankston, *Growing Up American.*

37. In addition to the three books previously cited, more than a dozen journal articles and book chapters that focus on Korean immigrants' religious experiences have been published thus far. See Kwon, Kim, and Warner, *Korean Americans and their Religions*, and chapter 2 of this book.

38. Anthony Alumkal, "Preserving Patriarchy: Assimilation, Gender Norms, and Second-Generation Korean American Evangelicals," *Qualitative Sociology* 22 (1999): 127–40; Anthony Alumkal, "Being Korean, Being Christian: Particularism and Universalism in a Second-Generation Congregation," in *Korean Americans and their Religions*, ed. Kwon, Kim, and Warner, 157–80; Karen Chai, "Competing for the Second Generation: English-Language Ministry at a Korean Protestant Church," in *Gatherings in Diaspora*, ed. Warner and Wittner, 295–332; Kelly Chong, "What It Means to Be Christians: The Role of Religion in the Construction of Ethnic Identity and Boundary among Second-Generation Korean-Americans," *Sociology of Religion* 58 (1998): 259–86; Pyong Gap Min and Dae Young Kim, "Intergenerational Transmission of Religion and Culture: Korean Christians in New York" (paper presented at the annual meeting of the Society for the Scientific Study of Religion, Washington, D.C., 2000); Soyoung Park, "The Intersection of Religion, Ethnicity and Gender in the Identity Formation of Korean-American Evangelical Women," in *Korean Americans and their Religions*, ed. Kwon, Kim, and Warner, 193–208.

39. To my knowledge, there are only three pieces of work, other than the chapter in this volume, focusing on Filipino immigrants' religious experiences: Edwin Almirol, "Church Life among Filipinos in Central California: Social Ties and Ethnicity," in *Religion and Society in the American West*, ed. Carl Guarneri and David Alvarez (Lanham, Md.: University Press of America, 1987); Artemio Guillermo, "Gathering of the Scattered: History of Filipino American United Methodist Churches," in *Churches Aframe: Asian Americans and United Methodism*, ed. Artemio Guillermo (Nashville, Tenn.: Abingdon, 1991); Steffi San Buenaventura, "Filipino Folk Spirituality and Immigration: From Mutual Aid to Religion," *Amerasia Journal* 22 (1996): 1–30.

40. Rick Bonu, *Locating Filipino Americans: Ethnicity and Cultural Politics of Space* (Philadelphia: Temple University Press, 2000); Yen Espiritu, *Filipino American Lives*

(Philadelphia: Temple University Press, 1995); Maria Roots, ed., *Filipino Americans: Transformation and Identity* (Thousand Oaks, Calif.: Sage, 1997); Pido, *Filipinos in America*.

41. Andrew Greeley, *The Denominational Society: A Sociological Approach to Religion* (Glenview, Ill.: Scott, Foresman, 1972); Will Herberg, *Protestant, Catholic, Jew: An Essay in American Religious Sociology*, 2d ed. (Garden City, N.Y.: Doubleday, 1960); W. L. Warner and Leo Srole, *The Social System of American Ethnic Groups* (New Haven, Conn.: Yale University Press, 1945).

CHAPTER ONE

A LITERATURE REVIEW WITH A FOCUS ON MAJOR THEMES

Pyong Gap Min

Traditionally, the sociological literature on immigration and religion in the United States was largely based on turn-of-the-century, Judeo-Christian religious groups. Since Judeo-Christian religions are congregation oriented, major sociological studies of Catholic and Jewish immigrant groups focused on religious congregations, while researchers in religious studies focused on religious faiths and rituals themselves. In particular, sociologists studying immigrant groups at the turn of the century emphasized the role of an immigrant or ethnic congregation in preserving ethnic culture and providing services for members of the congregation.

As will be shown shortly, many studies of post-1965 Asian immigrant groups have also emphasized the ethnicity and social service functions of Asian immigrant religious congregations. But they have also examined race, gender, and transnational ties relating to Asian immigrants' congregational and noncongregational religious practices. Moreover, some studies have emphasized the ethnicity function of Asian Americans' noncongregational domestic religious practices. This chapter will critically review the literature on Asian immigrants' religious experiences with a focus on these themes.

Ethnicity

The literature on religion and ethnicity is largely based on the experiences of turn-of-the-century white immigrant groups—mostly Catholic and Jewish. These Judeo-Christian immigrant groups do not differ from Protestant immigrant groups in that they practice their religious worship mainly through participation in a religious congregation. Thus, there is an abundance of the social science literature emphasizing the role of immigrant and ethnic congregations in maintaining ethnicity for immigrant and ethnic groups.[1]

Culture and identity are two major components of ethnicity. Close examination of the literature on religion and ethnicity indicates that immigrant/ethnic congregations help to maintain ethnicity by helping members of an ethnic/immigrant group to preserve their cultural traditions and ethnic identity. In their classic study of the assimilation patterns of Catholic and Jewish immigrant groups, W.L. Warner and Leo Srole assert that "the church was the first line of defense behind which these immigrants could organize themselves and with which they could preserve their group, i.e., system, identity."[2] According to S.M. Tomasi and M.H. Engel, the Italian Catholic parishes "functioned to maintain the ethnic personality by organizing the group around the familiar religious and cultural symbols and behavioral mode of the fatherland."[3] Robert Ostergren further elaborates the various ways in which ethnic churches helped white immigrant groups to preserve their language and culture:

> As the center of the community life, the church was charged with the responsibility of upholding the values and preserving the community with the cultural past. Most churches, for instance, made extensive efforts to preserve the language. Services in rural churches in the Upper Midwest were commonly held in the Old World language well into the early decades of the twentieth century. Church schools were established to instruct the young into the old language and congregations delayed as long as possible the eventual change to the keeping of official records into English. The church carefully observed the old holidays and customs, singing clubs preserved the traditional music, and women's organizations carried on folk crafts.[4]

Immigrant/ethnic churches also sustain ethnicity by providing their members with co-ethnic fellowship and social networks. African Americans before their emancipation were alienated from white society. Thus, the black church served for them as the family and community center. W. E. B. Du Bois said in *The Philadelphia Negro*, one of the classics on African Americans: "Its family functions are shown by the fact that the church is the center of social life and intercourse; acts as newspaper and intelligence bureau, is the center of amusement—indeed is the world in which the Negro moves and acts."[5] Meeting the need for fellowship and primary social interactions may be more important for immigrants, who are separated from relatives and close friends. As the Hebrew words for synagogue, *Beth Haknesseth* (place of gathering), denotes, the Jewish synagogue probably has played the most important role in providing communal ties for Jews settled in the United States, as well as in other parts of the world. It is also well known that Catholic parishes constituted territorial enclaves for many European immigrants in the later half of the nineteenth century.[6]

Contemporary Asian immigrant groups have transplanted not only Christian, but also many other non-Christian religions, such as Islam, Hinduism, and Buddhism, to the United States. Following the same theoretical perspective derived from the studies of the earlier white immigrant groups, recent studies of Asian immigrant groups have also stressed the ethnicity function of immigrant congregations.[7] For example, Prema Kurien has shown how Indian Hindus use their "religious organizations as means to forge ethnic communities and articulate their ethnic identities as Indian Americans."[8] Based on a survey of Vietnamese high school students, Carl Bankston and Min Zhou have concluded that "religious participation consistently makes a greater contribution to ethnic identification than any of the family or individual characteristics examined, except recency of arrival."[9] The results of a survey study of Korean churches in New York also reveal that maintaining Korean culture and enhancing co-ethnic social networks are two of the major functions of Korean immigrant churches.[10]

The preceding studies support the view that religion has positive effects on ethnicity mainly because participation in a religious congregation helps to maintain ethnic culture and co-ethnic social networks. Yet many non-Western religions do not put as much emphasis on participation in a religious congregation as do the Judeo-Christian religions. In particular, Hindus, Muslims, and Buddhists—mostly Asian immigrants—usually practice through family rituals and/or small-group prayer meetings without regularly participating in a religious congregation. Stephen Warner claims that even non-Christian religions in the United States are currently adopting *"de facto congregationalism* more or less on the model of the reformed Protestant tradition of the congregation as a voluntary gathered community."[11] Several researchers have indicated that Hindu, Muslim, and Buddhist immigrants in the United States participate in a congregation more often than they did in their home country, which is in partial support of Warner's claim about the convergence toward de facto congregationalism.[12] However, these non-Christian immigrants participate in a religious congregation far less frequently than Christian immigrants and probably less frequently than even native-born Christians.[13]

Due to their less frequent participation in a religious congregation, Hindu, Muslim, and Buddhist immigrants have a disadvantage for maintaining their ethnicity through various congregation-based activities. Yet we should not consider their lack of participation in a religious congregation as an indication of their religious inactivity, particularly with regard to the role of their religions in preserving their ethnic cultural traditions. The significance of religion for preserving ethnic culture is that the so-called ethno-religious groups have huge advantages over other ethnic groups in preserving their ethnic culture through religion because their religious values and rituals are inseparably tied to their ethnic values, customs, holidays, food, dress, and even music and dance. For example, Jewish Americans have been successful in retaining their cultural traditions mainly because their religious values and rituals are inseparably tied to their ethnic cultural traditions. Jewish religious holidays—Rosh Hashanah and Yom Kippur—have become Jewish ethnic holidays, while Jewish kosher food symbolizes Jewish ethnic cuisine.

The traditional literature on immigrant and ethnic religions, exclusively focusing on religious congregations, neglected to examine how observance of religious rituals at home helps members of an immigrant/ethnic group to preserve ethnic culture and identity. But the most recent studies of non-white Catholic and non-Christian immigrant groups shed light on this issue.[14] Based on studies of various immigrant groups in Houston, Ebaugh and Chafetz comment on the positive effects of "domestic religions" on preservation of ethnic culture and identity:

> Religious items representing ethnic culture include specific patron saints for Catholics, evidence of traditional ancestor veneration for Vietnamese Catholics, and Hindu saints veneration among some Parsi Zoroastrians, and religiously specific deity statues for Hindus. Home-centered religious devotions and celebrations of life-cycle events are also heavily tinged by the ethnic culture of participants. In these ways, the practice of domestic religion reinforces cultural identity, and women are centrally involved in such practices.[15]

I compared Indian Hindu and Korean Christian immigrants in their radically different ways of preserving ethnicity through religion.[16] Korean Christian immigrants participate in a Korean congregation very frequently; about 80 percent go to a Korean church once or twice a week.[17] Korean Christian immigrants preserve ethnicity mainly by practicing Korean culture (not necessarily Christian rituals) and increasing their co-ethnic fellowship through their active participation in a Korean congregation. By contrast, Indian Hindu immigrants, who participate in an ethnic congregation far less frequently than Korean Christian immigrants, maintain Indian ethnicity mainly by practicing religious rituals at home.

Social Services

Both studies of immigrant/ethnic congregations and those of social services reveal that Judeo-Christian religious organizations, especially Catholic ones, traditionally played a major role in providing various social services not only for the needy in their neighborhoods, but also for new immigrants and refugees in general.[18] Jag Dolan documents that by the middle of the nineteenth century Catholic parishes had become the centers around which neighborhood charitable societies were organized. Catholic organizations established many settlement houses in Chicago and other American cities especially to serve an increasing number of European immigrants.[19] A number of Catholic fraternity organizations of diverse nationalities were created in the early twentieth century to help new immigrants from Catholic countries. The synagogue played the central role in offering services for Jewish immigrants from Eastern European countries at the turn of the twentieth century. In a review article, Steven Gold argues that religious groups have advantages over government or other secular organizations in helping immigrants partly because they "offer a basis for equal interaction between native-born service providers and foreign-born recipients."[20]

Recent studies show that Asian immigrant Christian congregations play an active role in providing social services, but that they offer services largely to their own members.[21] As noted in the introduction, Korean immigrant churches have received more scholarly attention than any other type of Asian immigrant congregations. A few of the studies of Korean immigrant churches document a variety of services offered by them.[22] For example, according to my own study conducted in New York, Korean immigrant churches offer a number of services for their members including immigration orientation, counseling, educational services, job referral, and many other nonmaterial services.[23] While small churches provide services mainly through the head pastors' and other church leaders' direct aid to church members on an individual basis, large churches do so mainly through formal programs such as seminars and conferences. Despite their active involvement in providing services to their own members, for the most part Korean churches neglect to respond to the welfare needs of the Korean community as a whole. Other Asian immigrant Protestant and Catholic churches were also found to offer a number of services mainly to their members partly to attract more people to their organizations.[24]

It is interesting to see whether Asian immigrant non-Christian religious institutions—Buddhist and Hindu temples and mosques—offer social services comparable to Christian churches. A number of studies suggest that Asian Buddhist temples do provide services, but not to the extent Asian immigrant Christian churches do.[25] Z.Y. Yu comments with regard to Korean temples in Southern California: "Several temples maintain Korean language and cultural programs and provide many types of social services such as family counseling and senior citizen support."[26] Irene Lin describes social service functions of a Chinese Buddhist temple in Monterey Park,

California, as follows: "The abbess . . . emphasized free practical services for the overseas Chinese community: locating relatives and friends, helping immigrants find jobs by providing channels for networking, and organizing seminars to educate immigrants about American laws, customs, the educational system, and the job market."[27]

However, according to a study by Thuan Huynb, a Vietnamese Buddhist temple in Houston does not provide services with the exception of a youth class and a Buddhist doctrinal class for adults.[28] Piecemeal information also suggests that Hindu temples and mosques mostly remain as the place for worship without offering services.[29] Those who run such places of worship deliberately underestimate the social service functions of a religious congregation partly because they are afraid that social service provisions will weaken the religious part.

Race

No single story captures more clearly the distinctiveness of African-American Christianity than that of the Exodus. From the earliest days of colonization, white Christians had represented their journey across the Atlantic to America as the exodus of a New Israel; slaves identified as the Old Israel, suffering bondage under a new Pharaoh.

—Albert Raboteau, *A Fire in the Bones: Reflections on African-American Religious History*

In the United States where whites have dominated minority members, the latter have had qualitatively different experiences from the former in all areas of life. This is true of their religious experiences.[30] The above paragraph most succinctly points to the radically different meanings of Christianity and the Bible for European colonialists and African American slaves during the slavery period. Although slavery was abolished more than one hundred and fifty years ago, African Americans still suffer from the legacy of their earlier bondage and oppression.[31] Thus, even today African American Christian experiences basically differ from those of white Americans; liberation and communal solidarity are the central themes in their biblical stories, hymns, and rituals.[32] Although other minority groups in the United States fare better, they, too, encounter prejudice and discrimination. Accordingly, race should be treated as an important variable in understanding religious experiences of minority members.

Major studies of religious experiences of turn-of-the-century European immigrant/ethnic groups did not pay attention to race at all. When

Irish, Italian, Jewish, and other non-Protestant immigrants arrived in the late nineteenth and early twentieth centuries, they were considered separate races physically different from white Americans. But researchers began to study the turn-of-the-century southern and eastern European immigrant groups systematically forty years after their influx started, that is, when these groups were well into assimilation to American society.[33] It is not surprising, then, that studies of the Catholic and Jewish immigrants' religious experiences did not treat race as an important variable in their analysis. But it is surprising that recent studies of post-1965—mostly non-European—immigrant groups have neglected to examine the role of race in their religious experiences. For example, neither of two major edited volumes (*Gatherings in Diaspora* and *Religion and the New Immigrants*) on contemporary immigrant groups' religions has treated race or racialization as a significant category of analysis (although each has paid enough attention to the role of gender).[34] New immigrants are so nationalistic in their identity and so ethnic in culture that ethnic identity and ethnic culture may figure prominently in their religious experiences with their perception of the socially given racial category playing an insignificant role. This may be the main reason that researchers see many similarities between earlier European and contemporary immigrants' religious congregations in their ethnic identity, cultural retention, and fellowship functions.[35] Nevertheless, racial prejudice and discrimination that nonwhite immigrants encounter in both the religious and nonreligious contexts must have effects on their individual religious experiences and their organization of religious institutions.

Asian immigrants in the nineteenth and early twentieth centuries were targets of severe prejudice and discrimination.[36] The Chinese Exclusion Act and other anti-Asian laws at the end of the nineteenth and early twentieth centuries were passed partly due to the stereotypes and prejudice held by white Americans against Asians and partly due to the motives of white Americans to protect their economic interests. The migration to the United States of a large number of professional Asians since 1965 and the success of many U.S.-born Asian Americans have led to the change from negative to positive in most Americans' perception of Asian Americans. However, despite the model minority image, Asian Americans are still subjected to many negative stereotypes.[37] The age-old perception of Asian Americans as "perpetual foreigners" still embarrasses many U.S.-born Asian Americans.[38] Socioeconomically, Asian immigrants are generally underemployed, while U.S.-born Asian Americans encounter the glass ceiling problem.[39]

Asian Americans' historical and contemporary experiences with prejudice and discrimination and the emergence of many U.S.-born Asian American scholars in Asian American studies have contributed to the expansion of the literature treating race as a central theme in interpreting Asian American experiences. Yet there is a paucity of social science literature that has applied racial analysis to Asian Americans', especially Asian immigrants' religious experiences. In fact, as noted later, there is no single social science study that has used race or racialization in examining contemporary Asian immigrants' religious experiences.

In the introduction to *New Spiritual Homes: Religion and Asian Americans*, the only anthology of papers on Asian Americans' religious experiences, editor David Yoo emphasizes the importance of uncovering the connections between race and religion. He says:

> At the same time, the long standing presence of independent racial-ethnic denominations attests to how Asian American Christians have created institutions that reflect their concerns and cater to their own needs. Separate racial-ethnic churches, programs, and governing bodies within majority Euro-American religious institutions, moreover, suggest the complex and contested nature of Asian American Christianity.[40]

Despite the promising introductory comment by the editor, the volume does not include any social science study examining Asian Americans' religious experiences with a focus on the racial category. The only piece of work included in the volume that focuses on the theme of race is a theological reflection by a Korean American theologian, Sang Hyun Lee. In the reflection, Lee emphasizes his own and other Asian Americans' sense of marginality in the United States that is created by racial barriers, and he calls on the Asian American church and Asian American theology to "affirm its ethnic particularity against racism."[41] Other Asian American theologians have offered similar theological reflections focusing on the themes of Asian Americans' marginality and the role of Asian American theology in building a community where the marginalized can feel at home.[42]

Race is not a fixed category entirely based on physical differences, but a social construction created by the responses of minority groups to societal treatment. Asian immigrant groups, with their own language, unique cultural traditions, and history, are highly nationalistic or even provincial in their identity. Thus, few of them will adopt a pan-ethnic, Asian American label given by the dominant society. However, U.S.-born Asian Americans of different ethnic backgrounds have common experiences affected by racial lumping and other structural factors related to their adjustments in the United States. Accordingly, they hold varying degrees of a pan-Asian identity with significant individual differentials.[43] Some scholars have argued that the pan-Asian racial formation will be an important feature of Asian American experiences in the post–civil rights era.[44] It is interesting to see whether pan-Asian racialization will influence Asian Americans' organized religions and lead to pan-Asian congregations.

The mainstream media on the West and East Coasts have recently featured stories about the emergence of pan-Asian congregations.[45] *Pan-Asian congregations* is also a popular research topic for second-generation Asian American doctoral students; according to informal sources, a few doctoral students have chosen it as their dissertation topics. One of the dissertations has already been completed, and chapter 8 of this volume by Russell Jeung is based on his dissertation with information gathered in the San Francisco Bay area. As the first major study on the topic, Jeung's chapter sheds light on the formation of pan-Asian churches and their congregational cultures. His chapter reveals that evangelical and mainline pan-Asian church ministers hold different understandings of Asian American pan-ethnicity. The evangelical ministers draw pan-ethnic symbolic boundaries around similarities in church members' family upbringing and (professional) class background, while mainline ministers focus on the racialized experiences of Asian Americans and their ethnic heritages. Mainline ministers emphasize creating pan-ethnic churches that "integrate Asian cultural resources with Christian rituals and address racial justice issues." By contrast, his data show, evangelicals identify mainly with the broad American evangelical subculture rather than with Asian cultural traditions. Moreover, they emphasize that pan-ethnic churches should meet their members' individual psychological and emotional needs and should not be concerned with racial justice issues.

In examining pan-Asian racial formation in religion as well as in other areas of Asian American experiences, it is important to make a distinction between pan-ethnic coalitions at the collective level and pan-ethnic attachment at the individual level. As I have discussed elsewhere in more detail, political identity is central to pan-Asian coalitions, whereas private identity figures prominently in pan-Asian ethnic attachment in friendship and dating at the individual level.[46] Racial lumping and other structural factors have largely forced various Asian ethnic groups to make broad coalitions to protect common interests in politics, education, and other areas.[47] However, primordial ties—culture, history, and phenotype associated with Asian countries—have direct and indirect effects on the development of pan-ethnic attachment among Asian Americans at the individual level. While East (Chinese, Korean, and Japanese) or South Asians (Indian, Pakistani, and Bangladeshi) share many things within each cluster, the two pan-ethnic groups have significant differences in physical characteristics, culture (including religion), and premigrant historical experiences. Due to the within-group similarities and the between-group differences, East and South Asian groups maintain two separate pan-ethnic boundaries, which is supported by various data sources.[48]

Whether Asian Americans of different ethnic backgrounds participate in the same congregation is largely determined by their private identity, that is, their perceptions of similarities in physical characteristics, culture, and premigrant historical experiences, rather than their political identity. Because Asian Americans of East and South Asian origins, as previously noted, do not share commonalities in origin and culture, the two groups are least likely to participate in the same congregation. First of all, East and South Asians are divided by religion; as noted in the introduction, the majority of East Asians are Buddhists or Christians, while the vast majority of South Asians are Hindus or Muslims. As they do not share religions, they cannot attend the same congregations. Christians compose a small proportion of South Asian immigrants, and the proportion of Christians among second-generation South Asians is likely to increase in parallel to their acculturation.[49] But, due to the lack of other aspects of ethnic heritage, South and East Asian second-generation Christians are unlikely to participate in the same church.

Pan-Asian churches, in Jeung's study of the San Francisco Bay area, are largely attended by Chinese and Japanese Americans. Considering East Asian pan-ethnic boundaries, it is not surprising at all that Christians of two East Asian groups, Chinese and Japanese Americans, have established pan-ethnic churches in San Francisco.[50] There are large Filipino, Vietnamese, and Indian populations in San Francisco, which include many second-generation Protestants. But because of a lack of the similarities in ethnic heritage, most of these second-generation Christians are likely to feel uncomfortable sharing the place of worship with East Asian Christians. Emergence of East Asian Christian congregations is not limited to San Francisco. What journalists call "pan-Asian congregations" in Los Angeles are also East Asian congregations dominated by Japanese and Chinese American Christians and attended by a significant number of Korean Americans. Meanwhile, South Asians, who speak English well and who accept religion as a more important signifier of identity than national origin, do not have to wait for the second generation to have a pan-ethnic congregation. Muslim or Hindu immigrants from various South Asian countries sometimes participate in the same congregation.[51] Moreover, although at present we do not have data, second-generation Christians of various South Asian ancestries are likely to establish pan-ethnic churches among themselves. In view of this, it is misleading to use the term *pan-Asian congregations* to refer to pan-ethnic formation in organized religion among Asian Americans. Instead, we should use the terms *East Asian* and *South Asian* congregations.

Gender

Men and women learn their culturally assigned gender roles mainly through socialization. Historically, religion has played a significant role in offering cultural definitions of gender roles and legitimating gender hierarchy.[52] Through both teachings of the Bible and the organizational structure of the church, Christian religions have largely fostered the patriarchal ideology and gender hierarchy, although recently they have also been used as liberating forces for gender equality. Although women are more religious and more active in participation in churches in the United States, they play a subordinate role in performing rituals and holding leadership positions, including the clergy, in churches.[53] The Christian religions indigenized in Asian countries, with the exception of Philippine Catholicism, are likely to be more patriarchal and more sexist than those in the United States, which have gone through significant changes since the 1960s as a result of the feminist movement.[54] Moreover, Hinduism, Buddhism, and Islam have elements that support higher levels of patriarchy and sexism than American Christian religions, although levels of patriarchy and sexism within each religion are varied in different cultural contexts.[55] Given this fact, we can expect women to play a more subordinate role in Asian immigrant religious congregations—whether Christian or non-Christian—than in white American Christian churches.

A number of studies by social scientists and theologians have commented on women's subordinate role and the patriarchal customs supported by Asian immigrants' religions and/or practiced in Asian immigrant congregations.[56] I introduce three of these studies here.

In her study of an Indian Christian church, George reveals how Indian men from Kerala, most of whom were sponsored by their nurse wives and who lost their social status relative to their wives through immigration, have attempted to organize their Orthodox Christian immigrant congregation to enhance their male leadership.[57] In this attempt, they have not only reproduced the conservative Indian congregation in the United States, but also modified it to increase men's roles. In an interesting article, Kurien describes the complex process in which gender plays the central role in the creation of ethnic communities and cultures among Indian Hindu immigrants.[58] Because of their dominant role as religious and cultural producers, Indian Hindu women in the United States are able to reinterpret traditional gender images and constructs to their favor. However, as Kurien points out, their influence is largely confined to the family and community. It is the leaders of pan-Indian and pan-Hindu organizations, dominated by upper-class men, who formally codify and communicate what Indian culture and Hindu religion represent. These leaders make "the figure of the chaste, nurturing, and self-sacrificing Indian woman" the center of the Indian family values and work ethic. In her book, which focuses on Korean Christian immigrant women, A. R. Kim also shows how a Korean immigrant church perpetuates the traditional Korean patriarchal ideology and customs.[59] In her view, the Korean church legitimates the Korean patriarchal culture and women's traditional gender role by emphasizing women's self-denial and unconditional obedience to God on the one hand, and gender-based role differentiation within it on the other.

In discussing the effects of religion on women's subordinate role and status in the context of Asian immigrant communities, we should try to separate—no matter how difficult—the effects of religion from those of ethnic culture using comparative data. Let's take the Korean immigrant church as an example. In the previously mentioned book, A. R. Kim emphasizes the role of a Korean immigrant church in perpetuating traditional Korean patriarchal customs. She presents the Korean Confucian culture as the main cause of Korean immigrant women's continuously subordinate status and the Korean church as the mechanism for perpetuating the patriarchal culture.[60] In a similar study, J. H. Kim agrees that the Korean immigrant church is very patriarchal in ideology and rituals, but she views Christianity itself, rather than Confucian cultural traditions, as the main culprit of patriarchal customs practiced in Korean immigrant churches.[61] In his study of a second-generation Korean evangelical ministry, Alumkal makes a point similar to J. H. Kim's.[62] In his view, although members of a second-generation Korean ministry (evangelicals) are highly assimilated to American culture, they, too, accept many patriarchal customs. He argues that the persistency of patriarchy over generations of Korean American Christians supports the view that Christianity rather than Korean Confucian cultural traditions is mainly responsible for patriarchal customs practiced in Korean congregations.

There is no doubt that Christianity has patriarchal elements, as is evidenced by the fact that American Christians who are more religious accept more patriarchal values than those who are less religious.[63] This suggests that patriarchal customs practiced in Korean immigrant churches are partly influenced by the nature of religion itself. However, the issue is not whether a Korean immigrant or a second-generation Korean congregation is patriarchal or not, but to what extent it is patriarchal. Comparative data strongly suggest that Korean immigrant churches are far more patriarchal and sexist than both U.S. Christian churches, in general, and second-generation Korean congregations. For example, results of nationwide surveys of Presbyterians conducted by the Presbyterian Panel (1996) and the Racial and Ethnic Presbyterian Panel (1997) reveal that women compose only 8 percent of Korean elders compared to 44 percent of white elders.[64] The same data also show that Korean women elders have higher educational levels than male elders, suggesting that Korean women should have exceptionally high educational levels to be ordained as elders. [65] Given that elders exercise great power and authority in Korean immigrant churches, this data gives a glimpse of male domination there. Moreover, several studies have indicated that second-generation Korean Christians are critical of the male-centered structure of Korean immigrant churches and Korean immigrant families and that Korean second-generation ministry maintains more gender equality than immigrant churches.[66]

Transnationalism

Transnationalism, transnational ties, or transnational communities of contemporary immigrants are popular topics and research concepts.[67] To quote a widely used definition, *transnationalism* is "the processes by which immigrants forge and sustain multi-stranded social relations that link together their societies of origin and settlement." [68] Of course, transnationalism is not a new phenomenon applicable only to contemporary immigrants. As Nancy Foner has pointed out, European immigrants at the turn of the twentieth century, also lived transnational lives, maintaining ties with and allegiance to their European home countries.[69] However, by virtue of technological advances, changes in government policies in the host and home countries, and globalization of the economy, contemporary immigrants maintain close social, cultural, economic, and political ties with their home countries unimaginable to the earlier immigrants.

Transnational ties that immigrants maintain with their home countries have effects on their religious practices as well. As such, recent studies of contemporary immigrants' religious experiences, including *Gatherings in Diaspora* and *Religion and the New Immigrants*, have used transnational theory. Due to their physical proximity, Caribbean and Latino immigrant groups have advantages for maintaining ties with their home country. Thus, in religious experiences, as in other aspects of immigrant experiences, transnationalism has been applied more often to Caribbean and Latino immigrant groups than to other immigrant groups.[70] Because of physical distance, Asian immigrants cannot maintain as strong ties with their home countries as do Caribbean or Latino immigrants. Yet, Asian immigrants, too, live transnational lives, immensely affected by their ties with their home countries. There is no single study that has systematically examined the effects of transnational ties on Asian immigrants' religious practices, but the transnational theme emerges in several studies.[71]

Studies of transnationalism in general have usually focused on the individual immigrant's transnational ties and activities, regardless of whether those ties are sociocultural, economic, or political in nature.[72]

However, studies of transnational aspects of immigrants' religious experiences have focused on transnational ties in the organizational structure of the particular congregation under consideration.[73] Asian countries have developed several different varieties of Buddhism. During recent years, the establishment of Buddhist temples for Asian immigrants (for "ethnic Buddhism"), as well as for Americans, is a kind of "missionary activity" by central Buddhist organizations in Asian countries. Accordingly, Asian immigrant temples are inseparably tied to the central organizations. For example, Hsi Lai Temple in southern California is one of the several overseas branches of the Fo Kuang San of Taiwan established in the United States. As such, the temple is "administered by monks and nuns handpicked and sent from Fo Kuang San" and it has adopted the organizational hierarchy of the main monastery.[74] Boh Won Sa, a Korean immigrant temple in Boston, is more independent from the Chogye order in Korea than is the above-mentioned Chinese temple because it was founded with private donations collected locally. Yet, according to Chai, when "a monk was accused of misconduct," or when "the temple was seeking an additional monk or nun," it would call upon the Chogye leadership in Korea.[75]

Different forms of Hinduism represent Indian national and local religious and cultural traditions. Thus, Hindu religious leaders in India are seriously concerned with Indian Hindu immigrants maintaining their religion. A few studies have documented the involvement, in the forms of financial support, counseling, and advice, of Hindu religious leaders and architects from India in building temples in the United States.[76] In order to maintain religious orthodoxy, Hindu religious leaders from India continue to influence temples through lecture tours. As Johanna Lessinger puts it,

> One way in which faith and religious orthodoxy are promoted is through lecture tours which visiting Indian religious figures make around the U.S. Most of the major denominations arrange such tours. Leaders of religious foundations, saintly, learned men and women, or musicians specializing in a sacred repertoire travel through the U.S. giving sermons (often called "discourses"), concerts and public readings of the scriptures.[77]

However, it is "diaspora Hindu nationalism" that has attracted a great deal of scholarly attention as a more significant transnational dimension of Hinduism linking India and overseas Indian communities.[78] The *Hindutva* or Hindu nationalist movement is the political movement to make India a Hindu state and delegitimate minority religious groups in India. The movement, which started in the late nineteenth century, has become resurgent since the early 1980s, resulting in the victory of a Hindu political party (the Bharatiya Janata Party) in the national elections and increased physical violence against Christians and Muslims in India. Although most Hindus in diasporic communities do not accept the Hindu nationalist ideology, a wide variety of pan-Hindu organizations there have mobilized active support of the movement in the 1990s.[79] Kurien shows how a pan-Hindu organization in southern California supporting the Hindu nationalist movement and a pan-Muslim organization representing American Muslims from India construct Indian history and the ideal Indian state in radically different ways.[80] Although Hindu nationalist expression in the United States is different in meaning and implications from that in India, the two forms of Hindu nationalism are linked through transnational circuits of communication and exchange.[81]

Even Asian immigrant Christian congregations maintain moderate levels—although lower than Buddhist or Hindu temples—of transnational ties with their homelands. As is clear from discussions in many chapters of this book, Christian religions originally transplanted to Asian countries reflect local folk culture to a much greater extent than some Western people may believe. In particular, Syrian Christianity is almost indigenous to Kerala, India, with twelve hundred years of history.[82] Naturally, Indian immigrant churches of Syrian Christian ancestry (Catholic, Eastern Orthodox, and Protestant) are organizationally tied to, and under supervision of, the mother churches in India. Filipino Catholic immigrants, too, originate from a heavily Catholic country with a long history. As chapter 6 clarifies, Filipino Catholicism has incorporated much of Filipino folk culture in its adaptation to the country. In view of these facts, Filipino Catholic churches in the United States are likely to maintain some organizational ties with the Catholic hierarchy in the Philippines (although we do not have data on it).

Christianity in other Asian countries has a much shorter history than in India or the Philippines. Thus, immigrant churches attended by other Asian immigrants do not maintain direct organizational ties with the mother churches in their homelands. Yet they also maintain moderate levels of transnational ties. For one thing, some Chinese and Korean immigrant Protestant churches provide financial support for Christian organizations and rural churches in the homeland.[83] Asian immigrant churches and churches in the homelands often exchange invitations of ministers to give sermons, which is another form of transnational connection.[84] The invitations are facilitated not only by popularization of air travel but also by ministers' alumni connections.

Notes

1. Andrew Greeley, *Why Can't They Be Like Us? America's White Ethnic Groups* (New York: E. P. Dutton & Company, 1971); S. Rosenberg, *The New Jewish Identity*

in America (New York: Hippocrene Books, 1985); Timothy Smith, "Religion and Ethnicity in America," *American Historical Review* 83 (1978): 1155–85; S. M. Tomasi and M. H. Engel, *The Italian Experience in the United States* (Staten Island, N.Y.: Center for Migration Studies, 1971); Stephen Warner, "Work in Progress toward a New Paradigm for the Sociological Study of Religion in the United States," *American Journal of Sociology* 98 (1993): 1044–93; Stephen Warner, "The Place of Congregation in the American Religious Configuration," in *American Congregations*, vol.2: *New Perspectives in the Study of Congregations*, ed. James Wind and James Lewis (Chicago: University of Chicago Press, 1994), 54–99; W. L. Warner and L. Srole, *The Social Systems of American Ethnic Groups* (New Haven, Conn.: Yale University Press, 1945).

2. Warner and Srole, *Social System of American Ethnic Groups*, 160.

3. Tomasi and Engel, *Italian Experience in the United States*, 186.

4. Robert Ostergren, "The Immigrant Church as a Symbol of Community and Place in the Upper Midwest," *Great Plains Quarterly* 1 (1981): 225–38.

5. W. E. B. Du Bois, *The Philadelphia Negro* (New York: Schocken Books, 1967) 201.

6. R. M. Links, *American Catholicism and European Immigrants* (Staten Island, N.Y.: Center for Migration Studies, 1975).

7. Carl Bankston III and Min Zhou, "Religious Participation, Ethnic Identification, and Adaptation of Vietnamese Adolescents in an Immigrant Community," *Sociological Quarterly* 36 (1995): 523–34; Won Moo Hurh and Kwang Chung Kim, "Religious Participation of Korean Immigrants in the United States," *Journal of the Scientific Study of Religion* 29 (1990): 19–34; Kwang Chung Kim and Shin Kim, "The Ethnic Role of Korean Immigrant Churches in the U.S.," in *Korean Americans and Their Religions: Pilgrims and Missionaries from a Different Shore*, ed. Ho-Youn Kwon, Kwang Chung Kim, and Stephen Warner (University Park: Pennsylvania State University Press, 2001) 91–94; Prema Kurien, "Becoming American by Becoming Hindu: Indian Americans Take Their Place at the Multicultural Table," in *Gatherings in Diaspora: Religious Communities and the New Immigration*, ed. Stephen Warner and Judith Wittner (Philadelphia: Temple University Press, 1998), 37–70; Prema Kurien, "Religion, Ethnicity and Politics: Hindu and Muslim Indian Immigrants in the United States," *Ethnic and Racial Studies* 24 (2001): 263–93; Pyong Gap Min, "The Structure and Social Functions of Korean Immigrant Churches in the United States," *International Migration Review* 26 (1992): 1370–94; Paul Rutledge, *The Role of Religion in Ethnic Self-Identity: A Vietnamese Community* (Lanham, Md.: University Press of America, 1985); Raymond Brady Williams, *Religions of Immigrants from India and Pakistan* (Cambridge, U.K.: Cambridge University Press, 1988); Fenggang Yang, *Chinese Christians in America: Conversion, Assimilation, and Adhesive Identities* (University Park: Pennsylvania State University Press, 1999).

8. Kurien, "Becoming American by Becoming Hindu," 59. See also her article "Gendered Ethnicity: Creating a Hindu Indian Identity in the United States," *American Behavioral Scientist* 42 (1999): 648–70.

9. Bankston and Zhou, "Religious Participation, Ethnic Identification, and Adaptation," 530.

10. Min, "Structure and Social Functions of Korean Immigrant Churches."

11. Warner, "Place of Congregation," 54; Stephen Warner, "Immigration and Religious Communities in the United States," in *Gatherings in Diaspora*, ed. Warner and Wittner, pp.3–36.

12. John Fenton, *Transplanting Religious Traditions: Asian Indians in America* (New York: Praeger, 1988), 179; Thuan Huynb, "The Center for Vietnamese Buddhism Recreating Home," in *Religion and the New Immigrants: Continuities and Adaptations in Immigrant Congregations*, ed. Helen Rose Ebaugh and Janet Saltzman Chafetz (Walnut Creek, Calif.: AltaMira Press, 2000), 45–66; Kurien, "Becoming American by Becoming Hindu," 42; Eui-Young Yu, "The Growth of Korean Buddhism in the United States, with Special Reference to Southern California," *Pacific World* 4 (1988): 82–93.

13. According to a survey conducted in Queens, New York, in 1997 and 1998, 83 percent of Korean Christian immigrants attend church (in almost all cases a Korean church) once a week or more often compared to 22 percent of Indian Hindus. See Pyong Gap Min, "Immigrants' Religion and Ethnicity: A Comparison of Indian Hindu and Korean Christian Immigrants in the United States," *Bulletin of the Royal Institute of Inter-Faith Studies* 2 (2000): 130.

14. Ana Maria Diaz-Stevens, *Oxcart Catholicism on Fifth Avenue: The Impact of the Puerto Rican Migration upon the Archdiocese of New York* (Notre Dame, Ind.: University of Notre Dame Press, 1993); Ebaugh and Chafetz, *Religion and the New Immigrants*; Min, "Immigrants' Religion and Ethnicity," 122–40; Nancy Wellmeier, "Santa Eulalia's People in Exile: Maya Religion, Culture, and Identity in Los Angeles," in *Gatherings in Diaspora*, ed. Warner and Wittner, 97–122.

15. Ebaugh and Chafetz, *Religion and the New Immigrants*, 392–93.

16. Min, "Immigrants' Religion and Ethnicity."

17. Hurh and Kim, "Religious Participation of Korean Immigrants"; Min, "The Structure and Social Functions of Korean Immigrant Churches"; and Min, "Immigrants' Religion and Ethnicity."

18. Jay Doran, *The American Catholic Experience: History from Colonial Time to the Present* (Garden City, N.J.: Doubleday, 1985); Steven Gold, "Religious Agencies, Immigrant Settlement, and Social Justice," *Research in Social Policy* 5 (1997): 47–65; S. Jenkins, *Ethnic Associations and Welfare States: Services to Immigrants in Five Countries* (New York: Columbia University Press, 1988); Links, *American Catholicism and European Immigrants*; B. Nichols, *Religion, Refugee Work, and Foreign Policy* (New York: Oxford University Press, 1988); Marvin Olasky, *The Tragedy of Compassion* (Washington, D.C.: Regnery Gateway, 1992); Michael O'Neill, *The Third America: The Emergence of the Non-Profit Sector in the United States* (San Francisco: Jossey-Bass, 1989); Rosenberg, *New Jewish Identity*.

19. Doran, *American Catholic Experience*.

20. Gold, "Religious Agencies, Immigrant Settlement, and Social Justice."

21. Ebaugh and Chafetz, *Religion and the New Immigrants*, ch. 16, 17, and 18; Victoria Hyunchu Kwon, *Entrepreneurship and Religion: Korean Immigrants in Houston* (New York: Garland, 1997); Min, "The Structure and Social Functions of Korean Immigrant Churches"; Min Zhou and Carl Bankston III, *Growing Up American: How Vietnamese Children Adapt to Life in the United States* (New York: Russell Sage Foundation, 1998), ch. 4; Yu, "Growth of Korean Buddhism in the United States."

22. Hurh and Kim, "Religious Participation of Korean Immigrants"; Kwon, *Entrepreneurship and Religion*; Min, "Structure and Social Functions of Korean Immigrant Churches"; Pyong Gap Min, "Korean Immigrants in New York," in *New Immigrants in New York*, 2d ed., ed. Nancy Foner (New York: Columbia University Press, 2001).

23. Min, "Structure and Social Functions of Korean Immigrant Churches."

24. Ebaugh and Chafetz, *Religion and the New Immigrants*, ch. 16, 17, 18.

25. Ebaugh and Chafetz, *Religion and the New Immigrants*, ch. 3, 17, 18; Irene Lin, "Journey to the Far West: Chinese Buddhism in America," in *New Spiritual Homes: Religion and Asian Americans*, ed. David Yoo (Honolulu: University of Hawaii Press, 1999), 134–66; Yu, "Growth of Korean Buddhism in the United States"; Zhou and Bankston, *Growing Up American*, 98–99.

26. Yu, "Growth of Korean Buddhism in the United States."

27. Lin, "Journey to the Far West," 141–42.

28. Thuan Huynb, "Center for Vietnamese Buddhism," 45–66.

29. Ebaugh and Chafetz, *Religion and the New Immigrants*, 347; Min, "Immigrants' Religion and Ethnicity."

30. For African Americans' unique experiences of Christianity, see also Katharine Dvorak, *An African-American Exodus: The Segregation of Southern Churches* (Brooklyn, N.Y.: Carson, 1991); Walter F. Pitts, *Old Ship of Zion: The Afro-Baptist Ritual in the African Diaspora* (New York: Oxford University Press, 1993); Albert Raboteau, *Slave Religion: The "Invisible" Institution in the Antebellum South* (New York: Oxford University Press, 1978).

31. Andrew Hacker, *Two Nations: Black and White, Separate, Hostile, Unequal* (New York: Scribner, 1992).

32. Meridith B. McGuire, *Religion: The Social Context*, 4th ed. (Belmont, Calif.: Wadsworth, 1997), 259.

33. Herbert Gans, "Toward a Reconciliation of 'Assimilation' and 'Pluralism': The Interplay of Acculturation and Ethnic Retention," *International Migration Review* 31: 875–92.

34. The only exception is Elizabeth McAlister's chapter, entitled "The Madonna of 115th Street Revisited: Vodou and Haitian Catholicism in the Age of Transnationalism," in *Gatherings in Diaspora*, ed. Warner and Wittner, 123–62.

35. Peter Krivisto, "The Transplanted Then and Now," *Ethnic and Racial Studies* 13 (1990): 455–81; Warner, "Immigration and Religious Communities," 14; Williams, *Religions of Immigrants from India and Pakistan*, 3, 11.

36. Won Moo Hurh and Kwang Chung Kim, "The 'Success' Image of Asian Americans: Its Validity and Its Practical Implications," *Ethnic and Racial Studies* 12 (1989): 512–38.

37. Yen Espiritu, *Asian American Women and Men* (Walnut Creek, Calif.: Sage, 1997); Hurh and Kim, "The 'Success' Image of Asian Americans"; Mia Tuan, *Forever Foreigners or Honorary Whites: The Asian Ethnic Experience Today* (New Brunswick, N.J.: Rutgers University Press, 1999).

38. Pyong Gap Min and Rose Kim, *Struggle for Ethnic Identity: Narratives by Asian American Professionals* (Walnut Creek, Calif.: AltaMira, 1999); Tuan, *Forever Foreigners or Honorary Whites*.

39. Hurh and Kim, "Religious Participation of Korean Immigrants"; Joyce Tang, "The Career Attainment of Caucasian and Asian American Engineers," *So-*

ciological Quarterly 34: 467–96; Min Zhou and Yoshinori Kamo, "An Analysis of Earnings Patterns for Chinese, Japanese, and Non-Hispanic Whites in the United States," *Sociological Quarterly* 35 (1994): 581–602.

40. David Yoo, "Introduction: Reframing the U.S. Religious Landscape," in *New Spiritual Homes*, ed. Yoo, 7.

41. Sang Hyun Lee, "Pilgrimage and Home in the Wilderness of Marginality: Symbols and Contexts in Asian American Theology," in *New Spiritual Homes*, ed. Yoo, 218–31.

42. Jung Young Lee, "Marginality: Multi-Ethnic Approach to Theology from an Asian American Perspective," *Asian Journal of Theology* 7 (1993): 244–53; Fumitaka Matsuoka, *Out of Silence: Emerging Themes in Asian American Churches* (Cleveland, Ohio: United Church Press, 1995); Jitsuo Morikawa, "Toward an Asian American Theology," *American Baptist Quarterly* 12 (1993): 179–89; David Ng, *People on the Way: Asian North Americans Discovering Christ, Culture and Community* (Valley Forge, Pa.: Judson Press, 1996); Pet Phan and Jung Young Lee, eds., *Journey at the Margin* (New York: United Press, 1999).

43. Nazli Kibria, "College and Notions of 'Asian American': Second Generation Chinese and Korean Americans Negotiate Race and Identity," *Amerasia Journal* 25 (1999): 29–52; Pyong Gap Min and Rose Kim, "Formation of Ethnic and Racial Identities: Narratives by Young Asian-American Professionals," *Ethnic and Racial Studies* 23 (2000): 735–60.

44. Michael Omni and Howard Winant, *Racial Formation in the United States: From the 1960s to the 1980s* (New York: Rutledge, 1986); Dana Takagi, "Post–Civil Rights Politics and Asian-American Identity: Admission and Higher Education," in *Race*, ed. Steven Gregory and Roger Sanjek (New Brunswick, N.J.: Rutgers University Press, 1994), 229–42.

45. Tini Tran, "Pan-Asian Churches Emerging," *Los Angeles Times*, March 8, 1999; De Tran and Ariana Cha, "Congregations at the Crossroads: Asian American Christians Leaving Their Parent's Style of Worship Behind," *San Jose Mercury News*, April 12, 1998.

46. Pyong Gap Min, "Pan-Ethnic Boundaries among Asian Americans in the United States" (paper presented at the annual meeting of the American Sociological Association, Washington, D.C., August 2000).

47. Yen Espiritu, *Asian American Panethnicity: Bridging Institutions and Identities* (Philadelphia: Temple University Press, 1992).

48. Nazli Kibria, "Not Asian, Black or White: Reflections on South Asian Racial Identities," *Amerasia Journal* 22 (1996): 77–88; Nazli Kibria, "The Construction of 'Asian American': Reflections on Intermarriage and Ethnic Identity among Second-Generation Chinese and Korean Americans," *Ethnic and Racial Studies* 20 (1997): 523–44; Min and Kim, "Formation of Racial and Ethnic Identities"; Lavina Dingra Shankar and Rajini Srikanth, eds., *A Part, but Apart: South Asians in Asian America* (Philadelphia: Temple University Press, 1998).

49. According to a survey conducted in Queens, New York, based on a sample of randomly selected Indian surnames from the public telephone directory, 12 percent of Indian immigrant respondents chose Catholicism or Protestantism as their current religion. Since Indian Muslims may compose about 15 percent of the Indian immigrant population, the proportion of Christians among Indian

immigrants is likely to be less than 12 percent. See Min, "Immigrants' Religion and Ethnicity."

50. The Korean American population is one of the largest Asian groups in San Francisco, but second-generation Korean Christians can attend English ministry established in many Korean churches in the city.

51. Hoda Badr, "Al-Noor Mosque: Strength through Unity," in *Religion and the New Immigrants*, ed. Ebaugh and Chafetz, 196; Min, "Immigrants' Religion and Ethnicity."

52. Mary Daly, *The Church and the Second Sex* (Boston: Beacon, 1985); Janet Wilson James, ed., *Women in American Religion* (Philadelphia: University of Pennsylvania Press, 1980); Meredith B. McGuire, *Religion: The Social Context*, 4th ed. (Belmont, Calif.: Wadsworth, 1997), 121; Mary Neitz, "Inequality and Difference," in *A Future for Religion: New Paradigms for Social Analysis*, ed. William Swatos Jr. (Newbury Park, Calif.: Sage, 1993), 165–84; William Swatos Jr., ed., *Gender and Religion* (New Brunswick, N.J.: Transaction, 1993); Ruth Wallace, "Bringing Women In: Marginality in the Churches," *Sociological Analysis* 36 (1975): 291–303.

53. Robert Wuthnow, *The Restructuring of American Religion: Society and Faith since World War II* (Princeton, N.J.: Princeton University Press, 1988), 225–26.

54. For the effects of feminism on religion in the United States since the 1960s, see Edward Lehman Jr., *Women Clergy: Breaking through Gender Barriers* (New Brunswick, N.J.: Transaction, 1985); Swatos, *Gender and Religion*; Wuthnow, *Restructuring of American Religion*, ch. 9.

55. Nifufer Ahmed, Gladis Kaufman, and Shamin Naim, "South Asian Families in the United States: Pakistan, Bangladesh, and Indian Muslims," in *Family and Gender among American Muslims*, ed. Barbara C. Aswad and Barbara Bilge (Philadelphia: Temple University Press, 1996), 155–72; Katherine Young, "Upholding Norms of Hindu Womanhood: An Analysis Based on Reviews of Hindi Cinema," in *Gender Genre and Religion: Feminist Reflections*, ed. Morny Joy and Eva K. Neumaier-Dargyay (Waterloo, Ontario: Wilfred Laurier University Press, 1999), 173–76; Sheila McDonough, "The Impact of Social Change on Muslim Women," in *Gender Genre and Religion*, ed. Joy and Neumaier-Dargyay, 125–41.

56. Anthony Alumkal, "Preserving Patriarchy: Assimilation, Gender Norms, and Second Generation Korean American Evangelicals," *Qualitative Sociology* 22 (1999): 127–40; Sheba George, "Caroling with the Keralites: The Negotiation of Gendered Space in an Indian Immigrant Community," in *Gatherings in Diaspora*, ed. Warner and Wittner, 265–94; Sangeeta R. Gupta, ed., *Emerging Voices: South Asian American Women Redefine Self, Family, and Community* (Thousand Oaks, Calif.: Sage, 1999); A. R. Kim, *Women Struggling for a New Life: The Role of Religion in the Cultural Passage from Korea to America* (Albany: State University of New York Press, 1996); J. H. Kim, "The Labor of Compassion: Voices of 'Churched' Korean American Women," *Amerasia Journal* 22 (1996): 93–105; Pyong Gap Min, *Changes and Conflicts: Korean Immigrant Families in New York* (Boston: Allyn & Bacon, 1998), ch. 4; Naomi Southard and Ruth Nakashima Brock, "The Other Half of the Basket: Asian American Women and the Search for a Theological Home," *Journal of Feminist Studies of Religion* 3 (1987): 133–50.

57. George, "Caroling with the Keralites."

58. Kurien, "Gendered Ethnicity."

59. A. R. Kim, *Women Struggling for a New Life.*

60. In my studies of Korean immigrant churches, I provided a similar interpretation. See Min, "Structure and Social Functions of Korean Immigrant Churches"; Min, *Changes and Conflicts.*

61. Jung Ha Kim, "Labor of Compassion."

62. Alumkal, "Preserving Patriarchy."

63. Wuthnow, *Restructuring of American Religion*, 225–35.

64. Kim and Kim, "Ethnic Role of Korean Immigrant Churches."

65. Kim and Kim, in "Ethnic Role of Korean Immigrant Churches," show that 90 percent of Korean female elders, in comparison to 74 percent of their male counterparts, completed a four-year college education, although Korean men usually have a higher education than women in general.

66. Kelly Chong, "What It Means to be Christians; The Role of Religion in the Construction of Ethnic Identity and Boundary among Second-Generation Korean Americans," Sociology of Religion 59 (1998): 259–86; Soyoung Park, "The Intersection of Religion, Race, Ethnicity, and Gender," in Korean Americans and Their Religions, 193–208.

67. Linda Basch, Nina Glick-Schiller, and Cristina Szanton Blanc, eds., *Nations Unbounded: Transnational Projects, Postcolonial Predicaments, and Deterritorialized Nation-States* (Langhorne, Pa.: Gordon and Breach, 1994); Nina Glick-Schiller, "Transmigrants and Nation-States: Something Old and Something New in the U.S. Immigrant Experiences," in *The Handbook of International Migration*, ed. Charles Hirschman, Philip Kasinitz, and Josh DeWind (New York: Russell Sage Publications, 2000), 96–119; Nina Glick-Schiller, Linda Basch, and Cristina Szanton Blanc, "Transnationalism: A New Analytic Framework for Understanding Migration," *Annals of the New York Academy of Sciences* 645 (1992): 1–24; Steven Gold, "Transnationalism and Vocabularies of Motive in International Migration: The Case of Israelis in the United States," *Sociological Perspectives* 40 (1997): 409–27; Nancy Foner, "What's New about Transnationalism? New York Immigrants Today and at the Turn of the Century," *Diaspora* 6 (1997): 355–75; Michel Laguerre, *Diasporic Citizenship: Haitian Americans in Transnational America* (New York: St. Martin's, 1998); Alejandro Portes, Luis Guarnizo, and Patricia Landolt, "The Study of Transnationalism: Pitfalls and Promise of an Emergent Research Field," *Ethnic and Racial Studies* 22 (1999): 217–37; Michael P. Smith and Luis E. Guarnizo, eds., *Transnationalism Below* (New Brunswick, N.J.: Transaction, 1998).

68. Glick-Schiller, "Transmigrants and Nation-States," 7.

69. Foner, "What's New about Transnationalism?"

70. Luis Leon, "Born Again in East LA: The Congregation as Border Space," in *Gatherings in Diaspora*, ed. Warner and Wittner, 163–96; Peggy Levitt, "Local-Level Global Religion: The Case of U.S.-Dominican Migration," *Journal for the Scientific Study of Religion* 37 (1998): 74–89; Elizabeth McAlister, "The Madonna of 115th Street Revisited," 123–63; Kathleen Sullivan, "Iglesia de Dios: An Extended Family," in *Religion and the New Immigrants*, ed. Ebaugh and Chafetz, 148; Thomas Tweed, *Our Lady of the Exile: Diasporic Religion at a Cuban Catholic Shrine in Miami* (New York: Oxford University Press, 1997).

71. Simm Jacob and Pallavi Thaku, "Jyotti Hindu Temple: One Religion, Many Practices," in *Religion and the New Immigrants*, ed. Ebaugh and Chafetz, 229–42;

Kwang Chung Kim, Stephen Warner, and Ho-Youn Kwon, "Korean-American Religion in Transnational Perspectives," in *Pilgrims and Missionaries from a Different Shore*, ed. Kwon, Kim, and Warner, 3–24; Kurien, "Becoming American by Becoming Hindu"; Kurien, "Religion, Ethnicity, and Politics"; Vinay Lal, "Sikh Kirpans in California Schools: The Social Construction of Symbols, the Cultural Politics of Identity, and the Limits of Multiculturalism," in *New Spiritual Homes*, ed. Yoo, 87–133; Lin, "Journey to the Far West"; Fenggang Yang, "The *His-Nan* Chinese Buddhist Temple: Seeking to Americanize," in *Religion and the New Immigrants*, ed. Ebaugh and Chafetz, 67–87; Fenggang Yang, "Chinese Gospel Church: The Sinicization of Christianity," in *Religion and the New Immigrants*, ed. Ebaugh and Chafetz, 89–107.

72. Portes, Guarnizo, and Landolt, "The Study of Transnationalism," 20.

73. This is not surprising at all, given that social science studies of immigrants' religious practices have usually taken the congregation as the unit of analysis.

74. Lin, "Journey to the Far West," 140.

75. Karen Chai, "Intra-Ethnic Religious Diversity: Korean Buddhists and Protestants in Greater Boston," in *Korean Immigrants and Their Religions*, ed. Kwon, Kim, and Warner, ch. 16.

76. Jacob and Thaku, "Jyotti Hindu Temple," 239; Johanna Lessinger, *From the Ganges to the Hudson: Indian Immigrants to New York City* (Boston: Allyn & Bacon, 1995), 49–51; Williams, *Religions of Immigrants from India and Pakistan*, ch. 5.

77. Lessinger, *From the Ganges to the Hudson*, 51–52.

78. Kurien, "Becoming American by Becoming Hindu"; Kurien, 2000 "Religion, Ethnicity, and Politics." See also a special issue of *Ethnic and Racial Studies* 23 (2000), "Hindutva Movements in the West: Resurgent Hinduism and Politics of Diaspora."

79. Parita Mukta, "The Public Face of Hindu Nationalism," *Ethnic and Racial Studies* 23 (2000): 442–66; Biju Mathew and Bijay Prashad, "The Protean Forms of Yankee Hindusta," *Racial and Ethnic Studies* 23 (2000): 516–34; Arvind Rajagopal, "Hindu Nationalism in the U.S.: Changing Configurations of Political Practice," *Ethnic and Racial Studies* 23 (2000): 467–96.

80. Kurien, "Religion, Ethnicity, and Politics."

81. Rajagopal, "Hindu Nationalism in the US."

82. George, "Caroling with the Keralites," 271; Williams, *Religions of Immigrants from India and Pakistan*, 104–7; Raymond Williams, *Christian Pluralism in the United States: The Indian Immigrant Experience* (New York: Cambridge University Press, 1996).

83. Victoria Hyunchu Kwon, "Houston Korean Ethnic Church: An Ethnic Enclave," in *Religion and the New Immigrants*, ed. Ebaugh and Chafetz, 118; Yang, "Chinese Gospel Churches," 102–3.

84. Min, "Structure and Social Functions of Korean Immigrant Churches."

CHAPTER TWO

REBUILDING SPIRITUAL LIVES IN THE NEW LAND: RELIGIOUS PRACTICES AMONG SOUTHEAST ASIAN REFUGEES IN THE UNITED STATES

Min Zhou, Carl L. Bankston III, Rebecca Y. Kim

Southeast Asian refugees, primarily of Vietnamese, Cambodian, and Laotian national origin, are the largest and most visible refugee group to have settled in the United States since the mid-1970s. The story of Southeast Asians in America is one of very sudden and rapid growth, from a population of insignificant size in the early 1970s, to one of over a million people in the 1990s. The 1990 U.S. Census counted 615,000 Vietnamese, 128,000 Cambodians, 196,000 Laotians (almost half were Hmong), and some 200,000 ethnic Chinese from Southeast Asia. Even these figures probably understate the true size of these three national-origin groups because fertility levels are high and because continuing secondary migration within the United States has made it difficult to keep accurate records.[1]

Southeast Asian refugees have traveled a great cultural distance. They have come to postindustrial America from largely subsistence economies. Many refugees left interlocking kinship ties in small villages for a mobile, urban/suburban civilization. The religious institutions and practices linked to their ways of life in Asia were substantially different from those of the contemporary United States. Laotians and Cambodians come from a society that is overwhelmingly Theravada Buddhist. The Vietnamese come from a society that is shaped by Mahayana Buddhism and Confucianism. Even Vietnamese Catholicism, the religion of a substantial minority of people in Vietnam, has been so heavily influenced by indigenous traditions that it is frequently referred to as a form of "Confucianized Christianity."[2] Southeast Asians in the United States now live in a postindustrial society with a majority Protestant population that has been heavily influenced by its own varieties of Christian traditions and beliefs.[3] This chapter examines how Southeast Asian refugees are coping with these sudden and drastic cultural, social, and economic changes in the new land through the lens of their religious practices. We first provide a discussion of why and how Southeast Asian refugees have been resettled in America. We look at the challenges they face and at how they are faring in the new land. We then examine in greater detail the role of religion in facilitating the process of adjustment and in reconstructing the moral orders and spiritual lives of Southeast Asians in the United States.

The U.S. Involvement in Southeast Asia and Refugee Flight

The sudden emergence of Southeast Asians on the American scene was primarily the result of U.S. military involvement in Southeast Asia. The United States originally had little economic interest in the region. The development of the Communist bloc dominated by the former Soviet Union, the Communist takeover in China, the direct confrontation with Communist troops in the Korean War, and the threat of the Communist "domino" effect prompted a U.S. foreign policy to "contain" communism, pushing Americans into Indo-China.

The Vietnam War

In 1954 the French army was defeated by Ho Chi Minh's Viet Minh Front forces, and Vietnam was divided into two countries: the Democratic Republic of Vietnam (North Vietnam), headed by Ho Chi Minh, and the Republic of Vietnam (South Vietnam), headed by Ngo Dinh Diem. In response, the United States—acting on the primary foreign policy objective of containing international Communism—became increasingly dedicated to the preservation of Diem's anti-Communist government in South Vietnam. The U.S. government hoped that its support of South Vietnam would deter the expansion of power of communist North Vietnam and prevent communism from spreading to other Southeast Asian countries. Meanwhile, many U.S.-based voluntary agencies, including Catholic Relief Services (CARE), Church World Services, and others, were active in South Vietnam in response to the social disruption of war. Thus, the people of South Vietnam began to become better acquainted with Americans and American culture and better connected with Catholicism than their northern country folks.

In 1961, President Kennedy sent military advisers to South Vietnam to assist the beleaguered Diem government. However, Diem, born of a Catholic family and relying heavily upon Vietnamese Catholics and Catholic refugees from the north for his suppression of communist infiltration in the south, began to lose his popularity. In a country in which Buddhism dominated, Diem's favoritism toward Catholics created strong resentment, which opened up opportunities for the North Vietnamese–supported insurgents. These insurgents organized themselves as the National Liberation Front, known as the Viet Cong (Viet-namese guerrilla fighters who opposed the South Vietnamese government). Diem also made enemies of other religious groups, such as the *Hoa Hao*, the *Cao Dai*, and the *Binh Xuyen*, who opposed his Catholic favoritism.[4] In 1963, a military coup overthrew Diem. This coup apparently took place with the knowledge and consent of the American Embassy. The new leaders of South Vietnam proved less able to maintain control than Diem. By 1965, with the South Vietnamese government on the verge of collapse, President Johnson sent in ground troops to South Vietnam. American military and political leaders believed that they would be able to win the war by the end of 1967.

At the beginning of 1968, however, the Viet Cong forces of the south and the Viet Minh troops of the north launched the Tet Offensive, which undermined most Americans' confidence of winning the war. By the early 1970s, American political leaders began to realize that a quick military victory in Vietnam was extremely unlikely, that the American public was divided over the Vietnam War, and that continuing a war that was increasingly unpopular would mean committing American soldiers to an indefinite future. At the Paris peace talks in 1973, the United States agreed on a timetable for withdrawing American soldiers fighting in Vietnam and turning the war over to the South Vietnamese army with the support of American funding and continued training.

It turned out that the South Vietnamese government was no better prepared to defend itself than it had been in 1965. The U.S. Congress, reluctant to continue any backing at all for the domestically divisive war, cut off aid to South Vietnam, which seriously diminished the chances for survival of the disorganized and unprepared South Vietnamese government. In contrast, the North Vietnamese military, battle-hardened through years of fighting against the Americans and aided by the Viet Cong, found few obstacles in its way. In April 1975, Saigon, the capital of South Vietnam, fell to North Vietnamese troops. Vietnam was unified under the Hanoi government, and Saigon was later renamed Ho Chi Minh City.

The war produced over fifty-eight thousand American and about three million Vietnamese casualties. It also left in its wake nightmares, depression, antisocial behavior, and post-traumatic stress disorder that continue to affect Americans and Vietnamese Americans, as well as hundreds of thousands of refugees.

The U.S. Military Involvement in Laos and Cambodia

As in Vietnam, U.S. involvement in Laos and Cambodia was aimed primarily at the containment of Communism. Postcolonial Laos and Cambodia initially attempted to implement policies of neutrality. In Laos, Prince Souvanna Phouma succeeded in establishing a coalition government in 1957 after several years of patient effort to bring together pro-American rightists, nonaligned centrists, and the Pathet Lao communists.[5] However, the United States was not enthusiastic about this new coalition government because of the inclusion of the Pathet Lao. The United States thus actively intervened in the 1958 national election campaign to boost votes for non-Communists. When the election results turned out to strongly favor the leftists, the United States cut off aid to Souvanna's government, which eventually led to Souvanna's resignation and ended the Laos neutralist coalition.

Soon after, a civil war broke out between the Communist Pathet Lao and the Laotian Royalists. The Pathet Lao made significant advances with the assistance of the North Vietnamese Viet Minh forces and the Russians. At this point, the United States stepped in to form a mercenary army composed of Hmong tribesmen to fight the Pathet Lao and the Viet Minh. American forces also attacked the communist guerrillas with heavy aerial bombing. The war left massive casualties among the Hmong, who had fought on the U.S. side and were the main force holding back the Pathet Lao and North Vietnamese until 1973.[6] When the Pathet Lao came to power in 1975, the United States cut off aid to Laotian allies, forcing most Hmong and former Laotian Royalists to flee by air and overland to Thailand for asylum.[7]

During the turbulent wars in Vietnam and Laos in the mid-1950s and the 1960s, Cambodia basically maintained its neutrality under Prince Sihanouk's charismatic leadership and was able to enjoy peace and prosperity in a society that was largely agricultural, traditional, Buddhist, and isolated.[8] A 1970 coup d'état, led by Sihanouk's prime minister, Lon Nol, changed this, and the country was rapidly drawn into the Vietnam War. Cambodian history in the early 1970s was marked by governmental corruption, a near collapse of the national economy, the incursion of Vietnamese troops in the north of the country, and U.S. secret bombings of North Vietnamese border sanctuaries inside Cambodia. Phnom Penh, the Cambodian capital, fell to the Khmer Rouge, in mid-April 1975, a few weeks before Saigon fell to Communist forces. Several thousand military officers, government officials, and members of the country's elite managed to escape to Thailand. Most Cambodians, though, were swept up in the massive evacuation from the cities to the countryside that the Khmer Rouge undertook in order to create a new society. In the process, many died by execution, starvation, overwork, and illness.[9] It has been estimated that about 1.5 million Cambodians, out of a population of 8 million, vanished in the "killing fields" during Khmer Rouge rule between 1975 and 1978.[10]

In late 1978, the Vietnamese army invaded Cambodia and overthrew Pol Pot's government, forcing the Khmer Rouge to retreat to the jungles in the west along the Thai border. The Vietnamese invasion triggered a large flow of refugees from Cambodia to Thailand, creating crowded refugee camps that brought international attention to Cambodian suffering. During the massive refugee outflow, several Cambodian nationalist groups, including the Khmer Rouge, fought fiercely against the Vietnamese. The ensuing Cambodian civil war lasted until the late 1980s and almost completely dismantled the national economy and the traditional way of life.

The Refugee Exodus

Southeast Asian refugees fled their countries in different waves. Although Saigon, Vientiane, and Phnom Penh fell to the Communists forces roughly at the same time, only the Vietnamese had the privilege of "parole" to enter the United States immediately after the war, which allowed approximately 130,000 Vietnamese to land on U.S. soil. In December 1975, only 3,500 Hmong were paroled into the United States, while the majority of Hmong resistance forces and Laotian Royalists sought refuge in Thailand.[11] During that time, Cambodia, then renamed Kampuchea, restricted the movement of people, but some 20,000 Cambodians still managed to escape to Thailand during the Khmer Rouge period.

Another large refugee exodus, known as the second wave, occurred at the end of the 1970s when hundreds and thousands of refugees fled Vietnam by boat, creating the "boat people" crisis, and over land to China and Thailand. About a quarter of a million Vietnamese refugees went to China and some half a million were picked up floating in the open sea by the national guards of various countries. According to most reports, almost half the boat people perished at sea. The remaining half ended up in camps in Thailand, Indonesia, Malaysia, Singapore, the Philippines, and Hong Kong. Thousands of refugees also fled Laos and Kampuchea over land to seek refuge in crowded camps along the Thai border. Despite harsh repatriation efforts from the Thai government, about 600,000 Cambodians (15 percent of the country's population) and some 100,000 Hmong and 200,000 lowland Laotians (10 percent of the country's population) fled over land to Thailand.[12] The refugee exodus continued throughout the 1980s. Although the new governments did not plunge the three countries into bloodbaths, as so many had once feared, continuing political and religious repression, economic hardship, incessant warfare, and contacts with the outside world led many Southeast Asians to escape in search of better lives.

In sum, the Vietnam War and its expansion and the repressive regimes that followed the war left millions of people living in poverty, starvation, and constant fear in these three countries and forced many

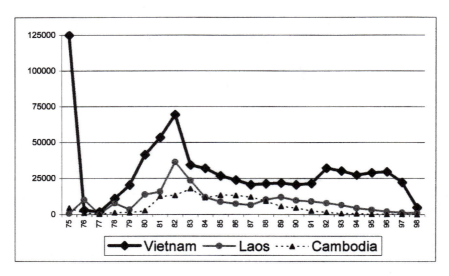

Figure 2.1   Southeast Asian Refugees Admitted to the United States by Year, 1975–1998
Source: *Statistical Yearbook of the Immigration and Naturalization Service, 1975–1998.*
Washington, D.C.: U.S. Government Printing Office.

others to flee from their homelands. One ironic consequence of the U.S. involvement in Indo-China is that a sizable part of Vietnam, Laos, and Cambodia is now in America.[13] As of 1998, over 724,000 refugees from Vietnam, 216,000 from Laos, and 132,000 from Cambodia were admitted to the United States. Figure 2.1 illustrates the influx. While the inflows from Laos and Cambodia have ebbed since the late 1980s, the influx from Vietnam has continued at a high level.

Resettlement and Adjustment

Patterns of Settlement and Socioeconomic Adaptation

Unlike most other immigrants, Southeast Asian refugees were pushed out of their homelands under extreme circumstances. They were therefore forced to leave without adequate preparation, had little control over when and where they could resettle, and lacked longstanding ethnic communities in host countries to provide assistance. Since U.S. refugee policy aimed at residential dispersion, Vietnamese, lowland Laotians and Hmong, and Cambodians were spread all over the United States, even in those states least populated by immigrants. However, sizable ethnic populations gradually converged in California. In the 1980 census, over a third of the Vietnamese reported living in California, and another 10 percent in Texas. By 1990, 46 percent of the Vietnamese had settled or resettled in the state of California alone, a 12-percentage-point increase. Texas had also acquired a large Vietnamese population, containing 11 percent of all Vietnamese in the United States. The 1980 census did not have a detailed breakdown of Laotians and Cambodians. However, by 1990, 46 percent of Cambodians in the United States lived in California, 10 percent in Massachusetts, and 8 percent in Washington, D.C. Similarly, almost 40 percent of Laotians and 52 percent of Hmong were concentrated in California. Outside California, the Hmong tended to concentrate in Wisconsin (18 percent) and Minnesota (18 percent).

Within states, the refugees tended to converge in a handful of metropolitan areas. For example, as of 1990, over three-quarters of California's Vietnamese population lived in four metropolitan areas—Orange County, Los Angeles, San Diego, and San Jose. In Texas, 44 percent of the Vietnamese resided in Houston. In Maryland and Virginia, 76 percent of the Vietnamese lived in Washington, D.C. In Washington State, 71 percent of the Vietnamese lived in Seattle. In Louisiana, close to two-thirds of the Vietnamese lived in New Orleans. This kind of concentration at the metropolitan level is due to secondary internal migration and subsequent international migration through family sponsorship. Though we have limited information on the magnitude of internal migration among Southeast Asian refugees, we know that secondary migration has occurred within a short period of time and that the primary motives for moving have been the establishment of an ethnic community and better economic conditions.[14] Thus, despite government policies aimed at dispersion, geographically centered ethnic communities have been formed, drawing in growing numbers of compatriots through word of mouth and through extensive kinship and family networks.

Refugees from Indo-China are distinct from contemporary immigrants from Asia in demographic and socioeconomic characteristics. With the exception of the first wave of evacuees from South Vietnam in 1975, most of the Southeast Asians were of rural origins, and the Hmong were primarily an illiterate tribal group. Many of them had minimal formal education, few marketable skills, little English-language proficiency, and scant knowledge of the ways of a highly industrialized society—attributes that would ease the passage into America.[15] Southeast Asian refugees are also significantly different from other post–World War II refugees, such as those that fled Cuba and the former Soviet Union. Most of the Cuban and Soviet refugees did not have to endure lengthy hardships in refugee camps and some were able to carry with them personal/financial assets of varying sorts.[16]

Table 2.1 shows the main demographic and socioeconomic character-istics of Southeast Asians in 1990. There were about 113 males per 100 fe-males among the refugees, except among the Cambodians, compared to 95 males per 100 females in the U.S. population. Southeast Asian refugees were much younger than the general U.S. population and showed a much higher fertility rate. These traits were especially notable among the Hmong. Over half of the individuals in this group were under fifteen years of age. Hmong women had a fertility rate three times higher than that of other American women. The Hmong were predominately foreign

Table 2.1 Characteristics of the Vietnamese, Laotians, and Cambodians in the United States, 1990

	Vietnamese	Laotian	Hmong	Cambodian	All Asian	All U.S.
% Female	47.4	48.3	48.9	51.7	51.2	51.3
Median age	25.6	20.5	12.7	19.7	29.2	33.0
Fertility per woman 35–44	2.5	3.5	6.1	3.4	1.9	2.0
% Under 15 years of age	26.5	38.1	55.3	40.9	23.7	21.5
% Female-headed households	15.9	11.3	13.6	25.4	11.5	16.0
% Foreign-born	79.9	79.4	65.2	79.1	65.6	7.9
% Immigrated after 1980	49.3	63.1	49.5	69.6	37.8	3.5
% Do not speak English very well	60.8	67.8	76.1	70.0	39.8	6.1
% Linguistically isolated	42.1	51.5	59.8	54.7	25.1	3.5
% Less than 5th-grade education	11.4	33.9	54.9	40.7	7.1	2.7
% College graduate or higher education	17.4	5.4	4.9	5.7	38.2	20.3
% In labor force	64.5	58.0	29.3	46.5	67.4	65.3
% Executive-professional	17.6	5.0	12.8	9.8	31.2	26.4
% Unemployed	8.4	9.3	17.9	10.3	5.2	6.3
Median family income	$30,550	$23,101	$14,327	$18,126	$41,583	$35,225
Per capita income	$9,033	$5,597	$2,692	$5,121	$13,806	$14,420
% Below poverty	25.7	34.7	63.6	42.6	14.0	13.1
% Receive public assistance	24.5	35.4	67.1	51.1	9.8	7.5
% Own home	40.1	24.0	11.1	19.7	48.3	64.2
Total Population	593,213	147,375	94,439	149,047	6,876,39	248,709,873

Source: U.S. Census of the Population, 1990, adapted from Table 9.3 (p. 247); Ruben Rumbaut, "Vietnamese, Laot-ian, and Cambodian Americans," in *Asian Americans: Contemporary Trends and Issues*, ed. Pyong Gap Min (Thou-sand Oaks, Calif.: Sage, 1995), pp. 230–67.

born. Among the foreign born, over 60 percent arrived after 1980, indicating that the Hmong are among the newest of the new immigrants. Except for the Cambodians, female-headed households were less common among refugees than in the U.S. population in general.

The initial group of refugees from Vietnam, and a small proportion of those from Laos and Cambodia arriving in the mid-1970s, came from privileged segments of their societies. These people include those most threatened by the new communist governments. Among them were generals, police officers, military officers, government ministers and civil servants, teachers, businesspeople, employees of American agencies and corporations, and members of the elite classes.[17] But these higher-status refugees were very diverse, ranging from fervent anti-Communists, religious conservatives, liberal intellectuals, to apolitical small business owners and farmers.[18]

Most members of this first wave came by airlift and were thus spared lengthy hardships while in flight, but the later arrivals had it much worse. The second and third waves of Southeast Asian refugees, especially those from Laos and Cambodia in the early 1980s, had to endure prolonged periods of extreme difficulties in overseas refugee camps before resettlement. Compared to the initial group, the later arrivals were also less skilled and were less likely to have had any urban experience. This background made the adjustment to America hard. Over 60 percent of the Southeast Asian refugees spoke English with difficulty or not at all, and many lived in linguistically isolated neighborhoods. With the exception of some of the Vietnamese, they were also poorly educated, with a disproportionately large number of people lacking minimum skills to compete in the labor market. Over a third of Laotians, half of the Hmong, and 40 percent of Cambodians barely had an elementary education. These limited educational backgrounds were related to low levels of labor force participation and high unemployment. The labor force participation rate was 58 percent for Laotians, 29 percent for the Hmong, and 47 percent for Cambodians. All of these rates were far below that of the U.S. adult population (65 percent).

Given the extremely unfavorable circumstances under which they fled their own countries and the severe cultural shock they encountered in the new land, the adjustment of Southeast Asian refugees to the United States has been remarkable. Among the Vietnamese, for example, labor force status improved from 1980 to 1990 in terms of labor force participation, proportions of year-round workers, self-employed workers, and professional workers. Median household incomes also increased during this decade. More remarkable, studies on the educational experience of the second generation reveal that Vietnamese young people have been attending college at a rate similar to that of Chinese and Koreans, and at a rate much higher than non-Hispanic whites in Los Angeles.[19] Even the Hmong, who came from a preliterate peasant background, and the more recently arrived Cambodians outperformed native-born English-only American students attending the same school in San Diego.[20] Nonetheless, Southeast Asians are still lagging behind their Asian American counterparts and the U.S. population by a significant margin in key socioeconomic areas, such as median household income, per capita income, poverty rate, dependency on public assistance, and home ownership. They also differ significantly from one another, with the Hmong trailing at the very bottom of the scale. Whether they will eventually achieve parity in socioeconomic status with other Asian immigrants and with native-born Americans still remains to be seen.

Having discussed the unique and enormous challenges that face Southeast Asians in the United States, we turn now to the role of religion in addressing these changes. We are interested in examining how religion can serve as a basis for reconstructing communities in diaspora and as a basis for rebuilding and maintaining the social identities of people in a strange new environment.

Religion as a Basis for Community Reconstruction and Social Identity

As we have seen, most Southeast Asian refugees came to the United States with few material belongings, little preparation for the sudden transition from agrarian to postindustrial living and radical cultural change, and no preexisting ethnic communities to receive them. Worse still for mutual assistance, the government resettlement policy dispersed them into completely unfamiliar environments. Federal and local governments implemented numerous resettlement programs, and American sponsors were enthusiastic in offering help to integrate the refugees. Still, the sponsors could not fully grasp the fact that the refugees had complex needs rooted in religious beliefs and practices, customs, diet, and traditional ways of coping with crises. Within a short period of time, the refugees started to cluster around their own people and to reconstruct, or create anew, interlocking systems of kin, friendship, and co-ethnic relations.[21] As these systems have consolidated over time, they have tended to become self-sustaining, self-perpetuating communities, similar to those of other immigrants.

What was the common ground for community reconstruction among these refugees, who were disoriented, displaced, and uprooted, with little control over where and when they could resettle? Prior research has found ample evidence suggesting that religion is an important source of psychological adjustment for immigrants, as well as for native-born Americans.[22] Recent studies have also consistently found that religious practices are central in promoting both psychological and economic adjustment.[23] The studies, however, generally lack specificity on how religions may contribute to immigrant adaptation and why religious practices may yield differential outcomes. To fill in this gap, we examine the structure and development of three Southeast Asian communities using ethnographic data. We believe that, while religion is a key cultural institution for reproducing and interpreting new forms of social relations, it can also enable a displaced group to resolve the tensions that have grown out of an entirely new set of environmental challenges. Drawing heavily and selectively on a religious heritage, group members can reconstruct or create a moral order and they can reorient old symbolic elements to a new environment. However, whether group members can successfully utilize their newly built collective identities and spiritual lives to meet new challenges in American life depends on historical patterns of homeland religious practices, specific conditions of refugee flight, the modes of incorporation, and the context of reception. The following case studies best illustrate the ways in which each ethnic community reconstructs its social and cultural lives by establishing a religious institution. In each case, the institution has been intended to serve as a cultural center. Each institution, however, also has implications for the social and economic adjustment of refugees and their children.

The Vietnamese Catholic Community of Versailles Village, New Orleans

General Background of Vietnamese American Catholicism

Vietnam is primarily a Buddhist-dominated country. Buddhism, which arrived in Vietnam from China, was the earliest foreign religion to put down roots in Vietnam. Buddhism, with about thirty million followers (or 52 percent of the total population in 1980) is also Vietnam's largest religion. Catholicism, with about three million followers, is Vietnam's second largest religion.[24] Vietnam's early contacts with Europe were primarily through Catholic missionaries, particularly Jesuits, who arrived in 1615, after they had been prohibited from entering Japan. France, as the most powerful Catholic nation in the seventeenth century, was especially active in supporting these religious endeavors through the *Société des Missions Etrangères*. Alexandre des Rhodes, a French Jesuit, was instrumental in establishing a formidable French Catholic presence in Vietnam. Des Rhodes and other missionaries distributed Christian literature printed in a romanized system of writing, later adopted throughout Vietnam and named *quoc ngu* (corresponding to the Chinese words *kuo-yu*, or "national language"). Through the work of missionaries, France had

47

become involved and influential in Vietnam during the seventeenth and eighteenth centuries, long before the arrival of French colonists.

During the Nguyen Dynasty in the early nineteenth century, the Vietnamese government sponsored a revival of Confucianism in an attempt to reestablish order using the Chinese model. Believing that the spread of Catholicism was a danger to the Confucian order, the government consequently initiated a policy of persecution of Catholics in 1825. The missionaries, however, continued to be active in defiance of the imperial prohibition on mission work. The French, who had helped to establish both the Christian missions and the Nguyen Dynasty itself, were meanwhile struggling to catch up in the nineteenth-century European competition for colonies. The French Emperor Napoleon III took up the cause of the Catholics in Vietnam and used their persecution as a reason, or a pretext, for invading the country and seizing Saigon and the three surrounding provinces in 1859. French domination of Vietnam continued until after the Second World War.

Catholicism put down deep roots in Vietnam, and Vietnamese Catholicism became a culturally distinctive faith, taking on such outward traits of Asian faiths as cultic attitudes toward ancestors and filiopietistic social relations. Nevertheless, some Vietnamese nationalists, especially the Communists, retained a deep suspicion of their Catholic compatriots. In turn, Vietnamese Catholics tended to view Communism as an ideology hostile to religion. In 1954, Vietnam split into a Communist-ruled north and a southern regime under the Catholic leader Ngo Dinh Diem. About one million northerners, between 600,000 and 800,000 of whom were Catholics, fled south on U.S. and French aircraft and naval vessels. Even after a military coup overthrew Diem in 1963, Catholics tended to oppose the northern Communists and their southern allies and to support the U.S. war effort in Vietnam. Thus, although Catholics make up only about 4 percent of Vietnam's population, one-fourth to one-third of all the refugees from Vietnam to the United States following the war were Catholic.

Vietnamese Catholics in America identified closely with their religion. There were approximately 200 priests and 250 nuns in the first wave of refugees to reach the United States in 1975.[25] The Vietnamese were among the largest ethnic group of vocations to the priesthood. In 1995 alone, 300 Vietnamese priests were ordained and 450 Vietnamese sisters entered religious orders. By the mid-1990s, about a quarter of the Vietnamese in the United States (or 270,000) were Catholic. The majority of the rest were Buddhist, and a small percentage adhered to the *Cao Dai* faith, a Vietnamese religion that blends elements of Catholicism, Buddhism, and Confucianism.[26]

In Vietnamese American Catholic communities, the church is often the center for holidays such as *Tet*, the Vietnamese lunar New Year.

Churches also host specifically religious holidays that are distinctive from those of other Catholics. There has long been a special reverence for the 117 Vietnamese Martyrs who died in the persecution of Catholics at the turn of the eighteenth through the nineteenth centuries. The Vietnamese Martyrs are considered spiritual ancestors of the believers, and their feast day, November 24, is a special day of devotion. The Vietnamese also have an ethnically specific Marian cult, during the second week in May, when they celebrate the Virgin Mary under the title of Our Lady of La Vang. This devotion also dates to the persecution, when a group of persecuted Catholics had a vision of the Virgin in 1798. The believers gave her the name of *Duc Phat Quan Am*, after the female goddess of Buddhism. Vietnamese Catholics also have their own versions of the marriage and funeral rites, intended to emphasize family relations and connections with ancestors.

Origins of the Vietnamese Catholic Church in Versailles Village

Vietnamese refugees began arriving in New Orleans in 1975. In that year, Associated Catholic Charities, one of the primary agencies in charge of refugee resettlement in the United States, placed one thousand refugees in the Versailles Arms Apartments on the eastern edge of town. The neighborhood, known as the Versailles Village, was then going through a time of economic hardship, partially as a result of the closing of a nearby NASA plant, making apartments available at a low cost. In 1976, another two thousand Vietnamese arrived on their own. While Associated Catholic Charities continued to settle Vietnamese in the area, many other Vietnamese were drawn by ties to friends, relatives, and former neighbors.[27]

Versailles Village was primarily black (57 percent) and Vietnamese (43 percent) as of 1990. While the two racial groups lived in close proximity, the Vietnamese were heavily concentrated in the area around their own Catholic church. Many of the newer streets in the vicinity of the church bear Vietnamese names. The residents in Versailles Village, blacks and Vietnamese alike, were struggling economically. The median family income of the census tract was only $17,440 in 1990, and over two-thirds of the families lived below the poverty level. The Vietnamese in this neighborhood had a median family income of only $15,841, and over half of the Vietnamese families lived below the poverty level. For the city of New Orleans as a whole, at the same time, the median household income was $18,477, and 27.3 percent of families were below poverty level.

In terms of education, the Vietnamese appear to be at a considerable disadvantage compared to their non-Vietnamese neighbors. While about 60 percent of the adult residents of the neighborhood were high school graduates, only 37 percent of the adult Vietnamese had finished high school. Unemployment among males in the labor force in the tract was 12.8 percent, and unemployment among Vietnamese males was even higher (16 percent). However, the Vietnamese were much less likely to live in female-headed households. Only 5.8 percent of Vietnamese families in the neighborhood were headed by females, compared to over one-fourth of all families. Despite the continuing poverty of the neighborhood, there is evidence that the Vietnamese achieved substantial upward mobility in the years since their arrival. For example, home ownership increased markedly, from only 15 percent in 1980 to over 37 percent in 1990, a greater than threefold increase. This is especially impressive when we consider that nearly 30 percent of these Vietnamese arrived in the United States after 1980 and over 10 percent arrived after 1985. Even this figure, however, does not take into account the growth in quality of housing for Vietnamese homeowners. During a walk or drive down the main streets of the neighborhood, even a casual observer can easily notice several large, new homes, either recently constructed or in the process of construction. All of these new homes are Vietnamese owned. Vietnamese home buying in the neighborhood had become so common that a Vietnamese developer, Mr. Hung Van Chu, created several new blocks, giving the streets Vietnamese names, such as *Tu-Do* ("Freedom") and *My-Viet* ("America–Vietnam"). Home buying in the neighborhood has significantly revitalized an otherwise rapidly deteriorating poor area. Since the 1980s, the Vietnamese have gradually moved out of the Versailles Arms apartments—the initial focal point of their settlement—into the neighborhoods or suburbs dominated by single-family housing.

As the Vietnamese in this location achieved upward mobility, one of their first communal actions was the establishment of a religious institution. The Vietnamese here are heavily Catholic. In a survey that we conducted of secondary school students living in the area, we found that 87.3 percent were Catholic, 10.4 percent were Buddhist, 0.7 percent were Baptist, 0.7 percent were *Cao Dai*, and 0.5 percent gave their religion as "other." In the early 1980s, community leaders applied to the local Catholic Archdiocese for permission to erect a church. In September 1983, the Archdiocese of New Orleans gave permission for the current large Vietnamese church to be built in Versailles Village. Funds were collected from Vietnamese Catholics throughout New Orleans and the Mary Queen of Vietnam Church was completed in May 1985.

Social Structure and Functions

Father Francis Bui, pastor of another Vietnamese church in Louisiana, explained why he thinks Vietnamese Catholic churches are needed: "We have the Vietnamese church to preserve Vietnamese culture and to pass on the language. If it wasn't for that, we could just assimilate into other churches for religion." Mary Queen of Vietnam Church in Versailles Village serves a number of explicit cultural preservationist purposes. Major Vietnamese festivals, such as the *Tet* celebration, take place in and around the church. A child development center on the church grounds is the site of classes in Vietnamese language, literature, and culture taught by lay volunteers.

The church is more than a mechanism for transmitting cultural heritage; it serves as the center of social organization for Versailles Village. The pastor of the church serves as chief spokesman and recognized leader of both church and neighborhood. He is supported by between one and two dozen influential neighborhood figures. A few of these people have influence because they have the prestige of high education and they can help people deal with the outside world in financial or legal matters; also, at least two of them are high school teachers. Others are wealthy business owners or successful owners of fishing boats who contribute financially to the church and to community projects.

At the church, people pass gossip and information. It therefore functions as a clearinghouse of useful communication, including communication about where jobs can be found. Although it was founded for the explicit or manifest purpose of providing a place for Vietnamese religious and cultural practices, it also fulfills the latent purpose of bringing people together where they can learn from each other what opportunities are available. "At church we find out everything that's going on," one respondent remarked. Jobs are among the things that are "going on" in this religious community. A number of respondents reported that they had found work in small shops owned by Vietnamese coparishioners through contacts at the church. It is true, of course, that they could have made these contacts elsewhere if the church had not existed. Nevertheless, the religious institution did bring people together in a place where they could exchange information about opportunities. Clerical and lay leaders of the church organize a market every Saturday, where Vietnamese people can earn money by selling foods, handicrafts, and other goods. Until the early 1990s, this market was actually held on the grounds of the church and it moved off the church grounds only because it grew too large.

Among the goods sold at the Saturday market are vegetables grown in gardens in wetlands on the outskirts of the neighborhood. The land on which these gardens are located was formerly owned by the New Orleans East Corporation, a private land development company. The Archdiocese of New Orleans reached an agreement with this company in 1978, obtaining permission for the Vietnamese to use the land. During the 1980s, the New Orleans East Corporation went bankrupt and the site of the gardens was purchased by the federal Resolution Trust Corporation (RTC). The RTC later sold the property to a New Orleans lawyer.

After negotiations by leaders of the Mary Queen of Vietnam Church on behalf of the gardeners, the lawyer agreed to lease the land to the church for a nominal fee.[28] Thus, the church has served not only as a place to obtain information about economic opportunities, it has also served as an organizational basis for pursuit of economic interests.

Social status in the community is closely linked to position in the church. Contributions from business owners and fishermen maintain the church and, although the pastor is the official spokesman of church and community, lay committees frequently determine church activities or church policies. One Vietnamese social worker who organized activities for troubled youth in the neighborhood told us he had to get the permission of the influential lay leaders of the church in order to carry on his work.

Monsignor Dominic Luong, pastor of the Mary Queen of Vietnam Church, has noted the increased role of the laity in Vietnamese American Catholicism in contrast to Catholicism in Vietnam: "The biggest change in the Vietnamese church here over the past two decades is the participation of the laity," said Luong. "The church in Vietnam is very clerical. Here the people are very involved."[29] This growing influence of lay power in Vietnamese Catholic churches has also been noted by others: "The demands on the Catholic Vietnamese community have been changing, too, as they progressed from docile obedience to the wishes of their local priests to involvement and leadership in parish life."[30]

Theravada Buddhist Community of Iberia Parish, Louisiana

General Background of Laotian American Theravada Buddhism

Although some of the minority groups of the Laotian mountains and highlands are animists, almost all of the ethnic Lao are Buddhists in their homeland. Many Laotians converted to Protestant Christian denominations in refugee camps in Thailand during the 1970s and 1980s or after arrival in the United States. These conversions were inspired in part by the psychological and philosophical upheavals of war and exile and in part by the fact that American church groups were the most active agencies in assisting refugees in Thailand and in sponsoring refugees in the United States. Nevertheless, a majority of Laotian Americans continue to profess Buddhism and many of the new converts to Christianity retain cultural elements of their older belief system.

Buddhism is divided into two schools of thought. The Northern School, known as Mahayana Buddhism, is the type of Buddhism found most often in China, Japan, Tibet, Korea, and Vietnam. The Southern

School, called Theravada Buddhism, predominates in Laos, Thailand, Cambodia, Burma (Myanmar), and Sri Lanka. Theravada Buddhists stress the importance of becoming a monk and achieving *Nirvana*, a state in which there is no self or rebirth, through one's own efforts. Mahayana Buddhists place more emphasis on help from *Bodhisattvas*, enlightened beings who have delayed achieving *Nirvana* in order to help others become enlightened.

The essence of the Buddhist faith is the belief that all worldly things are changing and impermanent. Those who are not aware of the impermanent nature of the world become attached to worldly things, and this leads to suffering. The suffering will continue as the soul goes through a cycle of rebirths, continually drawn back to worldly desires. Meditation and a moral, disciplined life can enable a believer to overcome desires. The soul that successfully overcomes all desires may reach *Nirvana*. The path toward *Nirvana* is governed by *Dharma*, one of the three central concepts of Buddhism. This word is frequently translated as "law," but it refers more broadly to the order of the universe and the Buddha's teachings on right order and belief.

The law of *Karma,* the second of Buddhism's three central concepts, controls life and rebirth. This law may be seen as a kind of spiritual accounting: Good deeds, or "merit," help the soul to be reborn in better circumstances and to earn rewards in the present life; bad deeds cause the soul to be reborn in worse circumstances and can bring about bad luck. For these reasons, "making merit" is a central part of religion for Laotians. If *Dharma* is a cosmological moral order, then *Karma* is a matter of whether or not one acts in accordance with this order. One can make merit through acts of kindness. However, becoming a monk or helping to support monks or a temple are the ways of making merit most highly regarded by Laotian people.

The *sangha*, the monastic community within which people can improve their own spiritual positions, is the third central concept of Buddhism. All Lao men are expected to become monks for a period of time, usually in early manhood, before marriage. It is also common for older men, especially widowers to become monks. Even in Laos, some men are not able to fulfill the ideal of entering the temple for a time. This is even more difficult for Laotian American men because of the demands of jobs and the scarcity of temples. Because the monastic community of the temple is so closely linked to making merit by becoming a monk or by supporting monks, establishing temples and adapting monkhood to American life are key religious problems for Laotian American Buddhists.

Laotian and Thai adherents to Buddhism usually combine their canonical Buddhism with noncanonical beliefs that are sometimes referred to as "folk Buddhism." A belief in spirits, or *phi* (pronounced like the English word "pea," but with a rising tone, as in a question) dates back to the time before the Lao were introduced to Buddhism, and the spirit cult has become a part of popular Buddhist practices.[31] Some of these spirits are the spirits of human beings following death, or "ghosts." Other *phi* are benevolent guardians of people and places, or malevolent beings who may cause harm and suffering.

Another important noncanonical element in Laotian Buddhism is the *khouan*, a mobile soul loosely attached to each human being. As one becomes involved with other people, one's own *khouan* has a tendency to become attached to them as well. The *baci* or *soukhouan* ceremony is one of the key rites of noncanonical Laotian Buddhism. The chanting of scriptures in the Pali language by a group of monks usually precedes the ceremony. Then, participants take bits of white cotton string as an elder layman calls upon the *khouan* to reenter the bodies of those present. The celebrants tie the cloth around one another's wrists. If one of those present is being especially honored, or has just returned from a journey, or is about to set out on a journey, or has experienced the death of a family member, those present will concentrate on tying the bits of cloth around this person's wrist, binding the soul to the individual.

Before tying the knot, celebrants will often place hard-boiled eggs or rice, symbols of fertility, into the palms of those whose wrists are being encircled. While tying, they will make wishes for those being honored, most often wishing them long life, good luck, and many children.[32] While it is by no means necessary that the ceremony be performed at a temple, or at any religious site, celebrants generally prefer to hold this ritual in a place that has some religious significance.

Origins of the Laotian Buddhist Community in Iberia Parish

Laotians began moving into Iberia Parish during the early 1980s, the peak period of Lao resettlement in the United States.[33] Their concentration in this area was a consequence of secondary migration in search of job opportunities. At this time, the federal Comprehensive Employment and Training Act (CETA) provided funding for training in pipe fitting, welding, and related skills in demand in the Gulf Coast region. When a few Laotians found this training, and the jobs that followed it, word of available employment spread through ethnic networks and others began moving to the region.

Those who arrived in New Iberia came with little capital, often relying on the help of friends and relatives and on the public assistance made available under the provisions of the U.S. Refugee Act of 1980. They had, therefore, relatively few choices in housing. They needed to seek the lowest possible rents, and many had to live in some form of public housing. Since they relied heavily on co-ethnics, they also tended to cluster together. For this reason, the Laotians initially established their first base in the southwestern part of the city, in a large apartment complex of federally subsidized section housing. As is the case with much public housing in the United States, this apartment complex is located in a poor, decaying area of the city. The neighborhood was an entirely black neighborhood before the arrival of the Lao. The houses are small and old, many of them with peeling paint and collapsing porches. Data from the 1990 census attest to the area's economic distress: The poverty level was extremely high with a median family income below $14,000; one-third of the families were headed by single females; and about 30 percent of households were receiving public assistance. It should be noted that these figures include the Laotians, among whom single female–headed families are still extremely rare.[34] The neighborhood also suffers from many of the social ills that plague America's poor neighborhoods. One local policeman that we interviewed referred to this area as "Dodge City" because of its frequent violence, much of which appears to be drug related. This is a neighborhood that fits the definition of a ghetto.[35]

Most Lao families contain at least two workers. Laotian male workers are concentrated in their occupational niches in pipe fitting and welding. Although the CETA training that initially drew the group to this southern city ended during the Reagan administration, it has become common for Laotian men with job skills to teach others. Those not in pipe fitting or welding are most often employed in seafood and restaurant jobs. Almost all of the women had extensive experience with sewing, embroidering, and related activities, since these were crafts traditionally passed from mother to daughter in Laos. These skills have enabled them to find work in regional textile mills. Many Laotian women found work just north of New Iberia, at a textile mill in St. Martinville. Thus, by the mid-1980s, almost all of the women were commuting to jobs in the north every day, while their husbands were commuting south to the Port of New Iberia. Even when both adults in a family held low-paying jobs, the combined incomes of two workers provided a base for upward mobility.

Like the Vietnamese in Versailles Village, there has been a trend of residential mobility. As early as the 1980s, Laotian families began to move out of the apartment complex into free-standing housing in the immediate area. Those who had managed to amass sufficient capital began to move further north, out of the neighborhood, into middle-class neighborhoods, generally settling in small clusters. By the mid-1980s, the Laotians had established clusters even further north within the city limits, purchasing comfortable suburban homes.

After the Laotians had established themselves sufficiently, they began planning to build their own community and cultural center. In 1986, a number of Laotian men generally recognized as leaders formed the

Temple Corporation, an association dedicated to building a Lao-style Buddhist temple that would be surrounded by an ethnic residential enclave. They found a tract of land in a semirural area on the northern edge of the county. The tract was relatively inexpensive, as it was outside of established residential, commercial, and industrial zones, and it was at that time unused for farming. The temple was completed a year later with surrounding streets renamed after provinces in Laos. Initially, most of the homes in the areas surrounding the temple were trailers, but members of the community set a rule that settlers would have to build a permanent home within five years of moving into the neighborhood. There was some flexibility in the enforcement of this rule, and as new people settled the area, approximately one-quarter of the homes were still trailers by 1996. However, about three-quarters were permanent buildings. According to our field interviews and observations, the newly built Laotian village held about four hundred residents in 1996. Laotians in other parts of the county regarded the temple as a center of cultural and religious traditions. During the early 1990s, the temple village began to run out of room for new households. As a consequence, the Lao started to establish homes on a stretch of land a little under a quarter mile to the west of the temple.

By the mid-1990s, there were about two to three thousand Laotians living in Iberia Parish, by our estimate. About 43 percent of Laotian households, according to our count, continued to reside within the apartment complex or its immediate environs. An estimated 19 percent of all Lao households were in the village immediately surrounding the temple. The temple village and the settlement just to the west of the village together contained 27 percent of all Laotian households in the parish (county). The rest were scattered in free-standing housing in small clusters throughout the parish. The temple, then, had not only become a regional center for Laotians, it had also become the core of a substantial Laotian residential concentration.

Social Structure and Functions

The temple was founded to express and preserve Laotian culture in the new environment. As one informant observed, "We need this place so that we can remember who we are." Driving in from the cane fields to the temple, the non-Laotian observer who has been to Southeast Asia may be struck by the sight of a colorful Theravada Buddhist temple in the middle of southwestern Louisiana. It is a bit like being transported from one part of the world to another. At the temple, the festivals and rites of Laos are faithfully reproduced.

Serving as a center of cultural identity may be viewed as the major manifest function of the temple. It also has important latent functions, though, notably latent functions of an economic character. In July 1998, one of the authors conducted an interview with the human resources director of a company constructing off-shore oil structures. The director estimated that about 15 percent of the company's five hundred welders, fitters, and other skilled craftsmen were Laotian. The economic as well as the cultural centrality of the temple became clear:

Interviewer: How do you get most of your new Laotian workers?

Respondent: One of our foremen is the financial manager at that Buddhist whatchmacallit. . . .

Interviewer: You mean the temple out in Cade?

Respondent: Yeah. People go to him for a job and he just refers them here.

In addition to connecting people with jobs, the temple also helps to connect people with homes. An adult daughter of one of the lay leaders in the temple community is employed by a bank in New Iberia as a loan officer in charge of mortgage loans. Fluent in both English and Lao, she is uniquely qualified to meet the needs of her employer and her ethnic community. Through her, the bank has access to a group of customers with a low default rate that it would otherwise miss. The new Laotian homeowners have someone who can translate for them and guide them through the financial maze of buying property. Most of the new Lao-owned houses around the temple and many of the Laotian homes throughout Iberia Parish have been financed with the assistance of this officer, who lives near the temple itself and frequently meets with customers at the religious site.

The temple is intended to preserve Laotian culture. This is a function temples in Laos do not have because the culture does not need to be preserved in the homeland. It also serves a variety of new economic needs by providing a place where network connectors can connect members of the group with jobs and financial resources. While reproducing Laos in America, then, the religious institution has changed in subtle ways that are not immediately evident from its colorful facade. These changes are in social structure, as well as in function.

In Laos, the *sangha* is the community of monks. It is the monks who are in charge of the religious affairs of the temple and who make decisions regarding religious matters. The laypeople support the monks with gifts of food and other offerings. The boundary between the monastic and the nonmonastic is also fairly porous. Ideally, all Laotian men should become monks at some point during their lives. However, none of the men that we talked to planned to become monks, even for a short time. As one of the informants explained: "We have jobs that we have to go to every day. Everybody has to work to get by. So we can't take time out to go into the temple. But we still hold Buddhism. We want to make merit, so we give to the monk who's there, and we can make merit through him."

The economic and social context of American society has encouraged two related trends that also seem to be characteristic of other Laotian Buddhist temples in America. First, monasticism has tended to shift from being a status that most, if not all, men occupy at some time to being a specialized, professional activity. Second, there has been a shift in power from the monk or monks to the laity, who find and employ the religious professionals.

After founding the temple, the Laotian community leaders of Iberia Parish located a Buddhist monk through their contacts with Laotian communities elsewhere in the United States, and they brought in this single religious figure to serve at the temple. When we asked interviewees what they would do if the single monk currently at the temple moved to another temple, they all had the same answer: They would seek to bring in another lifelong monk from another Laotian American community. The monastic order continues to lie at the heart of social relations, and it continues to be the chief mechanism for individual moral advancement, but monasticism has become a specialized job, rather than a stage of life.

Since the laity essentially hire the religious professional, decision making in the religious institution has shifted from the monks to a committee of laypeople composed of the same successful skilled craftspeople and small businesspeople who founded the temple. The author Phayvanh Phoumindr has noted a similar trend among Laotian Buddhist temples in Australia: "Temple projects in the new country are often started by lay community service groups, with some government funding. This means that the lay committee of the parent body like to continue the control of the temples, much against the wishes of many Buddhist monks who would prefer to look after their own religious affairs without the direction and interference of laypeople as was traditional in Laos."[36] If the shift to lay control has not led to conflict in the temple we observed, this may be a consequence of the fact that there is only one monk who has necessarily accepted the professionalization of his status.

The Cambodian Theravada Buddhist Community of Long Beach, California

General Background of Cambodian American Theravada Buddhism

Cambodians do not have a history of Catholicism, Christianity, or Confucianism. Less than 1 percent of the Cambodian population is Christian or Roman Catholic and about 90 percent of the Cambodians in Cambodia are Buddhists.[37] Like the Laotians, most Cambodians adhere to Theravada Buddhism. Introduced to Cambodia in about the thirteenth century, Theravada Buddhism is the official religion of Cambodia. Before the Khmer Rouge era, Buddhism was embedded in the national law of Cambodia and its teachings permeated everyday life and thought of Cambodians.[38] For the Cambodians as for the Laotians, the basic principle of Theravada Buddhism is that one earns merit toward a better life by being good and avoiding evil. Giving gifts and donations to the temple and the monks can be especially valuable ways of earning merit.[39] Emphasizing personal development and individual good behavior, it is believed that individuals must first attain enlightenment, or *Nirvana,* on their own, before they can help others to reach enlightenment.[40] Cambodian Buddhism is thus virtually the same as the Laotian Buddhism discussed previously.

Origins of the Wat Khemara Buddhikaram in Long Beach

The seeds of the Cambodian community in Long Beach were planted in the late 1950s with the establishment of an educational exchange program between Cambodia and the United States.[41] Under this exchange program, about one hundred students from Cambodia came to Long Beach and attended the California State University at Long Beach (CSULB). The exchange program was terminated in 1963 when Prince Sihanouk nationalized foreign trade and when diplomatic relations between the United States and Cambodia weakened.[42] When this occurred, many of the Cambodian students remained in Long Beach and established their new home in America.

The majority of Cambodians now settled in Long Beach came to the United States after Pol Pot's rule ended with the invasion of Cambodia by Vietnam in 1978.[43] About 120,000 Cambodians entered the United State in the five years following the Vietnamese invasion of Cambodian.[44] Since Long Beach already had an established Cambodian community, many relocated to Long Beach. According to the 1990 U.S. Census, 17,468 Cambodians resided in Long Beach, which has a total population of 429,233.[45] Within Long Beach (which has a majority white population), most Cambodians reside in inner-city neighborhoods with heavy black and Latino concentrations and few white residents.

Buddhism remains the primary religion in the Long Beach Cambodian community, although the community has witnessed significant conversion to Christianity, since about 12 percent of the Long Beach Cambodians are now Christians.[46] There are at least eight Buddhist temples in Long Beach, although most of the temples are actually monks' private residences and do not have the appearance or the functions of bigger temples.[47] Of the two official temples in Long Beach, *Wat Khemara Buddhikaram* (Khmer Buddhist Temple) is the bigger and the older. Established in 1982, this temple was built when the Cambodian Buddhists in southern California unanimously elected to purchase property for this purpose in Long Beach. In order to raise money to cover the building expenses—which was a little over a million dollars—the temple property was divided into twenty thousand shares at $50 each. The monk who headed the fund-raising to build the temple noted that in addition to the shares, it took several years of fund-raising through special ceremonies, individual donations, and a loan from the bank to build the temple. Since most of the Cambodian Buddhists were poor and on welfare, with little education and skills, individual donations reportedly ranged from $5 to $20. Unlike the Laotian case, a general increase in home buying or socioeconomic upward mobility did not precede the establishment of the Cambodian temples.

Cambodians are the most recent arrivals among the Southeast Asians in the Los Angeles–Long Beach metropolitan area and have the lowest levels of education, personal and household income, and home ownership. Ninety-five percent of Cambodians aged twenty-five years or older immigrated between 1980 and 1990 (compared to 58 percent for Vietnamese and 63 percent for Laotians). Only 5 percent of Cambodian adults are four-year college graduates. The median household income for Cambodians is $21,000, compared to $35,000 for Vietnamese and $27,000 for Laotians. Cambodians, foreign or U.S. born, also have the lowest personal incomes among the Southeast Asian refugee groups.[48] Only 19 percent of Cambodians own homes, compared with 44 percent of the Vietnamese.[49] Most of the housing units for Cambodian residents are run-down and located in ghettoized areas known for poverty and gang violence. Gang-related violence is prevalent in the Cambodian community. Cambodian gangs are known to extort protection money from co-ethnic individuals and businesses.[50] There is also gang violence between Cambodians and their Latino neighbors on the streets and in public schools.

Apparently, the Cambodian community has not gathered enough strength to influence the lives of co-ethnics as effectively as the Vietnamese in New Orleans and Laotians in New Iberia. Poverty and welfare dependency only partially explain this problem. What makes the community tenuous, we believe, is the lack of education and skills, compounded by a long history of colonization, postwar trauma in the homeland, recency of arrival, and a general distrust of authority and organization resulting from past colonial and war experiences. The Cambodians went through the most extreme hardships of all the refugee groups. Individuals who saw parents, spouses, children, and sometimes most or all members of their families die under horrific conditions during the Khmer Rouge period are common.

Even though Long Beach has the greatest concentration of Cambodians outside of Cambodia, there is no designated name for the Cambodian community and most inner-city Cambodian residents seem to simply merge into the urban underclass. The abbot of the temple and the fund-raising chairman reported to us that many Cambodians were poor and uneducated and that socioeconomic mobility of Cambodians did not precede or coincide with the development of the temple. Demographic data support these observations.

Social Structure and Functions

In both the Vietnamese and Laotian cases, the religious institution had a latent function of serving as a network center of economic activities, and there was a tendency in both toward an increase in the organizational power of the laity. These two tendencies are not immediately evident in the *Wat Khemara Buddhikaram* in Long Beach. The lack of an apparent economic function cannot be attributed to the fact that the Cambodian temple is a nonprofit, public benefit corporation under the laws of the State of California. Indeed, the other two religious organizations are also nonprofit corporations. The religious and lay leaders of all three organizations continually stressed that they saw the main functions of their institutions as religious, cultural, and social. Church and temple leaders and participants in all cases would have strongly opposed using the church or temple for personal benefit or economic gain. Opposition to the intentional use of religious institutions for personal gain is completely consistent with a latent economic function. Latent institutional functions are, by definition, neither intended nor sought after. Neither the Vietnamese nor the Laotians described previously would see themselves as "using" their church or temple for personal profit, and most would be understandably upset if it were suggested that they did so. In the Cambodian case, the absence of a discernible economic function for the temple appears to be a consequence of the dire financial and social situation of the temple's adherents. The temple does not provide them with a place to make contacts and exchange information about jobs and resources because there are so few resources to exchange. Similarly, the increasing power of the laity that we saw in different forms among the Vietnamese and the Laotians is not evident among the Cambodians because the latter have not yet achieved widespread socioeconomic mobility. Control therefore remains in the hands of religious specialists, as in the homeland.

The temple does, however, play a crucial social and cultural role for the Cambodians. Through the temple, fellow compatriots can preserve their cultural heritage, revive a sense of community, and share experiences of adaptation to their new home. The temple is used as a "Treasure-House" of Cambodian tradition where Cambodian arts; architecture; civilization; education; and physical, mental, and spiritual health can be stored and preserved. The Khmer Buddhist Monastery organizes at least seven traditional religious and cultural ceremonies for the Cambodian community each year. The annual New Year celebration, with rich Buddhist ceremonies, usually held on the 13th and 14th of April, is a particularly big event that draws hundreds if not thousands of Cambodians to the temple. The Buddhist monks and nuns also teach language courses to help Cambodian children learn Khmer language and culture. Sports and recreational activities are also made available by the temple to attract the younger generation of Cambodians. In addition, the temple provides opportunities for young Cambodian males in the community to get training and education as monks. First-generation Cambodians who suffer from post-traumatic stress and long-term depression as the result of the war and resettlement can also turn to the monks for help. Older Cambodians find comfort and a sense of belonging in the temple. Through offering spiritual and mental help, the temple contributes to the rebuilding of the Cambodian community. One member of the temple noted that the building of the temple was symbolic of rebuilding Cambodians' mental and spiritual well-being.

By rebuilding the Khmer cultural heritage, the Cambodians are able to renew trust, rebuild their self-esteem and dignity, and achieve gradual reunification with each other—something that has been broken by years of persecution and genocide. The temple publishes a monthly newsletter with topics dealing with Cambodian culture, tradition, and Buddhist teachings. It also conducts personal, family, and alcohol counseling to help Cambodians adapt to their new lives in America. Wedding celebrations and funeral gatherings are conducted in the temple. On various special occasions, all of the temple attendees gather together and eat traditional Cambodian foods with the monks. Last, the temple functions as a forum on community issues and a place where Cambodians can cooperate and extend friendships to other religious and nonreligious organizations to help support the Cambodians in the Long Beach community.

Unlike churches, temples do not have regular congregations that they can count. People simply come in and out of the temple, and some come only once or twice a year. The abbot of the Cambodian temple estimated that between ten thousand and fifteen thousand people come each year. People visit in especially large numbers when there are special ceremonies, as for the New Year celebration in April. The head reverend of the Long Beach temple noted that 85 to 90 percent of those who come to the temple are first generation. Only a few second-generation members come. He commented that the difference in religious involvement between generations could be due to the fact that the first generation had firm Buddhist beliefs before they arrived in America. Additionally, Cambodian parents, who usually possess low levels of education and lack familiarity with American language and culture, frequently have little control over their children. This makes it difficult for parents to encourage their children to visit the temple. Second-generation children are also sometimes uncomfortable sitting on mats for extended periods of time and listening to unfamiliar Buddhist chants in Pali (the sacred language of Cambodian and Lao Buddhists).

Though the temple has some trouble recruiting younger members, many Cambodians in Long Beach believe that the future of rebuilding the Cambodian community lies with the second generation. Since most of the educated and skilled elite were killed by the Khmer Rouge in Cambodia, the first-generation Cambodians in the United States have little education and limited English ability. As a result of the civil war experience, many first-generation Cambodians distrust their leaders. They feel that they have lost control over their own lives, and many are still haunted by the memories of genocide. As one member pointed out, they "have broken hearts" as a result of the war and refugee process. In a recent interview, a Cambodian community leader and political historian stated, "There is no leadership in the [Cambodian] community. People have lost faith. They don't trust leaders. They don't believe in themselves."[51] In contrast, the second-generation children are more educated than their parents and have greater familiarity with the new country. They are also more able than the first generation to detach themselves from the traumatic memories of genocide and refugee camps. In this way, the second-generation Cambodians, particularly those who are bilingual and maintain close ties to the temple and community, can help rebuild the Cambodian community and reunify the Cambodian people.

Discussion and Conclusion

The three religious organizations that we have examined here show both similarities and differences. In each of these three cases, the church or temple was founded explicitly to serve as a center for cultural identity. The religious institutions were established in order to give individuals a sense of who they are within a group and in order to create a basis for collective action. As Robert Bellah has pointed out, religion provides identity and motivation to groups and to individuals as members of groups.[52] In contrast to nonimmigrant congregations, though, the provision of collective identity and motivation for Southeast Asian refugees was self-consciously reconstructive in character. Previously, we quoted a Vietnamese pastor's words: "We have the Vietnamese church to preserve Vietnamese culture. . . ." The Cambodians and Laotians repeatedly told us much the same thing.

American Baptists or Catholics do not establish their churches to express or perpetuate some version of being American. In Vietnam, Laos, and Cambodia, similarly, adherents to local faiths do not see maintaining a cultural identity as the primary goal of a temple or church. For immigrants, however, religion becomes an essential symbol of ethnic identity, an emblem of the old life in the midst of the new. Ironically, Vietnamese Catholicism or Cambodian Buddhism becomes "more Vietnamese" or "more Cambodian" in America than in Vietnam or Cambodia as a result.

The employment of religion as a source of cultural identity is arguably more important for these refugees than it is for other immigrants. As we have pointed out in our overview of the backgrounds of these groups, they did not simply migrate from their homelands. They lost their homelands. Fleeing countries shattered by war, they lost the social statuses they occupied and the social structures that defined their lives. Because they arrived in America estranged, isolated, and dispersed, building new communities meant more than simply gathering together. They had to draw on their memories to create new communities of meaning.

Through participation in ethnically based religions, the refugee groups can make sense out of their new lives. They can, in Peter Berger's words, carve "an area of meaning . . . out of a vast mass of meaninglessness."[53] Rituals and ceremonies are critical to the production of meaning. Creating a web of cultural symbols in the new homeland has meant looking to the future, as well as to the past. For this reason, the temples and the church give a special emphasis to the socialization of the young. These are places where American-born or American-reared young people can learn the languages and customs that link their elders to memories of the homeland.

There is a broad similarity among these three religious organizations in the ways in which they help to define individuals as members of groups. Still, we also see some differences in the ways in which the religious organizations serve as bases for collective action. The Vietnamese and Laotian religious organizations that we have discussed served communities in the process of substantial upward mobility. The religious organizations were therefore affected by that mobility and helped to facilitate its continuation. The Vietnamese church and the Laotian temple were certainly not established for business purposes or to promote the financial well-being of their adherents. Nevertheless, they did serve latent economic functions by providing network centers for people who were achieving upward mobility and could assist each other. The Cambodian temple did not, as far as we could tell, play a major role in the economic adaptation of its adherents, although it was also an ethnic network focus. While it is possible that Cambodian Buddhists do informally exchange information about jobs and other opportunities as a consequence of religious participation, it appears that they have only limited information to exchange.

We can understand why the Cambodian religious organization differs from the other two by reflecting on how the challenges facing the Cambodians differ from those facing the other two groups. The Cambodians have suffered the most traumatic and drastic experiences in the troubled history of Southeast Asia. Haunted by memories of the genocidal Khmer Rouge years, the Cambodians are still chiefly concerned with mending their "broken hearts." They have not yet begun the struggle to create places for themselves in the economy of the New World. Hence, they continue to be economically marginal by almost all objective measures. Their collective action still revolves around basic social psychological adjustment, around trying to make some sense out of an anomic present and a chaotic past.

A second characteristic that sets the Cambodian organization apart from the other two is the relative lack of lay control over the religious institution. As we have seen, lay power in both the Vietnamese and Laotian institutions increased substantially, compared to churches and temples in their homelands. Organizing committees and raising funds tended to place power in the hands of the laypeople charged with these responsibilities. Here, again, it is important to note that the Vietnamese and Laotian communities were in a process of rapid socioeconomic adaptation. The adherents were becoming people who could exercise some control over their own lives and over their organizations. The Cambodians, traumatized and confused, with low levels of income, education, and home ownership, have relied on direction from traditional authorities. Since the refugees from Cambodia, in general, remain financially and psychologically unprepared to begin entry into the host society, the position of the monks may even have been enhanced. As representatives of the central social institution, the monks are often the only ones in the group who can achieve an understanding of the host society as well as that of the home country. The head monk of the *Wat Khemara Buddhikaram* has a doctorate degree. This makes him one of the few highly educated people in the Cambodian community. Among the groups experiencing rapid socioeconomic mobility, then, we find an increase in lay power. The relative lack of socioeconomic mobility results in an intensification of clerical power.

On this issue of lay control, we also see some differences between the Vietnamese and the Laotians, although both did display general trends toward increasing lay influence. These trends were much less marked, though, in the Vietnamese institution, because its religious figures were part of the established hierarchy of the American Catholic Church. The Laotian Buddhist temple, as a more radical transplant, saw a much greater expansion of the role of the laity accompanying mobility upward into American society. Thus, both the organizational fit between the immigrant religion and the American context and the socioeconomic position of the group shape changes in immigrant religious organizations.

A final area of variation among these groups concerned housing and settlement. Among the Vietnamese and the Laotians, the establishment of religious institutions followed the spread of home ownership. In the Vietnamese case, the church became the geographical center of a preexisting ethnic residential concentration. In the Laotian case, the temple was founded as people were moving into owner-occupied housing, but it was founded away from the initial site of settlement. These differences may be attributed to variations in the availability of land and housing. The Cambodian temple was established for people who had not yet managed to achieve substantial home ownership. The Cambodians were still largely confined to a low-income urban neighborhood. For this reason, the Cambodian institution was built outside of the Cambodian neighborhood, in a somewhat higher income Filipino-dominated area located about twenty minutes by car from the homes of most Cambodians. This temple has yet to give rise to a surrounding Cambodian settlement.

R. Stephen Warner has noted that the religions of new immigrant groups are both central to their lives in the new homeland and surprisingly under-studied.[54] We believe this three-part case study addresses this situation by providing some insight into the role of religion in the adaptation of Southeast Asian refugees in the United States. We have examined the critical part played by religious organizations among these newest pieces in the American mosaic. We have also attempted to suggest some general patterns. First, we have seen that all of the religious organizations have the manifest function of providing a sense of cultural identity and continuity to people who are struggling to make sense of new lives in a new world. Ironically, the religious institutions have come to symbolize home countries in ways that similar institutions in the home countries did not. Second, we have seen that religious organizations tend to take on unintended economic functions, particularly when immigrant communities are in the process of upward socioeconomic mobility. Third, socioeconomic position in the host country tends to reshape the organizational form of the immigrant religious institution. Among upwardly mobile ethnic groups, the influence of the laity increases. In a struggling, estranged group, traditional forms of clerical power can even be enhanced. Fourth, if there is movement into owner-occupied housing (usually a key aspect of upward mobility), a religious institution can provide both a geographical focal point and a place for exchanging information about housing opportunities. The patterns that we have identified here can, we believe, be found in other Southeast Asian communities and among other immigrant groups. We are therefore proposing the findings in this chapter as a basis for studying the role of religion in immigrant adaptation. Rebuilding spiritual lives, we suggest, is often a necessary basis for rebuilding communities.

Notes

This study was partially supported by a research grant from the Asian American Studies Center, University of California, Los Angeles.

1. Rubén G. Rumbaut, "Vietnamese, Laotian, and Cambodian Americans," in *Asian Americans: Contemporary Trends and Issues,* ed. Pyong Gap Min (Thousand Oaks, Calif.: Sage, 1995), 230–67.

2. Jesse W. Nash, *Vietnamese Catholicism* (Harvey, La.: Art Review Press, 1992); Carl L. Bankston III and Min Zhou, "The Ethnic Church, Ethnic Identification, and the Social Adjustment of Vietnamese Adolescents," *Review of Religious Research* 38 (1995): 18–37.

3. Carl L. Bankston III, "Bayou Lotus: Theravada Buddhism in Southwestern Louisiana," *Sociological Spectrum* 17 (1997): 473–89.

4. Gisèle Bousquet, *Behind the Bamboo Hedge: The Influence of Homeland Politics in the Parisian Vietnamese Community* (Ann Arbor: University of Michigan Press, 1991).

5. Sucheng Chan, *Hmong Means Free: Life in Laos and America* (Philadelphia: Temple University Press, 1994).

6. Chan, *Hmong Means Free.*

7. Timothy Dunnigan, Douglas P. Olney, Miles A McNall, and Marline A. Spring, "Hmong," in *Case Studies in Diversity: Refugees in America in the 1990s,* ed. David W. Haines (Westport, Conn.: Praeger, 1997), 145–66.

8. David P. Chandler, *The Tragedy of Cambodian History: Politics, War, and Revolution Since 1945* (New Haven, Conn.: Yale University Press, 1991).

9. Sucheng Chan, *Asian Americans: An Interpretive History* (Boston: Twayne, 1991).

10. Chandler, *The Tragedy of Cambodian History.*

11. Chan, *Hmong Means Free.*

12. Nathan S. Caplan, Marcella H. Choy, and John K. Whitmore, *Children of the Boat People: A Study of Educational Success* (Ann Arbor: University of Michigan Press, 1989); Chan, *Asian Americans*; Brian Wain, *The Refused: The Agony of the Indochinese Refugees* (New York: Simon & Schuster, 1981); Thanh V. Tran, "Sponsorship and Employment Status among Vietnamese Refugees in the United States," *International Migration Review* 25 (1991): 536–50.

13. Rumbaut, "Vietnamese, Laotian, and Cambodian Americans."

14. Beth C. Baldwin, *Patterns of Adjustment: A Second Look at Indochinese Resettlement in Orange County* (Orange County, Calif.: Immigrant and Refugee Planning Center, 1984).

15. Min Zhou and Carl L. Bankston III, *Growing Up American: How Vietnamese Children Adapt to Life in the United States* (New York: Russell Sage Foundation, 1998).

16. Cuban and Russian refugees are also older (median ages of 47 and 50, respectively, as of 1990), while Southeast Asian refugees comprise the youngest populations, with median ages of 26 or lower (13 for the Hmong). Russians, mostly Jews, also had the support of the Jewish community in the United States.

17. Beth C. Baldwin, *Capturing the Change: The Impact of Indochinese Refugees in Orange County, Challenges and Opportunities* (Santa Ana, Calif.: Immigrant and Refugee Planning Center, 1982); Kenneth A. Skinner, "Vietnamese in America: Diversity in Adaptation," *California Sociologist* 3 (summer 1980): 103–24.

18. Among the Vietnamese elite group, over half were Catholics and about a quarter were Buddhists. See William T Liu, Maryanne Lamanna, and Alice Murata, *Transition to Nowhere: Vietnamese Refugees in America* (Nashville, Tenn.: Charter House, 1979).

19. Lucie Cheng and Philip Q. Yang, "Asians: The 'Model Minority' Deconstructed," in *Ethnic Los Angeles*, ed. Roger Waldinger and Mehdi Bozorgmehr (New York: Russell Sage Foundation, 1996), 305–44.

20. Rubén G. Rumbaut, "The New Californians: Comparative Research Findings on the Educational Progress of Immigrant Children," in *California's Immigrant Children: Theory, Research, and Implications for Educational Policy*, ed. Rubén G. Rumbaut and Wayne A. Cornelius (La Jolla, Calif.: Center for U.S.-Mexican Studies, University of California, San Diego, 1995), 17–69.

21. Carl Bankston III, "Education and Ethnicity: Community and Academic Performance in an Urban Vietnamese Village," in *Beyond Black and White: New Faces and Voices in U.S. Schools*, ed. Lois Weiss and Maxine S. Seller (New York: State University of New York Press, 1997); Paul Rutledge, *The Role of Religion in Ethnic Self-Identity: A Vietnamese Community* (Lanham, Md.: University Press of America, 1985); Zhou and Bankston, *Growing Up American*.

22. Robert A. Witter, William A. Stock, Morris A. Okun, and Marilyn J. Haring, "Religion and Subjective Well-Being in Adulthood: A Quantitative Synthesis," *Review of Religious Research* 26 (1985): 332–42; Aaron Antonovsky, *Unravelling the Mystery of Health* (San Francisco: Jossey-Bass, 1987); Christopher G Ellison, David A. Gay, and Thomas A. Glass, "Does Religious Commitment Contribute to Individual Life Satisfaction?" *Social Forces* 68 (1989): 100–123; Melvin Pollner, "Divine Relations, Social Relations, and Well-Being," *Journal of Health and Social Behavior* 30 (1989): 92–104; Steven Stack, "The Effect of Religious Commitment on Suicide: A Cross-National Analysis," *Journal of Mental Health and Social Behavior* 24 (1983): 362–474; Christopher G. Ellison, "Religion, the Life Stress Paradigm, and the Study of Depression," in *Religion in Aging and Health*, ed. J. S. Levin (Thousand Oaks, Calif.: Sage, 1994), 78–121.

23. Bankston, "Education and Ethnicity"; Carl L. Bankston III and Min Zhou, "Religious Participation, Ethnic Identification, and the Adaptation of Vietnamese Adolescents in an Immigrant Community," *Sociological Quarterly* 36 (1995): 523–34; Yvonne Y. Haddad and Adair T. Lummis, *Islamic Values in the United States: A Comparative Study* (New York: Oxford University Press, 1987); Won Moo Hurh and Kwang Chung Kim, "Religious Participation of Korean Immigrants in the United States," *Journal for the Scientific Study of Religion* 29 (1990): 19–34; Peter Kivisto, "Religion and the New Immigrants," in *A Future for Religion: New Paradigms for Social Analysis*, ed. W. J. Swatos (Newbury Park, Calif.: Sage, 1993), 75–96; Nash, *Vietnamese Catholicism*; Bankston and Zhou, "Ethnic Church, Ethnic Identification, and the Social Adjustment"; Rutledge, *Role of Religion in Ethnic Self-Identity*; Zhou and Bankston, *Growing Up American*.

24. David B. Barrett, ed., *World Christian Encyclopedia* (New York: Oxford University Press, 1982).

25. Although we use some U.S. Census data to describe the Vietnamese parish in New Orleans, our data are chiefly qualitative. One of the authors of this chapter (Bankston) worked as an English-as-a-second-language teacher, a high school substitute teacher, and a volunteer with a youth group in the Vietnamese community of New Orleans from 1990 to 1995. During this time, he conducted both formal and informal interviews with residents and witnessed changes in community structure. Another author (Zhou) also did fieldwork in this neighborhood in 1994 and 1995. For details, see Zhou and Bankston, *Growing Up American.*

26. Dorothy Vidulich, "Religion Central for Vietnamese in U.S.," *National Catholic Reporter* 30 (October 14, 1994): 12–14.

27. Zhou and Bankston, *Growing Up American.*

28. For a newspaper report of these events, see Joan Treadway, "Gardeners' Meeting with New Landlord Fruitful," *Times-Picayune,* August 21, 1994, B3.

29. Quoted in Dorothy Vidulich, "Religion Central for Vietnamese in U.S."

30. Vidulich, "Religion Central for Vietnamese in U.S.," 12.

31. Stanley J. Tambiah, *Buddhism and the Spirit Cults* (New York: Cambridge University Press, 1976); Stanley J. Tambiah, *The Buddhist Saints of the Forest and the Cult of Amulets: A Study in Charisma, Hagiography, and Millennial Buddhism* (New York: Cambridge University Press, 1984).

32. On this ceremony, see also Anuman Rajadhon, *Essays on Thai Folklore* (Bangkok: The Intra-Religious Commission for Development and Sathirakoses Nagapradipa Foundation, 1988); Mayoury Ngaosyvathn, *Individual Soul, National Identity: The Baci-Sou Kh'uan of the Lao* (unpublished thesis, Cornell University, Ithaca, New York, 1989); Carl L. Bankston III, "Refuge," *Sycamore Review* 8 (1996): 54–66.

33. Our description of the Laotian Buddhist Community in Iberia Parish is based on fieldwork conducted throughout 1996 and 1997. One of the authors (Bankston) attended temple events and maintained social contacts with Laotians in the region throughout this period and after. In addition to information collected through this participant observation, we also conducted sixty-three unstructured interviews with Laotian immigrants. Again, we also make use of census data, although census information on the Laotians is more limited than the information on the Vietnamese.

34. Bankston and Zhou, "Religious Participation, Ethnic Identification, and the Adaptation of Vietnamese Adolescents"; Bankston and Zhou, "Ethnic Church, Ethnic Identification, and the Social Adjustment."

35. William Wilson, *When Work Disappears: The World of the New Urban Poor* (New York: Knopf, 1996).

36. Phayvanh Phoumindr, "Lao Community, Social Control, and Multiculturalism in Australia," *Lao Study Review* 1 (1995) (electronic journal available online at www.global.lao.net/laostudy).

37. Barrett, *World Christian Encyclopedia.*

38. MayMayko Ebihara, *Interrelations between Buddhism and Social Systems in Cambodian Peasant Culture* (New Haven, Conn.: Yale University Press, 1966), 175–247.

39. Mary Carol Hopkins, *Braving a New World* (Westport, Conn.: Bergin and Garvey, 1996).

40. Robert C. Lester, *Theravada Buddhism in Southeast Asia* (Ann Arbor: University of Michigan Press, 1973).

41. Suan Anne Needham, *Cultural Concepts of Literacy Learning and Literacy Uses in the Cambodian Community of Long Beach, California* (master's thesis, University of California, Los Angeles, 1992).

42. Donald P. Whitaker, Judith M. Heinmann, John E. MacDonald, Kenneth W. Martindale, Rinn-Sup Shinn, and Charles Townsend, *Area Handbook for the Khmer Republic* (Washington D.C.: U.S. Government Printing Office, 1976).

43. Hopkins, *Braving a New World.*

44. Anne M. Rynearson and Thomas A. Gosebrink, "Barriers to Censusing Southeast Asian Refugees," *Ethnographic Exploratory Report #10* (Washington, D.C.: Bureau of the Census, 1990).

45. However, various other sources estimate the population to be much larger; see Needham, *Cultural Concepts of Literacy Learning and Literacy Uses.*

46. Nadine Seldon, *Beyond the Killing Fields: Khmer Refugees in Long Beach* (unpublished paper, University of California, Irvine, 1989).

47. The qualitative data for the Cambodian Buddhist community in Long Beach was gathered from 1998 to 1999 by one of the authors (Kim) who resided in the Long Beach community for fifteen years. She attended the temple worship services and conducted personal interviews with Cambodian Buddhists and community members. She also conducted telephone interviews with community leaders and informants. In addition, census data was used to obtain information on Cambodians in Long Beach.

48. Data from the U.S. Census are for the Los Angeles CMSA (Los Angeles, Orange, Riverside, San Bernardino, and Ventura Countries) in 1990, cited in *The Ethnic Quilt*, by James P. Allen and Eugene Turner (Los Angeles: The Center for Geographical Studies, California State University at Northridge, 1997).

49. Allen and Turner, *The Ethnic Quilt.*

50. Pamela Bunte and Rebecca Joseph, *The Cambodian Community of Long Beach: An Ethnographic Analysis of Factors Leading to Census Undercount*, draft of final report to the Center for Survey Methods Research, Bureau of the Census (Washington, D.C.: U.S. Bureau of the Census, 1991).

51. Janet Wiscombe, "The Mighty Pen of New Phnom Penh," *Los Angeles Times*, April 26, 1998, E1.

52. Robert N. Bellah, *Beyond Belief: Essays on Religion in a Post-Traditional World* (New York: Harper & Row, 1976).

53. Peter L Berger, *The Sacred Canopy: Elements of a Sociological Theory of Religion* (New York: Doubleday, 1969), 23.

54. R. Stephen Warner, "Approaching Religious Diversity: Barriers, Byways, and Beginnings," *Sociology of Religion* 59 (1998): 193–215; R. Stephen Warner, "Immigration and Religious Communities in the United States," in *Gatherings in Diaspora: Religious Communities and the New Immigration*, ed. Stephen Warner and Judith Wittner (Philadelphia: Temple University Press, 1998), 3–34.

CHAPTER THREE

RELIGIOUS DIVERSITY AMONG THE CHINESE IN AMERICA

Fenggang Yang

R eligious diversity has never been strange to the Chinese. Traditionally, China has had many religions. Along with the three major religiocultural traditions of Confucianism, Daoism (Taoism),
and Buddhism there were many syncretic sects and localized folk religions. Meanwhile, many individuals followed an assortment of person-
alized eclectic practices without identifying themselves with any particular religion. Given these historical and cultural backgrounds, it is not
surprising to find that a religious diversity exists among contemporary
Chinese Americans or that a large proportion of them claim no religion.
What is remarkable is that Christianity appears to have become the
largest religion, and Christian churches have, in fact, become the predominant religious institutions among the Chinese in America. For example, a *Los Angeles Times* poll in 1997 reports that 44 percent of Chinese
Americans in southern California claim no religion, 32 percent are Christian (including 6 percent Catholics), and 20 percent are Buddhist.[1] Several surveys conducted in other metropolitan areas and the Canadian
census all report similar patterns: Christianity is the largest religion,
Buddhism the second, and close to half of Chinese claim no religion at
all. Organizationally, the latest counts report the existence of more than
800 Chinese Protestant churches, whereas the number of Chinese Buddhist temples and associations is less than 150.[2] This is in sharp contrast
to the situation in Chinese societies (Taiwan, Hong Kong, and mainland
China), where Buddhism is the largest religion and Christians remain a
small minority of between 1 and 5 percent of the population.[3]

More accurate estimates of religious practices and beliefs among the
Chinese in the United States and Chinese societies require more focused
surveys, which do not exist at this time. Without such surveys, this
chapter has to be based primarily on my own ethnographic research on
contemporary Chinese American religion in the past six years and com-
plemented by some historical documents, theses, and writings scattered
in scholarly publications.[4] To situate religious developments in their

historical and social contexts, I will first provide a short history of Chinese immigration and then provide a brief description of the current status of the Chinese community. Following this brief description, I will discuss three major religions among the Chinese in America: the Chinese folk religion, Buddhism, and Christianity.

History of Chinese Immigration

The Chinese were the first Asian group to immigrate in large numbers to the United States. Chinese immigration began in the late 1840s. This history may be divided into two stages, and each stage has several waves of immigrants. The first stage covers approximately the first hundred years.[5] Between the late 1840s and 1882, the first wave of laborers came to work in gold mines, railroad construction, agriculture, and fishing. This first wave of Chinese immigration was halted by the Chinese Exclusion Act of 1882. Between 1882 and 1943 the Chinese were excluded from immigration and naturalization, Chinese in America suffered severe racial discrimination and social isolation, and only a small number of Chinese managed to come to the United States. The ghetto-like Chinatown in major cities was the haven for those laborers and merchants working in Chinese restaurants, hand-wash laundries, gift shops, and domestics. After the Chinese exclusion laws were repealed in 1943, a small annual quota of 105 legal immigrants was established. Until the 1950s, almost all Chinese immigrants emigrated from rural areas surrounding Guangzhou (Canton) in the southern province of Guangdong. Until the 1960s, Chinatown was very much a "bachelor society" crowded by men. These male "sojourners" either failed to marry or were unable to bring their wives to the United States because of immigration restrictions. These first-stage immigrants have been referred to as *laoqiao* (earlier immigrants).

The Immigration and Naturalization Amendment Act of 1965 marks the beginning of the second stage of Chinese immigration. This and the following immigration laws grant an annual quota of twenty thousand immigrants for each country in the Eastern Hemisphere. Since 1965, Chinese immigrants, as well as refugees from Indo-China, have come in large numbers from several societies in several waves, including immigrants from Taiwan, Hong Kong, mainland China, and Southeast Asian countries. Consequently, the Chinese population doubled between 1970 and 1980, doubled again between 1980 and 1990, and reached 2.4 million in 2000 (see Table 3.1).[6]

Most of the post-1965 Chinese immigrants, like other Asian immigrants but in contrast with early Chinese immigrants, are characterized by their urban background, high educational achievement, and professional

Table 3.1: Chinese Population in the United States, 1860–2000

Year	Total
1860	34,933
1870	63,199
1880	105,613
1890	107,488
1900	89,863 (118,746) *
1910	71,531 (94,414)
1920	61,639 (85,202)
1930	74,954 (102,159)
1940	77,504 (106,334)
1950	117,629 (150,005)
1960	198,958 (237,292)
1970	383,023 (431,583)
1980	806,042 (812,178)
1990	1,645,472
2000	2,432,585†

* The numbers in parentheses are probably adjusted numbers including Hawaii and Alaska (see Yang, Chinese Christians in America).

† Does not include anyone who chose more than one category in the race question on the Census form.

occupations before immigration.[7] Due to the new immigration laws that established a preference system favoring skilled workers, many Chinese came first as students, then adjusted to the permanent resident status upon achieving graduate degrees and finding employment. Hence, most people work as professionals in nonethnic companies or as technocrats in governmental agencies. In the meantime, many less-educated laborers have come as well. While many Chinese Americans are on the high end of the socioeconomic spectrum, there is also a cluster on the low end. Many of the lower-class Chinese live in the inner-city Chinatowns of New York and San Francisco.[8] The ethnic economies have changed also: hand-wash laundries have disappeared, Chinese restaurants have boomed, travel agencies have arisen with service specialties for transpacific air routes, and real estate and insurance companies have Chinese agents for the growing markets among Chinese residents. Most new Chinese immigrants have bypassed the urban ghetto Chinatown and settled in ethnically mixed suburbs. For these new immigrants, the ethnic community is no longer a geographically separate enclave, but a community scattered throughout the metropolitan suburbs. Because they came during and after the civil rights movement, new immigrants usually suffer less discrimination than their predecessors, and the overall image of the Chinese in America has become one of the "model minorities."

The new Chinese immigration actually began earlier than many other Asian groups. Following World War II, tens of thousands of Chinese arrived as war brides and refugees and as international students.[9] In contrast to *laoqiao*, most of these people came not from Guangdong but from all over China, and many had received high school and college education before coming to the United States. Therefore, their backgrounds resemble those of the post-1965 immigrants, the *xinqiao* (new immigrants).

Diversity of the Chinese Population

An important characteristic of the contemporary Chinese population in the United States is the tremendous internal diversity. They come from very different societies and have very different linguistic, cultural, political, and socioeconomic backgrounds. According to the 1990 census, 69 percent of the over 1.6 million Chinese in the United States were foreign-born. Among them, 32 percent were born in mainland China, 15 percent in Taiwan, 9 percent in Hong Kong, and 13 percent in Vietnam and other Southeast Asian countries. These societies have been very different in social and political systems: Mainland China has been under the rule of the Chinese Communist Party since 1949; Taiwan has remained as the Republic of China under the rule of the Guomindang (Kuomintang) then the Democratic Progressive Party; Hong Kong was a British colony until 1997; and Vietnam experienced the sweeping Communist revolution in the 1970s. Of the 31 percent native-born Chinese Americans, many are second-generation children of the post-1965 immigrants, but a significant number of them belong to the third, fourth, or even fifth generation of earlier Chinese immigrants. As previously mentioned, there also exists a socioeconomic polarization. While the majority of Chinese Americans are highly educated professionals living in middle-class suburbs, there are also many less-educated laborers, especially recent immigrants from rural areas of China. They live in Chinatowns, work for minimum wages in garment factories and restaurants, and are struggling for a life in poverty.

Culturally, an obvious division exists between *laoqiao* (earlier immigrants) and *xinqiao* (new immigrants). The new immigrants "consider themselves more genteel, more literate, and more modern as most of them have lived in urban areas of China or Hong Kong. They feel that the [earlier] settlers who came from rural areas of the old country are bumpkins with unrefined manners."[10] Linguistic diversity has become very apparent.[11] Taishanese, commonly spoken by people from the Taishan district of Guangdong, was once the lingua franca in American Chinatowns, then it was replaced by the standard Cantonese spoken in the cities of Hong Kong, Macau, and Canton. Mandarin has become increasingly common inside and outside Chinatowns. Mandarin is the official dialect of China (*guoyu* or *putonghua*) that every educated Chinese is supposed to be able to speak, no matter what his or her mother tongue is. Meanwhile, some people from Taiwan cling to Taiwanese, which is a variation of Minnanese or Fujianese. Many Cantonese-speaking Hong Kong immigrants know little or no Mandarin. Moreover, many ethnic Chinese from Southeast Asia speak none of the Chinese dialects but Vietnamese, Malaysian, Tagalog, or English.

Similarly important, the sociopolitical background of new Chinese immigrants is very complex. From the 1950s to 1970s, most Chinese immigrants were the "uprooted" and "rootless" people. They were born in the mainland under the rule of Guomindang's Republic of China, escaped from wars or fled the Communist mainland, then wandered around in several places—Taiwan, Hong Kong, or Southeast Asia—before coming to the United States. Socially and politically, these sojourners often have connections with the Republic of China in Taiwan. Meanwhile, many also have strong attachments to their birthplace in mainland China and hold a vision of a united and strong Chinese nation. Also from Taiwan and Hong Kong are the sons and daughters of the sojourners. Growing up during the economic boom in Taiwan or Hong Kong, this generation generally has less attachment to mainland China than their parent generation, although their Chinese national identity can be similarly strong. Some Taiwanese natives, whose families have lived in Taiwan for three or more generations, have become sympathizers or supporters of the Taiwan independence movement. Beginning in the early 1980s, tens of thousands of students and scholars from the People's Republic of China have come to the United States. Many of them adjusted to immigrant status upon finding employment. After the Tiananmen Square incident in 1989, when the student-led democracy movement in Beijing was violently suppressed by the Chinese Communist government, the U.S. Congress passed the Chinese Student Protection Act in 1992, which granted 52,425 Chinese nationals permanent U.S. residence.[12] These mainland Chinese commonly have great concerns for China's economic modernization, political democratization, and unification of Taiwan and mainland China. In addition, since the mid-1970s, many ethnic Chinese came as refugees from Vietnam, Cambodia, and Laos. These diasporic Chinese had suffered doubly, first as Chinese minorities in host societies, and second as banished natives from Communists countries. Those ethnic Chinese from Malaysia, Indonesia, the Philippines, and other countries also experienced ethnic discrimination or political persecution.

All of the preceding cultural and sociopolitical groups share similar challenges from yet another group—the American-born Chinese (ABC) and the American-raised Chinese (ARC). These second-generation or

1.5-generation children of immigrants often speak English as their first or only language. Compared with their immigrant parents, ABCs and ARCs usually have greater concerns for social and political issues of the United States rather than those in Asia. ABCs and ARCs are often well assimilated culturally, socioeconomically, and structurally. On the other hand, however, because of very different family experiences, the internal diversity among ABCs and ARCs is also important.

Chinese Associations and Organizations

In the traditional Chinatown, the dominant ethnic organizations were *huiguan* and *tang*.[13] *Huiguan* were based on primordial sentiments, including home-district associations and clan (or same-surname) associations. For those who were unable to join a *huiguan*, there were *tang* (triads or secret societies), which were based on fraternal principles. Membership in these associations was not voluntary but often ascribed or forced on individuals. Above these separate and competing *huiguan* and *tang* was the umbrella Chinese Consolidated Benevolent Association (CCBA). The CCBA would coordinate and mediate among its member associations and represent the Chinese community to the larger society. These ethnic organizations provided many services to Chinatowns' Chinese, including housing and employment, social support and protection, credit union and financial help, medical clinics and evacuation services in case of death, and mediation service in case of disputes. Since the 1950s, when the anti-Communist McCarthyism was strong, the CCBA and most of Chinatowns' organizations sided with the Guomindang government in Taiwan (the Republic of China) and expressed opposition to the Chinese Communists in the mainland (the People's Republic of China).[14] Whereas formal religious institutions were almost absent in early Chinatowns, *huiguan* and *tang* had some religious dimensions in their organization and activities.[15] The same-district associations often kept shrines to their own local heroes and tutelary deities. The clan associations always performed rituals of venerating common ancestors, real or imagined. The triads commonly held cultic practices.

Amid the civil rights movement in the 1960s and 1970s, some new forms of Chinese ethnic organizations arose in various Chinatowns throughout the United States, including community service agencies, political organizations, and recreational clubs.[16] These new organizations promoted the interaction between ethnic Chinese and the larger society. Some of these organizations, such as the Chinatown Planning Council in New York City, brought in money with governmental financial programs to improve the social and economic situations of the Chinatown community. On the national level, a prominent new organization is the Organi-zation of Chinese Americans (OCA). Since its establishment in the 1970s, OCA has mobilized Chinese citizens to participate in American politics and society, lobbied the U.S. Congress and the administration on behalf of Chinese Americans, and reached out to rally other Asian Americans to fight for racial justice in American society. The OCA has headquarters in Washington, D.C., and branches in every metropolitan area where there is a sizable Chinese population.

Since the 1960s, the growing Chinese population and increasing het-erogeneity are accompanied by burgeoning growth of various Chinese as-sociations. Many new *tongxianghui* (same-district associations) have emerged, with either expanded boundaries to the province or a cluster of provinces. For example, in the Greater Washington area, there are provin-cial *tongxianghui* of Beijing, Fujian, Henan, Shandong, and Shanghai and associations across provinces and even countries, including the *Dongbei* (the three provinces of northeast China), the *Jiangzhehu* (the provinces of Jiangsu and Zhejiang and the city of Shanghai), and the *Indochinese Asso-ciation* (Chinese from Vietnam, Cambodia, and Laos). Compared with the old same-district associations (*huiguan*) in Chinatown, these new same-district associations (*tongxianghui*) are more voluntary than ascribed in membership, mostly for networking and social purposes. Because people live scattered in suburbs, interactions among association members are not as frequent and intense as in the traditional Chinatown organizations.

An entirely new type of Chinese organization is the alumni associa-tion of Chinese universities. In the Greater Washington area, there are more than thirty alumni associations of the major universities in Taiwan and mainland China. There are even more in the New York and Los An-geles areas. This reflects the educational achievement of many new Chi-nese immigrants before immigration. These alumni associations hold fre-quent activities including lectures, forums, karaoke, dancing, and so on.

Meanwhile, the number of Chinese weekend language schools (*zhongwen xuexiao*) has rapidly increased. In the Washington and Hous-ton areas, currently more than thirty Chinese schools each are teaching Chinese language and culture at levels from kindergarten to high school. These schools are not only for children, but also function as a weekly social occasion for parents. Some schools provide *qigong* or *taiji* classes for parents. The content of teaching at these Chinese schools is politically and culturally diverse. Most Chinese schools teach Mandarin, while a few teach Cantonese or Taiwanese. Most schools use textbooks imported from Taiwan, teach traditional Chinese characters, and adopt the traditional *bopomofo* spelling system. Recently, mainland Chinese have established Chinese schools for their children, which teach simpli-fied Chinese characters used in the People's Republic of China (PRC) and adopt the spelling system of *hanyu pinyin*. These pedagogical differences often have political implications—pro-PRC, pro-ROC, or pro-Taiwan independence.

Several Chinese language newspapers and monthly magazines are widely circulated in metropolitan areas. Some are nationally or even internationally syndicated, such as the *World Journal* daily and the *Sing Tao Daily*, reporting current events in Asia as well as local and national events that are of concern to Chinese in America. They are often backed by governmental agencies or business groups in Asia and have explicit or implicit political ideology toward Chinese politics. However, most of them also try to be inclusive in order to reach a wide audience. Some locally based newspapers and magazines exclusively focus on life in the United States, serve local ethnic businesses and residents, and promote ethnic Chinese unity and solidarity. Such ethnic media seem to have significant influence in terms of forging a sense of Chinese American community.

In sum, Chinese associations and organizations are numerous, diverse, and often unrelated to each other. Chinese people are divided based on political ideology, cultural orientation, and socioeconomic status in American society. These ethnic associations help maintain Chinese identity one way or another. However, sociopolitical tensions and frictions among these ethnic associations have fragmented the Chinese community.

With the preceding brief layout of the historical and social contexts, now let us examine various religious traditions and institutions among the Chinese in America. Briefly speaking, Christianity has become the most practiced institutional religion, Buddhism the second. Traditional Chinese folk religions have revived in the last two decades. Because various sectarian or cultic traditions have attracted few Chinese followers, the following discussion will focus on the traditional Chinese folk religion, Buddhism, and Christianity.[17]

Chinese Folk Religion and Cultural Practices

When the first wave of Chinese immigrants came to the American West Coast in the mid-nineteenth century, like their counterparts from other countries, they brought along their familiar gods and saints and established many temples. These temples are commonly referred to as "joss houses." The word *joss* is a corruption of the Portuguese word *deos*, meaning god. A joss house is thus a house of gods. The deities in those temples are from Buddhism, such as Guanyin (Kuan Yin), and Daoism, such as Yuhuang Dadi, and some are only known to a particular Chinese village or district. Charles Caldwell Dobie in 1936 made a detailed observation and description of the joss houses in San Francisco. He pointed out that

> It is hard to define a Joss House in Occidental terms. It is neither a church, nor a temple, nor a mosque. But it could easily have elements of all three. A Joss House is not a thing of sect and dogma. It is, to quote the Chinese themselves, simply a "place of worship." Into it may be poured any and all the religious faiths and influences that the Chinese have absorbed and modified in the sixty [sic] centuries of their civilization.[18]

In other words, a joss house was primarily for individual rituals and devotions, not for congregating with fellow believers or adhering to a set of clearly defined dogmas.

The first two joss houses were believed to be the Kong Chow temple and the T'ien Hou temple, which were built in the early 1850s in San Francisco under the auspices of the Kong Chow (Same-District) Association and the Sam Yap (Same-District) Association, respectively. The principal deity of the Kong Chow was Guan Gong (Kuan Kung), the god of wealth, and the T'ien Hou was the temple of the Queen of the Heaven (Tian Hou, T'ien Hou, or the Heavenly Queen). Both temples also had other minor gods.[19] In the second half of the nineteenth century, hundreds of joss houses were built on the West Coast, but most were abandoned soon after they were built. In San Francisco's Chinatown, there were at least fifteen joss houses in 1892. By the 1930s, however, only two joss houses were left there, and they had become showplaces for sightseers.[20]

After half a century, however, some joss houses on certain back streets of San Francisco's Chinatown have persisted or reopened.[21] Actually, the traditional Chinese folk religion, which worships a syncretic variety of gods with many festivals throughout the year, has been revived since the 1970s. This revival is brought mostly by the sudden influx of large numbers of refugees from Vietnam, Cambodia, and Laos, among them many ethnic Chinese. From Los Angeles to New York, from Washington, D.C. to Houston, many syncretic temples have been opened in the Chinatowns or built in suburbs.

In the 1990s in Houston, for example, Chinese from Indo-China (Vietnam, Cambodia, and Laos) have built three temples with magnificent Chinese-style architecture: the T'ien Hou, the Teo Chew, and the Guan Di. These temples represent the major forms of the contemporary Chinese folk religion in the United States. The T'ien Hou Temple worships the Heavenly Queen and Daoist deities, immortals, and some other gods as well. Tian Hou (Heavenly Queen) is a popular goddess in the coastal provinces of China and among the Chinese diaspora in Southeast Asia.

This sea goddess is believed to have the powers of protecting fishermen and sailors, healing, and answering all kinds of prayers. The Teo Chew Temple worships a major god named Bentougong along with various Buddhist and Daoist deities. Bentougong is the tutelary god in the Chao Zhou (Teo Chew) district of Guangdong Province. The Teo Chew Temple also houses the Teo Chew Association, which is for people who can trace their roots to Chao Zhou. The newest Guan Di Temple is dedicated to worshiping Guan Di, a historical figure in the third century who was praised as symbolizing loyalty and righteousness and deified as the god of wealth. A statue of Confucius is among the gods as well, but stands outside the main hall. The Guan Di Temple was established under the leadership of the Hai Nam Association, which is for people who claim Hai Nan (now a province in China) as their ancestral land.

These Chinese folk religious temples mainly serve immigrants from Indo-China, including some non-Chinese. They are open every day and welcome visitors and participants of various backgrounds. They often print materials in three languages—Chinese, Vietnamese, and English. Although each temple has its own major constituents, these temples do not have a formal membership system and the same people may participate in activities of several temples. No religious monks or nuns live in such temples; some lay priests and volunteers provide ritual facilitating and maintenance services. Individuals may come to the temple in daytime to say a prayer, conduct a divination in front of a god, or simply enjoy the familiar atmosphere deprived them in the larger society. Festival celebrations are mostly based on the Chinese traditional calendar system, although adjustment to a weekend schedule is often made. Important gatherings include the Chinese New Year, the Mid-Autumn (Moon) Festival, and the birthdays of Tian Hou, Guan Di, Guan Yin, Buddha, and other gods. Buddhist sutras and Daoist scriptures sometimes can be found in these temples.

The temples in Houston all have a weekend Chinese school teaching children the Chinese language, Chinese values, cultural customs, and martial arts. Preserving Chinese culture is one of the key motives of the founders of and donators to these temples. I also observed that few American-born or American-raised young people regularly attend temple activities. Growing up in American social and cultural contexts, receiving American education in public schools, and mixing with children of other ethnic and racial backgrounds, the children of these Chinese immigrants find it hard to maintain the unstructured beliefs and practices of their parents. In the past, the attrition of such temples established in the nineteenth century was in part due to the lack of interest in this religious heritage among the second and later generations.[22] Therefore, the continuity of these temples in their current form will depend on continual influx of immigrants more than on the maturing second and later generations.

Besides these temples, some Chinese maintain tablets of ancestors and altars of gods at home, observe *feng shui*, consult fortune-tellers, conduct divination, and practice *qigong*, all of which may be regarded as part of the traditional Chinese folk religion. *Feng shui* is a type of astrology using the concepts of yin, yang, five elements, eight *gua* (diagrams composed of three solid or broken lines), and stars to maximize harmony and minimize conflicts of a person with the surrounding environment. Practitioners consult *feng shui* masters in choosing the location of their houses and graveyards, decorating rooms, and selecting time for doing certain things, such as a wedding or opening a store. In the past few decades, *feng shui* has spread among many non-Chinese people. *Qigong* is a type of still or slow-motion meditation for the purpose of physical health, psychological peace, and spiritual enrichment. In the last two decades, hundreds of *qigong* schools have emerged and some have flourished throughout China, and a few *qigong* masters have ventured to North America. In the United States, two *qigong* schools have gained large numbers of practitioners, including some Caucasians: One is Yan Xin Qigong; the other is Falun Gong or Falun Dafa. Whereas older people and people with chronic disease usually practice *qigong*, a growing number of young and middle-aged people, including professionals who hold graduate degrees, have been attracted by Yan Xin Qigong and Falun Dafa. In July 1999, the Chinese government began to crack down on the cultic organization of Falun Gong. American and other Western media covered the events with apparent sympathy for the suppressed. This seems to have helped Falun Gong to gain non-Chinese followers in the United States. Interestingly, the spreading of *feng shui*, *qigong*, and other traditional Chinese folk religious practices has extensively used the latest technology—the Internet. A keyword search would generate a list of dozens or hundreds of Web sites and Web pages that provide a variety of information, instructions, publications, associations, and activity schedules on any of these practices. Joined with the postmodern New Age movements and information technologies, these cultic practices, as a whole, will persist even though particular groups or practices may emerge or diminish.

The nature of the folk religion makes it hard to know how widespread the folk religious practices are. Chinese folk religious temples do not have a formal membership system. Other folk religious practices are very individualistic in nature. No social surveys or polls, to my knowledge, have been designed to estimate the number of existing folk religious practitioners. Therefore, we do not know the numbers or proportions of Chinese in America who practice one type or the other of Chinese folk religion.

Buddhism

Although joss houses built by the earlier immigrants commonly had certain Buddhist deities and some individuals probably made personal devotions to Guan Yin (Kuan Yin, or Alalokitesvara Bodhisattva), it would be far-fetched to call those temples and practices Buddhist. Chinese Buddhism in more organized and less syncretic forms appeared in America along with the coming of *xinqiao* (new immigrants).[23]

As described earlier, Chinese new immigrants arrived earlier than other Asian new immigrants. Following the Chinese civil war (1945–1949) and the establishment of the People's Republic of China on the mainland (1949), many people fled to Taiwan and Hong Kong, some of them later came to the United States. The Buddhist followers among *xinqiao* were different from *laoqiao* not only in socioeconomic terms, but also in their religious orientation. They tended to distance themselves from syncretic religious practices and adhere to a relatively more pure form of Buddhism. This orientation happened in part because of their higher education than *laoqiao* and in part because of the influence of the Buddhist revival movement that had been going on for decades in China. This twentieth-century Chinese Buddhist revival insisted on orthodox Buddhism (*zheng xin fojiao*), modernizing the *sangha* (clergy) and lay organization.[24] After arriving in America, some lay believers gathered together to socialize with each other and to exchange experiences of learning the Buddha *dharma*. Before long, some Chinese Buddhists established nonprofit organizations and began to sponsor monks and nuns to immigrate to the United States. Those monks and nuns, who often had been masters of the most active lay leaders of the *xinqiao* Buddhist groups, had similarly fled mainland China and were wandering in Hong Kong or Taiwan.

Such lay-initiated Chinese Buddhist groups began to emerge in the 1950s. The first was the Chinese Buddhist Association of Hawaii, which was formed in 1953, sponsored a monk from Hong Kong in 1956, and constructed the Hsu Yun Temple in 1965. In San Francisco, the Buddha's Universal Church began in the early 1950s and dedicated its building in 1963. Another important group in San Francisco was the Sino-American Buddhist Association, which was organized in 1959, sponsored a monk from Hong Kong in 1962, built the Gold Mountain Temple in 1970, and since then has established several branch temples on the West Coast. In New York, the first Chinese Buddhist group was the Eastern States Buddhist Association, which was started in 1962 and completed the Mahayana Temple in 1971. This association sponsored more than a dozen monks and nuns from Taiwan, Hong Kong, Burma (Myanmar), and mainland China. Most of the monks and nuns then left to start their own groups, including the China Buddhist Association, the Buddhist Association of the United

States, the Eastern Buddhist Association, the Young Men's Buddhist Association of America, and the Grace Gratitude Buddhist Temple, in New York or other places.

Following the steps of pioneer monks and nuns, more monks and nuns came to America to gather their own followers. In 1972, a nun from Hong Kong, after traveling through major cities in North America, finally settled in Los Angeles and started the Western American Buddhist Association, the first Chinese Buddhist group in Los Angeles. Five years later, a monk from Taiwan, after visiting a New York temple for a while, formed the Buddhist Ortho-Creed Association in Los Angeles. In the late 1970s, Buddha Light Mountain Sect, under Hsing Yun, came to Los Angeles. After ten years of hard efforts, it constructed the grandiose Hsi Lai Temple, the largest and best-known Chinese temple in America.[25] In 1979, a monk from Taiwan, after spending seven years in New York, went out to explore Boston, Chicago, Washington, D.C., and finally settled in Houston and started the Texas Buddhist Association, the first Chinese Buddhist group in Texas. In the Northwest, a Taiwanese immigrant, Mr. Lu Shengyan, came to Seattle in the mid-1980s and founded his True Buddha Sect. Today there are more than a dozen True Buddha Sect branch temples in several metropolises in North America.

Overall, by the end of the 1990s, there were about 120 to 150 Chinese Buddhist groups (temples, associations, and centers) in the United States. Most of them are concentrated in the largest metropolitan areas of New York, San Francisco, Los Angeles, and Houston, whereas small groups are scattered in smaller cities of many states and university campuses. These Chinese Buddhist groups share three general characteristics: They tend to be organizationally independent, theologically (Buddhalogically) reformed, and institutionally ecumenical. First, most of the groups are locally organized and nondenominational. Many are lay organized small groups. For those well-established ones with a temple building, the resident abbot may be the heir of certain sectarian lineage, such as some Chan, Pure Land, or Tian Tai schools, but the temple does not belong to a hierarchical organization. On the other hand, some charismatic monks who have been able to gather followers in several places consequently have established several temples and centers under their names. The most successful Chinese monk may have been Hsuan Hua (1918–1995) of the Sino-American Buddhist Association. His teaching was a mixture of Chan, Pure Land, and Tian Tai schools. He led his followers and built the Gold Mountain Temple in San Francisco (1970), the Gold Wheel Temple in Los Angeles (1975), the Ten Thousands of Buddhas City in northern California (1976), the Gold Summit Temple in Seattle (1984), and the Gold Buddha Temple in Vancouver (1984).

Second, most Chinese Buddhist groups follow the reformed Buddhism that emphasizes "Buddhism in the World" (*ren jian fojiao,* or humanistic Buddhism) and/or Orthodox Buddhism (*zheng xin fojiao*).[26] One important exception is the True Buddha Sect, which has obvious elements of Mahayana Buddhism, Tibetan Tantric Buddhism, Daoism, and Chinese folk religion. The syncretic nature of the True Buddha Sect makes other Chinese Buddhist groups refuse to recognize it as an orthodox Buddhism, even though many groups themselves have various degrees of syncretism.

Third, most of the Chinese Buddhist groups in the United States are ecumenical with other major Buddhist traditions. Unlike Japanese Buddhists that have clear and distinct denominations or sects, Chinese Buddhists commonly practice both Chan and Pure Land Buddhism and frequently adopt Tian Tai and other traditions as well. Although some groups clearly emphasize one tradition over others, they are commonly open toward others, including Theravada and Varjana Buddhist traditions. For example, Fo Kuang Shan denomination and local groups such as the Texas Buddhist Association have been active in organizing and participating in ecumenical Buddhist activities.

While ecumenical in the religious sense, Chinese Buddhism in America is also making great efforts to cross ethnic boundaries. As a traditional religion brought in by immigrants, Chinese Buddhism continues primarily to serve Chinese immigrants. However, some non-Chinese, especially middle-class Caucasians, have been drawn into a few well-established Chinese temples under renowned monks. These temples, such as the Hsi Lai Temple of the Fo Kuang Shan and the Jade Buddha Temple of the Texas Buddhist Association, in responding to Euro-American inquiries, provide English instructions for meditation and sutra study. The most remarkable success in this regard was made by the Sino-American Buddhist Association under Hsuan Hua, which later turned into the Dharma Realm Buddhist Association. "By 1971, more than two-thirds of [Hsuan Hua's] disciples were Caucasians. . . . In 1972 at the Gold Mountain Monastery there were ten fully ordained monks and nuns—all but one of them Caucasian."[27]

However, the changes of this and other groups are not straight-line with a definite direction. The Dharma Realm Buddhist Association has not yet turned away from immigrants to become an American Buddhist group. In fact, after changing from a Chinese immigrant group in the 1960s to a mostly Euro-American group in the 1970s, it has changed back to a predominantly Chinese group in the 1990s. Euro-American monks and nuns now serve a majority of Chinese immigrant Buddhists.[28] In this and other Chinese Buddhist temples, Chinese and Euro-American believers interact on various levels. Although these temples regularly provide two services, one in English and one in Chinese, and the two services of-ten differ in format and content, I find that they cannot be described as "parallel congregations" that lack interaction with each other.[29] For exam-ple, in a Chinese Buddhist temple in Houston, most of the active lay be-lievers and leaders are middle-class professionals. The English-speaking immigrant lay leaders are heavily involved in the English ministry tar-geting Euro-Americans and American-born Chinese. Meanwhile, Euro-Americans are brought in to play active roles in combined services during important festivals.[30]

Several researchers have observed that the proselytizing efforts of the Chinese Buddhist temples are generally toward Euro-Americans be-sides Chinese immigrants. For example, Irene Lin finds that "Hsi Lai [Temple] strongly encourages and supports the joining of European American members," but pays little attention to attracting people of other Asian ethnic groups.[31] Having observed the same pattern at a Chi-nese Buddhist temple in Houston, Yang and Ebaugh suggest a theoreti-cal interpretation: When an immigrant religion (Chinese Buddhism, in this case) changes from a majority religion in the country of origin to a minority religion in the United States, the desire for establishing Ameri-can identity is a strong driving force for converting the perceived main-stream Americans—middle-class Caucasians.[32] Furthermore, in contrast to the great efforts of attracting Caucasians, the Houston temple has done little to integrate Chinese immigrants from different origins. More than 80 percent of temple members are from Taiwan and some are from Hong Kong and Southeast Asia. Very few mainland Chinese, the largest stream of Chinese immigration in the 1990s, have attended this temple regularly. The temple puts more resources on proselytizing among Caucasians than mainland Chinese or other Asians. In comparison, Chinese Christian churches in the United States have been very active in converting and in-tegrating Chinese from various origins, including mainland Chinese.[33]

The well-established Buddhist temples often have a Chinese school for teaching children the Chinese language, traditional values, and cultural customs. However, I have observed that the participation of the second generation in these temples is limited. Many Buddhist immigrant parents, who I interviewed in Houston, do not insist on their children becoming Buddhist practitioners. While the most active lay leaders strongly encour-age their children to go to the temple, many parents place moral and cul-tural education above religious education. They bring their children to the temple to learn Chinese language, moral values, and behavioral propri-eties. Regarding religious practice and belief, these parents frequently say that depends on each child's own karma. In the Houston temple, the Chi-nese school is large, with about three hundred students registered for weekend classes in Chinese language and culture. However, very few youths and young adults attend the religious services of the temple. Over-all, most of the regular participants in temple activities are middle-aged and older people, with a clear majority (60 to 70 percent) being women. At this time, with limited observation of the second generation in Chinese Buddhist temples, it is hard to predict whether the temples established by the immigrants will succeed in passing the religion onto their American-born and American-raised children.

Christianity

The history of Chinese Christianity in America is almost as long as that of Chinese immigration.[34] However, unlike European immigrants who transplanted their Protestantism and Catholicism to the New World, ear-lier Chinese Christian churches were missions started by American de-nominations.[35] Since the 1960s, however, new Chinese immigrants have established hundreds of churches by themselves.

Christianity is not a traditional Chinese religion. Its introduction to China has met many cultural, social, and political obstacles.[36] The first sig-nificant impact of Christianity on China was not felt until the sixteenth century when Jesuit missionaries found substantial success in the late Ming and early Qing dynasties. Later, Catholicism was banned by the em-peror, and Chinese Catholics were persecuted. Protestants began their missions in China in the early nineteenth century. However, their close re-lationships and simultaneous arrival with imperialists and opium traders caused great resentment by the Chinese people. Consequently, Christian-ity became stigmatized as the "alien" religion. "One more Christian, one less Chinese" was a common sarcasm visited on Chinese converts. For most Chinese, both elite and ordinary people, Christianity and Chinese-ness became incompatible, both culturally and politically. After the estab-lishment of the People's Republic of China in 1949, all foreign missionar-ies were expelled and the practice of Christianity was restricted. During the Cultural Revolution (1966–1976), all churches were closed and all reli-gions were completely banned for many years. After fleeing from the Communist mainland, some missionaries moved to Taiwan and Hong Kong to continue their missions, especially among people that fled from the mainland. Since the 1950s, there have been some Christian revivals in Taiwan and Hong Kong. Nevertheless, Christians have remained a small minority in both Taiwan and Hong Kong, composing around 5 percent of the population at the maximum.[37] The first Chinese Christian church in the United States was established in San Francisco in 1853 by a medical missionary, William Speer, who had been in China with the support of the Presbyterian Board of Foreign Missions. Four Chinese who had been converted in China became the charter members of this first Chinese church. Other denominations then started their own missions for Chinese laborers: Methodists in 1868, and Baptists, Congregationalists, and Episcopalians separately in 1870. By 1892, 11 denominations established 10 Chinese churches (including 3 in Canada), 10 Chinese Christian associations, and 271 Chinese Sunday schools and missions in 31 states.[38] Not surprisingly, the pastors of all the churches were Caucasian;[39] Chinese converts could serve only as assistants to white missionaries. During the decades of the Chinese exclusion acts (1882–1943), and in line with the exclusionist sentiments and policies toward the Chinese in the United States, these mission churches were treated mostly as extensions of China missions.[40] The goal was to Christianize the heathen Chinese and send them back to China to help American missionaries there. These early missions were not very successful in terms of converting the Chinese. It was clear that, as in the case of nineteenth-century China, the ratio of converts to the whole population was minuscule.[41] This was in part because of the anti-Chinese social environment and in part because of the missionaries' racist, nativist, and paternalist attitudes toward the Chinese.[42] Nonetheless, these churches provided a place for Chinese immigrants to learn English, to learn American values and lifestyles, to receive social services, and to meet non-Chinese Americans.[43]

In the first half of the twentieth century, most Chinese churches were still missions aided and supervised by American denominations. However, despite social, political, and economic hardships, some of these Chinese mission churches gained financial and leadership independence within the denominations, and some Chinese Christians formed a few nondenominational independent churches. By 1952, there were sixty-six Chinese Protestant churches in the United States: Forty-seven were denominational, five were interdenominational (sponsored by several denominations or a council of churches), and fourteen were independent of any denominational body.[44] During this period, a majority of Chinese church ministers were born in China. Most churches were small: The average membership size was 155. Some churches began to grow quickly after World War II.

Since the 1950s, the number of Chinese churches has rapidly increased, reaching seven hundred by 1994. Table 3.2 clearly shows this trend of fast growth in the number of Chinese churches in the United States.

In contrast to earlier Chinese churches, which were missions sponsored by Euro-Americans for the Chinese, most of the new Chinese churches were founded by Chinese immigrants themselves. Beginning in the late 1950s and early 1960s, Chinese students studying in American universities formed many campus Bible study groups (BSGs). As many

Table 3.2   The Growth of Chinese Protestant Churches in the United States, 1853–2000

Year	Number of Churches
1853	1
1890	7
1931	44
1952	66
1979	366
1984	523
1994	700
2000	819

Sources: Pang, Wing Ning, "Build Up His Church for My Kinsmen's Sake: A Study of the North American Chinese Churches" (paper presented to the North American Congress of the Chinese Evangelicals, June 23–28, 1980, Pasadena, California); Pang, Wing Ning, "The Chinese and the Chinese Church in America: A Preliminary Report for the Asian Ethnic Committee" (paper presented to the National Convocation on Evangelicizing Ethnic America, April 14–18, 1985, Houston, Texas); Lau, Yuet Shing, *Meizhou Huaquao Jiaohui* (Chinese Churches in America) (San Francisco: The Convention of Chinese Christian Churches, 1933); AFC (Ambassadors for Christ), *Directory of Chinese Churches, Bible Study Groups and Christian Organizations in North America* (Paradise, Pa.: Ambassadors for Christ, Inc., 1984, 1994, 2000).

students adjusted to permanent resident status under the new immigration act of 1965, many BSGs later evolved into churches. More churches then came to exist through efforts of church planting and schisms.

Besides the rapid growth, contemporary Chinese churches in America have two general characteristics: They are theologically conservative and organizationally independent. On the West Coast, where earlier mission churches for the Chinese are concentrated, many Chinese churches are affiliated with mainline American denominations. For example, in 1996 there were 158 Chinese churches in the San Francisco and Bay areas. Among them, 10 were Presbyterian churches (PCUSA), 7 were United Methodist churches, 6 were Episcopal churches, 5 were American Baptist churches, and 4 were Lutheran churches (Missouri Synod). However, a great number of new churches established by Chinese immigrants are independent, and those new churches that do affiliate with American denominations tend to favor those denominations that are theologically conservative and organizationally less centralized.[45] Nationally, about half of Chinese churches have no affiliation with American denominations; denominational churches tend to maintain a high degree of congregational independence. The largest group of Chinese churches belongs to the Southern Baptist Convention, which claimed about 150 Chinese churches in 1995. The second largest is the Christian and Missionary Alliance with about 60 Chinese churches in the United States.[46]

In traditional Chinatowns, Chinese Christian churches experienced tensions and conflicts with other Chinese immigrant organizations. For example, Melford S. Weiss notes that in "Valley City" in California, where the first Christian missions for the Chinese started in the 1850s, Chinese churches did not have representation in the Chinese Benevolent Association in the 1930s or in 1970.[47] In New York City, a Chinese Christian minister, Reverend Lee To, once served as the chairman of the Chinese Consolidated Benevolent Association in 1919 through 1921. Under his influence, the members of the Chinese Consolidated Benevolent Association decided to cast out the joss (their idol) from their council hall.[48] However, an anthropological study focusing on various voluntary associations in New York's Chinatown does not even mention Christian churches.[49] Among the studies of Chinatown communities, Betty Lee Sung unusually devotes a full chapter to positive influences of Christian missions in the Chinese community, which starts with the Chinese Community Church of Washington, D.C.[50] She has no discussion of how well the Chinese church was integrated in the power structure of other Chinatowns. Because of the short history of Chinatown in Washington, D.C., traditional Chinatown organizations had a limited influence. The Chinese Consolidated Benevolent Association, of which the Chinese Community Church was one of the founding organizations, was formed only in 1955. A Chinese Christian church so integral in the Chinatown community was not common in traditional Chinatowns. Although the number of Chinese Christian churches has increased rapidly in the last four decades, their influence in the ethnic community is still limited. One reason for this may be the extreme conservative theology in most Chinese churches, which calls for exclusive ministry of evangelization and refuses to cooperate with non-Christian organizations to work on social and political issues.

In many Chinese churches, a majority of immigrant members are adult converts from non-Christian family backgrounds. In contemporary pluralist American society, why have so many Chinese immigrants converted to conservative Protestantism? I find that at least four factors are important.[51] First, Third World experiences of the immigrants before coming to America and immigration experiences as racial minorities in the United States have intensified the desire for religious interpretations about the meaning of life and world events. Many Chinese were ruthlessly uprooted from China, then suffered difficulties as displaced persons and as immigrants in this strange land. Facing the rapidly changing and increasingly relativized society, many people longed for order, purpose, and rules. Second, these Chinese immigrants find conservative Protestantism attractive because it proclaims absoluteness, love, and certainty. The Chinese church serves as a haven for the homeless sojourners. Third, in the process of modernization, Chinese cultural traditions have been broken down. Meanwhile, these immigrants continue to cherish many traditional values, especially Confucian moral values. In conservative Christianity, these Chinese find a good match for their cherished social-ethical values. Fourth, the Christian identity also provides a universal and absolute ground on which these Chinese could selectively reject or accept certain cultural traditions, either Chinese or American. Overall, their construction and attainment of evangelical Protestant identity in the independent ethnic church have important contextual factors of modern China and America.

Becoming Christian and American does not mean that these Chinese immigrants are giving up their Chinese identity. While maintaining the universalism of the Christian faith or the inclusiveness of all peoples within the faith, these Chinese Christians also claim their Chinese cultural heritage.[52] They have made efforts to differentiate Chinese nonreligious traditions from religious ones and selectively preserve nonreligious traditional values, rituals, and symbols. For example, they celebrate the Chinese New Year, but without offering to the ancestors. Many accept and praise some Confucian values and philosophical Daoist notions, but reject religious Daoism and Buddhism. Meanwhile, the church helps American-born Chinese (ABCs) to maintain a Chinese cultural identity while facilitating their selective assimilation into American society.[53] The Chinese school is a common feature of contemporary Chinese Christian churches in the United States. In many metropolitan areas, it was often a Chinese Christian church that started the first Chinese school. The Chinese church also creates a generally favorable atmosphere for ABCs to learn the Chinese language and traditional values that are perceived as compatible with their evangelical Christian beliefs, including respecting parents, older people, and those in authority; preserving harmonious relationships; and being humble about oneself in talking with others. The church teaches thrift despite material prosperity; proclaims strict moral codes regarding smoking, drinking, and sexuality; and endorses stable marriages and intact nuclear families. The moral education of ABCs in the immigrant church is quite successful. Some common morally charged issues in American society, such as drugs, teenage pregnancy, and homosexuality, have rarely occurred among the young people in Chinese Christian churches. On the other hand, like the Korean churches described by Kelley Chong, the Chinese church also enforces gender- and age-based hierarchies.[54]

Generally speaking, Chinese immigrant churches have been successful in socializing the ABC children into Christianity. Through Sunday school classes and fellowship activities for children from kindergarten to college, Christianity often naturally becomes part of their lives. On entering college, away from immediate oversight by their parents, ABCs growing up in Chinese churches take divergent paths. Because of their religious indoctrination, few quit the faith or completely stop attending church.[55] Some remain committed to Chinese Christian groups. Indeed, Chinese Christian fellowships are noticeably active on many university campuses.[56] On the other hand, believing that the Christian faith transcends all worldly boundaries, many college ABCs take initiatives to explore and experiment with various nonethnic churches and groups. Many become active participants in the Campus Crusade for Christ, the Inter-Varsity Christian Fellowship, the Navigators, or independently organized Bible study groups and prayer meetings. However, the social reality of ethnic and racial classifications in pluralist American society bounce many ABC college graduates back to either the ethnic Chinese Christian community or to the pan-Asian American Christian church.[57]

In the last decade or so, some ABCs have joined other Asian American Christians to establish Asian American churches in metropolitan areas, especially on the West Coast but also in other metropolitan areas. Leaders of these churches claim that they are *truly* Asian American churches because the church membership is often a mixture of American-born Chinese, Koreans, Japanese, and Southeast Asians. These churches are monolingual in English and consciously target descendants of various Asian immigrants, especially East Asians. Reading their Internet Web pages and discussions on the listserv list of "Chinese American Christians," I find several common reasons given for establishing such churches. These include the facts that (1) these church members grew up in an ethnic (e.g., Chinese or Korean) church but want to speak only English in a less ethnically focused environment; (2) as Asians, they all look similar with yellow skin and black hair; (3) they share some residual Confucian or Asian values; (4) they have had similar experiences of being subtly or blatantly discriminated against by others in the larger society; and (5) some are children of inter-Asian marriages who find it difficult to remain in a church comprised of one particular ethnic group.[58] The number of such churches is still small, probably about two dozen at this time. How identities are formed and evolve in these churches remains to be observed.

Reflections on Assimilation, Ethnicity, and Transnationalism

Amid the cultural pluralism of the late twentieth-century American society, contemporary Chinese American religions have become increasingly diverse. Three traditions remain dominant: Chinese Buddhism has made significant advancements since the 1950s; some traditional folk religious practices have revived since the late 1970s; and Christianity has grown rapidly in the last four decades and has become the most practiced institutional religion among the Chinese in America. This religious diversity is associated with the heterogeneity of post-1965 Chinese immigrants who have come from various societies in several waves.

Overall, contemporary Chinese immigrants assimilate quickly into American society in cultural, socioeconomic, and structural aspects. Many Chinese have received American college and graduate education, work in companies of advanced technology and governmental agencies, and live in ethnically mixed suburbs. Actually, because of economic and cultural globalization, Americanization of cultural values and lifestyles often takes place before immigration and accelerates upon immigrants' arrival. Before coming to America, many Chinese had learned English in schools and had been exposed to some aspects of American culture through the mass media, Hollywood movies, and direct contacts with Americans visiting or working in Asia. Many people have adopted some American behaviors and lifestyles without immigrating to the United States. Upon arriving in the United States, universities and the media further facilitate their cultural assimilation and structural integration in American society.

However, in their religious practice, many Chinese immigrants stay in ethnic congregations. Actually, structural assimilation in their public lives—school, work, and politics—does not necessarily reduce their desire to congregate with fellow Chinese in their private, religious lives. It may, in fact, heighten such desire. As a home away from home, the ethnic religious congregation provides a familiar environment in which people can speak their native languages, eat ethnic foods, participate in shared rituals and cultural activities, and meet their nostalgia needs. As these needs are met and religious meaning is found, they can be better prepared or armed for interacting with others in public spheres of school, work, and politics. In other words, assimilation and ethnicity are not exclusive of each other. For Chinese immigrants in Chinese religious communities, many hold adhesive identities that add Chinese, American, and religious identities together.[59]

Transnational networks between the immigrants and the origin countries are another important factor in immigrants' identity construction. Because of the advancements in communication and transportation technologies, contemporary Chinese immigrants can, and often do, maintain close ties across the Pacific. Chinese Buddhist and folk religious temples import construction materials from China to build authentic Chinese temples in America. Chinese Christians and Buddhists frequently exchange visitors, preachers, ideas, materials, and resources between the United States and China. The religious changes in the Chinese American community have important impacts on the religious communities in Chinese societies, and religious changes in the Far East similarly influence the religious lives of Chinese Americans. Within this context of contemporary transnationalism, complete assimilation by giving up Chinese identity is neither possible nor necessary.

Notes

1. John Dart, "Poll Studies: Chinese Americans, Religion," *Los Angeles Times*, July 5, 1997, B5. The report is based on a survey of 773 ethnic Chinese in six counties in southern California, which was conducted in May 1997. Among the respondents, 19 percent said they were Protestant, 7 percent answered simply Christian, and 6 percent said they were Roman Catholic. At the same time, 20 percent identified themselves as Buddhists, and 44 percent claimed no religion. An unpublished survey of Chinese Americans in the Seattle area in the 1980s indicates similar patterns. The General Social Survey has too small a sample of ethnic Chinese (total $N = 78$ in the 1972–1994 cumulative data) for accurate estimates. Nonetheless, it is interesting to list its numbers here: 27 percent Chinese in the sample were Protestants, 22 percent Catholics, and only 14 percent other religions (including Buddhism). It is important to note that Chinese Protestant leaders tend to put much lower estimates of Christians among ethnic Chinese. Based on counting heads during typical Sunday services in Chinese Protestant churches in the San Francisco area, Rev. James Chuck concludes that Chinese youth and adult participation in Protestant churches is probably more near the 5 percent range (Chuck, *An Exploratory Study of the Growth of Chinese Protestant Congregations from 1950 to Mid-1996 in Five Bay Area Counties* [Berkeley, Calif.: American Baptist Seminary of the West, 1996], 15). Wing Ning Pang, an elder at a Chinese church in the Los Angeles area, gave a generous estimate of 10 percent of Protestants in the Chinese population in the United States (Wing Ning Pang, "Build Up His Church for My Kinsmen's Sake: A Study of the North American Chinese Churches" [paper presented to the North American Congress of the Chinese Evangelicals, June 23–28, 1980, Pasadena, California], 36.B). These low estimates include people who regularly attend Chinese churches every week. However, not every active church member is able to attend church every Sunday, and some Chinese Christians attend non-Chinese churches.

2. See Fenggang Yang, *Chinese Christians in America: Conversion, Assimilation, and Adhesive Identities* (University Park: Pennsylvania State University Press, 1999); Lingbo Yu, *Mei Jia Huaren Shehui Fojiao Fazhan Shi* (The Development of Buddhism among North American Chinese Communities) (Taipei: Xinwenfeng Press, 1996). In his "Chinese Buddhism in America: Identity and Practice" (in *The Faces of Buddhism in America*, ed. Charles S. Prebish and Kenneth K. Tanaka [Berkeley and Los Angeles: University of California Press, 1998], 17), Stuart Chandler also claims that "there are approximately 125 Chinese Buddhist organizations in the United States."

3. Statistics of Chinese Christians in China are hard to come by. In *Christianity in the People's Republic of China* (revised ed. [Atlanta: John Knox Press, 1986], 78), Thompson Brown comes up with numbers of 936,000 baptized Protestants,

3,274,740 baptized Catholics, 600,000 Protestant catechumens, and 194,712 Catholic catechumens, totaling 5,005,452 in 1949. This total would comprise about 1 percent of the total Chinese population of 450 million at that time. Overall, by 1949, when the Chinese Communist Party took power in mainland China, it had become evident that few of the Chinese people were likely to become Christians and that the missionaries' long-continued efforts, if measured in numbers of converts, had failed. See John King Fairbank, ed., *The Missionary Enterprises in China and America* (Cambridge, Mass.: Harvard University Press, 1974), 1. Since the late 1970s, Christianity has been the fastest growing religion in mainland China, but there is no informed and consistent estimate. The Chinese government-sanctioned statistics report about 4 million Catholics and 10 million Protestants, which would comprise about 1 percent of the total population of 1.3 billion. Some Christian organizations outside China claim that there are as many as 10 million Catholics and 60 million Protestants, which would be about 5 percent of the population. In Taiwan and Hong Kong, Christians account for about 5 percent of the population at the maximum. See Gail Law, ed., *Chinese Churches Handbook* (Hong Kong: Chinese Coordination Center of World Evangelism, 1981); Allen J. Swanson, *Taiwan Jiaohui Mianmian Guan* (Aspects of Churches in Taiwan: Retrospective and Prospective in 1980) (Taipei: Taiwan Jiaohui Zengzhang Cujin Hui, 1981).

    4. Some findings and analyses in this chapter have already been included in the following publications written by Fenggang Yang: "Chinese Conversion to Evangelical Christianity: The Importance of Social and Cultural Contexts," *Sociology of Religion: A Quarterly Review* 59 (1998): 237–57; "Tenacious Unity in a Contentious Community: Cultural and Religious Dynamics in a Chinese Christian Church," in *Gatherings in Diaspora: Religious Communities and the New Immigration*, ed. Stephen Warner and Judith G. Wittner (Philadelphia: Temple University Press, 1998), 333–61; "ABC and XYZ: Religious, Ethnic and Racial Identities of the New Second Generation Chinese in Christian Churches," *Amerasia Journal* 25 (1999): 89–114; *Chinese Christians in America: Conversion, Assimilation, and Adhesive Identities* (University Park: Pennsylvania State University Press, 1999); "Hsi Nan Buddhist Temple: Seeking to Americanize," in *Religion and the New Immigrants: Continuity and Adaptations in Immigrant Congregations*, ed. Helen Rose Ebaugh and Janet Chafetz (Walnut Creek, Calif.: AltaMira Press, 2000), 67–88; "The Chinese Gospel Church: The Sinicization of Christianity," in *Religion and the New Immigrants*, 89–108; "Chinese American Religions," in *Encyclopedia of Contemporary American Religion*, ed. Wade Clark Roof (New York: Macmillan Reference, 2000).

    5. Betty Lee Sung, *Mountain of Gold: The Story of the Chinese in America* (New York: Macmillan, 1967); Roger Daniels, *Asian America: Chinese and Japanese in the United States Since 1850* (Seattle: University of Washington Press, 1988); Sucheng Chan, ed., *Entry Denied: Exclusion and the Chinese in America, 1882–1943* (Philadelphia: Temple University Press, 1991); Kevin Scott Wong and Sucheng Chan, eds., *Claiming America: Constructing Chinese American Identities during the Exclusion Era* (Philadelphia: Temple University Press, 1998); Thomas W. Chinn, ed., *A History of the Chinese in California: A Syllabus* (San Francisco: Chinese Historical Society of America, 1969); Victor G. Nee and Brett de Bary Nee, *Longtime California: A Documentary Study of an American Chinatown* (Boston: Houghton Mifflin, 1973); Bernard P. Wong, *Chinatown: Economic Adaptation and Ethnic Identity of the Chinese* (New York: Holt, Rinehart and Winston, 1982).

6. Several special immigration laws have contributed to the accelerating increase of Chinese immigrants. They include the Indochina Migration and Refugee Assistance Act of 1975 (many Indo-Chinese refugees were ethnic Chinese), the Taiwan Relations Act of 1979 (which treats Taiwan as a chargeable country with an annual quota of 20,000), the Immigration Reform and Control Act of 1986 (13,752 Chinese in the United States were granted legalization), the Immigration Act of 1990 (which has raised the quota for Hong Kong from 5,000 to 10,000 per year), and the Chinese Students Protection Act of 1992 (52,425 mainland Chinese in the United States adjusted their status as immigrants).

7. See Wong, *Chinatown*; Pyong Gap Min, ed., *Asian Americans: Contemporary Trends and Issues* (Thousand Oaks, Calif.: Sage, 1995).

8. See Peter Kwong, *The New Chinatown* (New York: Hill and Wang, 1987); Jan Lin, *Reconstructing Chinatown: Ethnic Enclave, Global Change* (Minneapolis: University of Minnesota Press, 1998).

9. According to Chinn (*History of the Chinese in California*, 28–29), approximately 6,000 Chinese women came under the War Brides Act of 1945 and the G.I. Fiancées Act of 1946; 3,465 stranded Chinese students, visitors, and seamen adjusted status under the Displaced Persons Act of 1948; 2,777 Chinese adjusted status under the Refugee Relief Act of 1953; and the Refugee Escapee Act of 1957 and the Presidential Directive in 1962 permitted 15,111 Chinese refugees in Hong Kong to enter the United States. Also, the *1970 Annual Report* of the Immigration and Naturalization Service (table 6E) reports a total of 17,630 refugees from China between 1946 and 1966.

10. Wong, Bernard P., "Hong Kong Immigrants in San Francisco," in *Reluctant Exiles?: Migration from Hong Kong and the New Overseas Chinese*, ed. Ronald Skeldon (Armonk, N.Y.: M. E. Sharpe, 1994), 237.

11. While the written characters and basic grammars are the same across Chinese dialects, the numerous Chinese dialects are often mutually unintelligible.

12. Immigration and Naturalization Service, *Statistical Yearbook of the Immigration and Naturalization Service* (Washington, D.C.: U.S. Government Printing Office [GPO], 1996).

13. Stanford M. Lyman, *Chinese Americans* (New York: Random House, 1974); Lynn Pan, *Sons of the Yellow Emperor: A History of the Chinese Diaspora* (New York: Kodansha International, 1994); Edgar Wickberg, "An Overseas Chinese Adaptive Organization, Past and Present," in *Reluctant Exiles?*, ed. Skeldon, 68–84.

14. Actually, there were complicated reasons. Bernard P. Wong pointed out that identifying with Taiwan had many advantages. In so doing, one could avoid being labeled a Communist and gain much prestige. Leaders of the old overseas were invited to visit Taiwan and were decorated by high-ranking officials in Taiwan. In addition, pro-Taiwan Chinese community leaders often got better value on export/import merchandise and were able to obtain permits and visas for business activities more readily. But it is also important to note that some old overseas Chinese suffered from the revolutionary activities of the Chinese Communists. They and their relatives suffered from the various purges, land reform, and other movements in China. Some had been imprisoned and later had the opportunity to escape to America. These old immigrants, needless to say, are anti-Communist (*Chinatown*, 77).

15. See, for example, Wong, *Chinatown*, 17–21; Shih-Shan Henry Tsai, *The Chinese Experience in America* (Bloomington: Indiana University Press, 1986), 48–49.

16. M.S. Weiss, *Valley City: A Chinese Community in America* (Cambridge, Mass.: Schenkman, 1974); Wong, *Chinatown*.

17. For example, Chinese members are the majority at a Mormon Ward in the Washington, D.C., area. Mormon missionaries—often handsome young men speaking fluent Chinese—are very active in proselytizing among Chinese immigrants. Overall, however, very few Chinese have become Mormons, Jehovah's Witnesses, or Christian Scientists.

18. Charles Caldwell Dobie, *San Francisco Chinatown* (New York: D. Appleton-Century, 1936), 289–90.

19. Mariann Kaye Wells, *Chinese Temples in California* (master's thesis, University of California, 1962).

20. Dobie, *San Francisco Chinatown*, 287.

21. A Tian Hou Temple, devoted to the Heavenly Queen, closed down in the 1950s, but reopened in 1975. In the 1990s, it serves a small community of Cantonese-speaking Chinese. See S. Chandler, "Chinese Buddhism in America," 13–30.

22. Chandler, "Chinese Buddhism in America," 17.

23. Chinese Buddhism may also include Tibetan Buddhism. However, until very recently, there have been very few ethnic Tibetans in the United States. The lama Buddhist centers and temples in the United States are mostly patronized by Euro-Americans. See Amy Lavine, "Tibetan Buddhism in America: The Development of American Vajrayana," in *The Faces of Buddhism in America*, ed. Charles S. Prebish and Kenneth K. Tanaka (Berkeley: University of California Press, 1998), 129–46.

24. See Holmes Welch, *The Buddhist Revival in China* (Cambridge, Mass.: Harvard University Press, 1968).

25. See Irene Lin, "Journey to the Far West: Chinese Buddhism in America," *Amerasia Journal* 22 (1996): 107–37.

26. See Welch, *Buddhist Revival*.

27. Emma McCloy Layman, *Buddhism in America* (Chicago: Nelson-Hall, 1976), 155.

28. See S. Chandler, "Chinese Buddhism in America."

29. Paul Numrich, *Old Wisdom in the New World: Americanization in Two Immigrant Theravada Buddhist Temples* (Knoxville: University of Tennessee Press, 1996).

30. Yang, "Hsi Nan Chinese Buddhist Temple."

31. See Lin, "Journey to the Far West," 120; and S. Chandler, "Chinese Buddhism in America."

32. Fenggang Yang and Helen Rose Ebaugh, "Religion and Ethnicity among New Immigrants: The Impact of Majority/Minority Status in Home and Host Countries," *Journal for the Scientific Study of Religion* 41 (2001): 367–78.

33. See Yang, *Chinese Christians in America*.

34. The discussion here focuses on Protestantism. There are at least a dozen Chinese Catholic churches in the United States, and some can trace their history to the early twentieth century. However, little research has been done on Chinese American Catholicism. I mention Chinese Catholics several times in my book *Chinese Christians in America*.

35. Yuet Shing Lau, *Meizhou Huaqiao Jiaohui* (Chinese Churches in America) (San Francisco: The Convention of Chinese Christian Churches, 1933); Horace R. Cayton and Anne O. Lively, *The Chinese in the United States and the Chinese Christian Church* (New York: Bureau of Research and Survey, National Council of the

Churches of Christ in the United States, 1955); Wesley Woo, *Protestant Work among the Chinese in the San Francisco Area, 1850–1920* (Ph.D. diss., Graduate Theological Union, Berkeley, California, 1983); Timothy Tseng, *Ministry at Arms-Length: Asian Americans in the Racial Ideology of American Mainline Protestants, 1882–1952* (Ph.D. diss., Union Theological Seminary, New York, 1994).

36. See Julia Ching, *Chinese Religions* (Maryknoll, N.Y.: Orbis Books, 1993); Ralph R. Covell, *Confucius, the Buddha, and Christ: A History of the Gospel in Chinese* (Maryknoll, N.Y.: Orbis Books, 1986).

37. See Gail Law, *Chinese Churches Handbook*; Allen J. Swanson, *Taiwan Jiaohui Mianmian Guan* (Aspects of Churches in Taiwan).

38. Ira M. Condit, *The Chinaman as We See Him and Fifty Years of Work for Him* (Chicago: Missionary Campaign Library, 1900).

39. See Cayton and Lively, *Chinese in the United States*, 41; Woo, "Theological Themes."

40. Wesley Woo, "Chinese Protestants in the San Francisco Bay Area," in *Entry Denied: Exclusion and the Chinese in America, 1882–1943*, ed. Sucheng Chan (Philadelphia: Temple University Press, 1991), 213–45.

41. Woo, "Chinese Protestants," 217.

42. Woo, "Theological Themes"; Karl Fung, *The Dragon Pilgrims: A Historical Study of a Chinese-American Church* (San Diego, Calif.: Providence Price, 1989); Tseng, *Ministry at Arms-Length*.

43. James W. Loewen, *The Mississippi Chinese: Between Black and White* (Cambridge, Mass.: Harvard University Press, 1971); Weiss, *Valley City*; Pan, *Sons of the Yellow Emperor*; Wickberg, "Overseas Chinese Adaptive Organizations."

44. Lau, *Meizhou Huaqiao Jiaohui* (Chinese Churches in America); Cayton and Lively, *Chinese in the United States*.

45. See James Chuck, *An Exploratory Study of the Growth of Chinese Protestant Congregations from 1950 to Mid-1996 in Five Bay Area Counties: San Francisco, San Mateo, Contra Costa, Alameda, and Santa Clara* (Berkeley, Calif.: American Baptist Seminary of the West, 1996); Sharon Wai-Man Chan, *The Dynamics of Expansion of the Chinese Churches in the Los Angeles Basin* (Ph.D. diss., Fuller Theological Seminary, Pasadena, California, 1996); Wing Ning Pang, "The Chinese American Ministry," in *Yearbook of American and Canadian Churches, 1995*, ed. Kenneth B. Bedell (Nashville, Tenn.: Abingdon Press, 1995), 10–18.

46. See Yang, *Chinese Christians in America*; Yang, "Why Conservative Ethnic Churches Are Growing: The Case of Chinese Protestant Churches in the United States," Center for Immigration Research Working Paper Series, University of Houston, 1997.

47. Weiss, *Valley City*.

48. Julia I. Hsuan Chen, "The Chinese Community in New York: A Study in Their Cultural Adjustment 1920–1940,"(unpublished Ph.D. diss., American University, Washington, D.C. Reprinted in 1974 by R and E Research Associates, San Francisco, 1941), 43. Him Mark Lai, *Cong huaqiao dao huaren* (From Huaqiao to Huaren: Social History of the Chinese in the United States in the Twentieth Century) (Hong Kong: Joint Publishing Co., 1992), 143.

49. Chia-ling Kuo, *Social and Political Change in New York's Chinatown: The Role of Voluntary Associations* (New York: Praeger, 1977).

50. Sung, *Mountain of Gold*.

51. For a detailed analysis, see Yang, "Chinese Conversion to Evangelical Christianity."

52. For more detailed description, see Yang, *Chinese Christians in America*, ch. 5.

53. Those who immigrated to the United States as children with their parents are often referred to as American-raised Chinese (ARCs). Because of their similarities with ABCs in their identity construction, in this paper I use American-born Chinese, or ABCs, to mean the overall second generation of Chinese immigrants.

54. Kelly H. Chong, "What It Means to Be Christian: The Role of Religion in the Construction of Ethnic Identity and Boundary among Second-Generation Korean Americans," *Sociology of Religion* 59 (1998): 259–86.

55. This claim is based on my interviews conducted within midsized and large Chinese churches that have had good English ministries. Therefore, my findings may not apply to those ABCs who grew up in the churches established before World War II or small churches without effective youth ministries. Nonetheless, I think that Helen Lee's assertion of the "silent exodus" of second-generation young adults from Asian immigrant churches may be exaggerated. It may serve the purpose of alarming ministers who fear losing adherents. Moreover, Lee may overgeneralize second-generation Korean Christian experiences as East Asian Christian experiences. There are some estimates about the high dropout rates of Korean young people from immigrant churches (see Karen Chai, "Competing for the Second Generation: English-Language Ministry at a Korean Protestant Church," in *Gatherings in Diaspora*, ed. Warner and Wittner, 300), but, as far as I know, no informed estimates are available about the dropout rates of ABCs from Chinese churches. Some Korean American scholars, according to Karen Chai, observe that most grown-up second-generation Korean Americans do not attend their parents' churches. But this does not mean that they do not attend *any* church. Some well-assimilated second-generation Asian American Christians choose to attend nonethnic or multiethnic churches. In the 1990s, some pan-Asian American churches that specifically target English-speaking Asian Americans have emerged.

56. A quick Internet search of student organizations at various universities would find many active Chinese Christian groups. Cf. Rudy V. Busto, "The Gospel According to the Model Minority?: Hazarding an Interpretation of Asian American Evangelical College Students," *Amerasia Journal* 22 (1996): 133–47.

57. See Yang, "ABC and XYZ."

58. Russell Jeung has completed his dissertation in sociology, *A New People Coming Together: The Emergence of Asian American Pan-Ethnic Congregations*, at the University of California. His study is on churches in the San Francisco area, and Fong's reflection is based on his ministries in the Los Angeles area. For a reflection on pan-Asian American churches from a minister's perspective, see Ken Uyeda Fong, *Pursuing the Pearl: A Comprehensive Resource for Multi-Asian Ministry* (Valley Forge, Pa.: Judson Press, 1999).

59. See Yang, *Chinese Christians in America*, ch. 6. My interviews with Chinese American Buddhists find that they are also constructing adhesive identities—Chinese, American, and Buddhist—although the emphasis and strategies of identity construction differ from those of Chinese American Christians.

CHAPTER FOUR

"WE ARE BETTER HINDUS HERE": RELIGION AND ETHNICITY AMONG INDIAN AMERICANS

Prema Kurien

Introduction

Currently there are close to 2 million people of Indian ancestry in the United States,[1] making them the third largest Asian group in this country.[2] The 2000 census indicated that the Asian Indian population grew 105.87 percent between 1990 and 2000, and thus they are also one of the fastest growing groups in America. Despite this, current research on this section of the American population is woefully lacking. Indians are frequently overlooked in discussions regarding Asians in America and in Asian and Asian American programs around the country. Yet, as a group, Indians tend to differ from the majority of other Asian Americans in significant ways that have important consequences for community formation and ethnic mobilization in the United States.

This chapter examines these two issues in the context of studying the relationship between religion and ethnicity for Indian Americans. In the United States, religious organizations have provided the institutional framework to develop an Indian American community and identity. As the largest religious group among Indian Americans, the focus is particularly on Hindu Indians and the constructions of religious identity and of "Indianness" that they have developed. My primary research is based on a case study of three Hindu American religiocultural organizations representing the three different types of Hindu organizations that have proliferated among Indian immigrants in the United States—a *satsang* (religious congregation), a *bala vihar* (child development organization), and a Hindu umbrella organization. The first two types of organizations are noncommon in India and represent different strategies adopted by Indian immigrants to re-create a Hindu Indian environment and community in the United States. *Satsangs* largely target adults and celebrate and reenact religious practices. *Bala vihars* are directed at children and aim to teach them about the religion. Both these types of organizations are generally based on language and region of origin in India and thus may be considered "subethnic" organizations.[3] The goal of the umbrella Hindu organizations is to form a federation of the subethnic Hindu associations and to mobilize them for political activities in defense of Hindu interests.

After a brief overview of the two periods of Indian immigration to the United States and the characteristics of immigrants of each period, I turn to a discussion of religion and ethnicity among the early Indian immigrants in California and among the more recent immigrants in southern California. The case of the early Indians is particularly interesting because most of the predominantly Sikh immigrants intermarried with Hispanic women. Classified as "Hindu" by Americans, the Hindu identity of this group and their descendants was a constantly changing entity and "meant something totally different from [being] Hindu in . . . [the] homeland."[4] To a lesser extent, this is also the case among the more recent immigrants who have developed new types of organizations and definitions of identity as they have adapted to the American environment. In the third section, I focus on the three organizations that were the subject of my research and look at why these new forms emerged, the constructions of "Hinduness" and "Indianness" of these groups, and their implications for the Indian American community and for the wider American society.

Indian Immigration to America

Immigration is a selective process and therefore immigrant populations are rarely representative of the population of the home country. This is important to keep in mind as we discuss constructions of Indianness by Indian Americans. Immigration from India to the United States occurred during two different historical periods. The first phase was between 1899 and 1914 when around sixty-eight hundred Indians arrived in California. Most of the Indians were peasants from Punjab province and they took up farming in rural California. Around 85 percent of these immigrants were Sikhs, and another 10 to 12 percent were Muslim. Despite the fact that people from a Hindu background constituted less than 5 percent of this group, all of them were classified as "Hindu" in the United States.[5] These immigrants were largely male[6] and, due to the laws restricting Asian immigration and marriage across "racial" lines, most of them married Hispanic women.[7]

The second phase of immigration began after the passage of the 1965 Immigration and Naturalization Act. This immigration was largely family based and brought Indians from all over India and from a variety of religious backgrounds. It is now common to talk about two waves of post-1965 Indian immigration to the United States. The first wave of Indians came under the "special skills" provision of the act and were thus mostly highly educated, fluent English speakers from urban backgrounds, who entered into professional and managerial careers. This explains why Indians are among the wealthiest and most educated foreign-born groups in this country. According to the 1990 census, the median family income of Indians in the United States was $49,309, well above that for non-Hispanic whites, which was $37,630.[8] Also, 43.6 percent were employed either as professionals (mostly doctors and engineers) or managers, and 58.4 percent had at least a bachelor's degree.[9] The highly selective nature of the immigration can be seen by the fact that in the same year, the per capita income in India was $350, and only 48 percent of Indians were even literate (i.e., could read and write their own names).[10]

There are indications that the second wave of immigrants might bring down some of the high socioeconomic measures reported previously. Many of this group are relatives of the first-wave immigrants, sponsored under the "family reunification" provision of the 1965 act and do not have the same educational or professional status as the first wave. In 1996, for instance, of the total 44,859 Indian immigrants admitted, 34,291 were admitted under family sponsorship and only 9,919 in employment-based preferences.[11] Thus, such states as California, which have been the top destinations for this wave of immigrants, report that 10.2 percent of the Indian American population and 14 percent of Indian American children (compared to the national average of 9 percent) were living below the poverty line in 1995.[12]

Supporters of the Hindu nationalist *Hindutva* (Hinduness) movement (among whom number many Hindu American organizations and individuals) characterize India as a Hindu country. Although Hindus constitute the overwhelming majority, over 80 percent of the population, religious minorities are a significant presence in India, particularly given their location (most religious minorities are concentrated in urban areas and in a few regions of the country) and absolute numbers. Muslims comprise over 12 percent of the population, and there are more Muslims in India than in neighboring Pakistan, an Islamic state. Christians (both Protestants and Catholics) and Sikhs each constitute around 2 percent of the population.[13] Indian religious minorities also have a very long history in India, going back over sixteen centuries, in the case of Christians, and eleven centuries, in the case of Muslims.

There are no national or regional figures on the proportions of Indians in the United States belonging to various religions. However, indirect evidence indicates that Hindus are underrepresented in the United States in relation to their proportion in India, indicating the presence of significant numbers of Indian religious minorities in this country.[14] Among religious minorities, Sikhs and Christians seem to be particularly overrepresented. While upper castes form around only 25 percent of the Indian population, given the elite nature of the immigration to the United States, most Indian Americans are from this section of the population.

Over fifteen languages are officially recognized in India. Except for the north central area of India comprised of four states known as the Hindi-Hindu heartland (since it is dominated by Hindi-speaking Hindus), most other states in India were generally formed on the basis of language. Generally, states also have a distinctive culture and cuisine. In addition, states may have unique religious practices and deities as well as caste groups. According to the 1980 census, speakers of Hindi were the largest linguistic group among Indian Americans (as in India). Indians speaking Gujarati from the western Indian state of Gujarat were highly overrepresented in the United States and formed almost 20 percent of the population. Punjabi speakers (most of whom were probably Sikhs) were also overrepresented and formed around 8 percent of the Indian population in the United States.[15]

Immigration, Religion, and Ethnicity

Migration and relocation challenge many of the givens of life, such as culture and identity. Scholars have argued that religion often becomes more important for immigrants for a variety of reasons. First, Stephen Warner and other commentators indicate that the disruptions and questions raised by migration and resettlement in a new environment have a "theologizing" effect.[16] Many of the Indians I have spoken to mentioned that they had become more religious after coming to this country, where for the first time they had to think about the meaning of their religion and religious identity, which was something they could take for granted in India. In the immigrant context, religion also generally serves as a vehicle for the transmission of culture and provides the institutional framework for community formation.[17] According to Warner, this is particularly the case in the United States because Americans view religion as the most acceptable and nonthreatening basis for ethnic formation and expression.[18]

The literature on long-established overseas Indian settlements in various parts of the world shows that in each case, Indian traditions, cultures, and religions have been considerably reformulated and modified in the attempt to build an ethnic identity that is appropriate to the local context.[19] Raymond Williams puts this very well when he says that Indian American traditions and practices are "made in the U.S.A. . . . assembled . . . by relatively unskilled labor (at least unskilled by traditional standards) and adapted to fit new designs to reach a new and growing market."[20] The constructions of religion and identity discussed in the following sections should be seen in this light.

Religion and Ethnicity among the Early Immigrants

There are only a few accounts of the early Indian immigrants.[21] Karen Leonard's is the only one that focuses on constructions of ethnic identity among this group.[22] Thus, the following section draws heavily upon her work. Leonard, citing Oberoi, points out that boundaries between religious groups in Punjab were fluid at the turn of the century and that religion was not an important marker of difference.[23] The same was true in the California setting and there were good relationships among the Sikh immigrants (who, as mentioned, constituted the majority) and the Hindu and Muslim immigrants from Punjab. The Sikh temple at Stockton built in 1915 served as a cultural and social center for the whole Punjabi community.[24] The Sikh temple also played an important political function and was closely associated with the *Ghadar*, a radical movement originating in northern California whose mission was the violent overthrow of British rule in India.

Despite their intermarriage with Mexican women, the Punjabi men had little interaction with their wives' relatives and the wider Mexican American society due to prejudice on both sides. Thus, according to Leonard, "for better or for worse, the Hispanic women who married Punjabis became part of the men's social world."[25] However, since the mothers controlled domestic life, the culture and practices of the mothers predominated in the home. The children were given Spanish names, spoke Spanish, and adopted Catholicism. Most of the men "deliberately de-emphasized" their language, culture, and religion because they did not have the time or the ability to teach the language or explain the religion and culture.[26] In fact, the only time when Indian customs were followed was when the men died. Sikhs and Hindus were cremated and the appropriate death rituals were performed.[27] Leonard talks about the deep anxieties of some of the first-generation Punjabi men that proper death observances would not be carried out by their Punjabi-Mexican sons.[28]

However, when it came to the marriage of their children, distinctions of religion, caste, and race were emphasized by fathers, many of whom wanted to arrange the marriages of their children to suitable Indian or Indian American partners. Leonard states, however, that among the children themselves, marriages to other Punjabi–Mexican children were the least preferred option and most married Hispanics in Catholic ceremonies.[29]

Despite the fact that the Punjabi-Mexican children were brought up in the Mexican American culture, most of them identified themselves as "Hindu" or "East Indian." Initially, this was because of the prejudice they faced from the Mexican American society, but later, as their fathers' farms flourished, being "Hindu" was a means to distinguish themselves and their families from the largely working-class Mexican American population.[30] At the time, "Hindu" was the term applied to anyone from the Indian subcontinent (including present-day Pakistan). Thus, for the Punjabi–Mexicans, "being Hindu" meant identifying with certain values associated with the Punjabi Indian peasant immigrants (who were largely Sikh or Muslim) and had nothing to do with the Hindu religion. According to Leonard, it meant being a successful farmer; valuing the ethics of hard work, honesty, and hospitality; taking pride in one's Punjabi heritage; enjoying Punjabi American food, society, and politics; and having "a reverence for the 'holy book' from India, whether that was the Granth Sahib [the Sikh text] or the Quran."[31]

The religious cleavages that developed in the subcontinent, giving rise to the partition of India and Pakistan and the independence of the two countries in 1947, brought about changes in the relationships between religious groups among the Punjabi immigrants. Muslim immigrants began to develop separate religious associations and institutions and also to form Pakistani associations.[32] The second generation tried to counter these schisms by forming a "Hindustani" club in 1946 for children of all Punjabis. But Leonard also mentions that the children took pride in the newly independent nations of their fathers, and she refers to the selection of "Hindu" (Indian) and "Pakistani" queens in annual contests in the Punjabi-Mexican areas of California from the late 1940s.[33]

According to Leonard, the Punjabi-Mexican second generation was initially enthusiastic about the arrival of new immigrants from South Asia in the 1960s and participated in the religious institutions created or revitalized by the latter.[34] However, particularly in northern California where there was a large influx of immigrants, tensions developed between the two groups. The newcomers mocked and challenged the claims of the Punjabi–Mexicans to be Hindu (or Indian). The Punjabi–Mexicans reacted by distancing themselves from the new immigrants and stressing that they were American as well as Hindu.

Religion and Ethnicity among the Post-1965 Immigrants

In the United States as a whole, Indians are currently the most spatially dispersed immigrant group.[35] This spatial distribution creates obvious problems for ethnic formation. I will focus on the case of southern California since that is where I conducted my research. Compared to the East Coast and even the Midwest, California is a recent destination of the new Indian immigrants. Indian immigrants started arriving there in large numbers particularly after 1980. Thus, in 1990, 97.8 percent of Indians in southern California over twenty-five years of age were foreign born and 54.1 percent had immigrated between 1980 and 1990.[36] The corresponding national figures are 75.4 percent and 43.9 percent, respectively.[37] California was the top-ranked state of intended residence for Asian Indian immigrants between 1990 and 1993 with 19.3 percent of incoming immigrants stating that they intended to live there.[38] In 1996, again, California was the top choice among Asian Indian immigrants, showing that the movement of recent immigrants to California continued into the mid-1990s.[39]

Given the geography of southern California, Indians in this region are even more dispersed than in other major metropolitan areas. I see the process of ethnic formation as having occurred in three stages among Indian Americans in southern California.[40] Early Indian immigrants made some attempts to seek out and associate with fellow immigrants from India, but scattered settlement and small numbers made such occasions relatively infrequent. At this stage (early to mid-1970s), social groupings tended to be pan-Indian and organized events were largely sociocultural in nature.

The second stage started in the early 1980s. By this time, the first-wave immigrants were well settled and the group had a significant number of school-going children. The number of Indian immigrants had also risen substantially. At this stage, individuals felt the need to have a more structured basis for interacting with fellow Indians, and Indian American associations based on religion and regional/linguistic background in India mushroomed.[41] Such associations also tended to be fairly homogeneous in terms of caste and class background.

In the third stage (since the late 1980s), a reformulated pan-Indian Americanism has developed with the formation or revitalization of umbrella organizations, which provide a platform for Indian American concerns irrespective of region of origin. However, as religion had provided the basis for community and action at the earlier stages, pan-Indian organizations based on a religious platform have been more effective in developing a wider encompassing Indian American community and identity than secular organizations. It is at this third stage that organized versions of religious and ethnic identity were constructed.

Background of the Research

Description of the Three Organizations

The Kerala Hindu Organization (KHO) is a religiocultural organization of about fifty to seventy-five Malayalee Hindu families (Hindus speaking Malayalam, the language of Kerala in south India) that was established in 1991. Most members, both male and female, were professionals—mainly doctors, engineers, scientists, and accountants who had been in the United States for between twenty and thirty years. I was particularly struck by the fact that the women were as well educated and well placed as their husbands. In fact, there seemed to be only one case in which the woman was not currently working or studying. But even in this case, the woman had given up her career to raise her two small children. The KHO meeting took place on the second Saturday of the month in different locations (mostly member homes). There was a 2½-hour *pooja* (worship) consisting of prayers and the singing of *bhajans* (devotional hymns), followed by a potluck dinner. In addition to the monthly meetings, the KHO also celebrated the major Kerala Hindu festivals with religious and cultural programs.

The second group that I studied consisted of twelve Tamil Hindu families (Hindus speaking Tamil from the state of Tamil Nadu in south India) who met on the third Sunday of the month for a *bala vihar* meeting. The Tamil *bala vihar* (with a changing group of families) had been in existence since 1980. The *bala vihar* consisted of a 3½-hour session (again followed by a potluck dinner) divided into several short class periods, each dealing with a specific topic. Children learned about Hindu teachings, discussed Hindu philosophy, and were taught *bhajans* and *slokams* (chants). There was also a Tamil language class. The parents (mostly the mothers) were the teachers of the *bala vihar*. This group was also comprised mainly of professionals.

The Federation of Hindu Associations (FHA) was formed in 1993 and launched its major activities in 1995. The FHA was based in southern California but its leadership had close ties with like-minded individuals and organizations around the country. Most of its activists and leaders were wealthy, middle-aged, upper caste, north Indian businessmen. The goal of the organization was to unify Hindu Americans to "specifically pursue Hindu political interests."[42] Despite their professed goal, the FHA could not maintain internal unity, and in late 1998, a section of the organization broke away to form a parallel organization—the American Hindu Federation (AHF). The FHA, like other pan-Hindu American organizations, is a strong supporter of the *Hindutva* (Hinduness) movement calling for the establishment of a Hindu state in India. This movement has become the dominant force in Indian politics, and, at the time of this writing, the Indian party supporting the platform (the BJP) was in a coalition government with its allies.

Description of Research

I conducted an ethnographic study of the KHO between 1994 and 1996. In addition to attending monthly meetings and other functions, I visited the homes of many of the members and conducted semistructured interviews with them. In all, I interviewed one or both partners of eighteen married couples. I also conducted interviews with six of the teenagers. I talked more informally with many more women, men, and children as I participated in several activities with members of the group. My own position as a Malayalee immigrant and a professional helped me considerably. However, my Christian background did sporadically result in some discomfort on both sides.

I studied the Tamil *bala vihar* for a year (between 1995 and 1996). My fieldwork in this group consisted primarily of attending the monthly meetings and some other public events in which group members participated. I talked to members at the meetings but did not conduct detailed interviews with them. I chose to study these two groups because of my own linguistic and regional background (I am a Malayalee by ancestry, but grew up in Tamil Nadu and studied Tamil in school). However, Indians from Tamil and Malayalee backgrounds represent only a minority of Indians in the United States (around 11 percent).[43]

There are also distinct social, cultural, and historical differences between south India and the north. A key variation is in the degree of education, particularly of women. In general, women in south India are better educated than their counterparts in most other parts of the country. There is also a divergence between Kerala and Tamil Nadu in this respect, with Kerala having higher rates of education, in general, and female education, in particular, than Tamil Nadu. For all these reasons, members of these two groups should not be taken as representative of the average Indian immigrant (if indeed there is such a person, given the diversity of backgrounds of Indian Americans). However, most of the following discussion regarding the formation, function, and consequences of subethnic organizations is broadly applicable to Hindu Indian Americans.

Between 1996 and 1997, I attended some of the meetings and functions of the FHA. I also conducted in-depth interviews with the leaders.[44] Before this period and since then, I have been following their writings and the accounts of their activities published in Indian American newspapers.

Subethnic Hindu American Organizations

Formation and Function

Group religious activity is not typical in traditional Hinduism except during temple and village festivals. In India, Hindus worship largely as families or as individuals in their homes or in the temple. One of the primary reasons for the development of group forms of worship and learning among immigrants who have never been involved in such practices in the home country is the need for community. Immigration generally results in the isolation of the family from relatives and friends. For Indians who are generally dispersed in the suburbs, the monthly meetings are important since they are often the only time they meet other Indians.

Mr. Nair, the founding president of the KHO, told me that his motivation in founding the organization "was to develop a support group for Hindu Malayalees. Christians have the church as a support group, Hindus don't have anything." Other KHO members such as Mrs. Meena Shankar, while talking about the close friendships she had formed through the KHO, referred to the intense loneliness she had experienced in her early years in this country: "Arvind [her husband] would go off to work and the children to school and then I would be all by myself in the apartment. I have never been so alone. I did not know anyone around—I had no relatives and friends nearby. I cried a lot during this period." Many of the KHO members described the organization as "an extended family" and told me about the help members had provided them as they had to deal with such problems as death, divorce, and the loss of jobs.

As Mr. Ravi Panickar, the then secretary of KHO, indicated, the organization also helped members when it came to "practical matters." He explained: "We have doctors with different specializations from psychiatrists to cardiologists, engineers, accountants, businesspeople, scientists, and attorneys. So, whatever problem comes up, we have an expert who can help us." Earlier he had told me the story of how he had been harassed and exploited by attorneys as he tried to process his immigration papers, repeating several times during this narration, "If there had been an organization like the [KHO], nothing like this would have happened." He went on, "[At the time,] I did not know the American system . . . and we had no one to turn to for advice or help."

I have mentioned that in India, there are regional variations in Hinduism, culture, cuisine, and language. The main reason that organizations like the KHO form on the basis of subethnicity is because of these differences. For those of the immigrant generation in particular, there is a greater comfort level associated with interacting with people from the same subcultural background. They also enjoy the opportunity to speak and hear their native language, eat the different varieties of regional cuisine cooked by other members, and to reenact and celebrate rituals and festivals that they grew up with.

Some of the members indicated frankly to me that they attended the KHO meetings for "social reasons." However, for others, the religious aspect was important. Mr. Sharma, an executive member of the group, mentioned, "Growing up as Hindus in a Judeo–Christian environment can be difficult. There are so many misconceptions here about Indians and Hindus." He went on to say that one of the reasons that the KHO was formed was to correct these misconceptions. Mrs. Kala Ramachandran, another member, told me, "We are not fanatics, but being a Hindu organization, we believe very strongly that the Hindu religion and faith should be preserved forever. We believe that Hindu values have a big role to play in the future world and we are all proud of being Hindus."

For the more religiously oriented members, the KHO was a forum in which they could discuss the meaning and relevance of the Hindu scriptures and doctrines to their lives in the United States. Under the initiative of a few such members, a "Gita discussion" period was introduced toward the end of the *pooja* in which two verses of the *Bhagavat Gita* were translated and explained by Mrs. Kala Menon, followed by a group discussion. Several people also mentioned that they found the *bhajan* singing to be cleansing and uplifting. Mrs. Gowri Nathan, whose husband was unemployed and suffering from depression (he had sued his company for racial discrimination and won but refused to go back and work for the company after the nastiness of the trial), said she found the KHO meetings therapeutic since for those few hours, she could forget all her worries and find some peace of mind.

The teaching of Indian culture and values to their children was another reason cited by members for the formation of the KHO and their participation in it. As Mr. Sharma, a member of KHO, put it: "You know that children here go in search of their roots. We did not want our children to lose their heritage in a foreign environment and then have to recreate Alex Haley's journey!" Besides the needs of children, there are also increasing numbers of retirees and parents of immigrants who enjoy participating in such congregational activities. In addition are the large numbers of second-wave immigrants who have been continuously arriving in the country, for whom such organizations are important since "[t]hey provide a renewable continuity with religious organizations and traditions in India."[45]

Most of the reasons given for the formation and success of the KHO also hold true for the *bala vihars*. As a much smaller group, the *bala vihars* have an even stronger sense of community. Since most of the *bala vihar* session is spent expounding on and discussing Hinduism, the religious aspect is even more pronounced. The major difference between the KHO and the *bala vihar* as mentioned is that *bala vihars* are primarily oriented toward the children. Indian immigrants in the United States are often concerned that their children will pick up the negative aspects of teenage American culture, which they perceive to include sexual promiscuity, lack of respect for elders, violence, as well as drug and alcohol abuse. Their children, in turn, have to deal with the problems involved in negotiating their way between the values and practices learned at home and those they confront outside. Many parents realize that as individuals, they are not equipped to provide the answers and guidance required by the children. The *bala vihar* is an institution developed to bring both children and their parents together as "an extended family" to work through these issues. Unlike the KHO meetings, the Tamil *bala vihar* provided children with a lot of structured interaction time during which they could voice many of their concerns, particularly their struggles to try to balance their

Indian and American identities. Parents had the help and support of other adults to teach their children about Hinduism, Indian history and culture, and the Tamil language.

The effect the *bala vihars* can have on the youngsters is eloquently described by Hema Narayan, one of the students in the group, in her school essay on diversity (which won a national prize). Initially, she writes, she struggled to "fit in" by trying to be just like her classmates and rejecting her Indian identity. But, over time, as she began to learn more about her heritage and religion from her parents and the *bala vihar*: "I became more confident and sure of myself. With a wealth of knowledge by my side, I felt strong. I stood up to my classmates and introduced them to my beliefs. To my surprise, they stopped mocking me, and instead, wanted to know more. . . . I felt a sense of belonging, but not sameness, as though I were an individual piece adding color to the complete picture. I could fit in and still be different."

Other Consequences

I have mentioned that both the KHO and the Tamil *bala vihar* consisted of professionals. This is not accidental since there are both direct and indirect mechanisms to restrict membership to those with similar backgrounds and interests. New members are carefully selected so that they would "mix well with us" (in the words of Mr. Rajagopalan, director of the *bala vihar*) and would "fit in with the ethos of the group" (as Mrs. Kala Ramachandran, a committee member of KHO, put it). Indirect mechanisms such as the professional, upper-class atmosphere, the religious and cultural orientation of the activities, as well as the high achievements of the children of the group also seem to work to push out those who do not "fit in."

In fact, as I have argued in an earlier publication, the subethnic organizations are an important mechanism for maintaining and reproducing the socioeconomic status of the group.[46] Through their contacts, members help each other professionally and provide assistance in placing newcomers to the area and group members who have been laid off. However, even more crucial, is the indirect effect such organizations have on the second generation. Most of the college-going youngsters in both groups that I studied were enrolled in top universities. Not only was education strongly emphasized by the professional parents and their friends, but such groups also acted as informal information banks about success strategies that members could access and benefit from. Participating in the activities of subethnic organizations also facilitated educational success indirectly. The children who attended the KHO and the *bala vihar* manifested a strong sense of ethnic identity and pride, which, in turn, influenced their choice of peers (who tended to be largely Indian Americans or other high-achieving Americans who were respectful and supportive of Indian culture). As research has shown, the peer group is one of the most important determinants of how well teenagers do in school and college, and strong ethnic identity is positively correlated with academic achievement.[47]

Women play important roles in subethnic religiocultural associations. As a consequence of immigration, women's duties as teachers and transmitters of culture and tradition greatly increase.[48] Although both the KHO and Tamil *bala vihar* were headed by men, most of the activities that took up the bulk of time in the monthly meetings (such as the *bhajan* singing, the Gita discussion, and almost all of the class sessions of the *bala vihar*) were organized and led by women. In their pedagogical capacities, these women were able to provide a more egalitarian interpretation of the traditional gender constructs focusing on women's responsibilities by counterbalancing those accounts with others that emphasized the importance of male obligations and duties. However, since they were operating within an overarching patriarchal framework, women's agency in these associations tended to be largely confined to trying to obtain such "patriarchal bargains."[49] Teenage girls in such groups were encouraged to be high academic and professional achievers but were also expected to conform to the subtle but definite double standards imposed on them by the community.[50]

One of the indirect effects of organizations such as the KHO and Tamil *bala vihar* is that, as Hinduism becomes the nucleus around which to form community and develop ethnic pride and individual identity, members become more susceptible to the appeal of Hindu extremists who use the message of Hindu pride and unity to recruit supporters. The case of the KHO is a good example. While the leadership and most of its members went out of their way to emphasize that they were against Hindu "fundamentalism" and for pluralism (this was probably at least partly for my benefit as a person from a Christian background), the KHO was a registered member of the FHA, and FHA office bearers gave speeches promoting *Hindutva* at two of the functions organized by the KHO that I attended. The articles of FHA leaders were also printed by the KHO's annual *Souvenir* for the two years that I received them.

The second generation is particularly vulnerable to the appeal of Hindu nationalist organizations. The VHP, which has been at the forefront of the *Hindutva* movement in India, is particularly well established in American universities (often through its affiliate, the Hindu Students Council) and organizes cultural and religious programs and talks. As Indian American youth struggle to define their identity, organizations like the VHP that teach students about their "Hindu roots" are particularly attractive. Most of the time, the students are unaware of the political agenda of the organization and the way in which the money raised for it is used.[51]

Constructions of Ethnicity

From the comments and discussions at both the KHO and the Tamil *bala vihar*, it was clear that the members embraced and wanted to uphold the "model minority" image of Indian Americans. Thus, being Indian in the United States meant being affluent, highly educated, intelligent professionals, having "family values" and high-achieving sons and daughters. Those Indians who came to their attention (through the ethnic grapevine or the media) who lacked any of these characteristics were deemed to be exceptions, bringing disgrace to the good name of the community as a whole. The two groups also took special pride in their subethnic identities as Malayalee Americans and Tamilian Americans, which, to them, denoted Indians who were more educated and "cultured" and who accorded a higher status to women than their northern counterparts.

On several occasions I have heard members of the two groups (and many other Indian Americans that I have encountered) claim that they were "better Hindus here" and "more Indian" than many Indians in India. Both adults and children have told me that on their visits back to India, they realized that Indians were abandoning their cultural traditions and becoming more Westernized. Adults talked about Indian visitors to the United States who had praised them for the *satsangs* and *bala vihars* they had developed and who had told them that the expertise many of the Indian American children manifested in Indian music and dance was something they rarely saw anymore among the younger generation in India. Others mentioned that their relatives in India had remarked that their American-raised children behaved more respectfully and wore more modest clothing than Indian children of the same age. Several of the Indian American teenagers said that they knew more about Hinduism and Indian culture than their relatives in India and that they were surprised and shocked at how ignorant Indian youngsters were about their own culture.

Members of the KHO and Tamil *bala vihar* felt that, unlike many of their Indian counterparts, they have been able to maintain a balance between Westernization and Indianness by adapting to American life and drawing the best from it without losing their inner values and cultural integrity. As some members of the KHO pointed out, it is precisely the successful adaptation of Indians to American society and their ensuing prosperity that made them better supporters of Indian tradition, allowing them to sponsor prayer meetings, *poojas* and festival celebrations, the building of temples, and the visits of several cultural artistes from India.

Pan-Hindu American Organization

Formation and Function

The FHA is one of the many pan-Hindu organizations that mushroomed around the country in the 1990s, the same period that witnessed a resurgence of Hindu nationalism in India. According to the FHA leaders, it was the destruction of a sixteenth-century mosque in north India (which, according to *Hindutva* accounts, was built over an ancient temple) in December 1992 by *Hindutva* supporters that energized and inspired them to form their organization. FHA leaders promote a particularly aggressive brand of Hindu nationalism with vituperative diatribes against Indian Muslims and those Hindus who support secularism.

The FHA and other *Hindutva* organizations view India as a Hindu society whose glorious and ancient heritage and culture has been sullied by the invasions of the Muslims and the British as well as the postcolonial domination of "pseudo-secular" Indians.[52] A big grievance is that while India was partitioned on the basis of religion to create Pakistan, an Islamic state, Hindus were not allowed to have a Hindu state.[53] They also feel that minorities in India have been pampered with special government concessions (affirmative action) and that such programs discriminate against Hindus. All of this, according to the FHA, goes to show that the "secularism" of the Indian state is really an excuse for anti-Hinduism. They feel that only a Hindu state will be genuinely secular (here *secularism* means that the state will treat all religions equally) since only Hinduism is truly pluralistic.[54] According to the FHA, the modern pluralistic world "requires all religions to affirm [the] truth of other traditions to ensure tranquility."[55] Since only Hinduism fits this bill, it is the most suitable religion for the twenty-first-century world. Therefore, FHA sees as its mission the safeguarding of Hinduism "for our children, for the world."[56]

The FHA has organized and been involved in a variety of activities from its inception. It (along with other Hindu organizations around the country) sponsors the visits of *Hindutva* leaders from India to southern California. In the first few years of its existence, one or two of the most extremist of such individuals were given the "Hindu of the Year" award by the organization. FHA activists meet with other visiting Indian politicians and periodically send delegations to discuss issues with the Indian ambassador to the United States. The FHA also mobilizes donations for American politicians from southern California and meets with them to discuss the concerns of Indian Americans in an attempt to shape American foreign policy toward India.

The FHA leaders propagate their ideas by organizing and speaking at religious celebrations and through their copious writings, press releases, and frequent full-page advertisements in right-leaning Indian American newspapers such as the *India Post*. In 1996, they organized a seminar to discuss the protection and propagation of Hinduism that included many major figures in the Indian American *Hindutva* movement. Since 1996, they have been organizing a huge public open-air celebration in southern California for a major Hindu festival, which reportedly draws several thousand attendees every year. Over the past few years, they have been collecting funds to build what they term an "Ideal Hindu temple," which would be nonsectarian and where all the major Hindu deities would be given equal status.[57]

Claiming to represent Indian American Hindus, FHA leaders act as the watchdogs and defenders of Hinduism in America. Along with other American Hindu groups, the FHA has been involved in the campaigns against the "Om" perfume made by the Gap, a CD cover by a Sony artist that featured a distorted image of a Hindu deity, a *Simpsons* episode on Fox TV that caricatured the Hindu god Ganesh, and a *Xena* episode in which Hindu gods were characters.[58] In all of these cases, the Hindu groups have been successful in getting the concerned company to issue an apology and in most cases to withdraw the offending product or show.

Constructions of Ethnicity

As a publicity-seeking organization that projects itself as the voice of Indian American Hindus, the ethnic constructions of the FHA are much more clearly formulated and articulated than those of the subethnic organizations. Through its voluminous writings and the coverage it obtains in some Indian American newspapers, its ideologies are also widely disseminated.

For the FHA and other *Hindutva* groups, Indian culture and civilization are Hindu, true Indians are Hindus, and such groups as Muslims and Christians are resident aliens since they owe allegiance to religions that originated outside India. Although I have indicated that Indian religious minorities are overrepresented in the United States, bringing down the relative proportion of Indian Hindus when compared to India, FHA leaders still refer to Indian Americans as Hindus. FHA views Hindu Indian Americans as the proud descendants of the world's oldest living civilization and religion.[59] It counters the negative American image of Hinduism as primitive and bizarre by arguing that, contrary to American stereotypes, Hinduism is actually very sophisticated and scientific.[60] FHA leaders state that in ancient Hindu India, women were held in great esteem and that Hinduism gives women and men the same rights.[61] Thus, gender equality and respect for women are claimed to be an integral part of the Hindu tradition. The model minority label is used explicitly by American *Hindutva* leaders who attribute the success of Indians in the United States to their Hindu religious and cultural heritage, which, according to them, makes them adaptable, hardworking, and family oriented.[62] According to them, this heritage also makes Hindu Americans a truly secular and tolerant people. Together with their professional expertise (particularly in the fields of computers, medicine, and engineering), they believe that this makes Indians a group that has an important leadership role to play in modern America.

Rajagopal argues that the choice of Hinduism to represent an "Indian" identity has been a way for the predominantly upper caste immigrants to avoid their problematic racial location in this country.[63] Most Indians in the United States refuse to classify themselves racially but, if pressed, state that they are "Aryans." According to the conventional view of early Indian history (which is now discredited by most historians), the Aryans were a group from central Europe that invaded India around 1500 B.C., colonized the dark-skinned natives (now considered to be the lower castes), and established the religion and culture that developed into Hinduism. Thus, by labeling themselves Aryans, upper caste Hindus claim a racial identity close to that of Europeans.[64]

American *Hindutva* groups see themselves as the torchbearers and guardians of Hindu Indian tradition and values. According to Gopal Chaturvedi, a former FHA activist (and currently a leader of the newly formed American Hindu Federation), this is because Indians living outside India are able to understand India and India's problems more clearly. Other FHA members point out that Indians in the United States have greater resources (including access to modern communication methods) and power than Indians in any other part of the world and thus have the responsibility to use them to further the cause of Hinduism. They claim that they want to develop a model for Hindu pride, unity, and activism through their organization and then export the model to India.[65] In their speeches and full-page advertisements in the *India Post*, the FHA leaders stress the need for American Hindus to be more aggressive about defending and disseminating Hinduism.[66]

Consequences

Even though pan-Hindu organizations like the FHA may individually have only a limited direct influence and impact on Indian Americans, on Indians in India, and on the wider American society, the combined network effect of all such organizations and individuals can be significant. For instance, at the time of this writing, activists with *Hindutva* leanings had hijacked almost all of the local Indian American organizations in southern California, pushing out moderates and minorities. Such individuals have assumed leadership positions in secular groups such as the Federation of Indian Associations (FIA), political groups such as the Indo-American Political Foundation, and other Indian groups such as the Friends of India Society International (FISI). Their rabidly communal rhetoric has reinforced tensions between Indians of different religious backgrounds and has legitimized public expressions of religious chauvinism. This, in turn, will have a profound impact on the formation of Indian Americans as an ethnic group in the United States. If *Hindutva* leaders become accepted as the public voice for all people of Indian ancestry in this country, it could also adversely impact American foreign policy toward India and domestic policy toward Indian Americans.

The legitimization of the *Hindutva* discourse in the United States has also meant that individuals have been using aggressive Hinduness as a means to obtain status within the Indian American community and visibility outside the community. In the past few years, dozens of individuals and organizations, claiming their mission to be the defense of Hinduism, have tried to garner publicity for themselves by finding a Hindu cause to champion. When Hindu and Indian American organizations start using their clout to pursue companies that have "insulted" Hinduism, substantive issues of concern to the community at large, such as immigration laws, the treatment of immigrants, and racism, are neglected.

Conclusion

It is clear from the preceding discussion that the post-1965 immigrants from India have a very different construction of the meaning of a "Hindu American" identity than did the pioneer Indian immigrants. But just as the Sikh temple was closely associated with the militant nationalistic Ghadar movement, the religious organizations of the contemporary immigrants have become the centers of diasporic nationalism.

I have argued in this chapter that religion has become the basis for ethnic formation among Indian immigrants. My preliminary study of Muslim, Sikh, and Christian Indian Americans indicates that one important consequence of this tendency is that each of these groups has a very different construction of national and ethnic identity from each other and from Hindu Americans and, correspondingly, has a very different political agenda. This probably indicates that the Indian American community is going to develop deep schisms as the process of ethnic formation proceeds.

Notes

1. According to a preliminary report of the 2000 U.S. Census, there were 1,678,765 people of Asian Indian origin in 2000.

2. Next only to Chinese and Filipinos.

3. Pyong Gap Min and Rose Kim, *Struggle for Ethnic Identity: Narratives by Asian American Professionals* (Walnut Creek, Calif.: AltaMira, 1999), 26.

4. Karen Isaksen Leonard, *Making Ethnic Choices: California's Punjabi Mexican Americans* (Philadelphia: Temple University Press, 1992), 214.

5. Leonard, *Making Ethnic Choices*.

6. In 1930, 1,572 men for every 100 women. Leonard, *Making Ethnic Choices*, 23.

7. According to Leonard (*Making Ethnic Choices*, 66), around 80 percent of them married Hispanic women. After some initial legal restriction, the two groups were allowed to intermarry since they were both classified as "non-white." See Leonard, *Making Ethnic Choices*, 62–63.

8. The 1990 census figures from Mary C. Waters and Karl Eschbach, "Immigration and Ethnic and Racial Inequality in the United States," in *Majority and Minority: The Dynamics of Race and Ethnicity in American Life*, 6th ed., ed. Norman R. Yetman (Needham Heights, Mass.: Allyn & Bacon, 1999), 315.

9. The 1990 census figures cited in Larry Hajime Shinagawa, "The Impact of Immigration on the Demography of Asian Pacific Americans," in *The State of Asian Pacific America: Reframing the Immigration Debate, A Public Policy Report* (Los Angeles: LEAP Asian Pacific American Public Policy Institute and UCLA Asian American Studies Center, 1996), 113, 119.

10. World Bank figures, 1990.

11. Richard Springer, "Indians Jump to Third Place in Immigration to U.S.," *India West*, May 2, 1997, A22.

12. Richard Springer, "Poverty Persists Amid Indo-American Wealth," *India West*, August 18, 1995, C1.

13. 1990 census figures.

14. Fenton estimates that in 1985, around 65 percent of the Indian immigrants in America came from a Hindu family background. John Fenton, *Transplanting Religious Traditions: Asian Indians in America* (New York: Praeger, 1988), 28.

15. Peter Xenos, Herbert Barringer, and Michael Levine, *Asian Indians in the United States: A 1980 Census Profile*, no. 111 (Honolulu, Hawaii: Papers of the East–West Population Institute, July 1989), 10.

16. Timothy Smith, "Religion and Ethnicity in America," *American Historical Review* 83 (1978): 1175, cited in Stephen Warner, "Work in Progress toward a New Paradigm for the Sociological Study of Religion in the United States," *American Journal of Sociology* 98 (1993): 1062. See also P. Saran, *The Asian Indian Experience in the United States* (Cambridge, Mass.: Schenkman, 1985); and Raymond Williams, *Religions of Immigrants from India and Pakistan: New Threads in the American Tapestry* (Cambridge, U.K.: Cambridge University Press, 1988).

17. Richard Burghart, "The Perpetuation of Hinduism in an Alien Cultural Milieu," in *Hinduism in Great Britain: The Perpetuation of Religion in an Alien Cultural Milieu*, ed. Richard Burghart (London: Tavistock, 1987); John D. Kelly, *A Politics of Virtue: Hinduism, Sexuality, and Countercolonial Discourse in Fiji*

(Chicago: University of Chicago Press, 1987); David James Mearns, *Shiva's Other Children: Religion and Social Identity amongst Overseas Indians* (New Delhi: Sage, 1995); Steven Vertovec, "Hindus in Trinidad and Britain: Ethnic Religion, Reification and the Politics of Public Space," in *Nation and Migration: The Politics of Space in the South Asian Diaspora*, ed. Peter van der Veer (Philadelphia: University of Pennsylvania Press, 1995); Williams, *Religions of Immigrants from India and Pakistan*.

18. Warner, "Work in Progress toward a New Paradigm," 1058.

19. Steven Vertovec, *Hindu Trinidad: Religion, Ethnicity and Socio-Economic Change* (London: Macmillan, 1992); Parminder Bachu, *Twice Migrants: East African Sikh Settlers in Britain* (London: Tavistock, 1985); Verne Dusenbery, "A Sikh Diaspora? Contested Identities and Constructed Realities," in *Nation and Migration: The Politics of Space in the South Asian Diaspora*, ed. Peter van der Veer (Philadelphia: University of Pennsylvania Press, 1995), 17–42.

20. Raymond Williams, "Sacred Threads of Several Textures," in *A Sacred Thread: Modern Transmission of Hindu Traditions in India and Abroad*, ed. Raymond Williams (Chambersburg, Pa.: Anima Press, 1992), 230.

21. Bruce La Brack, *The Sikhs of Northern California 1904–1975: A Socio-Historical Study* (New York: AMS Press, 1988); Joan Jensen, *Passage from India: Asian Indian Immigrants in North America* (New Haven, Conn.: Yale University Press, 1988); Leonard, *Making Ethnic Choices*.

22. Leonard, *Making Ethnic Choices*.

23. Harjot S. Oberoi, "From Ritual to Counter-Ritual: Rethinking the Hindu Sikh Question, 1884–1915," in *Sikh History and Religion in the Twentieth Century*, ed. Joseph T. O'Connell, Milton Israel, and William G. Oxtoby with W. H. McLeod and J. S. Grewal (Toronto: Centre for South Asian Studies, 1988), 136–58; Leonard, *Making Ethnic Choices*, 25.

24. Leonard, *Making Ethnic Choices*, 90; La Brack, *Sikhs of Northern California*, 128–29.

25. Leonard, *Making Ethnic Choices*, 99.

26. Leonard, *Making Ethnic Choices*, 25.

27. Leonard, *Making Ethnic Choices*, 129.

28. Leonard, *Making Ethnic Choices*, 182.

29. Leonard, *Making Ethnic Choices*, 156–58.

30. Leonard, *Making Ethnic Choices*, 131–32.

31. Leonard, *Making Ethnic Choices*, 206.

32. Leonard, *Making Ethnic Choices*, 168.

33. Leonard, *Making Ethnic Choices*, 172–73.

34. Leonard, *Making Ethnic Choices*, 173–74.

35. Alejandro Portes and Ruben G. Rumbaut, *Immigrant America: A Portrait*, 2d ed. (Berkeley: University of California Press, 1996), 40.

36. James P. Allen and Eugene Turner, *The Ethnic Quilt: Population Diversity in Southern California* (Los Angeles: California State University at Northridge, the Center for Geographical Studies, 1997), 135.

37. Shinagawa, "Impact of Immigration," 101.

38. Shinagawa, "Impact of Immigration," 90.

39. Springer, "Indians Jump to Third Place," A22.

40. The three stages took place earlier on the East Coast and in the Midwest due to earlier settlement.

41. In Pyong Gap Min's study of Indians in New York, 53 percent reported that they attended a formal ethnic meeting at least once or twice a month. Pyong Gap Min, "Immigrants' Religion and Ethnicity: A Comparison of Indian Hindu and Korean Christian Immigrants in the United States," *Bulletin of the Royal Institute for Inter-Faith Studies* 2 (2000): 130 (table 2).

42. Statement made by the president of the organization at a banquet function. Sanjay Saberwal, "FHA Unity Banquet Raises $20,000 for Norwalk Temple, Support Emphasized at Sangeet Sandhya." *India Post*, July 28, 1995, D SW 6.

43. Xenos Barringer, and Levine., *Asian Indians in the United States*, 10.

44. Some of these were conducted by a research assistant who taped and transcribed the discussions for me.

45. Williams, "Sacred Threads of Several Textures," 252.

46. Prema Kurien, "Becoming American by Becoming Hindu: Indian Americans Take Their Place at the Multi-Cultural Table," in *Gatherings in Diaspora: Religious Communities and the New Immigration*, ed. R. Stephen Warner and Judith G. Wittner (Philadelphia: Temple University Press, 1998).

47. Laurence Steinberg, *Beyond the Classroom: Why School Reform Has Failed and What Parents Need to Do* (New York: Simon & Schuster, 1996); Margaret Gibson, *Accommodation without Assimilation: Sikh Immigrants in an American High School* (Ithaca, N.Y.: Cornell University Press, 1989); Min Zhou and Carl L. Bankston III, *Growing Up American: How Vietnamese Children Adapt to Life in the United States* (New York: Russell Sage Foundation, 1998).

48. S. Andezian, "Women's Roles in Organizing Symbolic Life: Algerian Female Immigrants in France," in *International Migration: The Female Experience*, ed. R. J. Simon and C. B. Brettell (Totowa, N.J.: Rowman and Allanheld, 1986), 254–65; K. Leonard, "Ethnic Identity and Gender: South Asians in the United States," in *Ethnicity, Identity, Migration: The South Asian Context*, ed. M. Israel and N. K. Wagle (Toronto, Canada: Center for South Asian Studies, University of Toronto, 1993), pp 165–80; M. de Leonardo, *The Varieties of Ethnic Experience: Kinship, Class and Gender among California Italian-Americans* (Ithaca, N.Y.: Cornell University Press, 1984).

49. D. Kandiyoti "Bargaining with Patriarchy," *Gender and Society* 2, no. 3 (1988): 274–90. For a more detailed discussion of the impact of immigration and settlement on Indian American women, see Prema Kurien, "Gendered Ethnicity: Creating a Hindu Indian Identity in the United States," *American Behavioral Scientist* 42, no. 4 (1999): 648–70.

50. See also discussions in S. D. DasGupta and S. DasGupta, "Public Face, Private Space: Asian Indian Women and Sexuality," in *Bad Girls, Good Girls: Women, Sex and Power in the Nineties*, ed. N. B. Maglin and D. Perry (New Brunswick, N.J.: Rutgers University Press, 1996), 226–43.

51. Lise McKean, "Political Capital and Spiritual Camps: The Vishwa Hindu Parishad in the United States" (presentation made at the 22d annual Conference on South Asia, Madison, Wis., 1993).

52. Federation of Hindu Associations [FHA], *Directory of Temples and Associations of Southern California and Everything You Wanted to Know About Hinduism* (Artesia, Calif.: no press, 1995), 76.

53. FHA, *Directory of Temples and Associations of Southern California*, 117.

54. FHA, full-page advertisement, "Will Hindus Become a Minority in India?" *India Post*, May 15, 1998, B17. Also Prithvi Raj Singh and Kanti Patel, FHA, "Cultural Nationalism," Letter to the Editor, *India West*, February 20, 1998, A6.

55. Prithvi Raj Singh "Discussing Religious Role Models," Letter to the Editor, *India Post*, March 14, 1997, A26.

56. President of FHA, Prithvi Raj Singh, in a discussion with research assistant, February 2, 1997.

57. FHA, full-page advertisement, "Ideal Hindu Temple," *India Post*, August 29, 1997, A27.

58. *Om* is a sacred word in Hinduism.

59. FHA, *Directory of Temples and Associations of Southern California*, 33.

60. FHA, full-page advertisements: "How to Be a Good Hindu," *India Post*, July 25, 1997, A15, and "To Our Hindu Youth," *India Post*, August 15, 1997, A51. Also FHA, *Directory of Temples and Associations of Southern California*, 33.

61. FHA, full-page advertisement, "Proud to Be a Hindu Woman," *India Post*, August 1, 1997, A15.

62. Kanti Patel in a discussion with FHA members February 9, 1997, by research assistant.

63. Arvind Rajagopal, "Better Hindu Than Black? Narratives of Asian Indian Identity," (paper presented at the annual meetings of the Society for the Scientific Study of Religion [SSSR] and the Religious Research Association [RRA], St. Louis, Mo., 1995).

64. In the early twentieth century, this Aryan invasion theory was challenged by members of the newly formed Hindu nationalist movement in India. These individuals reversed this theory, arguing that Aryans were indigenous to India and that the migratory movement had been from India to the West rather than vice versa. This idea has recently been picked up by some Indian scientists in the United States who have argued that they have found irrefutable scientific evidence to support the revised theory. Although the theory has been dismissed by most historians (Ratnagar, "Revisionist at Work: Chauvinistic Inversion of the Aryan Invasion Theory," *Frontline,* February 9, 1996, 74–80), it has generated considerable interest and excitement among Indian Americans.

65. Interview, February 9, 1997.

66. FHA, full-page advertisement, "A Call for Dharma Raksha," *India Post*, August 8, 1997, A15.

CHAPTER FIVE

A RELIGIOUS HISTORY OF JAPANESE AMERICANS IN CALIFORNIA

David Yoo

The men and women who left their native Japan in the late nineteenth century and early decades of the twentieth century to find
work in the United States left a country in the midst of major transition. Heavy land taxes exacted by the Meiji government to support the
modernization of Japan made it increasingly difficult for poorer farmers
to exist off the land, resulting in a growing number of Japanese who ventured outside the country. The first-generation immigrants (or Issei)
brought with them their hopes and aspirations, and also their world-
views—shaped by family and region, a budding Japanese national identity, and by the process of migration and settlement in the United States.
As part of this mix, religious institutions and communities played an important role in the negotiation of identity and experience.

The majority of the immigrants who entered the United States came
from Buddhist backgrounds since Buddhism was dominant in the southern prefectures that formed the core of the sending regions. Buddhism for
most of the Issei was tied to rituals connected to birth, marriage, and
death as well as to ethical ideas about behavior that linked one to family
and community.[1] In the United States, immigrants and their descendants
would create their own variation of Buddhism and also be influenced by
other religions such as Christianity. In terms of religious affiliation, a
Stanford University survey in the early 1930s found that 78 percent of the
Issei claimed affiliation with Buddhism while only 18 percent had taken
up the Christian faith. In a more comprehensive, if problematic, survey
taken by the War Relocation Authority (WRA) in 1942, 68 percent of all
immigrant internees reported a Buddhist affiliation compared to 22 percent Christian. The figures for the second generation (or Nisei) showed
gains for Christianity, but Buddhism still accounted for a greater percentage: 49 percent Buddhist and 35 percent Christian.[2]

This chapter examines the growth and development of Pure Land
Buddhism and Protestant Christianity among Japanese Americans in California, primarily from the onset of official migration in 1885 to the end of

World War II in 1945.[3] Though not comprehensive in scope, this case study traces the religious history of the most populous Japanese American state on the mainland. Japanese Americans in California, furthermore, were deeply affected by the concentration camp experience that has been such an influential feature of this group's past. In terms of method, sources, and narrative structure, the discussion is informed by a historical perspective. This angle of vision is warranted because unlike many other Asian groups, the formative migration that has shaped Japanese America took place prior to 1965. In fact, the bulk of immigrants entered during the period from the turn of the century until 1924, when restrictive legislation passed by the United States effectively shut the door to further arrivals. The Immigration Act of 1965 which reversed the 1924 act and which has produced such major growth among other Asian groups, did not spark large-scale migration from Japan—a country that by that time had begun its economic climb. In recent years, many Japanese coming to the United States have been international students and temporary corporate employees. Accordingly, turning our attention to the religious history of Japanese Americans may provide a helpful frame of reference for other Asian American groups whose stories have begun or been rejuvenated by the large influx of immigrants in the past thirty-five years.

Religious historians of the United States will recognize certain features of Japanese American experiences as reflected in those of many other immigrant groups, but this chapter contributes to the existing literature in two distinct ways. First, the case of Japanese Americans underscores the importance of the relationship between religion *and* race. Much of the scholarship has not taken into account how race has been a persistent and significant filter of experience. Despite its highly variable nature, race, as opposed to ethnicity, remained a persistent force in the lives of Japanese Americans that accentuated a lasting marker of difference. In the case of Buddhists, well outside a Judeo–Christian framework, the passage of time did little to remove the widespread suspicion that Buddhists could ever really become part of the fabric of American life. Doubly marginalized by virtue of race and religion, Buddhists were cast as the "other." For Japanese American Protestants, a shared faith with the dominant religious tradition of the nation was not enough to bridge the gap created by race. Although the prevailing assumption is that racial-ethnic Christians are more assimilated than their non-Christian counterparts, Japanese American Protestants consciously forged religious identities and organizations in opposition to the discrimination that they experienced. Whether Buddhist or Christian, Japanese Americans experienced racialized religion.

The second contribution of the case study is that it explores how religion factored into the identity formation of second-generation Japanese

Americans. As Nisei came of age during the 1930s and 1940s, many found in their religion spaces within which they wrestled with a range of issues, including what it meant to be Japanese American. Historians know relatively little about the experiences of the second generation, as assumptions of assimilation have rendered them invisible. How religion has been a part of this process is even more opaque, and this case study provides an opportunity to analyze the intersections of religion, generation, race, and American identity—major themes in our collective past as a nation.

As historian Yuji Ichioka has suggested, religious institutions were integral to the establishment of Japanese immigrant society in California. Protestant missions, in particular, provided a range of social services that enabled the largely young, male population in the late nineteenth century to make the adjustment to American society.[4] The Japanese government sanctioned its citizens to travel abroad in 1885 when economic and social changes created conditions favorable to migration. Those changes, which included thousands of displaced farmers, in conjunction with the efforts of American recruiters in search of labor meant that over 273,000 Japanese came to the United States in the years 1890 through 1930, including agricultural laborers, students, domestics, and entrepreneurs.[5] Like many immigrants during the nineteenth century, the Japanese who first came to the United States intended to work, save their earnings, and return to Japan. While some did return, many did not, and, in the process, Japanese America was born. Especially after the Gentleman's Agreement in 1907–1908, an agreement between the United States and Japan drastically curtailing labor migration, a shift began to take place to a more settled immigrant community. In California, agriculture represented a decision by many immigrants to invest their lives, literally, in American soil. The arrival of women and the rise of the second generation were accompanied by standard features of immigrant life such as the ethnic press, mutual aid societies, and temples/churches.[6]

Whether recently arrived or relatively well established, Japanese Americans faced hardships not only based on the rigors of migration and settlement in a new land, but also from a persistent race-based discrimination that would culminate in their incarceration during World War II. Inheriting the legacy of the anti-Chinese movement in California, Japanese Americans struggled to carve out their existence within a hostile environment. Laws barring them from naturalization and land ownership as well as other measures ranging from restrictive housing covenants to outright violence hindered individuals and families from gaining access to basic rights and privileges afforded to most other immigrants. Japanese Americans did their best to counter the prejudice that so infused their experiences, using the courts and other means to improve their situation. Immigrants who turned to the Japanese government on occasion found help, but only to the degree that policy fostered recognition of Japan's status as an emerging world power. The passage of the 1924 Immigration Act was widely seen as a slap in the face of Japan and Japanese Americans, and immigrants began to realize that the future would rest on the fate of their children. And so, despite the difficulties they faced, Issei and Nisei together moved forward, relying on the bonds of family and racial-ethnic community to navigate their life circumstances.[7]

Pure Land in America

Although Shin Buddhism traveled with the first immigrants to America, official missionary work, sanctioned by headquarters in Kyoto, did not begin until the end of the nineteenth century.[8] Temples and affiliated religious organizations addressed the needs of Japanese Americans. In an often hostile land, Buddhism offered sanctuary to its members and represented the development and growth of ethnoreligious communities in California.[9] In the years before the war, Jodo Shinshu Buddhism in the United States remained overwhelmingly Japanese American. A 1944 anthropological study indicated that this group accounted for 55,000 of 56,000 Buddhists in the United States.[10] By the time Kosei Ogura, a priest and graduate student in sociology from the University of Southern California, completed his thesis in 1932, the North American Buddhist Mission (NABM) had prospered. The humble work of two missionary priests and dedicated lay leadership resulted in thirty-five temples in the United States and Canada.[11] Clerics ministered to some 30,000 Japanese Americans. Kyoto maintained its lifeline to the work in North American through the selection of the bishop and the training of priests. In thirty years' time, approximately 170 priests had been sent to the United States to serve an average of nearly five years each.[12] While important ties to Japan remained, North American Buddhism showed signs of independence.

Lay leaders in Sacramento, for instance, legally incorporated their temple with the state of California in June 1901, but vested power in the board of trustees and *not* in the priests, effectively eliminating clerical control over temple life. In Japan, the priest and his family usually owned individual temples. Tradition dictated that the priesthood passed from one generation to the next and, with it, a sense of ownership. Trustees also broke new ground by setting priests' salaries and in controlling finances.[13] Although males claimed official lay leadership positions, women also exerted their own influence in temple life through Buddhist Women's Associations (or *Fujinkai*), which had been founded in 1900. At the core of religious activity in most temples, *Fujinkai* enabled women to develop networks and a sense of community. Their collective labor translated into service that included preparation of refreshments and food and organization of temple bazaars. The role of laywomen, however, extended far beyond the kitchen as they performed important social services for the immigrant community as well as raised critical funds for temple operations. Priests and male lay leaders alike quickly found that alienating the *Fujinkai* could spell real trouble. Women comprised the majority of adherents and often served as the glue that held the programs and activities of the temples together.[14] For women and men, the creation of important and powerful positions for lay leaders became a badge of prestige reflecting the fact that avenues for community involvement had been severely restricted by the decision to migrate to the United States.

Buddhists in America found themselves living in a society in which Christians wielded both religious and cultural power. Protestant missionaries often viewed followers of Buddha as heathen in need of conversion. The long history of anti-Japanese activity left Buddhists especially wary of public perceptions and misconceptions. Repeatedly, religion had been used against Nikkei as a sign of their incompatibility. As a strategy of survival, Buddhists, as had other religious groups, made adjustments to soften their differences from Protestant Christianity. Leaders recoded much of the terminology and outward practices—temples were called "churches" and priests, "reverends." Architecture also reflected Buddhism's new surroundings as most congregations opted for rather plain, nontraditional buildings instead of the traditional styles found in Japan. Inside, pews and lecterns gave the aura of a Protestant church.[15] An individualized, less-regularized format that characterized Shin Buddhism in the homeland gave way to a communal, scheduled worship on Sundays. Attending a morning adult service, one would typically find a format that included meditation, reading or chanting of Buddhist scripture, a sermon, *gathas* (songs), the burning of incense, and announcements. Sunday school programs for children, the Young Men's and Women's Buddhist Associations (YM/WBA), and Boy Scouts contributed to what sociologist Isao Horinouchi has called the "protestantization" of American Buddhism.[16]

Casting religious adaptation in Protestant terms, however, is misleading because it implies change that compromised the integrity of Buddhism. Few adherents would have mistaken what took place at the temple as anything but Buddhism. As with any transition, some may have disliked altered terms and forms, but a distinctively Japanese American Buddhism emerged. Upon entering the church on Sunday morning, for instance, one might stumble on pairs and pairs of shoes outside the sanctuary. Not only would one find shoeless worshippers inside, but also pews pushed against the walls with people sitting on the floor. Apart from the specific circumstances in the United States, Buddhism in general and the Jodo Shinshu school in particular exhibited a marked flexibility. As it made its way throughout Asia, Buddhism had a long history of being deeply affected by its surrounding cultures.[17] In explaining the adaptability of Buddhism, scholar Hajime Nakamura noted that "the doctrine of Buddha is not a system of philosophy in the Western sense but is rather a path. A buddha is simply one who has walked this path and can report to others what he has found. His standpoint is practical."[18] Given the Protestant bias of the United States, notions within Pure Land Buddhism akin to "salvation" and "grace" as well as an emphasis on the laity lent itself well to religious life in the United States.[19]

In relating to the changes and transitions within Buddhism among Japanese Americans, officials at the headquarters in Kyoto realized that rules of the old country did not always apply abroad. Minutes from the 1927 annual conference indicated that the Nikkei "seem now to be reconciled in the making of permanent homes in America," and in light of this, "the priest should help them to realize the American idea of 'Home Sweet Home' with the Lord Buddha as universal parent."[20] The charge to missionary priests by leaders in Japan acknowledged the contexts into which Buddhism entered the United States and also reflected a commitment to minister to Japanese Americans. A Buddhism and mixed traditional elements with newer modifications emerged that offered space and meaning to its adherents whose decision to sink roots in America and to raise families meant facing hardships and prejudice. Issei realized that they needed to stake their claims for a future in America with their children. The arrival of picture brides during the first two decades of the twentieth century enabled families to form, including the birth of the Nisei. Lay and clerical leaders who worked so hard to establish Buddhism in America naturally wanted to pass on their religious tradition.[21]

Under the aegis of temple life, the second generation gathered to worship and to share life's journey—religious and otherwise. Sunday school and Japanese language schools served as initial sites of contact with the faith. As they grew older, Nisei Buddhists (also known as Bussei) joined a variety of young people's groups. Through organizations, conferences, and publications, Japanese Americans created their own spaces within Buddhism. The YWBA and the YMBA became the primary vehicles for drawing the Nisei. Initially, at the turn of the century, the YMBA consisted of young immigrant men. But by the 1920s and 1930s, the YMBA and the YWBA became Nisei organizations, under the guidance of the Reverend Herbert Tansai Terakawa. Separate groups eventually united under the banner of the joint YMWBA and later as the Young Buddhist Association (YBA).[22]

The formation of the leagues for young men and women started a tradition of conferences that became a significant gathering place for Nisei Buddhists. Regional and statewide conferences drew hundreds of participants and enabled Nisei from different parts of the state to meet, develop friendships, and discuss not only their religious faith, but also a host of other issues.[23] A Nisei delegate heading to the seventh annual meeting of the YMBA in the spring of 1932 might have traveled by car with fellow Buddhists to the temple in Stockton. Standing in line to register, delegates craned their necks looking for relatives and friends. Name tags and programs in hand, men and women attended an opening service/ceremony and spent the day in a whirlwind of meetings, panels, and roundtable discussions. Official business ended at half past five in the afternoon, and hungry participants enjoyed a Chinese banquet dinner, featuring the culinary innovation, chop suey. An oratorical contest generally followed the meal. The second day consisted of more services and meetings, including the election of the next year's leaders. Delegates eagerly anticipated the evening social event that capped the two-day affair.[24]

Fred Nitta of the Watsonville Buddhist Church, legendary in Young Buddhist circles for his lifetime support of these groups, got his start at Stockton and recalled:

> As this was my first participation in the statewide conference where over 1,000 devoted young Buddhists of my own age assembled, the spiritual impact upon me was tremendous. I received great inspiration by direct contact with the leaders. . . . The friendly atmosphere created by the fellow young Buddhists from other cities made me feel at home. . . . It really surprised me to see so many capable boys and girls who believe[d] in the same Amida-Buddha as I [did] in the conference.[25]

Conferences and temple life not only occupied the energies of the second generation, but also allowed them to craft ways of seeing their world and their place in it. Religious faith helped other Bussei to cope with harsh realities of marginalization they encountered. Buddhism influenced the construction and negotiation of Japanese American identities. Like so many other children of immigrants, Nisei spoke about the challenges of living in two worlds and their plight of being a generation "in-between."

The tenuous nature of Japanese American identity was not lost on Manabu Fukuda. In 1934, as a contributor to the Buddhist journal *Bhratri*, Fukuda painted a bleak picture. By definition, a Nisei "[was] not an American nor [was] he a Japanese," but an unhappy and depressed person without a country. In looking for answers, however, Fukuda suggested that Japanese Americans could find acceptance in the "Land of Buddha."[26] Takeo Yamanaka of west Los Angeles reminded others that Buddhist faith in particular could sustain the second generation. Yamanaka recognized that missionaries and Japanese American Christians could give the impression that being Protestant somehow made one more fit for life in the United States:

> I once heard a person say, that only a real Christian, can be a true American. If that were so, then we Busseis couldn't be true Americans, could we? But is it true? Just because I don't happen to be a Christian, can you say that I am not a true American? We may be referred to the Constitution of the United States, and find written there, the guarantee that an American citizen, may worship whatever religion he chooses.

By invoking the U.S. Constitution, Yamanaka called on his rights to exercise the freedom of religion. As an American, he had indeed learned his lessons well. Prudence may have dictated that Buddhists be sensitive to their surroundings, but he wanted to dispel the notion that Christians possessed any greater claim to American identity. In fact, Yamanaka urged the spread of the faith since it so ably served Japanese Americans and any others who became Buddhists.[27]

Although religion at times divided Nikkei communities, Christians and Buddhists also shared not only a common ancestry and but also an existence in which racial concerns often overshadowed other important distinctions. Writers most frequently tackled issues of identity, expressing frustration over the second-class status of the Nisei in the United States. In seeking full recognition as Americans, the second generation wanted access to opportunities and a chance to enjoy a quality of life befitting citizens. Instead, the imprint of racial discrimination marred the experiences of men and women who simply desired that their racial-ethnic status not be used against them. Again and again, voices cried out for fair play and the opportunity to compete on equal terms. More than adolescent musings, the emphasis on identity spoke directly to the quality of life that these Americans could hope for in their native land.

While Nisei could not always control life circumstances, Florence Funakoshi urged the readers of the Buddhist magazine *Sangha* to be forceful and clear about who they were, especially in contexts that could perpetuate damaging stereotypes. Funakoshi sketched out a hypothetical but familiar scenario to illustrate her point: A young Nikkei in Los Angeles, gazing out the streetcar at the end of a day, felt the nudge of an elbow. Turning his head, John Nisei discovered an elderly woman sitting next to him who inquired, "I beg your pardon, sir, are you a Japanese or a Chinese?" John answered, "Neither, ma'am, I am an *American*!" To dispel misconceptions, public education extended beyond the classroom and into the streets. Funakoshi added: "[W]hether we be farmers, fruit-stand workers, students, or the envious holders of a white collar job . . . however large or small our contacts may be, like the boy on the streetcar, we must make them realize, 'We, too are Americans.'"[28] Historian Eileen Tamura has shown that the stress on American identity had much more to do with issues of access than with notions of wholesale assimilation.[29] Rather than becoming something they were not (European Americans), many members of the second generation claimed their status as Americans as a means of opening doors shut on the basis of their being "Japanese." "Americanizers" and casual observers alike mistakenly viewed outward signs of acculturation such as English language ability and interest in popular culture as a blanket attempt to shed one culture for another.[30]

For all their efforts to negotiate the complexities of being Japanese American, Bussei ran into difficulties as tensions mounted between the United States and Japan during the 1930s. An unwillingness by most Americans to distinguish between Japan and Japanese Americans placed an extraordinary burden on Nisei as the two nations headed down a collision course. Among Nikkei themselves, Bussei felt considerable added pressures of being religious outsiders. Japanese American Christians, on the other hand, had access to resources and support networks as part of larger Protestant denominations. As U.S.–Japan relations soured, Buddhism came under increasing attack and suspicion for its connection to things Japanese.

As war approached, loyalty and identity emerged as unavoidable issues within Japanese American Buddhism. As ethnic institutions, however, temples had never been limited strictly to religious concerns. Buddhism played a role in the lives of the Nikkei that went far beyond the numbers registered on membership roles or in statistical percentages. Conferences, journals, and campus groups helped Bussei to filter the ambiguities of being Japanese American through the lens of their religious tradition. Shared journeys included a common ancestry, immigrant parents, as well as the harsh realities of prejudice and racial discrimination. Bussei gravitated toward temple life because it helped them to negotiate their times and to construct their identities as Japanese Americans. Although religion did not supply easy answers, Buddhist belief did give the second generation a meaningful way of seeing the world and their place in it.

Protestant Presence

The Protestant presence among the Japanese in California, like Buddhism, centered around social services for newly arrived immigrants. Unlike Buddhists, however, Issei Christians moved within the religious contexts of American Protestant home missions, even as the first generation labored to establish their own churches. The ties to missionaries gave Issei access to a cultural capital that Buddhist counterparts did not enjoy, but also entailed operating within the paternalistic institutional setting that dated to the very founding of the immigrant community. Japanese who ventured to the United States discovered Protestant missions that offered English language classes, lodging, job information, and referrals. Early converts such as Kanichi Miyama and Kumataro Nonaka had come to America in 1875 and had been baptized by the Reverend Otis Gibson of the Chinese Methodist Episcopal Mission. Living and meeting in the dark and damp basement of the Chinese mission, student-laborers gathered by candlelight for Bible study and, when the candles went out, they slept in hastily constructed bunks that replicated the steerage accommodations Issei had endured crossing the Pacific. From those humble beginnings, Miyama and Nonaka with other Christians founded the Gospel Society in October 1877, an important group for the Japanese that later spawned similar organizations across several Protestant denominations.[31]

Gospel Societies, in turn, led to the formation of churches beginning with the First Japanese Presbyterian Church of San Francisco, organized on May 16, 1885. By 1919, the United Church of Christ claimed twelve congregations located in Japanese American communities ranging from the Bay Area to San Diego. The northern branch of the Methodist Episcopal Church had fifteen Japanese churches by the time of exclusion in 1924 and, by 1940, added another eight churches to reach a total of twenty-three. Thirteen Presbyterian and eight American Baptist congregations had been established throughout the state at the time of Pearl Harbor. Donald Fujiyoshi's study of Los Angeles in 1942 listed forty-six churches in ten southern California counties. Protestant groups such as the YM/WCA and the Salvation Army also worked among the Japanese.[32]

While linked to denominational structures, immigrant churches were Japanese American organizations with a high degree of ownership by their members and deeply rooted within the larger racial-ethnic community. According to Y. Caspar Horikoshi of the Wesley United Methodist Church in San Jose, "The Japanese Christian churches were not established as a separate institution. They were born out of the struggles of Japanese communities, as they faced many problems. The history of the Christian churches parallels the history of the Japanese people in this country."[33] Management and leadership of the churches fell largely to Japanese Americans because of culture and language—two factors that reinforced racial-ethnic foundations. Interestingly, attempts after the war to integrate the churches with other local congregations failed, even though language posed a lesser issue.[34]

The strong identification of immigrant churches as Japanese American institutions could complicate denominational relationships and efforts toward self-determination. Underscoring issues of power, Issei, denied naturalization rights and marginalized in other ways, relied on a missionary "defense" to represent their concerns. Unfortunately, immigrants discovered that beyond issues of immigration and exclusion, most Protestant patrons did little to critique the exploitation of Japanese labor or to challenge seriously the daily realities of racial discrimination. Moreover, many missionaries continued to defend the United States as a Christian nation whose manifest destiny included global supremacy.[35] Deference paid to missionaries by Japanese American Christians reflected their understanding of the relationship to Christ in hierarchical terms: as a servant to a master. In their study of Asian American churches, Michael Angevine and Ryo Yoshida have suggested that Japanese American Christians in the early 1900s struggled to develop their own sense of identity, but did so within the confines of a paternalistic nineteenth-century American Protestantism. The difficulty that Japanese American Christians had in separating their own efforts toward agency from their loyalties to missionaries could create situations that pitted one impulse against the other. In 1914, for instance, the formation of the San Francisco Japanese Church of Christ, a merger of the Congregational and Presbyterian churches, signaled an important step in Issei efforts to create an independent Japanese American denomination. At a special session meeting on November 17, 1914, discussion centered on separating the work of the Japanese YMCA from the Church of Christ—a move to loosen missionary ties. The entire body, with the exception of Presbyterian missionary Ernest A. Sturge, voted for the separation. Upon discovering Sturge's objections (the YMCA came under his care), the session reversed itself.[36]

Nevertheless, Japanese American Protestants continued to press for their own agenda within and across denominations, and the formation of federations of immigrant congregations represented an important development. Nikkei leaders in 1910 founded the Northern California Japanese Christian Church Federation (NCJCCF) "to keep up the morale of the community due to incidents of racial prejudice and persecution in business, school and work." The federation represented a move to address concerns that went beyond the boundaries of denominations and that recognized the common bonds of faith as well as Japanese American identity. The NCJCCF sponsored speakers, coordinated events and relationships between churches, and also explicitly included in its mission the education of the Nisei. The northern California segment of Young People's Christian Conference (YPCC) found staunch support from the NCJCCF.[37] Churches in southern California also joined forces. Sixteen parishes in the greater Los Angeles area formed the Southern California Church Federation, Japanese American in 1910, the same year as their northern counterparts. The federation programs included a successful Christian summer school on Terminal Island, which ran from 1932 until the outbreak of World War II. The churches believed strongly in serving the racial-ethnic community, and the southern California group organized a credit union, social center, and an orphanage.[38] In addition to federations that crossed denominational lines, Japanese American churches within the same denomination formed coalitions. The Japanese Presbyterian Conference (JPC), still operative today, created a lasting and important form of identification for Nikkei Presbyterians. Congregations often felt much more connected to and invested in the JPC than to their denomination.[39]

In laboring to build Japanese American churches, Issei leaders ministered to the needs of two generations. Nisei were the future of the churches, and immigrants encouraged their children to take part in the life of the congregation. The second generation inherited from their parents a desire to practice a brand of Christianity that spoke to their specific needs as a racial-ethnic group as well as a generation. Toward that end, the Young People's Union Church (YPUC) in San Francisco emphasized ministry to and by the second generation. In addition to formal services, the YPUC put together popular artistic productions that raised funds and increased visibility of the second generation.[40]

In addition to local efforts, Nisei Christians throughout California came together under the banner of the Young People's Christian Conference (YPCC). With direct ties to immigrant churches, the YPCC influenced its members primarily through local and regional conferences and experienced its peak years during the later 1930s and early 1940s. The YPCC concentrated its work almost exclusively on the Nisei, and its meetings enabled the second generation to meet and to discuss issues that they faced together as Japanese Americans and as Christians. The origins of the YPCC in many ways were linked to the life of Tokyo-born pastor Reverend Suzunosuke Kato. After completing theological studies at Butler University in Indianapolis, Kato settled in Berkeley, California, as the pastor of the Japanese Christian Church (Disciples of Christ) in 1923. Kato began his ministry at age thirty, and, as a relatively young minister, he directed much of his concern and energy to the second generation. On September 30, 1925, he launched the Fellowship Circle, a ministry for college students who attended the University of California. Less than a month later, on October 24–25, its first conference took place at the Japanese Methodist Episcopal Church in San Francisco. The registration brochure invited delegates from all parts of the state over the age of fifteen to participate.[41] Unfortunately, Reverend Kato did not live long enough to see the growth and the success of the YPCC. He succumbed to tuberculosis on August 28, 1926, in Los Angeles, where he had gone for the warmer and drier climate. Kato's legacy, however, lived on through the YPCC, which not only spread throughout California and the West Coast, but continued during the war and also enjoyed a strong postwar history among the younger Nisei and older Sansei.[42]

A key contribution of the YPCC came through its development of leadership skills as Nisei worked together to host conferences, and, unlike Issei organizations, two women held the top spot for the first five years of the conference. Margaret Tann served as chair in 1925 and 1926 while Sumile Morishita guided the YPCC for the years 1927 through 1929. After finishing her BA at the University of California (1927), Morishita went up the hill to the Pacific School of Religion, obtaining both an MA in religion (1929) and a Bachelor of Divinity degree (1930). Freshly minted degrees in hand, Morishita accepted the post of director of the young people's division of the Methodist Episcopal Church in northern California. She spoke extensively at churches and at conferences and continued as an active leader in the area until she set sail for Japan in the fall of 1934, where she went to teach and serve.[43] The organization aimed to raise Christian leaders who could then strengthen their local churches.

As the 1930s drew to a close, racial tensions at home and in Asia and in Europe weighed on the minds of Nisei who sought to make sense of their world in light of their commitments to Christianity. At the 1939 YPCC gathering, the delegates took part in a symposium that raised questions such as the following: What should the Christian attitude be toward citizenship? Is patriotism to one's country a really great quality? Is the Japanese American Citizens League (JACL) really necessary? The participants pondered whether race should and/or did make a material difference in their attitudes toward people and whether racial antagonism operated as an inherent element of human nature. In responding to the reality of race prejudice in their lives, the conferees talked strategy—how to defend oneself, whether there should be retaliation, and how much good, realistically, was education in diffusing racial discrimination. Interestingly, the organizers of the session asked the delegates to turn the question of race upon themselves. What attitudes did they hold and should their experience on the receiving end of discrimination act as a deterrent toward exhibiting the same behavior toward others?[44]

Unfortunately, the conference program did not list the answers, but the questions indicated something of the thought processes at work. The Sino-Japanese War, citizenship and loyalty, and race prejudice represented important concerns for American-born Japanese, and, in that respect, it is understandable that these subjects came up when Nisei Christians sat together at conference tables. As they came of age, the second generation faced a troubled world at home and abroad, and their connections to these events and realities surely prompted many more questions than answers. Michael Yoshii has suggested that the YPCC reflected the development of a "vocational consciousness" in which this generation sought to assess their place in history and to link this to a sense of Christian vocation.[45]

Deciphering their times did not prove to be an easy task, and many Nisei found in the Christian churches a place to gather with other second-generation men and women who shared much in common, including a basic worldview derived from Protestant Christianity. American-born Japanese undoubtedly associated and joined groups like the Young People's Union Church for other reasons, but the meetings offered an opportunity for people to come together as Japanese Americans. That fact touched almost everything about the process from standing in line to register to the evening socials that closed many conferences.

World War II and the Camps

Since the late nineteenth century, Buddhist temples and Christian churches have been a cornerstone within Japanese American communities. In the aftermath of Pearl Harbor and in the days leading up to the forced removal of Japanese Americans along the West Coast, religious leaders helped others with the daily tasks of survival.[46] In the concentration camps, temples and churches offered comfort and a source of meaning through a variety of religious activities. Religion, far from being an opiate, served as a venue in which Japanese Americans explored the meaning of their plight. Documents associated with religious life in the camps suggest how Buddhists and Christians assessed their incarceration, offering social commentary and engaging in a form of resistance. Consistent with their witness, racial-ethnic temples and churches continued to serve their constituencies. Religious institutions acted as (1) social service agencies; (2) sources of racial-ethnic solidarity; and (3) places of meaning and faith. Churches aided Japanese Americans in making the transition to the camps in concrete ways as ministers and lay leaders helped members pack and make other necessary arrangements. Temple and church buildings became storage centers since internees were allowed only two suitcases per person. Religion also supplied psychological and physical space for ethnic identification and solidarity and provided a means for assessing the war. The tradition of independent Japanese American congregations, well established for decades, continued during the war years. Buddhists and Christians supplied their own leadership, and this allowed them to gather together for a variety of purposes under religious auspices. Finally, Christianity and Buddhism, as expressions of faith, offered many Japanese Americans meaning, comfort, and hope—frameworks within which to respond to and interpret their lives.

Given the suddenness of internment, the social needs of the Japanese Americans far outstripped the ability of the churches to meet those needs.

The arrests of many Issei leaders exacerbated matters. Buddhist temples and Christian churches not only supplied workers who assisted families in every facet of their preparations, but also provided precious storage space in the sanctuaries, classrooms, and basements of church buildings. Lay leaders and clergy served as part of advance teams enlisted to ease the transition between the various stages of detention. Church networks assisted persons as they moved into their residential cubicles and adjusted to changes such as communal latrines, showers, and dining halls. Pastors took on roles as interpreters and mediaries between the administration and the internees in relaying policies and requests. In helping in such a wide variety of ways, the church leaders held positions that rivaled, if not surpassed, their prewar roles within the community.

Helping internees cope with the daily struggles of existence occupied much of the energy of clerical and lay leaders, but religious institutions, by their very presence, also offered Japanese Americans a racial-ethnic institution with which they could identify. Temples and churches supplied space that enabled people to work through their trials. One study of the Tule Lake camp in northern California argues that religion fueled resistance during the war and especially underscored the surge of Buddhist activity and folk beliefs/practices. In particular, religion helped combat the legacy of racism that predated the camps; it also tempered the attempts by the War Relocation Authority to use the camps as an opportunity to "Americanize" the internees. By upholding values such as filial piety, the family, and ethnic solidarity, religion affirmed key elements of the community.[47]

One form of resistance within the Christian circles also took shape in the reaction against a policy of "integration" that aimed to dismantle racial-ethnic churches. The WRA administrators hoped that geographic redistribution of Japanese Americans would break up ethnic ghettos of the West Coast so that other regions could "absorb" Issei and Nisei. Early resettlement of college-age students during the war, for instance, promoted the ongoing belief in education as a fundamental Americanizing influence. Many white American Protestant leaders did their part by encouraging Nikkei Christians to join white congregations. Historian Sandra Taylor has suggested that Protestant denominational policy meshed well with the assimilationist goals and objectives of the WRA.[48] Japanese American Christians, however, largely rejected the plans for "integration." The Reverend Paul Nagano stated that the churches played a pivotal role *because* they were centers of the ethnic community and sources of racial and ethnic identity.[49]

In terms of relations between Buddhists and Christians during the war, evidence exists that there was some interfaith cooperation. Joint services of worship took place, and, at one such event at the camp in Topaz,

Utah, Reverend J. K. Tsukamoto stated that the central geographic locations of both churches symbolized the role of religion in the lives of internees.[50] Both groups fell under the watchful eyes of the WRA—suspects by virtue of race. Daisuke Kitagawa and "Jack Sato" (a pseudonym) attributed cooperation among the groups to the massive dislocation experienced by all the internees. Leaders of both groups sought to care for people within a religious framework, and the pressing needs of internees kept leaders fully occupied. In a state of emergency, the "instant" parishes and their leaders often just managed to get by, and hence, may have minimized conflict.[51]

Resistance and interfaith cooperation illustrate how the churches acted as a base for ethnic solidarity. For many Japanese Americans, that sense of solidarity was enmeshed in religious faith commitments. Although highly diverse, religious beliefs sustained internees at various stages throughout the camps. Tashi Hori, president of the Manzanar YBA, reflected on how Buddhism had proven true during the trying times of the first year of the camps. "It has taught us to gain the highest perfection and preserverence [sic]," stated Hori. "This faith is a great gift in guiding our future life." In turning to their religion, Buddhists would find grounding in turbulent times.[52] Anthropologist Robert Spencer spent part of the war as a community analyst at the Gila River camp in Arizona. The social scientist noted that rites of passage such as birth, marriage, and especially death remained deeply connected to the faith tradition and practice of Buddhism. The observation of these rites formed an important part of the Buddhist legacy in the camps.[53]

In his wartime autobiography, "Frank Higashi" (a pseudonym) recalled that his Christian journey had been one of searching for real faith rather than outward forms based on habits or customs. Raised in Protestant churches in San Francisco before the war, Higashi turned to his faith during his current trials: "To me, the Christian way of life was the highest and the most satisfactory way of life, and one that was the closest to the democratic and the American way of life. I knew it to be a hard way of life, but one that can achieve happiness because it was unselfish in nature and regarded man as fellow brothers and as equals."[54]

In turning to their faith commitments as Buddhists and Christians, Japanese Americans sought meaning. Nikkei also received from and gave to churches and temple life. Social service, ethnic solidarity, and religious faith had of course been part of the Buddhist and Christian witness within Nikkei communities long before the war began. The experiences and testing that the churches had endured in the decades prior to Pearl Harbor served them well during the trauma of the war years.

Postscript

In the years following the war, Japanese Americans from California struggled to rebuild the homes, businesses, and communities that had been ravaged by incarceration. Temple and church leaders continued the legacy in the postwar that had been established in previous years. The Buddhist Churches of America (BCA), formerly the North American Buddhist Mission, which began its work among Japanese Americans in 1899, established forty-four temples in 1941, and by 1989, had added twenty new temples and seven fellowship groups. In order to train priests in the United States, BCA leaders founded the Institute of Buddhist Studies in 1966, a seminary and graduate school that has since become part of the Graduate Theological Union in Berkeley, California. Despite such developments, there has been an overall decline in numbers within the BCA. Figures from 1995 show that there are about 51,000 members, down from the 65,000 members listed in 1977. Enrollment in temple education programs has also dropped. In part, there has been an aging of both the priests as well as the membership, with fewer young people entering clerical and temple life. Alfred Bloom's study suggests that Pure Land Buddhism leaders need to find a balance between tradition and modernity that fosters an appreciation of Japanese heritage as well as the contemporary American setting.[55] Japanese American Protestant churches experienced new growth in the aftermath of World War II, but, like their Buddhist counterparts, have faced in more recent years an aging of the clergy and congregation. Although membership figures vary by denomination, it is clear that fewer young people are as actively involved in the churches as their elders. In some regions such as southern California, an interesting phenomenon has been taking place in which historic Japanese American churches have become spawning grounds for pan-Asian and multiethnic congregations. While it is beyond the scope of this chapter to assess the present circumstances of Japanese American Buddhism and Protestant Christianity, it is clear that numbers rarely ever tell the full story of what is happening within a given religious context.[56]

As for the religious history of Japanese Americans in California, how Japanese American Buddhists and Protestants negotiated their times provides insights into the issues of immigration, race/ethnicity, and religion. These stories contribute to a more nuanced understanding of the migration process, working against monolithic portrayals that conceal the differences that existed within immigrant groups and between generations. Japanese Americans, moreover, remind us that some immigrants, by virtue of race, chose from a fundamentally different set of ethnic choices that left them a "marked" people. Despite its dynamic and constructed nature, race nevertheless proved to be an enduring element of difference.

That difference extended even to those Protestants who stood under the umbrella of shared faith.

In serving Japanese American communities, temples and churches played a role in the lives of men and women that went far beyond the numbers registered on membership roles or in statistical percentages. Religious institutions offered an important form of community to Issei and Nisei alike, grounded in the very experiences that would give texture and shape to Japanese America.

Notes

1. Paul Spickard, *Japanese Americans: The Formation and Transformations of an Ethnic Group* (New York: Twayne, 1996), 54–56. More specific information on the Buddhism practiced by Japanese Americans is covered later in this chapter.

2. Edward Strong, *Japanese in California* (Stanford, Calif.: Stanford University Press, 1933), 168–70. Strong's survey projected that 51.5 percent of the second generation were Christians and 39 percent Buddhist. Also, 3.5 percent Issei and 7.5 percent Nisei indicated no affiliation, while a total of 13.2 percent (7.6 percent Issei, 16.1 percent Nisei) did not answer the question on religious affiliation. Strong's figures applied to those fourteen years of age and older; U. S. Department of the Interior, War Relocation Authority (WRA), *The Evacuated People: A Quantitative Description* (Washington, D.C.: Government Printing Office [GPO], 1946), 79. The WRA study included all persons evacuated and so included Japanese Americans outside of California. The remaining 16.3 percent from the WRA survey consisted of no response and other religions like Tenri-Kyo (0.04 percent). There is also some question as to the accuracy of reporting for the WRA survey, as some internees felt that Christian affiliation might be a safer claim given the wartime hysteria against them, Japan, and things Japanese. Strong and a later, separate study by sociologist Dorothy Thomas (based on selected internment camps) analyzed religious affiliation along other axes beside nativity, such as the Hawaii population, Kibei population, rural/urban, and male/female. Dorothy S. Thomas with the assistance of Charles Kikuchi and Richard Nishimoto, *The Salvage* (Berkeley: University of California Press, 1952), 65–71.

3. The vast majority of Buddhists belonged to the Pure Land or Shin Buddhist sect, and, likewise, most Christians were Protestants. There were, of course, others in both traditions, such as Roman Catholics, adherents of other branches of Buddhism, as well as other religions, but this chapter limits the focus to Pure Land Buddhism and Protestant Christianity in California. For general background on religion and Japanese Americans, see Yuji Ichioka, *The Issei: The World of First Generation Japanese Immigrants, 1885–1924* (New York: Free Press, 1988); Tetsuden Kashima, *Buddhism in America* (Westport, Conn.: Greenwood, 1977); Ryo Munekata, ed., *Buddhist Churches of America, 75 Year History, 1899–1974* (Chicago: Nobart, 1974); Shigeo Kanda, "Recovering Cultural Symbols: A Case for Buddhism in the Japanese American Communities," *Journal of the American Academy of Religion* 44 (1978): 445–75; Charles S. Prebish and Kenneth K. Tanaka, eds., *The*

Faces of Buddhism in America (Berkeley: University of California, 1998); Brian Masaru Hayashi, *"For the Sake of Our Japanese Brethren": Assimilation, Nationalism and Protestantism among the Japanese of Los Angeles, 1895–1942* (Stanford, Calif.: Stanford University Press, 1995); Sumio Koga, ed., *A Centennial Legacy: History of the Japanese Christian Missions in North America, 1877–1977* (Chicago: Nobart, 1977); Ryo Yoshida, "A Socio-Historical Study of Racial/Ethnic Identity in the Inculturated Religious Expression of Japanese Christianity in San Francisco, 1877–1924" (unpublished Ph.D. diss., Graduate Theological Union, Berkeley, California, 1989).

4. Ichioka, *The Issei*, 16–19.

5. Spickard, *Japanese Americans*, 7–23.

6. Ichioka, *The Issei*, 3–5, 7–12.

7. Ichioka, *The Issei*, 4–6.

8. The major role of Jodo Shinshu Buddhism in Hawaii could have easily been the focus of the chapter; for more information on this subject, see Louise Hunter, *Buddhism in Hawaii* (Honolulu: University of Hawaii Press, 1971); Eileen H. Tamura, *Americanization, Acculturation, and Ethnic Identity: The Nisei Generation in Hawaii* (Urbana: University of Illinois Press, 1994), 203–10. Also of interest: Mark R. Mullins, "The Organizational Dilemmas of Ethnic Churches: A Case Study of Japanese Buddhism in Canada," *Sociological Analysis* 49 (1988): 217–33.

9. For background on Shin Buddhism in America, see Munekata, *Buddhist Churches of America*; Kashima, *Buddhism in America*; Kanda, "Recovering Cultural Symbols"; William C. Rust, "The Shin Sect of Buddhism in America: Its Antecedents, Beliefs, and Present Condition" (unpublished Ph.D. diss., University of Southern California, Los Angeles, California, 1951); Minimai Ratanamani, "History of Shin Buddhism in the United States" (master's thesis, College of the Pacific, Stockton, California, 1960); Donald Tuck, *Buddhist Churches of America*, (Lewiston, N.Y.: Edwin Mellen Press, 1987). For inclusive studies of Buddhism in the United States, see Emma McCloy Layman, *Buddhism in America* (Chicago: Nelson-Hall, 1976); Charles Prebish, *American Buddhism* (North Scituate, Mass.: Duxbury Press, 1979).

10. U.S. Department of the Interior, War Relocation Authority, Community Analysis Report, No. 9, "Buddhism in the United States," May 15, 1944, 3. A small number of European Americans adopted Buddhism. Thomas A. Tweed, *The American Encounter with Buddhism, 1844–1912* (Bloomington: Indiana University Press, 1992).

11. The North American Buddhist Mission was reorganized as the Buddhist Churches of America during World War II (1944) to formally cut ties with Japan. Kashima, *Buddhism in America*, 59–61.

12. Kosei Ogura, "A Sociological Study of the Buddhist Churches in North America with a Case Study of Gardena, California, Congregation" (unpublished master's thesis, University of Southern California, Los Angeles, 1932), 34–36, 85.

13. Isao Horinouchi, "Americanized Buddhism: A Sociological Analysis of a Protestantized Japanese Religion" (unpublished Ph.D. diss., University of California, David, 1973), 119; Robert F. Spencer, "Japanese Buddhism in the United States, 1940–46" (unpublished Ph.D. diss., University of California, Berkeley, 1946), 77–82.

14. Kashima, *Buddhism in America*, 23, 137–39. Ryo Munekata, interview, July 21, 1995, Los Angeles, California.

15. Horinouchi, "Americanized Buddhism," 115–16, 155, 187–88. He states that cost factors, as much as anything else, also entered decisions about architectural style; Kashima, *Buddhism in America*, 41; Spencer, "Japanese Buddhism in the United States," 57.

16. Kashima, *Buddhism in America*, 129; Horinouchi ("Americanized Buddhism") coins the term "Protestantization" in his study of Buddhism.

17. Frank E. Reynolds and Charles Hallisey, "Buddhist Religion, Culture, and Civilization," Tamaru Noriyoshi, "Buddhism in Japan," and Araki Michio, "The Schools of Japanese Buddhism," in *Buddhism and Asian History*, ed. Joseph M. Kitagawa and Mark H. Cummings (New York: Macmillan, 1987), 3–28; 159–74; 267–75.

18. Hajime Nakamura, "The Basic Teachings of Buddhism," in *Buddhism in the Modern World*, ed. Heinrich Dumoulin (New York: Macmillan, 1976), 3.

19. Noriyoshi, "Buddhism in Japan,"167–68; Michio, "Schools of Japanese Buddhism," 272–73; Nisji Utsuki, *The Shin Sect: A School of Mahyana Buddhism* (Kyoto, Japan: Publication Bureau of Buddhist Books, 1937), 1-15; Munekata, *Buddhist Churches of America*, 28–35; Tuck, *Buddhist Churches of America*, 202.

20. "Instructions to the Ministers of the Mission," North American Buddhist Mission, Annual Conference Minutes, 1927, reprinted in Rust, "Shin Sect of Buddhism in America," 344–47.

21. Ichioka, *The Issei*, ch. 7.

22. Fred Nitta, "The YBA Movement in America," manuscript history, 1966. Personal archives of Dr. Ryo Munekata, Los Angeles, California.

23. Valerie Matsumoto's work on the farming community of Cortez touches on the role of religious groups as a space for socialization; *Farming the Home Place* (Ithaca, N.Y.: Cornell University Press, 1993), 53–54, 77–86. Although conferences during the early years were technically single sex, it was quite common for either the YMBA or the YWBA to send members to the other's conferences.

24. *Bhratri* 2 (July 1932). This journal was published occasionally, and, hence, the volume numbers, page numbers, and other citation information varied from issue to issue. In every case, I have cited it as fully as possible; Nitta, "YBA Movement in America," 3, 19–21.

25. *Bhratri* 2 (July 1932); Nitta, "YBA Movement in America," 11–12.

26. *Bhratri* 2 (July 1934): 22.

27. *Sangha* (February 1941); this represents the extent of the citation information. Institute of Buddhist Studies Archives, Berkeley, California.

28. *Sangha* (February 1941).

29. This perspective, from my reading, runs throughout Tamura's 1994 monograph (*Americanization, Acculturation, and Ethnic Identity*). See p. 198 for an example.

30. On Americanization, see Edward Hartmann, *The Movement to Americanize the Immigrant* (New York: Columbia University Press, 1948); and for California, David Herman, "Neighbors on Golden Mountain: The Americanization of Immigrants in California and Public Instruction as an Agency of Ethnic Assimilation, 1850 to 1933" (unpublished Ph.D. diss., University of California, Berkeley, 1981).

31. Ichioka, *The Issei*, 16–28

32. William Bryant, ed., *The Church's One Hundred Years in the Japanese American Community* (San Francisco: Christ United Presbyterian Church, 1988), ii–23; Koga,

Centennial Legacy, 46–47, 62–97, 108–252; *Official Journal*, Pacific Japanese Mission of the Methodist Episcopal Church, 1924; *Official Journal*, Pacific Japanese Provisional Annual Conference Methodist Episcopal Church, 1940. The northern and southern branches of the Methodist Episcopal Church in the United States, which had split over the issue of slavery, reunited in 1939; Donald Fujiyoshi, "A Study of the Educational Program of the Church School of the Japanese Christian Church and Institute of Los Angeles" (master's thesis, University of Southern California, Los Angeles, 1942), 20.

33. Koga, *Centennial Legacy*, 36.

34. Hirochika Nakamaki, "The History of the Japanese Christian Churches and the Consciousness of Japanese Christians in Sacramento, California," in *Japanese Religions in California*, ed. Keiichi Yanagawa (Tokyo: Dept. of Religious Studies, University of Tokyo, 1983), 258–65.

35. Yoshida, "Socio-Historical Study of Racial/Ethnic Identity," 60–61, 152.

36. Yoshida, "Socio-Historical Study of Racial/Ethnic Identity," 60–61; Michael J. Kimura Angevine and Ryo Yoshida, "Contexts for a History of Asian American Presbyterian Churches: A Case Study of the Early History of Japanese American Presbyterian Churches" (unpublished paper, December 1989), 23–24, 27. I thank Rev. Angevine for giving me a copy of the paper.

37. Koga, *Centennial Legacy*, 37, 112–15.

38. Koga, *Centennial Legacy*, 37, 188–89.

39. Angevine and Yoshida, "Contexts for a History of Asian American Presbyterian Churches," 20.

40. Bryant, *Church's One Hundred Years*, 57–59; *Nichibei Shimbun*, May 13 and 16, 1933, and June 24, 1934.

41. "A Biographical Sketch of Reverend Suzunosuke Kato" (unpublished paper, n.d.); Program Guide/Conference Registration, Young People's Christian Conference, October 24–25, 1925. I thank Mr. Tadashi Fujita of Berkeley, California, for access to his private papers.

42. Tadashi Fujita, "Biography of Rev. Suzunosuke Kato" (unpublished paper, n.d.); Lester Suzuki, "The Significance of the NCYPCC" (unpublished paper), 2–5. I thank Rev. Lester Suzuki for copies of his work on Japanese American Christianity.

43. Suzuki, "Significance of the NCYPCC"; *Nichibei Shimbun*, November 3, 1927, February 16 and June 28, 1930, February 3 and March 14, 1932, and September 28, 1934. There is a discrepancy in the newspaper reports concerning the date of Morishita's marriage to the Rev. N. Oda, but it appears that the wedding took place on June 4, 1932.

44. Northern California YPCC Conference Program (1939), in private papers of Tadashi Fujita, Berkeley, California.

45. Michael Yoshii, "The Young People's Christian Conference: The Formation and Development of a Nisei Christian Youth Movement" (unpublished paper in possession of author), 19. Yoshii incorporates theologian Paul Tillich's concept of "vocational consciousness." I thank Rev. Yoshii for providing me a copy of his paper.

46. The literature on the incarceration of Japanese Americans is extensive. Two helpful works that provide an overview are Roger Daniels, Harry H. L. Kitano,

and Sandra Taylor, eds., *Japanese Americans: From Relocation to Redress* (Seattle: University of Washington Press, 1991); and Michi Weglyn, *Years of Infamy: The Untold Story of America's Concentration Camps* (New York: William Morrow, 1976).

47. Gary Y. Okihiro, "Religion and Resistance in America's Concentration Camps," *Phylon* 45 (1984): 220–33.

48. Sandra Taylor, "'Fellow-Feelers with the Afflicted': The Christian Churches and the Relocation of the Japanese During World War II," in *Japanese Americans: From Relocation to Redress*, ed. Roger Daniel (Seattle: University of Washington Press, 1991), 123–29.

49. Budd Fukei, *The Japanese American Story* (Minneapolis: Dillon Press, 1976), 133.

50. Japanese Evacuation and Resettlement Study (JERS), Bancroft Library, University of California, Berkeley, call no. 67/14c, Box H, Folder 3.51 (cited henceforth as JERS with box and folder nos.). In some cases, records required keeping the person's identity confidential. In those cases, I have used names in quotes and placed ** next to the box and folder information.

51. Daisuke Kitagawa, *Issei and Nisei* (New York: Seabury Press, 1967), 67–71; JERS, **R20. 86.

52. JERS, O2. 78.

53. JERS, K8. 58.

54. JERS, **B12. 35.

55. Information for this paragraph taken from Alfred Bloom, "Shin Buddhism in America: A Social Perspective," in *The Face of Buddhism in America*, ed. Charles S. Prebish and Kenneth K. Tanaka (Berkeley: University of California, 1998), 31–47.

56. Jane Iwamura's essay on Asian American religious identity offers insightful suggestions about how we might view the landscape in the past as well as the present. Jane Iwamura, "Homage to Ancestors: Exploring the Horizons of Asian American Religious Identity," *Amerasia Journal* 22 (1996): 162–67.

CHAPTER SIX

FILIPINO RELIGION AT HOME AND ABROAD: HISTORICAL ROOTS AND IMMIGRANT TRANSFORMATIONS

Steffi San Buenaventura

Introduction

In the first half of the twentieth century, more than two hundred thousand Filipinos migrated to the United States, mostly to Hawai`i and California. This earlier movement and the change in the 1965 immigration law have created an impressive one million-and-a-half Filipino American population base by 1990. Much has been written about aspects of Filipino immigration but there has been very little mention of the religious experience of Filipinos, both in historical and contemporary times. This historical piece on the study of Filipino religion is an initial contribution to growing body of Filipino American historiography and to an emerging collection of scholarly works in the field of Asian American religion.[1]

The first half of this chapter examines the roots and colonial legacy of Filipino spiritual beliefs against the cultural landscape of "home" in the Philippines, while the second half covers the history of Filipino immigrant religious experiences "abroad" in America. This integrated historical approach is important because these two dimensions are embodied in the story of Filipino immigration, not only in the early 1900s, when Filipinos left their native soil to explore American colonial boundaries overseas created by the U.S. acquisition of the Philippines, but also in the present transnational setting of the new century, in which Filipinos are active participants. Known for their strong religious beliefs, it can only be correctly assumed that, in their journey abroad, Filipinos have brought, and continue to bring, with them their religious traditions and spiritual practices.

Although predominantly Roman Catholic, the Filipino people are more diverse than is commonly acknowledged when it comes to faith and worship because of centuries of exposure to many forms of belief systems from contacts with other cultures in the home site. The dominance of Catholicism in the Philippine population has under-standably overshadowed the proportionately smaller number of these diverse faiths. However, all these religious experiences have flourished in a common cultural soil, nurtured by a Filipino indigenous belief system and enriched by the intersections of these different religious traditions with one another, over time. The Philippine Census of 1990 shows that out of 60 million Filipinos, 83 percent were Roman Catholics while 5.5 percent and 4.5 percent were Protestants and Muslims, respectively, and the remaining 6 to 7 percent identified themselves with the Philippine latter-day Christian religion, the *Iglesia ni Cristo*, and as Aglipayan, Buddhist, and "Born-Again Christians" (a new category in the 1990 Philippine Census).[2]

A fundamental set of beliefs that has permeated Filipino culture is folk religion, that is, the animistic belief system of the indigenous population before Islamic and Western contact and Christianization. Native religion found its place in Spanish Roman Catholicism and vice versa, and the syncretic product of this religious encounter has often been referred to as "folk Catholicism" or "folk Christianity" in the Philippine Studies literature. The concept has also been applied to the elaborate Catholic rituals and religious celebrations, added over time as part of popular worship, which many Filipinos have often chosen to embrace over the doctrinal directives of going to Mass every Sunday and approaching the clergy for the sacraments. This chapter begins with an overview of the intricacies of Filipino native beliefs and mystical practices outside, and as part, of the Christian religion in relation to Spanish colonial Catholicism; and in juxtaposition to twentieth-century American Protestantism and the historical events that had begun to shape Filipino nationalism and sense of peoplehood on the eve of U.S. colonization and of Filipino immigration to America.

Religion and Spirituality at Home

> Although the Spaniards were the conquerors and the Filipinos were the conquered, the meeting of these two cultures was not a one-sided process in which the Spaniards remade Filipino society into an exclusively Hispanic image. Much of the preconquest culture survived the conquest. . . .
>
> —John Leddy Phelan, *Hispanization of the Philippines: Spanish Aims and Filipino Responses, 1565–1700*

The Christianization of the Filipino people, from nearly four centuries of Spanish Catholicism followed by almost half a century of American

Protestant influence, has set them apart from the rest of their Southeast Asian neighbors. The religious traditions of their Southeast Asian neighbors have been rooted not only in the religions of Buddhism, Hinduism, and Islam, but also in indigenous animism and ancestral worship. Because of the historical development of the archipelago under Western dominance and the evolution of a common Christian identity that served to consolidate the Filipinos as a people, non-Filipino scholars and outside observers have often excluded the Filipino national experience from the common regional history of the non-Christian, generally "anti-Western" peoples of Southeast Asia.[3] Instead, they have linked Filipino identity to a long-established legacy of Westernization that came with the two continuous Philippine colonial experiences. "Spain brought the Philippines into the orbit of Western civilization from which they have not departed since the sixteenth century," writes John Leddy Phelan. "As a direct consequence of Spanish colonization, the Filipinos are unique for being the only Oriental people profoundly and consistently influenced by Occidental culture for the last four centuries."[4] By the time Protestant Christianity was formally introduced by American missionaries in 1898 and became an accepted religion by the predominantly Catholic population, the Filipinos had already become well known for their strong Christian legacy. When the Philippines obtained its independence in 1946, joining the emerging Third World independent nation states in the postwar era, it proudly proclaimed its status of being "the only Christian country in Asia"——a distinction of which the majority of Filipinos have been most proud.

Colonization and Conversion

Phelan argues that unlike the violent conquest-by-the-sword of Mexico and Peru, the Spanish colonization of the Philippine archipelago was primarily a conquest-by-the-cross, whereby Spanish missionaries "envisioned their work as a 'spiritual conquest' of the minds and hearts of the natives, a supplement to, and the ultimate justification for, the military conquest."[5] The Spanish missionaries, such as the Jesuit Pedro Chirino, described indigenous life at the point of initial contact in their chronicles.[6] They encountered inhabitants of the islands who were practitioners of animism who embraced both monotheistic and polytheistic ideas represented in a primary god (*bathala*) and a pantheon of godly spirits (*anito, diwata*) inhabiting the interconnected universe of nature, the earth, and the subterranean world. They worshipped their ancestors and believed in life after death and in a final resting place (*calualhatian*). The culture of the natives integrated both the sacred and the secular and included epic poems and songs about creation and "fabulous genealogies" recited in the oral tradition; purification rites and rituals for venerating the dead; and material offerings and prayers to the gods of the invisible world. Furthermore, a class of women priestesses and priests (*babailan, catalonan*) led the people in the rituals of worship and healing and in defending native practices.[7]

To eradicate the natives' "false belief in the divinity of their idols . . ." the missionaries injected vivid elements of Christian worship and capitalized on the native belief "in invisible spirits and in an after-life and in demons, enemies of men, of whom they are very much afraid because of the terrors and misfortunes they have always received from these evil spirits—so much so that one of us, by means of a *well-painted picture of hell*, has converted a very great number of them [emphasis added]."[8] Toward the end of the sixteenth century, after fifty years of vigorous missionary work, Chirino reported on the state of native conversion and relationship with the missionaries in this light:

> I am moved to devotion when I see men like savages come down from the mountains and ask for Baptism on bended knees, and children like angels many of them already knowing their prayers though I know not who has taught them. . . . There was so great a hunger and longing to hear the things of God and to learn the doctrine all night long they never ceased, now one group and now another, to sing and pay homage to God in their own homes.
>
> And they soon began to be baptized, and to assist the Spaniards, and to deal with our men with so much intimacy and confidence that they came to crave the honor of making us kindred by marriage and of serving us by means of their lands and industry.[9]

Despite their one-sided view, these chronicles have been invaluable in building the primary foundation by which knowledge of pre-Hispanic Filipino society has been acquired and its history reconstructed by today's scholars. However, Philippine historian William Henry Scott refers to these "official documents of the Spanish colonial regime," as "parchment curtain" (as in "iron curtain") in that they represent a "state control of information . . . prevent[ing] the modern Filipino from forming a clear picture of his ancestors' conditions." He also points to sources that indicate that vast areas of the archipelago were still untouched by the process of Christianization in the late seventeenth century and that there were numerous "unconverted Filipinos" in Spanish-controlled provinces in the late 1800s.[10] There was, of course, the perennial shortage of priests to minister to millions of natives in remote communities, which experienced only occasional and rare clerical visits.

Dual Process of Conversion

The Christianization of the Philippines, particularly in the first two centuries of its consolidation, does not represent a simple "evolutionary progression" of the history of Hispanic rule as Phelan and other historians may have suggested, argues Vicente L. Rafael. After all, evangelization had to have occurred in the arena of language and linguistic transmission and needed to have been filtered through the language of the ruler and the ruled in the process of translation—whether written or oral, in both the giving and receiving of the Christian message. Rafael emphasizes this "double process at work" by examining sources written in the vernacular (in this case, Tagalog) that encompassed the substance and strategy of conversion, revealing a differing world of meaning and intent between the Spaniards and the natives.

> Translation, by making conceivable the transfer of meaning and intention between colonizer and colonized, laid the basis for articulating the general outlines of subjugation prescribed by conversion; but it also resulted in the ineluctable separation between the original message of Christianity (which was itself about the proper nature of origins as such) and its rhetorical formulation in the vernacular. For in setting languages in motion, translation tended to cast intentions adrift, now laying, now subverting the ideological grounds of colonial hegemony.[11]

Regardless of how Filipino Christianization is extracted and critiqued, an established consensus among scholars is the reciprocal nature of religious conversion.[12] The spiritual capture of the native population would not have proceeded as it did had it not been for the general openness with which the people received the new faith, Phelan contends. With religion very much ingrained in their way of life, the natives took an active role in the reformulation and interpretation of the new spiritual order, thus denoting a conversion process that was far more complex than a simple procedure of the removal and replacement of faith.

The coming of Christianity to the islands was preceded by the Muslim conversion of the native tribes in the southern region of the archipelago that had started two centuries earlier. The Muslim conversion is revealing of how the inhabitants embraced a major religion earlier without relinquishing their traditional beliefs. Arab traders first introduced Islam in the mid-fourteenth century from the south, through Borneo to Sulu, and the southern coast of Mindanao. It also reached the western coasts and found its way along a few scattered areas all the way to Luzon, to the north. It would have spread to the rest of archipelago had it not been preempted by Spanish colonization.

In studies of Muslim and tribal groups at the beginning of the American administration in the Philippines, Najeeb M. Saleeby observed that "the daily life of the common people is dominated by innumerable superstitions and beliefs which are foreign to the Islamic creed . . . [having] kept the religion of their pagan fathers and the bulk of the superstitions of their primitive forefathers and what they have now is not pure Islamism, but the aggregate of past and present creeds." Before Muslim conversion their "form of heathenism [was] very similar to that of the coast-pagans of the Bisaya [Visayan] Islands . . . and is the same religion that the ancient Tagalogs had."[13] Nevertheless, Philippine Islamic historian Cesar A. Majul insists that this in no way makes Islam "syncretic" but that Muslim Filipinos have taken preserved precontact beliefs to be a part of their Islamic religion. "Much in the pre-Islamic belief system and customary law (adat) which was indigenous to Malay peoples in general, and to the people of Mindanao and Sulu in particular, was simply carried into the new and friendly faith to which they gave their allegiance," adds Peter G. Gowing.[14]

Folk Christianity

The planting of Roman Catholicism on missionary soil, half a globe away from the center of Spanish Christendom, marked the growth of a Western religion that flourished over three centuries among the succeeding generations of the vast majority of the Philippine population. However, it did not necessarily replace a native belief system that easily absorbed elements of Christianity with indigenous mysticism. The inclusion and integration of some of the very fundamental elements of native spirituality in the cultivation of the Western religion in the archipelago were immediately apparent to the early American colonial scholars who were quick to make note of it. For example, James Alexander Robertson remarks that "the readiness with which the early Filipinos embraced the Faith does not mean that the old forms and beliefs were discarded in their entirety, nor that they have yet altogether disappeared."[15] Phelan characterizes this phenomenon of Filipino conversion as the "Philippinization of Catholicism": "As it was, there were virtually two religions. One was the Catholicism of the Spanish clergy and the Spanish colonists, and the other was the folk Catholicism of the Filipinos, a cleavage which was sharply delineated along racist and linguistic lines."[16]

The concept of "folk Catholicism" has been interjected in a number of ways in contemporary Philippine scholarship.[17] Jesuit social scientists, in particular, have been concerned with reconciling the faith and culture of Philippine Catholicism and the "double standard" by which Filipinos observe the teachings of the Church but freely supplement their "official" faith with cultural celebrations and social usages contributed and validated by various communities. Some of these observances are the penitential devotions during Lent and the rich religious and cultural celebrations of year-round *fiestas*, including elaborate town processions during the feasts of saints and the Virgin Mary. Assuming a Hispanized (i.e., Catholic) Philippine society, Frank Lynch attributes most of these traditional observations to "Spanish folk origin . . . [which] have received local elaboration and embellishment" as part of the development of the popular Christian culture of the society.[18] Or, presented from the perspective of a psychologist, Jaime Bulatao suggests:

> Perhaps the co-existence of the Catholic religion together with the old traditional beliefs in spirits and *herbolarios* [practioners of folk medicine] is itself another manifestation of the "split-level" [Christianity] phenomenon, with the difference that the Catholic religion, by prescription in the course of time, has itself obtained a somewhat stronger hold on the Filipino psyche. Nevertheless, in large part its doctrines still remain an abstract conceptual scheme unassimilated into the living dynamics of the culture.[19]

Protestantism did not escape the broader implications of "folk Christianity" either, seeing that "folk Protestantism" also exists and "is identifiable in some parts of the country. . . ," write Douglas J. Elwood and Patricia Ling Magdamo. "It should not be assumed . . . that this fusion is limited to Catholicism . . . [for] many [Filipino] Protestants believe in spirits and magic."[20] Similarly, in an Ilocano municipality in northern Luzon, Raul Pertierra recounts that during healing rites, "the invocation is addressed to the ancestors and any spirits that may have caused the patient harm" accompanied by a "short Catholic prayer, like the Hail Mary or, in the case of Protestants, a biblical passage."[21]

Furthermore, folk Christianity—Catholic and Protestant—has been a convenient conduit that has allowed many Filipinos to cross the institutional boundaries between the two Christian religions, if not because of dogma, certainly for cultural reasons. An anthropological study of a rural community in the central region of the Philippines conducted in the 1960s by F. Landa Jocano provides a microcosmic representation of the intersecting dimensions of folk Catholicism and folk Protestantism. In "the patterning of Christian experience in Malitbog [a pseudonym]," Jocano observes that "many Roman Catholics who joined the Protestant group later re-embraced Roman Catholicism, because the latter is apparently more in keeping with the structure and content of Malitbog culture than the former" and contains religious elements more suited to "traditional ways of believing and thinking." In the case of Protestantism, "most people . . . are not quite prepared to intellectualize the philosophy of Christianity as embodied in the Bible."[22] Or, as Pertiera observes in an Ilocano community, Protestant folks fulfill ancestral obligations in a similar fashion as their Catholic counterparts in the spirit of kinship. Both "educated and conventionally devout Catholics and Protestants resort to the non-Christian tradition when the need arises" without any feeling of moral transgression.[23]

Popular Religion

There is, however, another dimension of Philippine religion that is grounded in the historical legacy of nativistic movements, which abounded in the Philippine landscape since early colonial encounters and which continues to occupy a distinct traditional presence in present-day society. Native religion (embodying precontact beliefs whether in its "pure" or syncretic state) flourished separately from and in opposition to Catholicism in many ways, enkindling religious groups and movements that remained primarily nativistic in nature while at the same time maintaining a millenarian and folk Christian character.[24] Today, these movements continue to represent a diverse range of categories, all the way from obscure religious groups to long-established organizations, from the countless *Rizalista* cults that revolve around the national hero, Jose Rizal, to the groups that have incorporated as religious organizations.[25]

The phenomenon that has received much attention in recent decades has been the renowned tradition of the Mount Banahaw religious groups, set in the midst of the spiritual atmosphere of a mystical mountain that has nurtured native religion over the centuries and has attracted throngs of rural and urban pilgrims on the trek to spiritual discovery. Once viewed by mainstream society and the clergy as "fatalistic, superstitious, fanatical and dehumanizing," the Banahaw movements have now become an acceptable symbol of Philippine popular religion and have become situated in the context of Pope Paul VI's 1975 encyclical, *Evangelii Nuntiandi,* on popular piety. Jesuit theologian Vitaliano R. Gorospe cites the pope as saying: "We wish to speak about what today is often called popular religiosity. One finds among the people particular expressions of the search for God and for faith, . . . these expressions were for a long time regarded as less pure and were sometimes despised, but today they are almost everywhere being rediscovered."

Once a critic of the Banahaw "cults," Gorospe does not now advocate others to believe in Banahaw and its religious beliefs. His overall message is that "[i]n Banahaw live the simple, marginalized Filipino life, illumined by faiths at once familiar and strange. Learn from them."

Vicente Marasigan, another Jesuit theologian, elaborates on the phenomenon of "Banahaw religiosity" through an experiential immersion in the barrio of Kinabuhayan ("life source") in Mt. Banahaw by living among the members of the religious community of *Tatlong Persona Solo Dios* ("Three Persons in One God") and also translating a ninety-page rough typescript document (written by twelve elders who performed this task guided by the Voice) on the life of their mystic father and teacher, Agapito Illustrisimo. Marasigan writes:

> This present study is an attempt to share with the readers the intellectual, or more accurately, the epistemic, conversion that I personally underwent. I have learned not only to revitalize the meanings and values from my Western education, but also to respect the indigenous meanings and values revealed in the symbols of popular piety. I hope this sharing will contribute to a self-correcting process of communal understanding, communal judgement and communal decision about the people's search for God and the faith.[26]

Past religiopolitical and military suppression of these movements did not erase their presence in the consciousness and life of a population that generated and nurtured them in the first place. Oral tradition and folkloric narratives validate their enduring influence on the culture as older generations today still recount the stories of their elders about the latter's first-hand involvement in these movements in an earlier time;[27] and instead of portraying them as fanatical, contemporary writings now celebrate these socioreligious movements as native articulations of empowerment.

Religion and Nationalism

Historians have traced the formation of these movements as having "formally" begun with the religious uprising of the *Cofradia de San Jose* led by Apolinario de la Cruz in 1840 in the Tagalog province of Tayabas (now Quezon). This and the subsequent religious movements bearing similar character became a historical landmark of a changing Philippine society in the nineteenth century and have been popularly referred to as *colorum*. This generic term derived from the name of the Cofradia group which reemerged, decades after the Spanish authorities executed de la Cruz in 1841, proclaiming the sainthood of de la Cruz. Historian David R. Sturtevant presents these popular movements as having formed the core of the peasant revolts that erupted during the latter part of the nineteenth century and the agrarian uprisings of the early twentieth: "Few if any movements between 1840 and 1930 were organized around purely economic symbols. Few if any, furthermore, made the redistribution of land a basic objective. If a connecting link or common theme existed in the outbreaks, it was a religious or supernatural element." He considers these revitalization movements as a response to the "cultural tensions" in the society in the "complex clash" between "customary and modern tendencies" as agrarian economic conditions began to change while traditional values remained entrenched.[28]

Reynaldo C. Ileto, on the other hand, takes the interpretation of these movements out of Sturtevant's application of Robert Redfield's "little and great tradition" paradigm and rejects the stereotypic assessment of this phenomenon by other scholars as "aberrations" vis-à-vis the structural balance in the society or as a simplistic carryover heritage from a "feudal and colonial past." He argues that "folk traditions . . . have latent meanings that can be revolutionary. This possibility emerges only by regarding popular movements not as aberrations, but occasions in which hidden or unarticulated features of society reveal themselves to the contemporary inquirer."[29] Extracting meaning and evidence from vernacular sources ("poems, songs, scattered autobiographies, confessions, prayers and folk sayings"), Ileto presents these popular movements as having drawn impelling inspiration from the revolutionary nature of the life and teachings of Christ as embodied in the *pasyon* (Passion of Christ) and imbibed in the consciousness of rural folks through the traditional Lenten readings (*pabasa*) of the *pasyon*: "The most provocative aspect of the pasyon text is the way it speaks about the appearance of a 'subversive' figure, Jesus Christ, who attracts mainly the lowly, common people (*taong bayan*), draws them away from their families and their relations of subservience to the maginoo [the privileged or wealthy], and forms a brotherhood (*catipunan*) that will proclaim a new era of mankind."[30] He argues that these popular movements speak of the generative power of rural folks, moved by some of their most fundamental cultural values and internalized Christian virtues consistent with the spirit of peasant protest against oppression and for liberation, which intensified the rising tide of nineteenth-century nationalism into a revolution for independence and beyond.

To the hispanized members of the educated elite (the *ilustrado* class) as epitomized by Rizal, the dramatic demonstration of the power of the religious orders and their racial contempt for the secular native clergy came in 1872 when three native priests—Jose Burgos, Mariano Gomez, and Jacinto Zamora—were falsely accused of having instigated a local mutiny and were publicly executed.[31] The impact of this historic moment paved the way for the *ilustrado* campaign for reforms conducted from Europe, the Propaganda Movement (1872–1892), which unintentionally paved the inevitable revolutionary path of the separation from Spain.

A Filipino National Church

With the revolution of 1896, a movement for the creation of a Filipino revolutionary church also surfaced, resulting in a schism from the Roman

Catholic Church and the establishment of the *Iglesia Filipina Independiente,* or the Philippine Independent Church, in 1902. Popularly referred to as the Aglipayan religion (after its religious head, Ilocano native priest Gregorio Aglipay) and an apostasy denigrated by Catholics, the movement added to the complex Philippine "religious situation" involving the still unresolved postrevolutionary issues regarding the disposition of Catholic Church properties (e.g., friar-owned lands) against the demands for their return to Filipino control.[32] The Independent Church seized parish churches, claiming that they were built out of native labor and resources in the first place and would now serve as places of worship for the millions of defecting Filipino Catholics. In 1906, the issue of church ownership was decided by the Philippine Supreme Court in favor of the Roman Catholic Church, after which Aglipayan support and membership declined tremendously, reportedly from a very high estimate figure of three to four million down to around a million and a half by 1918.[33]

The decline in the Philippine Independent Church's popularity and the question of its institutional and doctrinal integrity were affected by several fundamental issues. The first issue was that it did not have apostolic succession since Aglipay was not a duly consecrated Catholic bishop before he became the spiritual head of the Independent Church. Having kept their distance from Aglipay and his earlier attempt for apostolic validation, the American Protestant missionaries eventually saw the Philippine Independent Church as a "Philippine Reformation"—a "genuine people's movement," which "in effect . . . continued the ideological momentum of the revolution," according to Lewis Bliss Whittemore.[34] Over time, however, the revolutionary origins of the Independent Church and its inherent nationalism became increasingly counterproductive to its spiritual and material growth and irrelevant to the national public interest (but, understandably, not to a steadfast rural and heavily Ilocano following). Under the new leadership of the next generation of church leaders, the Independent Church reached out to the Philippine Episcopal Church for the training of its clergy and petitioned for official apostolic succession, which the U.S. Episcopal House of Bishops approved in November 1947.[35] In April 1948, three bishops of the Philippine Independent Church were consecrated in Manila by three Episcopalian bishops in the Anglican succession. The following statement was printed in the program commemorating the event:

> While the *Iglesia Filipina Independiente* will always cherish and maintain its independence and take pride in the record of its people in laying the foundation of national as well as ecclesiastical independence, it rejoices that in this service of Consecration the validity of its Orders is secured and very close cooperation with the Episcopal Church made possible. It

is expected that in the future, by action of the two Churches, a Concordat may be concluded between them authorizing inter-communion."[36]

In September 1961, "a Concordat of full communion" between the Philippine Independent Church and the Episcopal Church was established. It marked the inclusion in the Christian community of what began as a nationalist schismatic or reformation movement (depending on a Catholic or Protestant view), now "a young church . . . brought back into contact with historic Christianity."[37]

Catholic Interests and Protestant Gains

The earlier rhetoric and activism that accompanied Protestant advocacy of American acquisition of the Philippines were naturally alarming to the American Catholics, whose overall concern was the protection of Catholic interests and institutions in the archipelago from Protestant influence and the inevitable changes about to be introduced by the American regime.[38] Catholics and Protestants openly disputed issues based on religious ideology and institutional interests in the American media and in their respective press as part of the strategy to influence the diplomatic and political formulation of U.S. government policies in the Philippines. The Catholics, however, found themselves on the defensive lest their support of the Catholic interests during the Spanish–American War and criticisms of U.S. policies in the Philippines be interpreted as anti-American, unpatriotic, and dictated by Rome. A known Republican and supporter of President William McKinley, Archbishop John Ireland of St. Paul, Minnesota, declared in a press interview in March 1898 that "no true American Catholic will think of espousing the case of Spain against that of this country [just] because the former is a Catholic nation."[39]

American Catholics, especially those who embraced the Americanist position of Archbishop Ireland, also embraced the idea that the same principles of religious liberty that gave American Catholicism the right to co-exist with Protestantism and other religions in America—and to flourish, in spite of past anti-Catholic persecution—would serve to uphold the state and growth of Philippine Catholicism as well: "If Catholicism had prospered in the free society of the United States it should prosper in an American controlled Philippines."[40] Putting the Protestant issue aside, however, the Catholic Church in the Philippines was faced with a more immediate internal problem of a dysfunctional clergy. Constantly short of priests, the colony had always depended on the religious orders from Spain for the maintenance of missionary services. Now depleted as a result of deaths, imprisonment, retirement, and voluntary repatriation to Spain, the friar population of 1,012 in 1898 dipped to 246 by the end of 1903; and of the 825 Filipino priests in 1900, about 200 to 300 defected to the Independent Church. Twenty-five years later, the Philippine Catholic Church, headed by the American archbishop of Manila, Michael O'Doherty, was still addressing the issue of clerical shortage, this time juxtaposed against a competitive landscape that now included Protestant presence and institutions.[41]

The new order of things also included the "Americanization" of the Catholic Church in the Philippines, starting with the entry of new missionary priests and nuns from the United States and Europe who took over the Catholic schools and founded new ones. A Protestant missionary, Frank Laubach, referred to it as the "Catholic Counter-Reformation," citing, in particular, the impressive "pedigrees of the twenty [American Jesuit] priests who arrived in 1921" and the subsequent groups who were to form the new faculty of the Jesuit universities in the Philippines. Another Protestant missionary commented: "Protestants have forced a marked reform in the Roman Catholic Church. We have forced her to put in more energetic young priests, and they are beginning to make reforms."[42]

The coming of Protestantism ended the Roman Catholic monopoly on Christianity in the Philippines, but its goal of converting the Filipino Catholic population en masse did not exactly materialize. Most Filipinos chose to identify with the religious legacy of Spanish colonialism but, just the same, many welcomed the religion of the Americans for it represented religious choice and liberation from the ever powerful control of a state religion.[43] Among those who rejoiced in the coming of the Protestants were *ilustrados* such as Paulino and Nicolas Zamora, father and son, who traveled the path to Protestantism even before the Americans came. A nephew of Father Zamora, one of the three priests executed in 1872, the elder Paulino was exiled to a Spanish penal colony in the Mediterranean for obtaining a Bible, which he read in secret against the law. When he returned to the Philippines around late December 1898, "his son Nicolas joyfully told him of the new atmosphere of religious liberty in the islands and of the Protestant services that the Americans were holding in Manila . . ." and of the first Protestant service held on the Islands on August 28, 1898, by Chaplain George C. Stull, with the First Montana Volunteers and a member of the Methodist Montana Conference.[44]

The Zamoras were crucial role models and represented a modern breed of native religious leaders in the landscape of the new American religious order. Educated in the Spanish Jesuit institution in Manila, devoutly religious and eloquent in Spanish, English, and several native languages, Nicolas impressed Bishop James M. Thoburn—the first Episcopal representative of the Methodist Episcopal Church Missionary Society in charge of South Asia, who first visited the Philippines in 1899—and was ordained by Thoburn the following year as deacon in the Methodist Episcopal Church.[45] However, Zamora's case was the exception as most early Filipino Protestant converts began as much-needed translators and field assistants to the American missionaries and as "native workers" or "Filipino helpers" relegated to lower positions of leadership. The heavy percentage of "unordained preachers" and the slow progress of native participation at the higher levels of missionary work prompted Reverend Walter N. Roberts in 1907 to comment that "[t]here was very little of the feeling [among the Filipinos] that the movement is 'ours with God.' It was still a foreign movement, started in the Filipino community, under the care of [American] missionaries."[46] Even Zamora did not receive full acceptance among Church leaders who were critical of his work. The coup de grâce came in 1909, when he formed an independent native Methodist church, the *Iglesia Evangelica Metodista en las Islas Filipinas*, taking with him twelve hundred members of the Methodist Church and claiming three thousand more defections by 1910. "The demand for self-determination and proper recognition, which is like a rising tide in every country, came more rapidly in the Philippines than the missions could prepare themselves for it."[47] The case of Zamora and subsequent defections from other denominations led to the formation of a number of indigenous "Independent Protestant Churches" as well as to changes in Protestant Church policies encouraging self-supporting, indigenously run churches. "Philippine nationalism has affected the churches . . . almost wholly in terms of related issues of national independence and development of ecclesiastical self-direction. Religious support for the former has been expected by Filipino nationalists, while nationalists in turn have agitated for ecclesiastical independence and Filipino leadership (or "Filipinization") in the churches and related institutions."[48] Nevertheless, Protestantism had become an enduring legacy of American colonialism in the Philippines and its influence would greatly affect Filipino immigrant life in America.

Religion and Immigration

In the journey of the Filipinos to Hawai`i and the United States soon after American colonial rule was established in the Philippines, one can assume that, for a people with a strong tradition of beliefs, religion had to have had a special place in their sojourn to America and that, in crossing the vast ocean between two continents, the early Filipino immigrants brought with them not only their cultural heritage and language but the world of their native spirituality, both folk and Christian. The thousands who traversed the way to Hawai`i and America were not only Catholic and Protestant Filipinos, but believers and practitioners of nativist religion and also charismatic leaders in popular religious movements described earlier.[49] The contract laborers who pioneered the first decade of the mass movement to Hawai`i in 1910—following the initial recruitment attempt in 1906 by the Hawaiian Sugar Planters' Association (HSPA), which produced only fifteen workers—came from remote rural areas where folk religious belief systems permeated the lives of men, women, and children.

Among these early arrivals was a youth, Lorenzo de los Reyes, from the Tagalog province of Tayabas, the home region of Apolinario de la Cruz and the colorum movement.[50] As a child, Reyes was raised in the mystic tradition of Mt. Banahaw and left the Philippines for Hawai`i as a minor—after Halley's comet appeared in 1910—on a journey abroad in search of a mystical mission. After working in the Ewa plantation on O`ahu less than a year, he departed in 1911 for San Francisco where, some years later, he met a charismatic Filipino immigrant from the Visayan province of Cebu, Hilario Camino Moncado, who also came as recruited labor to Hawai`i in 1914 and who moved to California the next year. In 1925, under the leadership of Moncado, Reyes and eleven other charter members formed the foundation of a mutual aid association in Los Angeles, the Filipino Federation of America, which was designed as a "quasi-religious" fraternal organization directed at the thousands of mostly single and young male Filipinos arriving in California without women and families in the 1920s and the early part of the 1930s. However, the Federation was distinctively different from the rest of the Filipino associations with similar benevolent objectives because it required its members to abstain from the "vices" of gambling, drinking, smoking, and going to taxi-dance halls, which had become the stereotypic behavior attributed to all Filipinos during this time of heavy migration into California. This image of a "clean organization" and "moral Filipinos" appealed to white society at this time when Filipinos were perceived to be a "social threat" in California and on the West Coast. Thus, Moncado was able to solicit the support of key people in the Los Angeles white community, who primarily saw him and the Federation as a useful agency for controlling Filipino immigrant conduct.

The high visibility of Moncado's leadership was a clear contrast to the quiet personality and blurred profile of Reyes, who directed the spiritual development of the organization. While Moncado and Federation officers pursued the stated "material" objectives of the organization, such as lobbying for Philippine independence and reaching out in friendship to mainstream America, the soft-spoken and gentle-mannered Reyes supervised the voluntary initiation of incoming members, consisting of special prayers and fasting. He guided the more receptive individuals—many of whom had been exposed in their youth to Philippine native mysticism before coming to America—into forming the spiritual core of the Federation. Their beliefs began to embrace deep and fundamental elements of Filipino mysticism, at the center of which was the evolving "divine" persona they attributed to Moncado's charisma and "supranatural" prowess, as they could clearly deduce, beginning with his material accomplishments as the leader of the Federation and from many other "miraculous" circumstances. Taking inspiration from Moncado, they also integrated cultural elements culled from the popular movements that flourished in the California scene at that time—such as ideas from the New Thought "religion," Physical Culture, and "raw food" vegetarian diet—and were influenced by selected features of kabala and numerology and the Protestant practice of quoting passages from the Bible, all of which found their way into the religious "principles" of the Federation along with Filipino folk religious traditions and the belief that Moncado was a reincarnation of Christ through Jose Rizal.

The Filipino American communities in Hawai`i, and on the U.S. mainland condemned the Federation as a colorum organization and the "hocus-pocus" opportunistic machinations of Moncado, but hardly anyone was truly aware of Reyes's role in shaping the religious character of the movement. In 1930, Reyes and dedicated spiritual members moved to Hawai`i, and succeeded in attracting a solid following from the huge population of plantation laborers transplanted to an island setting similar to the Philippines. Two years later, accompanied by about two dozen spirituals and re-enforced by others who followed later, Reyes returned to the Philippines to oversee and expand the colonies already established in Mindanao by earlier Federation repatriates. This voyage home brought back a Filipino socioreligious movement from abroad—created out of immigrant native beliefs and practices in the first place and shaped by immigrant social and cultural experience in America—a collective religious experience that had come full circle, attracted a local following in the Philippines, and soon evolved as small, distinct religious sects in the home country.[51]

Filipino Protestant Evangelists in Hawai`i: Ygloria and Company

Reyes was among a 2,915-person cohort of contract laborers (*sakada*) that arrived in Hawai`i in 1910, the year that ushered in the mass movement of Filipino workers to the U.S. territory.[52] By the time the Filipinos came, however, other immigrant groups recruited by the HSPA had already become settled in a plantation system that also encouraged the Christianization of its labor force. Because of the Protestant origins of the sugar industry (started and controlled by the children of the original Boston missionary families that brought Christianity to the islands in 1820), the creation of ethnic missions within the Congregational and Methodist Churches was a natural step in inculcating Christian teachings and virtues to the "Asiatic" plantation workers and in instructing them in American democratic principles through the process of Americanization.[53] To them, it was also necessary to nurture the Christian religion among the converted workers so as to ensure the continued civilizing effect of Christianity on their outlook and conduct.

Upon the influx of Filipino immigration, the Congregational Hawaiian Board of Mission through the Hawaiian Evangelical Association (HEA) initiated its "Filipino work" and added a Filipino department to others established earlier—the Hawaiian, Portuguese, Chinese, and Japanese. For the same evangelical reasons, but also to prevent having a "Filipino social problem"—the large numbers of arrivals, being mostly single, young, male laborers with little or no schooling from the large peasant sector of Philippine society—the Protestant missionaries worked on the assumption that the Filipinos needed special Christian moral guidance.

The establishment of Protestant institutions in the Philippines at the turn of the century had started to bear fruit, even for the distant mission in Hawai`i, which automatically turned to Manila's Ellinwood Bible Institute in the search for a Filipino evangelist to minister to the *sakada* population. The communication that began in 1911 between Reverend William Brewster Oleson, head of the HEA Filipino department, and Reverend George Wright, director of Ellinwood, centered on only one candidate, Simon Ygloria, who was wholeheartedly endorsed by Wright. Impressed and convinced by Wright's absolute confidence in Ygloria (in spite of Oleson's initial concern about Ygloria's health), the HEA agreed that Ygloria "is the man we want and that he will do good work among his countrymen in Hawaii." On the night of February 8, 1913, Simon Ygloria "was ordained by the Presbytery of Manila to the Gospel Ministry." On February 11, he sailed for Hawai`i on the ship, *Shinyo Maru.*[54]

Oleson had made earlier arrangements with George F. Renton, manager of the Ewa plantation, one of O`ahu's oldest, to base Ygloria's work there where many Filipino workers were assigned. Ygloria was to receive $1,200 for the first year (with an increase later), with $600, plus expenses, to come from the Hawaiian Board of Mission and the rest of the salary was to be donated on a monthly basis from five other plantation managers. Oleson wrote each man the same message: "We believe the time is ripe for some earnest effort among the Filipinos now among us, and are sure that what may be done will inure to the advantage of the plantations in no small degree."[55]

In the field, Ygloria encountered Filipino Catholics who objected to his proselytizing. Ygloria wrote to Oleson:

> You know that all this people from the Philippines were born and trained in Catholic religion, especially the old folks which is so fanatic and idolatry, when they heard of the words "Protestante" which they hate, and many are afraid for their priest very often told them that this people [the Protestants] are Satanic and condemned by God. They toold [sic] not come near to them . . . that's why in the Philippines and over here now in Hawai`i, this old folks are the hardest than the young to full [pull] them out of their old belief . . . however, here in Ewa which is the center of my works, there are number of young men are interested in the Gospel of our Lord Jesus Christ, which is the ful [sic] Salvation for the souls.[56]

However, he also met some plantation workers who attended Protestant schools in the Philippines, such as six "boys" from the Iloilo [a Visayan province] Baptist School, who indicated that "they have already made the profession of faith in the Philippines, one Presbyterian among them." Ygloria also was quick to identify and nurture potential evangelists. In the Waialua plantation camp under his care, he met Rufo Agustin, who arrived in 1915 as a labor recruit with a wife and a baby and was a former preacher from the Visayan province of Capiz. Ygloria seized this opportunity and succeeded in having HEA hire Agustin as his assistant, at the same time helping Agustin's financial situation.

Ygloria was the "first [Protestant] missionary from the Philippines to any other country," claims Laubach, but there were other evangelists before Ygloria who came to Hawai`i as labor recruits rather than as hired church workers. Jose Alba was recruited from the province of Negros Occidental in the Visayas, and like Ygloria, he converted to Protestantism as an adult and was persuaded by Reverend Harry Henderson Steinmetz of the American Baptist Missionaries in the Philippines to go to Hawai`i to work among the *sakada* workers. Alba arrived in September 1910 with his wife and children and was assigned by HSPA to Kaua`i where his evangelical background came to the attention of the Board of Mission organization on the island. He was ordained in 1915 and became pastor of the Filipino church on Kaua`i and was later assigned to the Big Island.[57] Both the Congregational Church and the Methodist Mission were involved in promoting the Filipino mission and formed a comity to avoid overlap in evangelical jurisdiction.[58] The former continued to support Ygloria and Alba and also commissioned Flaviano Santa Ana from the Philippines in 1916 to preach at Olaa and Pahoa in the Big

Island. Santa Ana was then assigned on O`ahu, where he was ordained in 1932 and became the pastor of the Filipino Waipahu Evangelical Church, a position in which he served until 1950.

In 1917, Pedro F. Royola arrived on Maui as a missionary from the Philippines, was stationed at the Puunene plantation, and handled the Filipino work in Central Maui. By the time the HEA brought in another evangelist, Pedro Racelis, to work in Waialua in1921 (and later in Papaikou Congregation Church on the Big Island), Ygloria's health had deteriorated from the pioneering years of his ministry. He was confined to the Kula Sanitarium on Maui and died of tuberculosis on September 28, 1922, at the age of thirty-eight. "In Hawaii he worked against great odds trying to bring his countrymen to a higher standard of Christian character," wrote Laubach, who also reiterated the praise Hawai`i had given of Ygloria: "Although quiet and self-effacing to an extraordinary degree, Mr. Ygloria exerted a strong influence upon all those with whom he came in contact. He was everywhere recognized as a leader of the best type. . . . His influence was island-wide. Thus in many respects he was to Hawaii what Jose Rizal was and is to the Philippines."[59]

From Hawai`i to California

Hawai`i had become a different place by the time of Ygloria's death. For one thing, the Filipino ministers who arrived in the 1920s found themselves in the middle of the growing struggle for power between the HSPA and an increasingly militant labor movement, which was spearheaded by the plantation's largest (and an earlier) ethnic group, the Japanese, now matched by the growing Filipino labor activism under the leadership of Pablo Manlapit. Both groups joined forces in the 1920 islandwide strike, with the Filipinos receiving much attention in the Kauai "Filipino Strike" of 1924.

Just as the workers were confronted with having to support or oppose the strikes, the Filipino evangelists and church ministers were also placed in a dilemma of having had to take sides between the HSPA and organized labor. One strong-willed and progressive minister, Reverend Nicolas C. Dizon, for example, who was recruited earlier by the Methodist Church to work among the Filipinos on the plantation, disagreed with the HSPA labor policies, left the plantation, and instituted his own Filipino ministry in the city of Honolulu. He established a Reading Room, sold translated copies of the Bible in several major Filipino languages, as well as Ilocano, Tagalog, and Visayan dictionaries and other books for improving people's lives, and published a diatribe against Moncado and the Federation.[60] However, most of the Filipino ministers supported the HSPA and had little or no choice in the matter because their ministry and livelihood were subsidized by the HSPA and the Protestant Mission. It was, therefore, not uncommon in those days for workers opposed to plantation management to accuse some of these ministers as having been hired by the HSPA to spy on the labor-organizing activities on the plantations. The labor disputes also made it difficult for a minister to intercede for clemency, as Reverend Mauricio Valera had done on behalf of Filipino workers arrested "for causing trouble" and who, like Pascuale Cabico at Ewa Plantation, were consequently evicted from their plantation homes. Valera's action angered Renton, the plantation manager, and thus, even ministers were themselves subject to HSPA suspicion and surveillance.[61]

Discouraged by the labor unrest in the islands, many Filipinos left in sizeable numbers, beginning around 1923, to escape the strike situation and look for work and new opportunities in California and on the West Coast. As the California State Department of Industrial Relations 1930 report on Filipino immigration to California indicates, there were 31,092 Filipinos admitted to the state between 1920 to 1929, a majority of whom (including hundreds of women, particularly in the earlier years) came from Hawai`i. Many of them headed for the "Little Manila" area of Stockton, where they joined many others arriving directly from the Philippines. The Filipino expatriate colony had gained notoriety for its frontier-like atmosphere, where the lifestyles of thousands of the majority of Filipino "bachelors" were projected against the backdrop of vices.[62] Yet, like the plantation community in Hawai`i, the men, and the small population of women, children, and a core of families in Stockton, all struggled individually and collectively to dignify their experience and attain a decent life in America through mutual help and, for others, by being active Christians.

"In the early years, there was no Catholic project among the Filipinos in Stockton. Fortunately, a few brave dedicated Protestants saw the need for a Mission to reach out to the spiritual and physical needs of the Filipinos," recalls Reverend Sebastian N. Inosanto. Dr. Henry C. Peterson, a physician and former president of the Stockton Board of Education, and his wife established the Lighthouse Mission at 131 Lafayette Street, in the heart of downtown Little Manila. "In this Mission a big hall was used for religious services, and the basement was converted into a dormitory to house the students and single men from farms. During the depression years this couple labored among the Filipinos, helping them in any way possible. They had a kitchen in the basement of the Lighthouse Mission where they fed the hungry and gave them shelter for the night."[63]

From this mission evolved a congregation of regular Filipino worshippers and it led to the establishment of the Filipino Christian Fellowship in 1931 by Reverend Vicente Zambra. Zambra was affiliated with the Presbyterian Silliman University in the Philippines before coming to

Stockton in 1925 (with Inosanto) and underwent religious training at San Anselmo Seminary in San Francisco, where he obtained a bachelor's degree in theology. With the financial support from the Presbyterian, Methodist, and Baptist Churches, the fellowship was able to acquire a piece of property at 341 South Hunter Street and "continued its work under the banner 'United Filipino Church' . . . started under the ministry of Reverend Pablo Estrera from Watsonville." Estrera replaced Zambra, who had been transferred to Sacramento.

On October 30, 1942, thirty members organized the Trinity Presbyterian Church in which Inosanto and Vicente Acoba were ordained Elders. Members of Trinity moved to its present site on West Eighth Street in 1957. Inosanto wrote in 1974 that the members agonized over the name of the new church:

> Great names such as Lighthouse Mission, Filipino Christian Fellowship and United Filipino Church of Christ presented themselves. The Filipino Presbyterian Church of Stockton was almost adopted, but that name gave way to the non-racial name, Trinity Presbyterian Church. Though the church was primarily commissioned to work among Filipinos, it must operate with open doors to all peoples on God's earth. So today Trinity is a church of many nations. The church has a Navajo woman, several Spanish Americans, Mexicans, Anglos, and Negroes. There are also some Portuguese in the membership.[64]

Charter members Angelina Bantillo Magdael and Leticia Bantillo Perez recounted this dilemma (in 1993) and were also quick to add Koreans to the list of multiracial membership.[65]

A Christian Fellowship in Los Angeles

Much of the initiative for the evangelization of Filipinos in the early days of immigration to the mainland came from American Protestants with former ties to the Philippines, either as former missionaries (e.g., evangelical, medical) and residents, or civil servants in the colonial government. Christian outreach—through Bible studies, fellowships, and community socials—was also mobilized by local churches and organizations as they became increasingly concerned for the welfare and moral behavior of a growing population of Filipinos. In the big urban center of Los Angeles, for example, the work among Filipino working students and transient farmworkers came from religious and Christian service institutions, such as the Methodist–Episcopalian Church and the Goodwill Industries. There, the Filipino Christian Fellowship started as an organization of Christian Filipinos who pledged "loyalty to the ideals and aspirations of [the Philippines]" and "promise[d] to put into practice . . .

the principles and teachings of our Lord and Saviour, Jesus Christ," according to Severino F. Corpus. They also had the objectives of promoting "the moral, physical, and social well-being of the Filipinos in Southern California," and "be[ing] an active agency in the solution of their problems."[66] The organization grew out of the informal fellowship started by Disciples of Christ (DOC) missionary couple, Royal and Eve Dye, from a gathering of a small number of working students who met regularly for Bible class and social activities in the Dyes's back garden. In 1928, a Filipino evangelist from the Ilocos Norte province, Silvestre Morales, came as a member of the Philippine delegation to the World Sunday School Convention in Los Angeles. Through a written introduction from an American missionary in his home region, he met the Dyes, was persuaded to stay after the convention, and worked closely with Mrs. Dye to launch the Filipino Christian Fellowship. As the membership and its activities grew, the Fellowship was accommodated at the First Christian Church at Eleventh and Hope Streets.

> The First Christian Church was used only on Sunday mornings—for the Bible Class and the morning worship. The afternoon activities were held in the midst of a crowded "Filipino town" where pool halls, gambling dens, and other vices were rampant. On Weller Street in a small place between First and San Pedro Streets, the Filipino Christian Fellowship offered a new kind of entertainment. Band music, drama, native songs, devotional hymns, forum discussions, games, and educational lectures were the services rendered to everybody. The hall was filled to its capacity.[67]

Soon after, a "Filipino Center" affiliated with the Fellowship group was established—"a Christian Home for Filipinos, wherein they live under a Christian influence." It consisted of an apartment house and four bungalows at 718 West First Street, accommodating from forty to fifty men, and served as a home for the residents and a community center for Filipinos. Consequently,

> The numbers of adherents of the Filipino Christian Fellowship were growing by leaps and bounds; therefore in that dingy hall in the Majestic Hotel next to the Filipino Center, the Filipino Christian Church came into being. Mr. Silvestre Morales became the first minister. Instead of going to the First Christian Church, husbands, wives, and children and unmarried people thronged to Mr. Morales' church.[68]

In 1933, with the financial support of some generous DOC Protestants in southern California, such as Charles C. Chapman, the Filipino Christian Church was formally instituted. The fellowship organized more Bible classes, introduced the Christian Endeavor, affiliated with the national

Filipino Students' Christian Movement based in New York, and sponsored a number of clubs—Debating, Athletic, Drama, Choir, and the Jurisprudence Society. However, the fellowship could not sustain itself in a different post–World War II Filipino community, but the Filipino Christian Church survived and is still an active church today in the heart of Los Angeles's Filipino Town.

Catholic Centers and Clubs

The Catholic Church was certainly concerned about preserving and protecting the faith of Catholic Filipinos against the strong influence and powerful reach of the Protestants both in the Territory of Hawai`i and the U.S. mainland. However, there were no Filipino priests available to work among the growing Filipino immigrants, to begin with. Besides, the Catholic way of expecting the people to come to the church for Mass and formal devotions and to the parish priest for the sacraments was intimidating, to say the least, and not as immediately effective as the Protestant tradition of bringing Bible classes and fellowships right into people's homes. Furthermore, the Protestant orientation of the plantation management in Hawai`i and close working arrangement with the HEA worked to the disadvantage of the Catholic Church. One prominent member of the Filipino community in Honolulu remembers thinking that the Protestants had more privileges. Raised as a Catholic in the Philippines, he decided to convert to Protestantism in Hawai`i, furthered his education on the mainland, returned to the territory after World War II and became a successful businessman, converted back to Catholicism, and has been an active leader in the Filipino Catholic Club ever since.[69]

The Catholic Church began more active work among the Filipinos in the twenties, and could not avoid noting the presence of fifty thousand Filipinos in the territory by that time. Father Reginald Yzendoorn observes that the earlier immigrants, who were mostly bachelors, were "rather indifferent Catholics" and "did not create much of a problem in the first few years." He mentions that succeeding waves included "married couples and girls," that the "great majority of the Filipino Catholics . . . are poorly instructed in their religion," and "among those of the [Ilocano] tribe are many Aglipayans or as they call themselves, Independientes" and that, "from the beginning," the priests diligently visited their camps, "inviting them to the divine services, speaking to them in Spanish or in pidgin-English."[70] In Honolulu, the Catholic Church established "three small Filipino centers . . . to attract and instruct the children," starting with Iwelei's "modest Catholic Filipino Clubhouse" with a kindergarten, plus two other centers in Kalihi-kai and Liliha, which closed down for lack of funds.

Like the Protestants, the Catholic Church was concerned about the deterioration of the faith and morals of the young, heavily male, working population of Filipinos. In San Francisco, according to an earlier research by Jeffrey M. Burns, "Protestant missions, sponsored by such groups as the YMCA, attempted to assist the Filipinos, and raised fears in Catholic circles that the Filipino was being lost to the Protestants."[71] To counteract the influence of the Protestants, the Archdiocese established a Filipino Catholic Center in 1920, which consisted of a boarding house and recreation facilities where young Filipino men could live comfortably and congregate, away from the clutches of vice. Unfortunately, the center was not well managed and was too constricting to many of the Filipinos, some of whom preferred the freedom of the boarding house of a Filipino fraternal organization, the *Caballeros de Dimas Alang*.[72]

There was also the Church effort to assist Filipinos in Seattle, according to Burns:

> Ministry to the Filipinos began in the 1920s in Seattle, as Archbishop O'Dea was asked by the Archbishop of the Philippines to assist the growing Filipino community in his archdiocese. O'Dea placed the Filipinos under the care of the Maryknoll Fathers at Our Lady Queen of Martyrs, the Japanese national parish. Ministry to the Filipinos was assisted by the Young Ladies' Institute and the Knights of Columbus. By 1928 in Seattle, there was a Filipino study club, a Filipino Legion of Mary, and the Catholic Filipino Club (which flourished throughout the West Coast). In 1929, a small hall at the church was given to the Filipinos, which became the center for their monthly business meeting and social affairs. In the 1930s, they actively participated in the St. Vincent de Paul Society.[73]

Unfortunately, Filipinos also encountered the strong and overt discriminatory practices in white America's houses of worship—Catholic and Protestant—in different towns and cities. In Salinas in the early 1930s, for example, "Although a majority of the early Filipino arrivals were Catholics they were not readily accepted by Salinas Catholic churches," writes Edwin B. Almirol.[74] A seventy-eight-year-old retired farmworker he interviewed in the mid-1970s recalled that the Filipinos "were ushered into one corner in the last back pews . . . so we joined the Protestant church with the hope that we would be treated better." Another old immigrant added that "to be accepted then, we thought that being Protestant would help, but it did not really matter much. We were different and different was equated with inferiority. We were treated like dirt by the Americans, regardless of whether we professed to be Catholics or Protestants."

It is easy to understand why religion did not play a more pivotal role in the daily lives of Filipinos in America in the twenties and thirties, although many profited from the Protestant fellowships and Catholic clubs created especially for them. These were "segregated" from the mainstream congregation to begin with, but it was an arrangement that was mutually comfortable and convenient since many Filipinos also preferred to be among themselves.[75]

Postwar and Post-1965 Immigration

World War II caused a shift in the American perception of Filipinos as a brave and accomplished people loyal to America. This switch in attitude and certain changes in immigration laws, combined with the overall postwar circumstances in the forties and fifties, contributed to a different Filipino American community in contrast to the earlier decades of expatriates. Many became citizens, more women came, older men started to marry and raise late families, the small cohort of American-born second generation entered adulthood, and immigrants with professional background and students seeking graduate education started to come. In 1946, the Catholic Church had begun to recognize the presence of a permanent Filipino American population by designating St. Columban's Church in the Filipino town district of Los Angeles a national parish.[76] Valentin R. Aquino mentions the existence of "the Filipino Catholic Church" on Belmont and First Streets in 1952, a "church building . . . supported and maintained by [its] members. . . . Up to the present time there is no Filipino Catholic priest."[77]

The postwar immigrants themselves provided the strong incentive for the revitalization of Catholicism in an emerging ethnic community for, among the small influx of newcomers, especially the women and families, many were practicing Catholics; furthermore, some of those who came to study in the fifties were priests and nuns who were sent by their superiors for advanced degrees in education, theology, and canon law in Catholic universities. In the late forties, a Filipino priest, Osmundo Calip, came to the United States to study in Washington, D.C., met with Filipino groups across the country in his travels, and began to prod them into organizing Filipino Catholic clubs. On December 4, 1948, he went to Hawai`i where he was enthusiastically received by the majority of the Filipino population, especially those from his native Ilocos region. He organized the first Filipino Catholic Club in St. Theresa's parish on Kaua`i in 1949, followed by other parishes: "Father Calip's approach in his crusade was basic and simple but proved to be very effective. He stayed for several days or weeks at each parish he visited. He held masses and visited the homes of the Filipinos. By involving the community leaders, including the plantation managers, he held numerous community meetings. His sermons from the pulpits were centered on the people's return to spiritual life. But he also reminded them of their families in their motherland."[78]

The clubs were structured under the direction of the parish priest, followed by the creation of Island Councils from all the parish units, and centralized under the Diocesan Congress of Filipino Catholic Clubs, which held its first annual convention on Oahu in 1951. Father Calip returned to the Philippines that year and the Catholic Clubs continued to flourish, particularly as more "complete" Filipino families began to settle in Hawai`i, preceded in 1946 by the last mass labor migration of more than seven thousand men, women, and children from the Philippines. Moreover, the diocese began to recruit women religious orders from the Philippines—such as the Maryknoll Sisters' mission in the Philippines, and the native order of the Dominican Sisters of the Holy Rosary—to teach in the Catholic schools in Hawai`i.[79]

The passage of the Immigration and Nationality Act of 1965 brought large numbers of individuals and whole families to Hawai`i, where Filipino immigration under the "family reunification" category was most pronounced. The new immigration was starting to grow rapidly when Sister Grace Dorothy Lim of the Maryknoll Sisters arrived from the Philippines in 1969 to teach in the parochial schools in Honolulu. She immediately became involved with the immigrant apostolate, which eventually led to the founding of the Catholic Immigration Center in 1980, based at St. Theresa's Church on School Street. The center addressed the immediate needs of the new immigrants, who were mostly Filipinos, and recently arrived Chinese, Koreans, Vietnamese, and Pacific Islanders.

The absence of Filipino priests—at a time when conducting pastoral work among a growing population of newcomers was greatly needed—became an even more critical issue at this time. As early as 1938, "a visiting priest from Manila, Father Ignacio Cordero, recommended that a Filipino priest be assigned to work in the Hawai`i community," an idea that was apparently brought to the attention of the archbishop of Manila. In 1980, Bert Mendoza, the lawyer-president of the Filipino Community of Los Angeles "wrote to Cardinal Timothy Manning asking why the Church had made no visible attempt to reach out to Filipinos, and why St. Columban's Church, the only Filipino Catholic Church in the whole United States, continued to be under a non-Filipino priest when there already were a number of Filipinos priests in the area."[80] In Hawai`i, with only a few local-born Filipino clergy among tens of thousands of predominantly Ilocano immigrants, it became crucial to have Filipino priests in the ethnic ministry who spoke the language of the immigrants—an issue which Sister Grace began to address in 1974. Since then, fourteen Ilocano-speaking priests from the Philippines have served under the sponsorship of the Church and the Filipino Catholic community.[81] In the late eighties, the

Bishop of Hawai`i created an office of Filipino Ministry, appointing Sister Grace as Director and Vicar for Ethnic Ministries in the Roman Catholic Church in the state of Hawai`i.

Protestant Churches, Popular Religion

Protestant missionary work among the early Filipino immigrants produced impressive results to the benefit of the community. In Hawai`i, for instance, an impressively large number of the leaders in the Filipino community (before the influx of the post-1965 immigration) had been second-generation (local-born) Protestant Filipinos, who were raised on the plantation and were members of the old Filipino plantation churches. On the other hand, the Filipino Methodist mission in Honolulu merged with the Congregational Filipino mission and became the Filipino United Church outside of the plantation. In 1953, it officially became the Aldersgate United Methodist Church located to the present day in the heart of Honolulu's multiethnic immigrant community, and it has been a church community in which many urban Filipino "old-timers" and "newcomers" have congregated.

The Philippine Independent Church also played a visible role among Hawai`i's largely Ilocano population, many of whom were Independientes or followers of the Aglipayan church in the Philippines. In communion with the Episcopal Church since 1948, the Independent Church was invited by Bishop Harry S. Kennedy of the Hawai`i Episcopal Diocese in 1955 during an Episcopal general convention to send a Filipino priest to the islands. On August 12, 1959, Reverend Canon Timoteo Quintero arrived in Honolulu, and on August 30, he held his first Ilocano service in St. Paul's Church (officially, the St. Andrew's Parke Chapel) beside the St. Andrew's Episcopal Cathedral in downtown Honolulu, marking the establishment of the Philippine Independent Church in Hawai`i. Father Quintero served as pastor for thirty-eight years and saw the church grow from the thirty-six attendees during his first service in 1959 to a congregation of about six hundred active members and several hundred adherents in 1997, the year he retired. In 1969, Father Quintero transferred from the Independent Church to the Episcopal Church but continued to serve the Filipino congregation at St. Paul's.[82]

On the U.S. mainland, the United Methodist Church initiated the formation of various Asian ethnic caucuses, which articulated the need for more churches. The work of Filipino caucuses of the Pacific and Southwest Annual Conference, for instance, provided "impetus to the formation of Filipino United Methodists churches in the United States," according to Artemio R. Guillermo, and the "[b]eneficiaries of this caucus movement were the old established ethnic churches and the embryonic ethnic fellowships that were already gestating in white churches."[83] Jenny

Espiritu, a fifth-generation Filipino American Methodist born of professional immigrant parents who came in the seventies, corroborates this pattern in her account of the Filipino United Methodist Church of the Inland Empire (FUMCIE), which began as an outreach program of the San Gabriel (California) United Methodist Church in September 1990 and became a recognized, chartered church of the United Methodist in 1993 after it moved to Riverside county. Whereas Espiritu's family attends a regular Methodist church, many Protestant Filipinos "are not comfortable with the fellowship presented by Anglo Protestant churches." And, although FUMCIE's Pastor Marcos foresees the church's multicultural growth because of "interracial marriages and children . . . [he believes] that FUMCIE will continue as long as Protestant Filipinos have a desire for fellowship among their Filipino brothers and sisters in faith."[84]

In contrast to the more established churches that sought to combine the experiences of the old with the new immigrants, the newcomers of the sixties started to bring new religious faiths from the Philippines as a "mission of migration." The *Iglesia ni Cristo* (INC)—a latter-day Philippine Christian religion with a mass following in the Philippines, founded in 1914 by Felix Manalo, a proclaimed "angel from the east"— was first introduced to the United States in 1968 by way of Hawai`i by his son-successor, Eraño. INC churches have since been established in thirty states and in fifty countries (outside of the Philippines and the United States) on different continents of the world, thus making this independent Philippine religion, known for its strong anti-Catholic position, an international church institution with a goal of universal membership. The INC under Eraño Manalo has a tight and centralized power base (as with his late father) in the Philippines, where all ministers of the church (including non-Filipinos) undergo rigid religious training according to INC rules and beliefs. The INC has a following of more than three million in the Philippines.[85]

Of immediate and direct concern to the Catholic Church and lay leaders of Filipino Catholic Ministries is the popularity of the *Banal na Pagaaral* (BNP, meaning Sacred or Holy Learning), a devotional group founded in the Philippines in 1968 and led by Remedios Carreon (now Remedios Rios Stuart and referred to as "Ate Salve" by her followers), who claims an "indwelling" of and possession by an ancient revered spirit "Mahal na Inkong," who personifies God. Translocated from Manila to California during the late eighties to early nineties and in its newly constructed headquarters in Ontario (Riverside County) in October 1996, BNP has attracted a strong following in the Philippines and among Filipino Catholics in the United States and elsewhere. The Church has banned the BNP essentially on the issue of "indwelling" and because BNP continues to claim that it is a devotional movement within the Catholic

Church and that its religious activities have been centered on Eucharistic vigils, prayer devotions to Our Lady of Fatima and other saints, and special weekend retreats (earlier held in Catholic parishes with the consent of the parish priest unaware of the Philippine Church's ban).[86]

A more recent group within the Catholic charismatic movement in the Philippines, *El Shaddai*, has also attracted mass followers at home, and migrating members have continued the movement overseas. Founded by a popular radio personality, Mike Velarde, *El Shaddai* was tolerated by the Philippine Catholic bishops until the movement's recent public position supporting the government's push for a constitutional amendment and other issues (e.g., the death penalty) that the Church opposes. In spite of the controversial status of the charismatic organization, Filipino Catholics in the United States and elsewhere, particularly among the Overseas Contract Workers (OCW) and especially those involved in the Church's charismatic movement, continue to identify with *El Shaddai* and observe its religious practices—from abroad.[87]

Filipino American Catholicism in the Nineties

In spite of an estimated million Filipino Catholics in the United States, "[t]he Filipino Catholic community has been one of the least recognized in the country" either because members are mistakenly regarded as Hispanic due to their surnames or because they are taken for granted since they communicate well in English and are then expected to adhere strictly to the "American style" of Catholicism.[88] For these reasons, many Filipino Catholics have stopped going to church or have sought other religious groups more welcoming of them and more relevant to their needs. The Catholic Church has responded to this problem by revitalizing its Ethnic Ministries (in lieu of the earlier American Church tradition of creating national parishes) and increasing its efforts to recruit, in this case, Filipino clergy and laypeople to these agencies,

Fortuitously, in a 1992 estimate, the new immigration also included close to seven hundred Filipino priests, most of whom acquired regular parish or diocesan assignments in the United States with their bishops' permission. Yet, many of them "would not be involved with Filipino apostolate but would be serving in American parishes or in hospital chaplaincies" while others had personal issues to deal with.[89] Father Arturo Balagat was among the new arrivals in 1991 who answered a call to work in the diocese of San Bernardino (southern California) in 1992, He has since been assigned as a parish priest in Corona, and currently, in Ontario (Riverside County), he is the director of Filipino Ministry for the Inland Empire comprised of the San Bernardino and Riverside Counties, where 29,312 Filipinos lived in 1990. He works closely with the head of the Diocesan Asian Pacific Islanders Ministry, Father Romy Seleccion. Seleccion is one of three

Filipino priests from the LaSalette religious order in the Philippines, which was contracted by the diocese to take charge of St. Christopher Parish in Moreno Valley, a multicultural community with a substantial concentration of Filipinos. Both priests—one secular, the other religious—exemplify the formal participation of Filipino priests in the U.S. Catholic Church's current efforts to attend to the pastoral needs of a growing population of immigrant and native-born Catholics, particularly in southern California, with its heavy concentration of Filipinos and other Asian American Catholics, such as the Vietnamese.

In New York, the Filipino Apostolate was established in 1995 as a program of the Intercultural Affairs of the Archdiocese with the appointment of Father Erno Diaz as the first archdiocesan director. In addition to its pastoral mandate, the Filipino Apostolate sponsors "an annual Filipino Liturgy at St. Patrick's Cathedral to foster unity and solidarity among Filipino Catholics in the archdiocese as well as to show Filipino presence and Philippine Catholic heritage." Since the late eighties and the early nineties, this heritage has become increasingly visible in churches with substantial Filipino parishioners who have introduced Philippine Catholic practices, particularly the *Simbang Gabi* (a novena of evening Mass ushering the coming of Christmas), popular Marian devotions, and a weekly or monthly celebration of a "Filipino Mass" (conducted wholly or partly in Tagalog or another Filipino language), accompanied by the singing of Philippine hymns by a "Filipino Choir."[90]

An example of the mobilization of Filipino Catholics in a national project with specific religious and cultural significance to Filipinos in the Philippines and now, to Filipino Americans, was the installation of the replica statue of Our Lady of Peace and Good Voyage, the "Virgin of Antipolo," in one of the alcoves in the crypt of the Basilica of the National Shrine of the Immaculate Conception in Washington, D.C.[91] It was a costly, four-year project that involved ecclesiastical approvals, mobilizing community support and resources both nationally in the United States and in the Philippines, raising at least $400,000, and coordinating a complex network of volunteer personnel and activities in the two countries. This transnational project culminated in the inauguration of the chapel in August 1997. The goal was to establish a Filipino Marian shrine and chapel in "America's Catholic Church," to include Filipino representation among the basilica's "numerous chapels which convey a remarkable story of faith, devotion, struggles and triumphs of the United States as a nation of immigrants" and which "also tell the story of the development of the Church in this country, of the many hard working men and women who, through much sacrifice, laid the foundation of their communities and ensured the promotion of Catholic faith in their new land." An appropriate choice, the Virgin of Antipolo (the original is in a national shrine in Antipolo, Rizal, just outside of

Manila) has been venerated for centuries by Filipinos as the patron of "Peace and Good Voyage," with specific reference to her legendary voyage on the Manila–Acapulco galleons.[92] Her installation in the National Shrine stands as a symbolic reminder of the celebration and blessing of the ongoing voyage of Filipinos abroad.

Conclusion

Filipino mass immigration overseas began as a colonial sojourn to Hawai`i and America at the beginning of the twentieth century. Today, it is a diasporic phenomenon that has expanded beyond the boundaries of the United States into transnational spaces connecting the home country with other places of destination as well. Although Filipinos have turned to other migratory locations, the United States continues to be a pivotal site because of its historical role in the movement abroad and due to the large Filipino American population that will stay strongly connected to the Philippine home community.

Knowledge of the early history of immigration of Filipinos to the United States has been limited to the narratives of the economic and social struggles of the pioneer sojourners and very little is revealed about the religious issues that affected their lives and survival abroad. On the other hand, the continuous flow of hundreds of thousands of "new immigrants" since the liberalization of immigration in 1965 has compelled major religious institutions to become involved with immigrant ministries in preserving the faith and maintaining the spiritual well-being of the newcomers. The Catholic Church, in particular, has become a very relevant agency of the new immigration because many of the recent arrivals are Catholics—not only Hispanics from the Western Hemisphere but also some Asian immigrant groups, such as Filipinos and Vietnamese. Because of the absence of statistics on religious affiliation, one can only assume that a great majority of 1.45 million Filipino Americans (according to the 1990 census) would identify themselves as Catholics, since a majority of the Filipinos in the United States is "foreign-born" from the Philippines. A limited set of statistics from the Office of Pastoral Research and Planning of the Archdiocese of New York shows Catholic adherents in the United States to be almost 54 million in the 174 dioceses within the nine census regions.[93] Once again, one can only assume that since the Filipinos comprise the only predominantly Catholic ethnic group among 10.5 million Asian Americans (they are also the second largest, next to the Chinese), the figures for the Asian Americans, especially those in diocesan areas where Filipinos and Asian American populations are concentrated (e g., Mid-Atlantic and Pacific regions have

1 million or more and 3.6 million Asian people, respectively), reflect Filipino American, albeit immigrant, Catholic presence.

Unlike the spiritual frontiers of the earlier decades of migration, today's new immigration is filled with the rich and diverse religious experiences of new arrivals as they enter already-established communities of faith and worship in the United States, which are welcoming of their "instant" participation. Many also come with an activist intent of introducing or continuing new doctrinal beliefs and devotional rituals such as first represented by the INC in the late sixties and exemplified by the more recent movements of BNP and *El Shaddai* in the nineties. Among the much newer participants in the transmovement of religious beliefs are the Christian Pentacostal churches which have found their way to the Philippines from the United States in recent decades but which are being replanted as branches of the Philippine churches by Filipinos moving to America. The Kingdom of Jesus Christ of Eagle Rock is one example. Founded in Davao City (in Mindanao), the close-knit, one-hundred-member southern California church was established in 1997 as a branch of a Philippine Pentacostal church, which "claims 100,000 active members worldwide and has a strong missionary focus."[94] Thus, today's Philippine religions are not only meant for Filipino religious practice at home but are intended for translocation to America and to other global destinations as well.

The contemporary religious practices of Filipino Americans, in general, reflect the diversity of faith in the home country and also the religious choices available to immigrants in American society. Thus, while the second-generation American-born Filipino youth generally choose to follow the religion of their immigrant families, many also exercise their religious freedom by choosing to embrace a different faith as part of growing up in America. Perhaps the degree of religious understanding on the part of immigrant parents is in keeping with the tolerance that Filipinos have traditionally exhibited toward the acceptance and practice of different religions, beginning with their native belief system.

Most Filipinos at home and abroad will continue to reflect the predominant influence of Catholicism, in particular, and the Christian faith, in general. However, many others will also persist in expressing the diversity of their spirituality, including folk Christianity and popular religion, regardless of institutional or "official" religious affiliation. Similarly, just as their ancestors had a rich legacy of religious choices and experiences, Filipino Americans today, whether immigrant or American-born, have before them similar opportunities for exercising religious options in a transnational and postcolonial world, in contrast to the restrictive boundaries once imposed on Filipinos by Christianity and colonialism. The narrative of the Filipino American religious experience is a new work in progress, an exciting story with a rich beginning, but one that is still evolving.

Notes

1. See David K. Yoo, ed. *Spiritual Homes: Religion and Asian Americans* (Honolulu: University of Hawaii Press, 1999), including my chapter, "Filipino Folk Spirituality and Immigration: From Mutual Aid to Religion." The first section of this chapter is discussed in detail in a forthcoming book, Steffi San Buenaventura, *"From Below and From Within": Nativism, Ethnicity, and Empowerment in a Filipino American Experience, 1925–1995.*

2. Republic of the Philippines, *1995 Philippine Yearbook* (Manila: National Economic and Development Authority, National Census and Statistic Office), 266 (statistics sheet provided by Alice Mak, librarian in charge of Philippine Studies/Southeast Asian collection at the University of Hawaii Hamilton Library). It is not known under which category the rising membership in popular Christian Pentecostal religion is included.

3. In the first edition of D. G. E. Hall's celebrated post–World War II book, *A History of South-East Asia* (London: St. Martin's, 1955), the Philippines was totally omitted in any of the chapters or subsections of the book, not even as a country listed in the subsection on "After the War, 1945–50." In the second edition (1964), the Philippines was finally acknowledged in three of the total forty-eight chapters.

4. John Leddy Phelan, *Hispanization of the Philippines: Spanish Aims and Filipino Responses, 1565–1700* (Madison: University of Wisconsin Press, 1959), 161.

5. Phelan, *Hispanization of the Philippines,* 11.

6. Pedro Chirino, *Relacion de las Islas Filipinas* (The Philippines in 1600), trans. Ramon Echevarria (Manila: Historical Conservation Society, 1969); some of the frequently cited works include "Relacion de las Islas Filipinas" (1582) by Miguel de Loarca, "Los Costumbres de los Tagalos" (ca. 1590) by Fray Juan de Plasencia, *Sucesos de las Islas Filipinas* (1609) by Antonio de Morga, *Labor Evangelica* (1626) by Francisco Colin; some were republished, edited, and/or translated in later periods, and others appeared in the original Spanish and English translation in Emma Helen Blair and James Alexander Robertson, *The Philippine Islands, 1493–1803,* 55 volumes (Cleveland: A. H. Clark, 1903–1909).

7. These religious revolts are discussed in the Blair and Robertson volumes and also in Nicolas Zafra, *Philippine History through Selected Sources* (Quezon City: Alemar-Phoenix Publishing House, 1967) and other Philippine history texts.

8. Chirino, *Relacion,* 297.

9. Chirino, *Relacion,* xii, 238.

10. William Henry Scott, *Cracks in the Parchment Curtain and Other Essays in Philippine History* (Quezon City: New Day, 1982), 1, 18.

11. Vicente Rafael, *Contracting Colonialism: Translation and Christian Conversion in Tagalog Society under Early Spanish Rule* (Durham, N.C.: Duke University Press, 1993), 4, 21.

12. This is also true of other cultures and societies.

13. Najeeb Saleeby, *The Origin of the Malayan Filipinos,* papers of the Philippine Academy, vol. I, part 1 (Manila: Philippine Academy, 1912), 10–11. See also Saleeby's earlier publications: *Studies in Moro History, Laws and Religion* (Manila: Bureau of Printing, 1905); *The History of Sulu* (Manila: Bureau of Printing, 1908).

14. Gowing, *Muslim Filipinos—Heritage and Horizon* (Quezon City: New Day, 1979), 26, 67. Cesar Majul's extensive and seminal works in this area include: *Muslims in the Philippines* (Quezon City: University of the Philippines Press, 1973) and "The Role of Islam in the History of the Filipino People," *Asian Studies* 4 (August 1966): 303–15. Contemporary anthropological studies of Muslim groups basically reiterate earlier scholarship about the religion of Moro Filipinos that is both Islamic and folk. See Eric S. Casino, "Ethnoecology of the Jama Mapun Islanders," in *Society, Culture and the Filipino*, ed. Mary R. Racelis (Metro Manila: Ateneo de Manila University Press, 1979) and his book, *The Jama Mapun: A Changing Samal Society in the Southern Philippines* (Quezon City: Ateneo de Manila University Press, 1976).

15. James Alexander Robertson, "Catholicism in the Philippines," *Catholic Historical Review* 3 (1918): 382–83.

16. Phelan, *Hispanization of the Philippines*, 88.

17. See, for example, Frank Lynch, SJ, "Organized Religion: Catholicism," in *Area Handbook on the Philippines*, Human Relations Area Files (Chicago: University of Chicago, 1956), 476–686; Jaime C. Bulatao, SJ, *Split-Level Christianity* (Quezon City: Ateneo de Manila University Press, 1966); and John J. Caroll, "Magic and Religion," in *Philippine Institutions*, ed. John J. Caroll. (Manila: Solidaridad, 1970), 40–74. In 1958, "a group of Roman Catholic and Protestant professionals" began to hold annual meetings in Baguio City (a mountain "resort" north of Manila) "to learn about the dynamics of cultural encounter" and "to explore ways by which their own cross-cultural experiences can be more fruitful." A selected compilation of the papers presented at the Baguio Religious Acculturation Conferences from 1958 to 1968 was published in *Acculturation in the Philippines: Essays on Changing Societies*, ed. Peter G. Gowing and William Henry Scott (Quezon City: New Day, 1971).

18. Frank Lynch, SJ, "Folk Catholicism in the Philippines," in *Society, Culture and the Filipino*, ed. Mary Racelis Hollinsteiner (Quezon City: Institute of Philippine Culture, Ateneo de Manila University, 1979), 125. Refer also to F. Landa Jocano, "Filipino Catholicism: A Case Study in Religious Change," *Asian Studies* 5 (1967): 42–64.

19. Jaime Bulatao, "Comments," in *Acculturation in the Philippines*, ed. Gowing and Scott, 74. Refer also to Jaime Bulatao, *Split-Level Christianity.*

20. Douglas Elwood and Patricia Ling Magdamo, *Christ in Philippine Context* (Quezon City: New Day, 1971), 18.

21. Raul Pertierra, *Religion, Politics, and Rationality in a Philippine Community* (Quezon City: Ateneo de Manila University Press, 1988), 126.

22. F. Landa Jocano, "Conversion and the Patterning of Christian Experience in Malitbog, Central Panay, Philippines," in *Acculturation in the Philippines*, ed. Gowing and Scott, 61–62, 71. Refer also to Jocano's *The Traditional World of Malitbog* (Quezon City: Community Development Research Council, University of the Philippines, 1969).

23. Pertierra, *Religion, Politics, and Rationality*, 138, 141.

24. Throughout centuries of Spanish rule, native dissent erupted in a sustained pattern in different localities in the archipelago in the form of minor and major rebellions against the imposition of excessive tributes, forced labor, land-grabbing

practices, and other abuses, and even as protest against the Christian faith itself. An abbreviated list of these rebellions is provided by Teodoro A. Agoncillo and Milagros C. Guerrero, *History of the Filipino People* (Quezon City: R. P. Garcia, 1973). Blair and Robertson document these movements, dispersed in the 55 volumes of *The Philippine Islands.*

25. For some selected references, see Propspero R. Covar, "Religious Leadership in the Iglesia ng Watawat ng Lahi," in *Filipino Religious Psychology,* ed. Leonardo N. Mercado (Tacloban City, Philippines: Divine Word University Publications, 1977), 109–26 and other articles in the volume. Some of these religious groups are considered "sects" and appear in Douglas J. Elwood, *Churches and Sects in the Philippines: A Descriptive Study of Contemporary Religious Group Movements* (Dumaguete City, Philippines: Silliman University, 1968). See also Douglas Elwood, "Varieties of Christianity in the Philippines," in *Studies in Philippine Church History,* ed. Gerald H. Anderson (Ithaca, N.Y.: Cornell University, 1969), 366–87.

26. Vitaliano Gorospe, *Banahaw: Conversations with a Pilgrim to the Power Mountain:* (Manila: Bookmark, Inc., 1992), 6, 60. Vicente Marasigan, *A Banahaw Guru: Symbolic Deeds of Agapito Illustrisimo* (Manila: Ateneo de Manila University Press, 1985), 2.

27. San Buenaventura, "Filipino Folk Spirituality and Immigration." in Yoo, ed., *Spiritual Homes.*

28. David Sturtevant, *Popular Uprisings in the Philippines, 1840–1940* (Ithaca, N.Y.: Cornell University Press, 1976).

29. Reynaldo Clemeña Ileto, *Popular Movements in the Philippines, 1840–1910* (Quezon City: Ateneo de Manila University Press, 1979), 13.

30. Ileto, *Pasyon and Revolution,* 21.

31. See John Schumacher, *The Propaganda Movement, 1880–1895* (Manila: Solidaridad, 1972) and *Revolutionary Clergy: The Filipino Clergy and the Nationalist Movement, 1850–1903* (Quezon City: Ateneo de Manila University Press, 1981); Cesar Adib Majul, "Anticlericalism during the Reform Movement and the Philippine Revolution," in *Studies in Philippine Church History,* ed. Anderson, 152–71.

32. The founder and brains behind the Philippine Independent Church was Isabelo de los Reyes, an Ilocano *ilustrado* nationalist and labor organizer who convinced Father Aglipay to be the ecclesiastical head of the Filipino church.

33. In *Religious Revolution in the Philippines,* 2d ed. (Quezon City: Ateneo de Manila University Press, 1961), Pedro S. Achutegui and Miguel A. Bernad used the 1903 and 1918 Philippine census to refute the Philippine Independent Church's claim of 4 million membership at the height of the movement, but they also suggest the other extreme estimate of the membership having been lower than 1 million; in vol. 1 of *Religious Revolution,* 222–27. Most scholars seem to settle for the 1.5 million figure.

34. Cited in Lewis Bliss Whittemore, *Struggle for Freedom: History of the Philippine Independent Church* (Greenwich, Conn.: Seabury, 1961), 180–81.

35. There were several attempts by individual associates to rescue Aglipay from apostasy but these failed. Aglipay, on the other hand, had contacted Bishop Brent of the Episcopal Church as well as the Old Catholics in Switzerland earlier in the schism in an attempt to begin to explore the issue of apostolic succession.

36. Whittemore, *Struggle for Freedom,* 180–81.

37. Richard L. Deats, *Nationalism and Christianity in the Philippines* (Dallas: Southern Methodist University Press, 1967), 85–87; Ramon A. Alipit, "The Position of the

Philippine Independent Church," *South East Asia Journal of Theology* 4 (July 1962): 32; William Henry Scott, "The Philippine Independent Church in History," *East and West Review* 28 (1962): 11.

38. For an extensive treatment of this subject, see Frank T. Reuter, *Catholic Influence on American Colonial Policies, 1898–1904* (Austin: University of Texas Press, 1967). For a thorough history of the American Protestants in the Philippines, refer to Kenton J. Clymer, *Protestant Missionaries in the Philippines: An Inquiry into the American Colonial Mentality* (Urbana: University of Illinois Press, 1986).

39. Cited by Reuter, *Catholic Influence on American Colonial Policies,* 8. Within the American Catholic hierarchy itself, there was disagreement as to the appropriate way to handle the Philippine situation: Some bishops took the "anti-imperialist" position but the majority embraced an Americanist policy in the acquisition of the Philippines. See also Thomas T. McAvoy, CSC, *A History of the Catholic Church in the United States* (Nortre Dame: University of Nortre Dame, 1969), 316.

40. Reuter, *Catholic Influence on American Colonial Policies,* 17.

41. Reuter, *Catholic Influence on American Colonial Policies*, 155. Achutegui and Bernad provide these estimates of Filipino clerical defection to the Independent Church from the figures drawn by James Robertson, James LeRoy, and Frank Laubach and come up with their very low estimate of less than one hundred in *Religious Revolution*, 228. Friar statistics are also mentioned in Laubach, *The People of the Philippines: Their Religious Progress and Preparation for Spiritual Leadership in the Far East* (New York: George H. Doran, 1925), 114; M. J. O'Doherty, "The Religious Situation in the Philippines," *Ecclesiastical Review* 74 (1926): 29–138.

42. Laubach, *People of the Philippines*, 450–54.

43. Only 124,575 of the Philippine population, for example, were listed as Protestants in the 1918 census (or 1.3 percent) out of 10 million people.

44. Richard L. Deats, "Nicolas Zamora: Religious Nationalist," in *Studies in Philippine Church History*, ed. Anderson, 327; Homer C. Stuntz, *The Philippines and the Far East* (Cincinnati: Jennings and Pye, 1904), 415. It is not clear exactly when Paulino was exiled from the Philippines; Deats mentions his return as having been after the Treaty of Paris (December 10).

45. Stuntz, *Philippines and the Far East*, 427. Like his father, Nicolas Zamora read the Bible in secret when this was forbidden during the Spanish regime. He considered becoming a priest but decided instead to take up law at the University of Santo Tomas but abandoned his studies to join the 1896 Revolution. With much immediacy, Bishop Thoburn secured the authority of the South Kansas Conference, then in session, for the official membership of Nicolas in that conference with a special motion for ordination.

46. Stuntz, *Philippines and the Far East,* 450–54; Roberts, *The Filipino Church* (Dayton, Ohio: Foreign Missionary Society, 1936), 40–41; Laubach, *People of the Philippines*, 336.

47. Laubach, *People of the Philippines*, 305.

48. Deats, *Nationalism and Christianity in the Philippines*, 6.

49. Including the famous Pedro Calosa who led the Tayug rebellion in Pangasinan province in the thirties. See Sturtevant's interview, *Popular Uprisings*, 269; also San Buenaventura, "Filipino Folk Spirituality and Immigration."

50. For the following discussion, refer to my articles: "Folk Spirituality and Immigration"; "The Master and the Federation: A Filipino-American Social Movement in California and Hawaii," *Social Process in Hawaii* 33 (1991): 169–93; and "Nativism and Ethnicity in a Filipino-American Experience" (unpublished Ph.D. diss., University of Hawaii at Manoa, 1990).

51. The Federation experience was historically specific to America and Hawai`i and could not have been transplanted in its original form—as a mutual aid and fraternal organization created partly out of Filipino immigrant needs—to the Philippines. Its spiritual component, however, had a natural place in the home country, such as what evolved from the spiritual colony that Reyes started. Out of the original group of repatriated Federation members evolved several sects: Equifrilibricum Iglesiarium (1945), Equifrilibricum World Religion (1956), Moncadian Sheepfold Equi Frili Bricumian Gospel (1958), Moncadian Church of the Philippines (1959), and Universal Religion of the Equifrilibricum Universum (1959) as listed in Douglas J. Elwood, *Church and Sects in the Philippines: A Descriptive Study of Contemporary Religious Group Movements* (Dumaguete City: Silliman University, 1968) as cited in "Nativism."

52. Between 1910 and 1934, and including the last cohort of recruits in 1946, about 150,000 Filipino contract laborers came to Hawaii via HSPA direct recruitment.

53. The materials in this section come primarily from my work in progress on "Filipino Protestant Evangelists: Spiritual Mission and Immigrant Labor in Hawai`i and California, 1912–1946," and my earlier paper, "American Protestantism, Filipino Evangelists and Immigrant *Sakada* Labor in Hawai`i, 1910–1946," presented at the annual meeting of the Organization of American Historians held in Chicago on March 28, 1996.

54. Wright to Oleson, October 19, 1912, response to Oleson's letter of September 10, 1912; HEA File. I am grateful to the Hawaiian Mission Children's Society and chief librarian, Marilyn L. Reppun, for the archival data on Ygloria and the early Filipino evangelists.

55. Oleson to Renton, April 22, November 13 and 19, 1912; Oleson to Andrew Adams, J. Gibb, G. Chalmers, W. W. Goodale, and E. K. Bull, November 13, 1912; Gibb to Oleson, November 15; Renton to Oleson, November 18, Bull to Oleson, November 20. HEA File: "Churches-Ewa."

56. The following information and quotations have come from Ygloria's letter to Oleson from Ewa, September 15, 1913. HEA File: "Ygloria."

57. My interview data on the Filipino Protestant evangelists have come from Rosalie Golez Alba Valera, "Nanay and Tatay" (unpublished manuscript, July 1982, Hilo, Big Island); interviews with Rosalie Valera and Lily Alba Alicuben, February 5, 1996 (Hilo). The children of Reverend Alba, Rosalie and Lily, have provided me with more extensive information about their father and the other Filipino ministers; and so has the son of Reverend Pedro Racelis, Pedro "Pete" Racelis Jr., in a series of conversations and an interview in July 1993 (Aiea, Oahu). Helen Nagtalon-Miller has also shared so much of her knowledge about the Protestant community life in Hawaii from her experiences growing up in an active Protestant family in Waipahu. See also *The Friend* (Honolulu), especially the October 1913 issue.

58. Because of space limitations and the deliberate focus on the Congregational mission, it is not possible to discuss the Methodist work in Hawai`i. For some historical account on this subject, refer to Alex Ravelo Vergara, "Filipino Ministry in Hawaii: Past, Present, and Future" (Doctor of Ministry diss., Claremont School of Theology, Claremont, Calif., 1986).

59. Laubach, *People of the Philippines*, 268–70.

60. The initial pieces of information on Reverend Dizon have been pulled together from earlier interviews and conversations with Protestant members of the Filipino community, especially Helen Nagtalon-Miller, the late Inez V. Cayaban, and the late Reverend Arsenio Manuel. In gathering material artifacts for a Bishop Museum historical-cultural exhibition on the 75th anniversary of Filipino Immigration to Hawai`i, then curator Gaylord Kubota and I came across several books by Dizon, which were featured in the exhibition. See also San Buenaventura, "The Master and the Federation"; and San Buenaventura, "Hawaii's '1946 *Sakada*,'" *Social Process in Hawaii* 37 (1996): 81–82; Dizon, *The "Master" vs. Juan de la Cruz* (Honolulu, Hawaii: Mercantile Press, 1931).

61. George F. Renton to Norman Schenck, February 29, 1932, May 13; Schenck to Renton, March 1, May 16, HEA File "Churches-Pahu-Ewa." Valera was the son-in-law of Jose Alba.

62. Louis Bloch, *Facts About Filipino Immigrants into California,* California State Department of Industrial Relations, special bulletin no. 3 (1930). See also Steffi San Buenaventura, "Filipino Immigration to the United States," in *Asian American Encyclopedia,* ed. Franklin Ng, managing ed. John D. Wilson (New York: Marshall Cavendish, 1995), 445–46; and Carol Hemminger, "Little Manila: The Filipino in Stockton Prior to World War II," part 1, *Pacific Historian* 24 (1980): 21–34, and part 2, *Pacific Historian* 24 (1980): 207–20.

63. "The Story of Trinity Presbyterian Church of Stockton, California," (Stockton, October 1974, mimeographed), 7.

64. "The Story of Trinity Presbyterian Church of Stockton, California," 11.

65. "The Story of Trinity Presbyterian Church of Stockton, California," 11. I am grateful to Angel Bantillo Magdael and Letty Bantillo Perez for the interviews in Stockton in 1993 and for allowing me to make a photocopy of Inosanto's article. Refer also to a quotation of Magdael in Fred Cordova, *Filipinos: The Forgotten Asian Americans* (Dubuque, Iowa: Kendall/Hunt, 1983), 168.

66. Corpus, "An Analysis of the Racial Adjustment Activities and Problems of the Filipino-American Christian Fellowship in Los Angeles" (master's thesis, University of Southern California, Los Angeles, 1938), 44f. Much of the information on the Filipino Christian Fellowship and the Filipino Christian Church comes from Corpus; also from several conversations with Royal Morales, son of the late Reverend Silvestre Morales, and Doroteo Ines (Los Angeles, 1997), and the late Primo Quevedo (Inglewood, 1993), who were both members of the Filipino Christian Fellowship and Church.

67. Corpus, "An Analysis of the Racial Adjustment Activities and Problems," 37.

68. Corpus, "An Analysis of the Racial Adjustment Activities and Problems," 38.

69. Steffi San Buenaventura, "Old and New Immigration: Catholic and Protestant Filipinos in Twentieth Century America" (paper presented at the

Western Historical Association, California Meetings, Sacramento, October 17, 1997).

70. Reginald Yzendoorn, *History of the Catholic Mission in the Hawaiian Islands* (Honolulu: Honolulu Star-Bulletin Limited, 1927), 238. In my interviews and conversations with the old Filipinos in the late seventies and early eighties, many did mention the camp visitations of Caucasian priests (some Portuguese), but they indicated not having been able to communicate with the priests (or of avoiding them) because of the language barrier (most Filipinos, especially rural people, did not speak Spanish and spoke little English) and the fact that they were *puti* (white).

71. Jeffrey M. Burns, *The Catholic American Parish: A History from the 1850s to the Present,* vol. II, ed. Jay P. Dolan (New York: Paulist, 1987), 68–69.

72. Archives of the Archdiocese of San Francisco, Filipino Catholic Center files. I am grateful to Archdiocesan archivist, Jeffrey M. Burns, for the use of the Filipino materials in the Archdiocesan Archives.

73. Burns, *Catholic American Parish,* 68

74. Edwin Almirol, "Church Life among Filipinos in Central California: Social Ties and Ethnicity," in *Religion and Society in the American West,* ed. Carl Guarneri and David Alvarez (Lanham, Md.: University Press of America, 1987), 308.

75. Doroteo Ines dramatizes an incident in which a Filipino experiences discrimination in a Protestant church service in a film he made in Los Angeles in 1937, *A Filipino in America,* restored by the Pamana Foundation (Los Angeles) in 1998; see Fred Cordova's brief chapter on "Church and Religion," in his book *Filipinos: Forgotten Americans,* 167–74. Royal F. Morales, author of *Makibaka 2: The Filipino American Struggle* (Laoag, Philippines: Crown Printers, 1998), son of Reverend Silvestre Morales and a community leader in Los Angeles, has corroborated these incidents of discrimination in Los Angeles churches against Filipinos in a number of conversations.

76. Francis J. Weber, *John Joseph Cantwell* (Hong Kong: Cathay Press, 1971), 130.

77. Valentin Aquino, "The Filipino Community in Los Angeles" (master's thesis, University of Southern California, Los Angeles, 1952), 50.

78. Oscar Portugal, "Filipino Catholic Clubs of Hawaii," 1999 edited version, most likely published in the FCC 1999 Anniversary Program, following the clubs' golden anniversary celebration (one page, no pagination), provided by Sister Grace Dorothy Lim, MM, Director of Filipino Ministry, Vicar for Ethnic Ministries, Archdiocese of Hawaii.

79. On the 1946 immigration, see San Buenaventura, "Hawaii's '1946 *Sakada,'*" *Social Process in Hawaii* 37 (1996): 81–82; Maggie Bunson, *Faith in Paradise: A Century and a Half of the Roman Catholic Church in Hawaii* (Boston: St. Paul Editions, 1977), 202, 204.

80. "Filipinos in Religion," in *The Filipinos in Hawaii . . . the First 75 Years, 1906–1981* (Honolulu: Hawaii Filipino News, 1981), 111. St. Columban's Church is run by the Columban religious order, which established a mission in the Philippines after World War II.

81. Conversation and correspondence with Sister Grace Dorothy Lim, Mount St. Mary College, Los Angeles, August 11, 1999, and Honolulu, January 4, 2000,

respectively; and from previous association with Sister Grace in Honolulu in the late seventies. Henry Sabog from Waipahu is the first Hawai`i-born Filipino priest and is now retired. The others are Marvin Samiano from Lihue, Alfred Rebuldello from Papaiko, and Roland Pacdoan, who was actually born in Bohol province but came to Hawai`i as a deacon.

82. Ed Kennedy, "Vicar of St. Paul's to End 38-Year Odyssey," *Honolulu Advertiser*, May 10, 1997, B3.

83. Artemio G. Guillermo, ed., *Churches Aflame: Asian Americans and United Methodism* (Nashville, Tenn.: Abingdon Press, 1991). See especially chapter 5 by Artemio Guillermo, "Gathering of the Scattered: History of Filipino American United Methodist Churches," 91–112.

84. "Protestant Filipinos: Rebels of the Catholic Faith," a paper written for an Ethnic Studies class at the University of California, Riverside (June 10, 1999), 16–17. Espiritu's great-great-grandmother converted to Protestantism after her husband was killed in 1897 (fighting in the Philippine Revolution of 1896), and she blamed the Spanish friars for having been directly responsible for his death. Espiritu gives a couple of reasons for the discomfort in mainstream churches: Older Filipinos complain about not being able "to understand the accent of Anglo ministers as well as the expressions they use[d] to conceptualize a sermon. Other Filipinos [are] not able to find the Christian fellowship they had in the Protestant churches in the Philippines."

85. Robert R. Reed, "Migration as Mission: The Expansion of the *Iglesia ni Cristo* Outside the Philippines," in *Patterns of Migration in Southeast Asia*, Occasional Paper No. 16, ed. Robert Reed, the Center of South and Southeast Asia Series (Berkeley: University of California, 1990). For the directory and photographs of INC churches, see Iglesia ni Cristo, *God's Message* (The Magazine of the Iglesia ni Cristo), special issue, "25 Years in the West, 1968–1993."

86. I have had initial conversations about the BNP with a number of individuals (including BNP members) and members of the Filipino Ministry of the Diocese of San Bernardino and its president, Willie Bogaoan, and also with students in my Filipino American history classes at UCLA (in 1992), and more recently at UC Riverside. See Banal na Pag-aaral, *The Fulfillment of Our Dream*, Special Inauguration Issue (Ontario, Canada: October 19–24, 1996), which was made available to me by Rachelle Sarmiento.

87. The inevitable conflict between the Church and *El Saddai* came out in the open when the issues of "Charter Change" and "Visiting Forces Agreement" were publicly debated and the Church led the government opposition to, and with Velarde and the *El Shaddai* membership siding openly with, Philippine president Joseph Estrada. *Saksi* television news program, channel 18, Los Angeles, September 17, 1999, broadcast; *Philippine News by RealPinoy.com*, "Bishops Target El-Shaddai Leader"(week of September 12, 1999, http://realpinoy.com/news/1999/sep/week2/2.htm).

88. From "The Pastoral Care of Immigrants from the Philippines," 1992 (no author), a six-page essay provided by Cecile Motus, Coordinator of Ethnic Ministries in the Office of Pastoral Care of Migrants and Refugees, United States Catholic Conference, Washington, D.C.

89. "The Pastoral Care of Immigrants from the Philippines."

90. Reverend Erno Diaz, *Filipino Apostolate Handbook of the Archdiocese of New York*, 1997, 6 (provided by Willie Bogaoan); see also, Joe Vargo, "Filipinos Keep Traditions Alive in Month of Faith," *The Press-Enterprise* (Riverside, California), May 25, 1997 (Sunday), B4b.

91. For the history and details of the project, see Noemi M. Castillo and Reverend Michael G. Kyte, OP, *Journeying with Mary* (Journeying with Mary Foundation, September 1996).

92. Castillo and Kyte, *Journeying with Mary*, 24, 39.

93. "Catholic Dioceses by Census Region," n.d.; four pages of statistics from the Archdiocese of New York provided by Cecile Motus.

94. Sally Ann Connell and Mitchell Landsberg, "7 Die, 7 Hurt in Van Crash on Church Trip," *Los Angeles Times*, October 23, 1999 (Saturday), A1, A19; This article provided background information about the church and was further corroborated by a two-minute interview of church members and their pastor in the Eagle Rock (southern California) church in connection with this accident, *KABC Evening News* (5 P.M.), channel 7, Los Angeles.

CHAPTER SEVEN

CARTOGRAPHY OF KOREAN AMERICAN PROTESTANT FAITH COMMUNITIES IN THE UNITED STATES

Jung Ha Kim

"What are the specific intellectual, social, and ethical charges to which we wish to commit ourselves?" and "[h]ow can we make certain that our work does not simply trail the issues facing our community but is useful for analyzing and addressing real problems outside [and inside] the academy?"[1] These are questions raised by Elaine H. Kim's presidential address at the annual meeting of the Association of Asian American Studies held at Cornell University and the subsequent reasons that I decided to partake in the challenging task of documenting a social history of Korean American Protestant faith communities in the United States. For as Min asserts in the introduction to this volume, the very paucity of comprehensive analysis of the state of Asian American religions in the United States is an important charge to which I wish to commit myself by writing this chapter. As a Korean American churched woman whose academic training predominantly comes from the fields of religious studies and social sciences, an attempt to write a comprehensive social history of Korean American Protestantism in the United States has been, indeed, an intellectual and ethical challenge. Aware of both limitations and peculiarities of theoretical and methodological assumptions in these fields of studies, there are at least two complex political and academic undercurrents that I seek to address in this chapter: (1) the new academic enthusiasm of remaking Asian traditions and Asian American religions in the United States as "new" and "foreign";[2] and (2) the heavy-handed cultural assimilation approach to delineate organized religion's impact on various Asian American communities.[3] These two trends in academia coincide with the rapidly changing racial-ethnic demographic compositions of the United States on the one hand, and the influence of globalized capitalism and the advanced technology of the late twentieth century that addle national boundaries and the transnationality of cyberspace on the other hand.

These and other macro- and micro-dynamics of everyday life in the United States notwithstanding, real experiences of Korean Americans as a racial ethnic people point to concrete human struggle, community building, and negotiating demands of religion and of everyday survival. As Finke and Stark argue in *The Churching of America*, the history of American religion is not the history of religious ideas, but "the history of human actions and human organizations."[4] Durkheim also asserted nearly a century ago that "[t]here can be no society which does not feel the need to upholding and reaffirming at regular intervals the collective sentiments and the collective ideas which make its unity and its personality."[5] Korean Americans living in the United States also have gathered and formed various communities of their own, upheld and reaffirmed the collective sentiments and ideas, incorporated survival strategies, and negotiated identities as both individuals and a racial-ethnic group from their own social locations. Consequently, this chapter emphasizes the centrality of the Korean American agency for documenting the state of Korean American faith communities in the United States. In other words, this chapter is less a history of how organized religion impacted its adherents than the story of how people formed and experienced religious communities from their own historically situated lives.

As many have argued, if religion is an important lens through which people construct meanings and negotiate intricacies of everyday life experiences, there seems to be a peculiar affinity between Korean Americans living in the United States as a people and Christianity as a religion in the past one hundred years of Korean American history. This is not to say that virtually all Korean Americans practice Christianity or that they share the same definition, understanding, and experiences of being Christians in the United States. Nor does the astonishing phenomenon of some 75 percent of Korean Americans being churched take away the fact that the rest of Korean America is comprised of Buddhists, Chun-do-Kyo-in, B'hai, multireligious people, Confucians, atheists, and people with no formal religious affiliation. Rather than highlighting the multireligious aspects, however, I have attempted to probe the agency of Korean Americans in forming and experiencing their own *kyo-whe* (which literally means, the [Christian] church, in Korean) as faith communities. Two main reasons for using the term *faith communities* rather than using the conventional name of *Christian church* are the following. First, while experiences of religion and spirituality are considered private matters in the mainstream United States, Korean Americans tend to experience them as both ethnic and communal matters.[6] As such, the clear demarcation between the private and the public and the much assumed separation between the church and the state are less relevant to understanding Korean American religion. Put differently, the "Korean" aspect of forming and experiencing Christianity often takes precedence over traditionally categorized names of religions, such as Buddhism, Confucianism, Taoism, Christianity, and Shamanism.

That is not to say that Korean Americans do not differentiate various religious boundaries, but that what Korean Americans mean when they use these religious categories is more insightful and instrumental to understand Korean American religious experiences as a whole. This leads to the second reason for using the phrase *faith communities* in this paper. What Robert Wuthnow has observed as "a patchwork quilt" of making American religion also applies to understanding Korean American religion. Wuthnow aptly agues that Americans who were "cradle-to-grave members of their particular traditions" at the beginning of the twentieth century and whose "spirituality prompted them to attend services and to believe in the preaching of their churches and synagogues" are now piecing together "their faith like a patchwork quilt" in the first few years of the twenty-first century.[7] Although responding to different life circumstances from different social locations, Korean Americans also have woven together various religious traditions and demands of everyday life in the United States into a peculiar religious patchwork quilt called the *kyo-whe*. This patchwork of *kyo-whe* is said to resemble the complex interplay among religions and traditions as exemplified in some scholars' naming of Korean Americans as "churched Confucians" or "Confucian Christians"[8] and "Confucian Buddhist Christians."[9] An attempt to assign a name to this type of eclectic and integrated religious experience as either "syncretic" or "folk" or "additive spirituality" is not the main concern of this chapter. Rather, the usage of *faith communities* denotes the inadequacy of using conventional religious categories for understanding Korean American religion and also emphasizes the peculiar juxtaposition of religion, culture, and the politics of identity in Korean America.

Documenting a social history of Korean American Protestant faith communities in the United States is more than an assemblage of dates, acts, and names, as an Asian Americanist, Gary Y. Okihiro asserts. Pointing to a new way of documenting a history called "family album history," Okihiro explains that "a family album history is inspired by the strands in Asian American history that reach to those regularly absent from the gallery of 'great men,' to activities excluded from the inventory of 'significant events,' and to regions usually ignored by the worlds of science."[10] As such, it overcomes limitations imposed by deeply masculine accounts of historical recordings, communal histories written by outsiders, and forgotten and omitted stories of the dispossessed. Just as individual family albums may "help to define a personal identity and locate its place within the social order and to connect that person to others, from one generation to the next, like the exchanging snapshots around family and friends,"[11] ethnic family albums can help to probe the intricate relationship between individuals and their community and to uncover emerging themes and paradigms of their lived experiences.[12] Employing family album history as both a methodology and a construct is not only instrumental for writing a social history of Korean American Protestant faith communities, but is advantageous in another way: It fills the gap in census data and in other quantitative studies. For unlike national census forms used in other European and Latin American countries, "the U.S. Census never asked citizens to report their personal religious affiliations," and "Korean" as a racial-ethnic category in the U.S. Census did not appear until the year 1970.[13]

By defining the social history of Korean American Protestantism as the history of Korean American actions and their community formations, and by employing family album history as both a methodology and theoretical construct, this chapter is organized around four historical periods: (1) 1903–1950; (2) 1950–1968; (3) 1968–1988/1992; and (4) 1988/1992–present. Each historical period is segmented according to how Korean Americans formed and experienced their own faith communities on the one hand, and how they responded to the broader sociopolitical structures of their times in the United States, on the other hand. For each historical segment, an overview of demographic characteristics of Korean Americans, the meaning and experiences of faith communities, and, when applicable, selected stories of lived experiences are offered—"narrative matters," and these stories can provide deeper understanding of the agency of Korean Americans in negotiating their own racial-ethnic identities, religion, economic opportunities, and gender (re)construction in the United States.[14]

Not so much to reiterate the popular misnomer of all Korean Americans being "new" immigrants, I offer lengthier discussions on the contemporary state of Korean American religion in the United States as an attempt to highlight the fundamental change that took place in Korean American faith communities and demographics since the late 1960s. With the sweeping transformation taking place in Korean America and the United States at large during the past three decades or so, several issues have emerged out of Korean American faith communities: the intergenerational conflict along the line of language proficiency/preference; the shifting visibility and leadership in the Korean American community at large; the political intersection across lines of geography, class, gender, and generation; and the emergence of pan-ethnic faith communities in Asian America. Although these and other emerging themes and experiences of the contemporary Korean America are too complex to allow for full satisfying analysis in this chapter, I attempt to provide discussions to further generate future explorations.

The Exile Community, 1903–1950

Just as discussions of the discovery of gold in California, labor shortages on Hawaiian plantations, and the building of intercontinental railroads in the middle of the nineteenth century provide the irreplaceable econopolitical context for documenting Chinese American history in the United States, discussions of the role of Christian missionaries spreading a peculiar "gospel" about the United States as "the heaven on earth" and the "land flowing with milk and honey" to offset the ethnic labor politics on Hawaiian plantations at the dawn of the Japanese annexation of the Korean peninsula became the oft-cited econoreligious context for understanding Korean immigration to the United States.[15] Along with the civil unrest caused by famine, poverty, and constant attacks by and influences of foreign powers—the push factors—Christian missionaries from the United States seized the opportunity to recruit new Korean converts for both spiritual and economic causes—the pull factors. Take, for example, Hollace Newton Allen,[16] the first Protestant missionary from the United States who went to Korea in September 1884.[17] As a Christian missionary, he provided an important "pulpit service" for officially arranging Korean labor immigration with Hawaiian plantation owners[18] to break the labor unrest and to force down wages of their predominantly Japanese workforce.[19] Hollace G. Underwood, the Presbyterian missionary who went to Korea in April 1885, and Henry G. Appenzeller, the first United Methodist missionary who arrived a month later, also actively cooperated with the United States Ministry of Labor to recruit Korean laborers for Hawaiian plantation owners.[20] Thus, the early eclipse of Korean immigration points to not only transnational politics among Korea, Japan, and the United States, but also the interplay of economic and religious undercurrents. A closer examination of the "pulpit service" offered by Christian missionaries during late nineteenth century in Korea provides a critical lens to understand the history of Korean American experiences of Christianity in the United States. Immigration policies that impacted Korean Americans not only shaped their migration and resettlement patterns, but also reconfigured religious experiences.

Although there are a few records of Koreans traveling to the United States as early as 1888,[21] the entrance of Koreans as labor immigrants to the United States started in 1903.[22] On January 13, 1903, 101 Koreans—composed of 55 men, 21 women, and 25 children—entered Honolulu, Hawaii.[23] During the first three years, from 1903 to 1905, a total of 7,226 Koreans came to work on Hawaiian sugar plantations. Among them, approximately six thousand were adult males, whose ages ranged from their early twenties to their late thirties, and some one thousand women, with several hundred children. Some scholars have pointed to this pattern of the Korean "family" labor unit as a distinct characteristic that set them apart from virtually all-male laborers from China and, to a lesser degree, from Japan.[24] Clearly, the sex ratio of the first wave of Korean immigrants was far from balanced; but, compared to the highly skewed sex ratio among Chinese and Japanese laborers at the time, experiences of the "mutilated family" were not as widely spread among Korean male laborers.[25] Further, there were at least two other distinct demographic characteristics of these first 7,226 Koreans that defy attempts to homogenize them as unskilled proletariat from Korea.

First, although they were all treated as unskilled or semiskilled laborers by Hawaiian plantation owners at the time of their arrival, only about 60 percent remained in Hawaii by 1905 and only about 50 percent by the time Japan officially annexed Korea in 1910. Approximately 1,000 returned to Korea, another 2,000 moved to the mainland United States (mostly to California), and 1,033 were reported to have immigrated to Mexico in 1905.[26] This trend of "moving on" among the first wave of Korean immigrants can be explained from several vantage points, but their diverse social class backgrounds prior to entering the United States also provides an important clue. They were semiskilled urbanites, low-ranking government officials, peasants, ex-soldiers, students, and political refugees from Korea.[27] Other records also illustrate that they were originally from Inchon, Pusan, Wonsan, Chinnampo, and Seoul, all fairly large "metro" cities and port cities.[28] These metro and port cities were also known as important religious sites in which massive and zealous Christian conversions were taking place in Korea. For example, it is now a well-documented fact that some 40 percent of the first 101 Koreans who came to the United States in 1903 were from the same Christian church in Inchon, the Youngdong Church of Reverend George Herbert Jones.[29] Further, Korean and Korean American scholars estimate that approximately 40 to 60 percent of all Koreans who came to the United States before 1905 were converted Christians.[30] Indeed, for Koreans, the ticket for the voyage across the Pacific Ocean came with the price tag of obtaining a (new) religious identity.

The Korean labor immigrants' religious affiliation was another distinct characteristic that set them apart from the earlier Chinese and Japanese laborers. Once they arrived in the "Christian country," Korean laborers formed the Hawaii Methodist Church in November 1903, within the first several months of resettling in the United States, and the Hawaii Korean Anglican Church in February 1905. The first Koreans who ventured onto the mainland established the San Francisco Korean Methodist Church in September 1903 and the Los Angeles Presbyterian Church in September 1905.[31] All four of these early Korean churches were formed prior to the termination of Korean immigration in 1905 by the Japanese government, and they were the first Korean American faith communities in the United States.

From 1910 until the passing of the Immigration Act in 1924, which prohibited entrance of Asian immigrants, a total of 1,066 picture brides came into the United States.[32] In addition to picture brides, some 900 students, intellectuals, and political refugees who had been involved in the anti-Japanese movement in Korea also came to the United States by 1924. Since no official Korean immigration took place from 1924 to 1950, no data is shown in records of the U.S. Immigration and Naturalization Services during this historical time period.

The lived experiences of Korean Americans at the time were doubly impacted by racial discriminatory immigration policies of the United States and Japan's colonization of Korea, which Elaine H. Kim calls the "double colonialism of Korean immigrants."[33] This "double colonization" has effectively limited the growth of the Korean American population and impeded both political and economic development of Korean American communities in the United States. Being completely cut off from any possible diplomatic assistance from Korea and opportunities to allocate a source of merchandise for business trade from their homeland during the Japanese annexation of Korea, Korean Americans were utterly left alone to survive in a strange land. Documenting a history of Korean Americans during this time period, Elaine H. Kim states that it was a time to "express the particular anguish of the exile deprived even of the sustaining illusion of a triumphant return 'home' after a life of toil in a country where she/he felt hated" even "long after the Japanese occupation was formally ended in 1945."[34] The exile experience of Korean Americans was further reiterated by the fact that no Korean-born person could become a naturalized U.S. citizen until the passage of the McCarran Walter Act in 1952.

Given the legal constraints barring Korean Americans from becoming U.S. citizens, Korean Americans' nationalism to actively participate in the movement for Korean independence from Japan may have been further ignited. Along with *Taehanin Kungminhoe* (Korean National Association), numerous churches were established to support the Korean provisional government in Shanghai, another Korean exile to China, from 1919 into the 1940s. Indeed, most surviving records from this time period testify to unusually frequent gatherings at the church and active participation of "churched" Korean Americans in the Korea Independence Movement. The importance of the Christian church providing a physical site for Korean Americans to gather together to "donate significant portions of their wages to support the provisional government" and providing a religious cause for its adherents to repeatedly sign and send numerous petitions to U.S. president Theodore Roosevelt advocating Korean national independence cannot be exaggerated.[35]

As a racial-ethnic institution, the Korean American church also hosted and trained its own political leaders for the cause of Korean independence. Among many Korean American Christian politicians, perhaps, the story of Syngman Rhee can depict a particular experience of religion and community in Korean America at the time. Syngman Rhee, who became the first president of the Republic of Korea (ROK) after Korean independence from Japan, was a labor immigrant who arrived in the United States in 1905. After studying at Harvard and Princeton, Rhee formed the *Hanin Tongnip Kyohoe* (Korean Independence Church) in Hawaii and pastored churched Korean Americans during the 1920s. Korean independence from Japan was achieved in 1945, and, with the landing of the U.S. troops in South Korea and the Soviet troops in North Korea, he returned to Korea in 1946. As a result of the UN-supported separate elections in South and North Korea, Syngman Rhee became the first president of South Korea. Throughout his thirty-odd years of political life in both the United States and Korea, the Korean Independence Church in Hawaii provided "a base for his political activities."[36]

This is not to say that virtually all Korean Americans living in the United States had converted to Christianity by 1950, but they had become extensively and predominantly a "churched" population. Whether Korean Americans attended the church predominantly for the political cause or for religious reasons, their experiences of Christian religion do not point to a dichotomy between politics and religion. Moreover, the much-assumed separation between the church and the state in the mainstream United States was foreign in the context of the Korean American church from its inception at the turn of the century. Here, an attempt to fit Korean American experiences of Christianity into a sociologically derived index along the line of theocracy and totalitarianism also fails.[37] For their experiences of faith communities points to a continuum between politics and religion and between Koreans abroad and in the homeland. As a people in exile whose experiences are marked by double colonialism, Korean Americans have formed and founded their faith community in the United States in their own racial-ethnic churches. By 1950, there were "32 [Christian] congregations serving 2,800 Koreans" in Hawaii alone and "a similar number of Christian churches on the mainland."[38] These churches became the main community centers to address multifaceted survival needs of their adherents, and they provided programs and services such as translation and interpretation, job placement, counseling, legal aids, conflict resolution strategies, and language classes.

Rather than attempting to categorize Korean American experiences of religion along the line of ethnic and political, applying Edward Said's notions of filiation and affiliation may be helpful here. Said claimed that while filiation is based on "natural" and/or blood-related bonds, affiliation is based on individuals making free choices to become members of a social group or organization.[39] Given this difference between filiation and affiliation, Korean American religious experiences during this historical time seem to be more in tune with filiation than affiliation. Put otherwise,

Korean Americans have formed and experienced faith communities based on their shared racial and ethnic filiation in the United States. To say that the first faith experiences of Korean American faith communities are largely filiational is to contradict what has been traditionally derived categories and the paradigm for studying religion based on the assumption that it is largely of affiliational ties. For what brought Korean Americans together to form a faith community is not necessarily their affiliation with the same religious identity, but their shared experiences of being "Korean" in the United States during this historical time period.

The Hybrid Community, 1950–1968

While formation of filiational religious communities and strengthening ethnic bonds may be characteristics of the exile people, the faith communities of the second wave of Korean immigrants to the United States after 1950 resemble a peculiar combination of exile and immigrant models. Defining main differences between exiles and immigrants rests largely on two concepts and experiences: dislocation and home base. *Exile* is defined as "the condition of voluntary and involuntary separation from one's place of birth" and is often offset by "continuous bonds to the lost homeland," whereas immigrants are people who made conscious decisions to leave the birthland, in order to reestablish a new home based in the new country.[40] Since most of the second wave of Korean immigrants came to the United States as three distinct groups—(war) orphans, wives of U.S. servicemen, and students—their experiences of dislocation and home base vary along the continuum of voluntary and involuntary leaving of the birthplace and of intentionally or unintentionally naming the United States as their own home base. Hence, the second wave of immigrants from Korea point to other diverse and hybrid characteristics of Korean American communities in the United States.

From 1955 to 1966, 6,293 Korean orphans were adopted in the United States, mostly through the Holt Adoption agency.[41] The racial composition of these orphans was as follows: 46 percent "white Koreans," 13 percent "black Koreans," and the rest, 41 percent, "full Koreans."[42] Although the adoption of Korean children continues still today, a majority of the 6,293 war orphans were "Amerasians" and what Velina H. Houston calls the "Asian hybrid" produced by the Korean war.[43] Besides a few nationwide studies of adopted Korean orphans by D. Kim in 1972, D. Kim and S. P. Kim in 1977, and Hurh and Kim in 1984, very few, if any, systematic studies or information are available. Some religious and humanitarian attempts to address issues and problems of Korean adoptees in the United States have been initiated recently. The Korean Community Presbyterian

Church of Atlanta, (P.C., U.S.A.), for example, launched its annual "Festival for Adopted Families" in 1996. And by 1999, the church's annual ministry for Korean adoptees and their families had gown to a gathering of 280 family members. The church hopes "to turn the event into a true festival with booths that offer everything from ethnic food to cultural information and resources to help parents understand their children."[44] Integrating stories and experiences of Korean adoptees in the history of Korean America, however, is another important chapter that is yet to be written.

Under the 1952 McCarran Walter Act, another understudied and silenced category of Koreans started to enter the United States: Korean wives of American GIs.[45] From 1951 to 1964, 6,423 Korean women came to the United States as "war brides" or "GI wives." Mainly due to the U.S. military presence in South Korea, this influx of Korean immigrant wives continues today. For example, the average number of Korean wives of U.S. servicemen coming into the United States was approximately 1,500 per year during the 1960s and about 2,300 per year in the 1970s.[46] A few scholars have documented demographic characteristics and marital adjustments made by Korean wives of GIs.[47] Living in strategically isolated locations near military bases and being culturally segregated from their co-ethnics for out-marrying, experiences of Korean wives of U.S. servicemen are rendered secondary in both Korean American communities and the United States at large. Many of these Korean wives sponsored their relatives from Korea to bring them to the United States under the Immigration Act of 1965, but crediting them as the very backbone of contemporary Korean America is yet to be accomplished.

In addition to these two hybrid and silenced groups of Korean Americans, an estimated five thousand students also came to the United States between 1950 and 1965. Very little has been documented about this group of people for yet another reason. A majority of these students eventually and inevitably became un- or under-documented aliens in the United States. Since the student visa stipulates that the duration of legal stay in the United States is to be determined by the attainment of academic credentials or other reasons for terminating study, most Koreans who overstayed their visas "naturally" became illegal aliens. Realizing the fact that the very pillars of the Korean American community have once been "illegal aliens" in the United States, perhaps, is unsettling. It is even more unsettling to be reminded that these Korean Americans utilized religion, Christianity, as their very survival mechanism in the United States.

Caution against an overemphasis on the important functions U.S. missionaries played in Korea and in Korean American lives is well intended, because the history and content of Korean American Protestant faith communities in the United States attest to the agency of Korean Americans.

When assessing the access to socioeconomic resources, however, the religious identity of Korean Americans and their ties to U.S. missionaries demonstrate a clear and strong correlation to the immigrants' survival and economic success in the United States. For example, Kyung Won Lee, who came to the United States in 1950 and became "a pioneer Korean American journalist in English," testifies to the missionary zeal to offer scholarships to Koreans studying Christian theology at colleges and universities in the United States.[48] Reflecting his own status as "one of the original FOBs" (fresh-off-the-boats) in 1950, K. Lee claims that most Korean immigrants during the 1950s were Christians: "[W]e were targets of Christian embrace."[49] He continues, "Koreans who had some connection with a church could get a scholarship, but I never had any connection with the church, so I came on my own. The others had scholarships."[50] U.S. missionaries actively recruited Koreans to study Christian theology and to spread Christianity, and they offered scholarships to those Koreans who would become Christians and study theology. At the time of the political and economic upheaval in the divided Korea, many (male) Koreans made decisions to put their souls in the hands of U.S. missionaries in exchange for a ticket to the "land flowing with milk and honey." Hence, professing the correct religious identity along with a contact with U.S. missionaries were two direct causal factors for Korean American survival in the United States. Given these historical memories of infusing a religious identity with educational opportunities, it is no surprise to find so many Korean Americans aggregate in their own faith communities in searching for survival resources and spiritual solace.

The Immigrant Community, 1968–1988/1992

Lumping together all Korean Americans living in the United States as a monolithic category called the "post-1965 immigrants" calls for a critical reexamination of the history and politics of immigration policies.[51] Too often, literature focuses on remaking Korean (and Asian) Americans as all new and post-1965 immigrants, and their religions as various attempts to transplant ethnic traditions in the United States; this points to the tenacious process of mythmaking based on the assumed "teleology of Americanization."[52] The teleology of Americanization entails conceptualizing immigrants, their cultures, and "racial-ethnic differences largely as a matter of something 'left behind.'"[53] This type of insistence on "a time before U.S. entry and on cultures separate from U.S. Anglo-identity" is also called the "immigration logos."[54] This immigration logos plays an irreplaceable role in depicting Korean Americans and other Asian Americans as all-foreign and therefore un-American. From the perspectives of the teleology of Americanization and the immigration logos, racial-ethnic identity of Korean Americans is perceived as fixed, static, and often affiliated with a language proficiency (or lack thereof). If one adopts another view, however, the view that ethnicity is never fixed but something that is always being made anew, just as in the politics of individual identity formation, the agency of the people and their complex negotiations along the axes of socioeconomic status (SES), language, generation, gender, and transnational ties become more salient and urgent constructs for documenting a social history of Korean American faith communities. And this is "when and where I enter" the discussion of lived realities of the post-1965 Korean immigrants and their experiences of religion in the United States.[55]

Systematic and detailed information on Korean Americans living in the United States has become available since 1970, because that was the first year the term "Korean" as a distinct ethnic name was used on the U.S. Census, replacing the previously used "other Asian" category. The U.S. Census counted 70,598 Koreans living in the United States by 1970; 357,393 by 1980; 798,849 by 1990; and one million by 2000.[56] Clearly, these census data demonstrate a drastic increase in the Korean American population in theUnited States; within the decade from 1970 to 1980, the Korean American population increased almost 500 percent, and during the decade from 1980 to 1990, another 100 percent. Under the 1965 Immigration Act, immigrants from European countries accounted for only 10 percent of all immigrants, while 43 percent came from Asia and 41 percent from Latin America and the Caribbean by 1987. And during the period of 1981 to 1990, nearly 50 percent of the naturalized citizens were born in Asia.[57]

A closer look at demographic characteristics of the Korean American population, however, points to two distinctive SES (socioeconomic status) groups of the post-1965 Korean immigrants. While Koreans who came into the United States under the 1965 Immigration Act were mostly well-educated, middle-class professionals, Koreans who arrived under the Immigration and Nationality Act Amendment of 1976 (and the Immigration Reform and Control Act of 1986)—which limited the number of entries for professionals by favoring family reunification of U.S. citizens—were a variety of educated people from skilled backgrounds.

Given these demographic differences, how have the pre-1976 (and the post-1965) and the "late first-generation immigrants" (post-1976 Korean Americans) formed and experienced faith communities?[58] Did the early and the late first-generation immigrants differ in their resettlement patterns in the United States? Did Korean Americans form various faith communities based on their own SESs? How did the post-1965 Korean immigrants relate to the pre-1965 co-ethnics?

Critiquing the mere lip service given to the importance of class as another political factor that can determine an identity in multicultural society, Edna Bonacich argues that "class relations are not relations of identity, but relations of dominance and resistance."[59] Although the concept of class or SES came to mean class "background" in contemporary America, Bonacich urges to "avoid confusing the class from which one has come with class into which one is moving."[60] And this distinction between the "class from" and the "class to" is instrumental in understanding faith communities of post-1965 and post-1976 Korean immigrants. For, regardless of various class backgrounds, most Korean Americans tended to consider their present SES in the United States as a temporary, and therefore transitional, stage to achieving their own American dream in the land of opportunity. Put otherwise, Korean Americans may have originally come from different class backgrounds, but tend to perceive themselves as the (upper-) middle-class-to-be in the United States. This robust striving to achieve the American dream, in effect, enabled Korean Americans to continuously form and experience faith communities across class lines in the United States. This is not to depict Korean American faith communities as truly inclusive and egalitarian religious institutions, but to emphasize the significance of the "striving class" (and not so much of class background) in the Korean American mind-set.[61]

The significance of the concept of "striving class" among Korean Americans and their experiences of faith communities across class lines are subtexted by at least two closely intertwined macro- and microdynamics. First, Korean (and other Asian) Americans are "racialized" and therefore locked out of the broad labor market in the United States.[62] Since they were originally recruited as cheap labor and often isolated and suppressed as a racial-ethnic "minority," they "could not be a part of the working class and certainly could not develop strong American class consciousness."[63] This economic isolation, in turn, contributed to "the distortion of capital formation within [Korean] American communities."[64] Second, even as Korean Americans are rendered as another racial-ethnic minority in the United States, most of the post-1965 first-generation immigrants' simplistic understanding of race precludes them from critical assessment of their own American dream. Their crude perception of race follows something like this: "We are Asians! We look different! Therefore, we are being discriminated against! The remedy is to work harder and to show the Whites that we are just as good if not better."[65] Indeed, work harder, they do. Approximately 60 percent—an exceptionally high level—of Korea Americans are self-employed and/or work within the ethnic enclaves, and their length of daily labor is often stretched from 10 to 12 hours.[66] Experiencing a keen sense of status inconsistency between their propensity to be self-employed and their high educational backgrounds, first-generation Korean Americans often turned to their own ethnic church for both social and spiritual solace. For it is within their own faith communities that Korean Americans can acquire respectful status as deacons, elders, and other community leaders. Some sociologists point to this yearning for the status of power and privilege as the main causal factor for the Korean American church's schismatic tendency.[67] That is to say, Korean Americans (especially men) tend to hop around from one church to the next and/or split the church in order to acquire higher socioreligious status.

Juxtaposing the presently bipolarized class situation, status inconsistencies, and the undying efforts of striving for upward mobility in the future, Korean Americans congregate in their own churches by enthusiastically embracing a peculiar gospel of equating Korean Americans as "God's chosen people." It is no surprise, then, to find that a prominent Korean American theologian's articulation of Korean immigrants as a faithful people obediently responding to God's call to make pilgrimages to God's promised land, America, swept Korean American faith communities throughout the 1980s.[68] The mode of pilgrimage and the searching for the spiritual home in God's promised land is also reflected in the high rate of mobility and church hopping among Korean Americans as they move from one place to another and from one church to another to find an economically and spiritually secure home. Among five hundred questionnaire surveys mailed to Korean American families in the Greater Atlanta area in 1992, for example, 287 were returned for incorrect address or with moved-with-no-further-information stamps on them.[69] And from the most recently conducted nationwide survey on never-married Korean American women, 58 participants out of 62 on which data was collected (94 percent) reported that they had moved within the past four years. With such highly mobile and scattered adherents, who willingly commute a distance to attend their own faith communities, Korean American churches are not neighborhood churches. The Presbyterian Panel Study and the Racial Ethnic Presbyterian Panel Study sponsored by the United Presbyterian Church found that "Koreans, even those living in the large metropolitan areas with Korean churches in their neighborhood, indicated that their church is located 10 miles or more away from their residence."[70] In contrast, 17 percent of African Americans, 24 percent of Hispanics, and 10 percent of European Americans travel ten miles or more to attend their churches.[71] In short, Korean Americans have not only become synonymous with a highly "churched" population, but also self-selected survivors as God's "chosen people" en route to religious pilgrimage in the United States. Accordingly, Korean American success is now God's will and that every obedient subject of God's will should congregate together faithfully to bring about God's will here on earth.

There is another often-neglected aspect of understanding Korean American faith communities: the feminization of church attendance. Korean women, both in Korea and in the United States, are more likely than Korean men to attend and actively participate in the church.[72] Although this differs from church to church and from region to region, Korean American women make up 60 to 65 percent of the Korean American church attendees. As a numerical majority in their own faith communities, they actively participate in educational and other service-intensive efforts as Sundays school teachers, hostesses of church banquets, and organizers of garage sales to raise church funds. Regardless of their irreplaceable services to the church, Korean American women often find their contributions have been rendered secondary.[73] Among Korean American churches that are officially affiliated with the Presbyterian Church of the United States of America, for example, only 8 percent of church elders are women, whereas 92 percent are men. By analyzing the nationwide data on gender discrepancies in the Korean American Presbyterian Church, Kim and Kim conclude that "Korean females have to be older, more educated, and richer [than Korean males] to be ordained as elders."[74] Further, among eighty-one ordained Korean American clergywomen in the United Methodist denomination, only twenty-seven are appointed and accepted into Korean American churches, while the rest hold positions in non-Korean churches, educational institutions, or other nonparish ministries. And virtually all twenty-seven clergywomen (except two) who serve the Korean American church are appointed either as assistant/associate pastor or as youth/educational minister under the supervision of the senior Korean American male clergy.[75] In sum, while Korean American women constitute a clear majority of church attendance, opportunities in church leadership are rarely available to them.

Several studies attempt to offer explanations for sexism in the Korean American church by emphasizing the ethnic component of the organization. That is to say, the Korean American church is the main (and at times, the only) ethnic institution in which immigrant men can attain socioreligious status and gain self-respect. If immigration is an "enormously disruptive" and "disorienting" experience, it also presents itself with a special opportunity to reshape and transform people, both male and female. And if immigration is, indeed, "a theologizing experience,"[76] the Korean American church needs to service its adherents, both male and female, as a mediating institution between the patriarchal Korean customs and the Americanized Christian values. It is this deeply gendered context of the Korean American church, what Huping Ling observes as a major difference between the Korean American and the Chinese American churches, that becomes obvious. Arguing that Chinese churches were "far less indispensable to Chinese women than to Korean immigrant women," Ling highlights how the church played different roles in the adaptation of Chinese American and Korean American women. While "Christian churches served as windows of the mainstream American life to Chinese immigrant women and attempted to accelerate the Americanization," Korean American churches "functioned as community organizations that resembled the patriarchal social structure in Korea and consciously preserved Korean tradition."[77] Put differently, the main mechanism by which the Korean American church attempts to impede "the Americanization of Korean immigrants" is through practicing and re-inforcing patriarchy in the name of preserving Korean culture in the United States.[78] Indeed, with the rapid numerical growth of the Korean American church, its deeply gendered subculture also has been (re-)rooted in the American soil.

The Hyphenated American and Transnational Community, 1988/1992 to Present

The year 1988 was the first year the "return migration" of Korean American families to South Korea took place in significant numbers; and the year 1992 brought about profound leadership changes in Korean American communities.[79] The significant influx of reverse migrants and the sudden and sweeping leadership change in any community begs for explanation, and Korean American communities in the United States are no exception. What follows, then, is a brief discussion of the two historical events in 1988 and 1992 and how they impacted the new Korean American consciousness. To classify the years 1988 and 1992 as a watershed time period marking the Korean American community as transnational and hyphenated in the United States is to recognize the significance of both micro- and macrochanges in the formation of the Korean American consciousness.

The capital of South Korea, Seoul, hosted the World Olympic Games in 1988. The glaring display of economic boom and industrial progress depicted on television screens caused both pride and a keen sense of dislocation in the Korean American consciousness. The remembered "home land" many had left behind was plagued by political repression, economic struggle, and was in need of swift and fundamental social reformation, if not revolution. The South Korea portrayed on television screens during the Olympic games, however, was full of happy and proud smiling Koreans who seemed untouched by poisonous racism. When asked to share opinions on various social issues on television screens, Koreans voiced their own thoughts with unashamed self-confidence, without worrying about foreign accents. It was as if, while Korean Americans struggled to turn their life journeys in the United States into "success stories" by putting in extra hours of hard labor in order to actualize the American dream, the entire country of South Korea made itself a huge success story—an "economic miracle" by becoming a member of the "five little dragons" (or "tigers") in the global economy.[80] Experiencing this cognitive dissonance, significant numbers of Korean Americans started to pack their belongings to make the trip back across the Pacific Ocean in 1988. *The Korean Journal* and *The Southeast News* reported that approximately 3,000 Korean Americans in 1988 and 4,000 in 1989 (reverse) migrated to South Korea.[81] According to the *New York Times*, the number of reverse migrants ranged between 5,000 and 6,000 each year from 1990 to 1995.[82] Parenthetically, data released by the U.S. Immigration and Naturalization Service also illustrates the steady decline in the number of Korean immigrants to the United States from 1988 to 1991 and the more drastic decline from 1992 to 1995.[83]

Several years after the 1988 Olympic Games in Seoul, from April 29 to May 2, 1992, much of the south-central spread of Korea-town in Los Angeles was broken into, looted, and burned to the ground. As of May 6, 1992, the estimated damage to property and business loss of Korean-owned businesses in Los Angeles amounted to $346,962,394.[84] Thousands of Korean Americans lost their means of livelihood and the ability to at least dream the American dream. The shock and the rage against the Rodney King verdict and the aftermath of the L.A. "riot"/"uprising" was not contained within the city of Los Angeles alone, but spread throughout the United States. New alerts and finger-pointing against "different" racial and class boundaries went on for some time as people attempted to make sense of what had happened in their own communities. The whereabouts of the National Guard and the Los Angeles Police Department during the riot/uprising was investigated; African American residents blamed rude Korean American store owners; Korean Americans pointed at Hispanic American looters; and Hispanic Americans criticized African American violence. Headlines in Korean newspapers, such as "Korean Americans as Sacrificial Lambs" and "The American Dream Gone to Ashes," pointed to the utter despair, rage, and sense of injustice experienced by Korean Americans during the riot/uprising.[85] In fact, the impact of the L.A. riot/ uprising brought about such a fundamental change in the Korean American consciousness that Korean Americans call the incident the "*Sa-I-Ku*."[86] The literal meaning of the *Sa-I-Ku* is "4-2-9" in Korean. Indeed, the *Sa-I-Ku* and its aftermath led Korean Americans to reassess their own socioeconomic and political locations in the United States. And their urgent need to give voice to the shared experiences prompted both explicit and implicit shifts in the landscape of Korean American community leadership rather rapidly. Korean Americans who were fluent in English rose up to vocalize experiences of the *Sa-I-Ku* from a Korean American perspective. To name the loss and rage and to demand at least financial compensation, the Korean-speaking community leaders, who enjoyed virtually sole access to the leadership positions, found themselves relying on the English-speaking (often called second-generation) Korean Americans.

This leadership change, from the predominantly Korean-speaking first generation to the mostly English-speaking Korean Americans in the community, was not necessarily a "natural" generational shift in leadership as in other racial-ethnic communities, but was mostly a result of a particular historical event that necessitated such a drastic change. That is to say, since the influx of Korean immigrants in 1968, the Korean American (faith) community leadership positions tended to be handed down to and replaced by new first-generation immigrants from Korea rather than the second generation. Since the community leadership was not transmitted from the first generation to the second and subsequent generations, the predominantly English-speaking second-generation Korean Americans tend to form their own new faith (and other social) communities, often set apart from first-generation-oriented organizations. These English-speaking faith communities are increasingly becoming pan-Asian rather than insisting on ethnically specified, hyphenated Korean as a salient organizational identity, as Russell Jeung's chapter in this volume documents. Given that 72.7 percent of Korean Americans are born outside of the United States[87] and 51.6 percent of Korean Americans "do not speak English very well,"[88] the emerging trend of the English-speaking Korean Americans representing Korean American communities at large also demands a closer look and further probing. Of particular interest here, however, is that a combination of the turbulent economic uprootednesss of the *Sa-I-Ku* and the cognitive dissonance stemming from the 1988 Olympic Games in Seoul resulted in the fundamental change: the carving out of a political space that enabled the predominantly English-speaking Korean American generation(s) to gain both voice and visibility in the context of Korean America and the mainstream United States, on the one hand, and a blurring of the traditionally drawn boundary between Koreans and Korean Americans via fluid and migratory movement transnationally, on the other hand. The surge of the English-speaking "generation," then, needs to be examined as a necessary survival strategy of Korean Americans living in the post-1992 United States, rather than merely as a "natural" phenomenon.

It is often assumed that each and every generation "will change, develop, or be socialized anew in the on-going process of negotiating generational emergence"[89] and that religion as an important sociocultural institution would provide "a crucial narrative structure that calls upon a known world, even as that world shifts and adapts to new faces."[90] What is meant by *generation* and the *generation conflict* in the context of the Korean American faith community? How do different generations of Korean Americans experience their own faith communities?

Terms such as *generation* and *generation gap* are often used to describe a wide range of differences in Korean America. Although the "new" or "young" generation of Korean Americans consists not only of the second generation but also the 1.5, third, and subsequent generations, and mixed-race Korean Americans, the fixation of the predominantly English-speaking Korean Americans as the "second generation" seems to have taken place. Put otherwise, despite wide generational variations, Korean Americans often refer to the first generation as "parents" (i.e., adults and Korean speaking) and the "second" generation as "children" (i.e., perpetually young and English speaking). The fact that generational lines are neatly drawn based on people's preferences for and proficiency with language skills also strengthens the perceived demarcation between the "foreign-born" immigrant generation and the "assimilated" U.S.-born/grown Korean Americans. Thus, a few words of caution may be necessary. Just as in the case of the "immigrant logos," "generation gap" as a construct needs to be examined closely. Take, for example, the ways in which the generation gap discourse was understood during the 1960s in the United States. The gap was described at the time as "between college age students and their parents"; but a number of later studies demonstrated that the college students actually "shared the social and political views of their parents more often than not."[91] As the older-age cohort of baby boomers approach retirement age, the generation gap is now perceived as the conflict between workers and retirees. Perhaps in the near future, this conflict may be proved more of a mirage than reality, as in the 1960s. Moreover, regardless of new expressions of generation gap within the particular historical time period, gerontologists and other social scientists tend to agree that an "old-age bloc" and/or a politics of age is yet to be developed in the United States.[92]

Articulating the flexible and ever-changing experiences of the generation (gap), Bengston, a life course scholar, discusses "generation" in largely four different ways: (1) generation as an age cohort, usually of five- or ten-year intervals of birth group; (2) generation as a social and biological succession and as family position; (3) generation as a subset of birth cohorts who share a group consciousness based on experiencing the common historical events; and (4) generation as a cohort group determined by either peer personality or fertility/demographic characteristics.[93]

Given these varieties of meanings and uses of the term, can *generation* be operationalized as a useful concept and a measurement with which to understand complex experiences of religion in Korean America or will it lend itself to more debate and confusion? Lack of a set of clear and obvious differences between generations such as language preference notwithstanding, recent studies on the English-speaking generation's experiences of religion point to a peculiar juxtaposition of (re)claiming the racialized identity in the context of the color-blind and universalized Christian faith communities. For example, David Kim's and Anthony W. Alumkal's studies document the English-speaking generation's critique of their first-generation immigrant parents for holding fast to the ethnic priori rather than the religious identity in their church. The main reason to coalesce and gather into a faith community for the second generation is to uphold their religious identity and not so much of their ethnic iden-tify.[94] Helen Lee's and Minho Song's studies report the phenomenon of the "quiet exodus" among the English-speaking Korean Americans from their Korean-speaking parents' churches.[95] These studies cite reasons for leaving the first-generation immigrant church as mostly linguist and reli-giously based. For instance, most of the formal liturgy at the Korean American church is conducted in Korean, and its full-time clergy tend to minister more readily to the first generation and their needs. Min and Kim's study also substantiates a sign of the "quiet exodus": Only 42 per-cent of their telephone survey respondents reported that they presently participate in the Christian church, while some 77 percent reported that they had participated in the church during their childhood. Other results from the same study, however, point to a relatively high rate (65 percent) of respondents' affiliation with Christianity.[96]

While some studies report the general dissatisfaction and conflict ex-perienced by the English-speaking Korean Americans in the heavily ethnicity-identified Korean American church, other studies discuss the contemporary trend of building the pan-Asian church. Kelly Chung's study in the Chicago area and Karen Chai's ethnographic study of the English-speaking Korean American church in the Boston area, for exam-ple, both highlight the complex process and rationales among church members for attending a Pan-Asian church.[97] While some pan-Asian churches preach "Christ over culture" by upholding Christian identity over ethnicity, others preach the "Christ in culture" by making symbolic linkages between religious and ethnic identities.[98] So, in the minds of "the church members, being a good Christian is synonymous with ac-cepting traditional Korean cultural values."[99] By highlighting the dy-namic nature of identity negotiation as Koreans, Americans, and Chris-tians among the second-generation Korean Americans, Karen Chai sees the pan-Asian church mainly as the place of mediation. Claiming the "distinctiveness of the pan-Asian church," Chai discusses the agency of the second-generation Korean Americans who manage to package the best of both worlds: selectively remembering and preserving Korean cul-ture while offering (conservative) evangelical openness to non-Korean Americans. Although these selected studies of the 1.5 and subsequent generations' experiences of the pan-Asian church are based on a particular region and tend to be ethnographical approaches, they point to a clearly emerging trend: While forming a faith community based on the shared ethnic identity is less relevant for the English-speaking generation, their racialized and religious identity in the United States plays an instrumental role in forming their own pan-Asian faith communities.

Why does occasional focus on generations and a generation gap emerge at some periods of history and not others? Why conceptualize the historical period from 1988/1992 to the present as mainly the time of generational conflict? Here, Mannhiem's understanding of generation is helpful in addressing these questions. Unlike other scholars who define *generation* as more or less an age/birth cohort, Mannhiem emphasizes the importance of sharing the same social change and events as a group to form "generational uniqueness."[100] For him, generation is not determined so much by sharing the same demographic characteristics such as birth cohort or age group, but by sharing the group consciousness, which results from experiencing common historical events of significance. In this sense, Korean Americans who experienced the keen sense of cognitive dissonance during the 1988 Olympic Games in Seoul and/or the "generational uniqueness" via the *Sa-I-Ku* mark a new generation of Korean Americans. This preference for defining *generation* as a matter of attaining and sharing the group consciousness is also consistent with the increasingly blurred boundaries among nation states in the late twentieth and early twenty-first centuries. As Elaine Kim has noted, "[Y]esterday's young Korean American immigrants have labored beside his immigrant farm-worker parents in segregated rural California. . . . Today's young Korean Americans probably watched 'The Wonderful World of Disney' on television in Seoul as a child and today rents Korean-language videos at a Los Angeles mini-mall store."[101] Through rapid communication technologies and affordable mobility, Korean immigrants and their subsequent English-speaking generations are able to maintain multiple relations and identities across the Pacific Ocean, which in turn enable them to adapt to current life circumstances in the United States. Further, since the post-1988/1992 Korean American community is maintaining transnational ties in different ways than the earlier immigrants, remapping of immigration and migration processes and reconceptualization of the new religious situations are urgently needed.

In short, the status of faith communities in the hyphenated and transnational Korean American community is quite different from that of the earlier immigrants. On the one hand, the fact that over 70 percent of one million Korean Americans are faithfully attending their own 3,500 churches every Sunday deserves recognition. As Stephen Warner states, for example, "Korean Americans are so well organized religiously and so reflective about their religious experience in the United States that they offer the student of American religion an ideal opportunity to explore the parameters of recent change."[102] The conceptual paradigm and categories for studying the relationship between religion and race-ethnicity based on the earlier immigrants' experiences, on the other hand, need to be challenged. Raymond B. William's rhetorical question "How do you add on rooms to a house for a growing family?" points to the danger of thinking that "new immigrants can be squeezed into already existing rooms or that new rooms or temporary lean-tos can be added without changing the basic structure of the house."[103]

Concluding Remarks

Along with the call to struggle with adding "rooms to a house for a growing family," I close with a series of questions that are relevant to addressing such a struggle. What are the cultural and political dynamics within which Korean Americans find themselves as a deeply churched population in the United States? What does it mean to experience the ongoing and rapid growth of the Korean American church while most mainstream Christian denominations have been experiencing decline in the past three decades? As the predominantly English-speaking Korean Americans form and experience filiational and/or affiliational faith communities of their own, what issues, concerns, and theologies will be incorporated into their experience of religion? While English-speaking Korean Americans turn to their pan-Asian, reethnicized Korean American churches or become unchurched, will they continue to hold fast selective memories and rituals that make them "Korean," as the first-generation Korean immigrants have done?

As Goellnicht asserts, I also believe that all historical analysis is always "partial, incomplete, and provisional."[104] In a way, history is "nothing other than the reconstruction and redistribution of a pretended order of things, the interpretation or even transformation of documents given and frozen into monuments."[105] What I have attempted in this chapter is, then, a provisional social history of Korean Americans in the United States by making their religious experiences the center of such a reconstruction. The sweeping scope and formation of Korean American faith communities that this chapter has attempted to chronicle provide a picture of dynamic change of community and the agency of the people that is anything but simple. Faith communities of Korean Americans as important media through which people act, gather, and live out their lives by remembering and reshaping their own sense of their peoplehood in multicultural America shall continue to unfold.

Notes

1. Elaine H. Kim's presidential address at the 1993 annual meeting of the Association for Asian American Studies is reprinted as "Beyond Railroads and Internment: Comments on the Past, Present, and Future of Asian American Studies," in *Privileging Positions: The Sites of Asian American Studies*, ed. Gary Y. Okihiro, Rony Alquizola, and K. Scott Wong (Pullman: Washington University Press, 1995), 11–19.

2. Selected literature that addresses the problem of remaking Asian Americans' presence and their religions as "new" are Jung Ha Kim, "Sources Outside of Europe," in *Spirituality and the Secular Quest*, ed. Peter H. Van Ness (New York: Cross Road, 1996), 53–71; Harry Kitano, *Race Relations*, 5th ed. (Upper Saddle River, N.J.: Prentice Hall, 1997); and Okihiro et al. eds., *Privileging Positions: The Site of Asian American Studies* (Pullman: Washington State University Press, 1995). I also offer further discussion on the topic in this chapter under the subheading "The Immigrant Community, 1968–1988/1992."

3. Here, the term *cultural assimilation approach* to study Korean/Asian American faith communities refers to the tendency of examining religious organizations of Asian Americans as mainly ethnic institutions rather than as the process and the outcome of racial formation in the United States. For further criticism of the cultural assimilation approach and the salience of race in lives of Korea/Asian Americans, see Michael Omi and Howard Winant's *Racial Formation in the United States from the 1960s to the 1990s*, 2d ed. (New York: Routledge, 1994); and David Yoo, ed., *New Spiritual Homes: Religion and Asian Americans* (Honolulu: University of Hawaii Press, 1999).

4. Roger Finke and Rodney Stark, *The Churching of America, 1976–1990: Winners and Losers in Our Religious Economy* (New Brunswick, N.J.: Rutgers University Press, 1992), 5.

5. Emile Durkheim, *The Elementary Forms of the Religious Life*, trans. J. W. Swain (New York: Free Press, 1965), 464.

6. Literature on the privatization of religion in the United States is extensive, both in the fields of social sciences and theology. Robert Bellah et al., *Habits of the Heart: Individualism and Commitment in American Life*, (Berkeley: University of California Press, 1985), for instance, is a book that provides both an overview and information on the extent of privatized religion in mainstream America.

7. Robert Wuthnow, *After Heaven: Spirituality in America Since the 1950s* (Berkeley: University of California Press, 1998), 2.

8. See Ai Ra Kim, *Women Struggling for New Life: The Role of Religion in the Cultural Passage from Korea to America* (Albany: State University of New York Press, 1996), especially chapters 2 and 3.

9. See Kyeyoung Park, *The Korean American Dream: Immigrants and Small Business in New York City* (Ithaca, N.Y.: Cornell University Press, 1997).

10. Okihiro et al., *Privileging Positions*, 93.

11. Okihiro et al., *Privileging Positions*, 94.

12. Sociologically put, this conceptualization of the interplay between "history and biography and the relations between the two within society" is called "sociological imagination." See C. Wright Mills, *The Sociological Imagination* (New York: Grove Press, 1961), 6.

13. Finke and Stark, *The Churching of America*, 6.

14. David Yoo, *New Spiritual Homes*, 10.

15. Sucheng Chan, *Asian Americans: An Interpretive History* (Boston, Mass.: Twayne, 1991); Lucie Ching and Edna Bonacich, eds., *Labor Immigration under Capitalism: Asian Workers in the United States before World War II* (Berkeley: University of California Press, 1984); Kitano, *Race Relations*.

16. Rev. H. N. Allen was not the first Protestant missionary to Korea, but the first missionary from the United States. In 1832, Rev. C. Gutzlaff from Germany was the first Protestant missionary ever to enter Korea, after some years in China first. For further information on both Allen's and Gutzlaff's work in Korea, see Yong-Suk Oh, *Hankook Kidokkyo ei Konan* (The Persecution of Christianity in Korea) (Seoul, Korea: The Institute of Korean Christian Cultural Studies, 1985).

17. Kywang-Mok Lee, *Kewahaki Kwangsuhjibanh kwa Kiddokkyo* (The Kwansuh Region and the Spread of Christianity during the Open Policy Period) (Seoul, Korea: The Institute of Korean Christian Cultural Studies, 1983).

18. Jung Ha Kim, *Bridge-Makers and Cross-Bearers: Korean American Women and the Church*, (Atlanta, Ga.: Scholar's Press, 1997); and Wayne Patterson, *The Korean Frontier in America: Immigration to Hawaii, 1896–1910* (Honolulu: University of Hawaii Press, 1988).

19. Nancy Abelmann and John Lie, *Blue Dreams: Korean Americans and the Los Angeles Riots*, (Cambridge, Mass.: Harvard University Press, 1995); and Park, *Korean American Dream*.

20. Lee, *Kewahaki Kwangsuhjibanh kwa Kiddokkyo* (Kwansuh Region and the Spread of Christianity); and Oh, *Hankook Kidokkyo ei Konan* (Persecution of Christianity in Korea).

21. The Korea–America Treaty was signed in 1882. Cited in Patterson (*Korean Frontier in America*), both Abelmann and Lie's (*Blue Dreams*) and Park's (*Korean American Dream*) books documented some "twenty-odd ginseng merchants," along with another handful of Korean students and diplomats.

22. Bong-Youn Choy, *Koreans in America* (Chicago: Nelson-Hall, 1979); Warren Kim, *Koreans in America* (Seoul, Korea: Po Chin Cha, 1971); and Kitano, *Race Relations*.

23. W. Kim, *Koreans in America*, 10.

24. The first group of contracted laborers from Japan entered Hawaii in 1868. The group comprised 141 men, 6 women, and 1 child. See Jere Kahahashi Takahashi, *Nisei/Sansei: Shifting Japanese American Identities and Politics* (Philadelphia: Temple University Press, 1997), 15–16.

25. Kitano, *Race Relations*, 169.

26. L. Houchins and C.-S. Houchins, "The Korean Experiences in America, 1903–1924," in *The Asian American*, ed. N. Hundley (Santa Barbara, Calif.: ABC-Clio, 1976), 135; and Kitano, *Race Relations*, 269.

27. Chan, *Asian Americans*; Kitano, *Race Relations*; and Patterson, *Korean Frontier in America*.

28. Chae-Kun Yu, "The Correlates of Cultural Assimilation of Korean Immigrants in the U.S.," in *The Korean Diaspora*, ed. Hyung-chan Kim (Santa Barbara, Calif.: ABC-Clio, 1977), 36.

29. Rev. G. H. Jones was a missionary sent from the United States by the United Methodist Church. He was also known by the adopted Korean name, Won-shi Oh. Along with his main parish, the Youngdong Church in Inchon, Rev. Jones also had close connections with other "branch" churches in Seoul and Pusan.

30. San Oak Cho, "A Study of Korean American Churches and Their Growth in the U.S." (unpublished Ph.D. diss., Fuller Theological Seminary, Pasadena, California, 1984); and Lee, *Kewahaki Kwangsuhjibanh kwa Kiddokkyo* (Kwansuh Region and the Spread of Christianity).

31. Cho, "Study of Korean American Churches."

32. In her book (*Korean American Dream*), Kyeyoung Park indicates that based on *The Annual Report* (1995) of the Immigration and Naturalization Service 1,100 picture brides came to the United States from Korea during this historical period.

33. Elaine H. Kim, "Korean American Literature," in *An Interpretive Companion to Asian American Literature*, ed. King-Kok Cheung (New York: Cambridge University Press, 1997), 158.

34. Kim, "Korean American Literature."

35. Elaine H. Kim and Eui-Young Yu, eds., *East to America: Korean American Life Stories*, (New York.: New Press, 1997), 369.

36. Kim and Yu, *East to America*.

37. Robert Booth Fowler, *Religion and Politics in America* (Metuchen, N.J.: Scarecrow, 1985); and Ronald L. Johnston, *Religion in Society: A Sociology of Religion*, 5th ed. (Upper Saddle River, N.J.: Prentice Hall, 1977).

38. Kitano, *Race Relations*, 269.

39. Edward Said, "Secular Criticism," in *Critical Theory Since 1965*, ed. Hazard Adams and Leroy Searle (Tallahassee: Florida State University Press, 1986).

40. Shirley Geok-Lin Lim, "Immigration and Diaspora," in *An Interethnic Companion to Asian American Literature*, ed. King-Kok Cheung (New York: Cambridge University Press, 1997), 296.

41. Won Moo Hurh, "How They Fared in American Homes: A Follow-up Study of Korean American Children," *Children Today* 6 (1967): 102.

42. Won Moo Hurh, "Marginal Children of War: An Exploratory Study of Korean-American Children," *International Journal of Sociology of Family* 2 (1972): 16; and Ministry of Health and Social Affairs, *A Handbook of Korea* (Seoul, Korea: Korean Overseas Information Services, 1967).

43. Velina Hasu Houston, "The Past Melts the Future: A Cultural Essay," *Amerasia Journal* 17 (1991): 79.

44. Cheryl Crabb, "Families Celebrate Korean Kid's Culture," *Atlanta Constitution*, September 13, 1999, D4.

45. Some Asian wives and children of U.S. servicemen entered as nonquota immigrants under the War Bride Act of 1945. But the McCarran Walter Act of 1952 is important for understanding Koran wives of U.S. servicemen. Further, unlike Chinese brides who mostly married co-ethnics, Korean wives of servicemen "more often than not married non-Asian men"; see Espiritu, *Asian American Women and Men*, 56.

46. Chan, *Asian Americans*, 140.

47. Bok-Lim Kim, "Casework with Japanese and Korean Wives of Koreans," *Social Case Work* 53 (1972): 272–79; and Pyong Gap Min, "Korean Americans," in

Asian Americans: Contemporary Trends and Issues, ed. Pyong Gap Min (Thousand Oaks, Calif.: Sage, 1995), 199–231.

48. Kim and Yu, *East to America,* 1.

49. Kim and Yu, *East to America,* 10.

50. Kim and Yu, *East to America,* 11.

51. Designating the years 1988/1992 as a dividing point in Korean American history is nothing but my own attempt to reconstruct and make better sense of the history of Korean American religions in the United States. I see the years 1988 and 1992 as the two most significant, eventful years in regard to understanding contemporary Korean American experiences. For instance, if South Korea's hosting of the Olympic Games in Seoul in 1988 was the key event that impeded Korean Americans from coming to terms with their experiences of "cognitive dissonance," the *Sa-I-Ku,* otherwise known as the L.A. uprising in 1992, was a wake-up call for Korean Americans to reassess their complacent dreaming of the "American dream" in the United States. By probing the significance of these two historic events, I argue that Korean Americans at large have experienced the transition from being predominantly an immigrant community to a more conscious transnational community in many respects.

52. Hyun Y. Kang, "Remembering Home," in *Dangerous Women: Gender and Korean Nationalism,* ed. Elaine H. Kim and Chungmo Choi (New York: Routledge, 1998).

53. Kang, "Remembering Home," 250.

54. Shirley Geok-Lin Lim, "Immigration and Diaspora," 297, 292.

55. Paula Giddings, *When and Where I Enter: The Impact of Black Women on Race and Sex in America* (New York: Morrow, 1984).

56. U.S. Bureau of the Census, *1990 Census of the Population, Asian and Pacific Islanders in the United States* (Washington, D.C.: Government Printing Office [GPO], 1993). Other statistical data from the U.S. Census, 1970, 1980, and 1990, were cited in Kitano, *Race Relations;* Min, "Korean Americans"; and Park, *Korean American Dream.* These data released by the U.S. Census are inevitably conservative.

57. Raymond B. Williams cites other statistical data to substantiate the claim that the United States is rapidly moving toward "the first universal nation" in *Christian Pluralism in the United States: The Indian Immigrant Experience* (New York: Cambridge University Press, 1996), 25.

58. The term, "late first-generation immigrant" is borrowed from Raymond Brady Williams, *Christian Pluralism in the United States,* 10

59. Edna Bonacich, "The Site of Class," in *Privileging Positions,* ed. Okihiro et al., 67.

60. Edna Bonacich, "The Site of Class," 68.

61. While there are churches that serve particular classes, occupations, and gender groups in South Korea, no Korean American church claims to serve a particular people of specific social categories exclusively. For example, there are at least two well-established Protestant churches in South Korea in which the majority of adherents are *yeonaein* ("artists"), such as actors/actresses and singers; and the Women's Church was also formed in the late 1980s by feminist women theologians who criticized the masculine perspectives and articulations in *ming-jung* theology (which is often translated as the theology of "commoners," the "op-

pressed," and "grassroots people"). Most founders of the Women's Church were educated in Bible colleges and/or seminaries in the United States.

62. Omi and Winant, *Racial Formation in the United States*.

63. Peter Kwong, "Asian American Studies Needs Class Analysis," in *Privileging Positions*, ed. Okihiro et al., 74.

64. Peter Kwong, "Asian American Studies Needs Class Analysis," 75.

65. Peter Kwong, "Asian American Studies Needs Class Analysis," 76.

66. An in-depth analysis of Korean American labor participation and its impact on their family lives has been conducted. Pyong Gap Min, for example, documented an unusually high percentage of self-employed Korean merchants in the greater Atlanta area and in the United States in general: "An Exploratory Study of Kin Ties among Korean Immigrant Families in Atlanta," *Journal of Comparative Family Studies* 15 (1984): 75–86. See also his books, *Ethnic Business Enterprise: Korean Small Business in Atlanta* (New York: Center for Migration Studies, 1988) and *Caught in the Middle: Korean Merchants in America's Multiethnic Cities* (Berkeley: University of California Press, 1996). See also Ivan Light and Edna Bonacich, *Immigrant Entrepreneurs: Koreans in Los Angeles, 1965–1982* (Berkeley: University of California Press, 1988).

67. Won Moo Hurh and Kwang Chung Kim, "Religious Participation of Korean Immigrants in the United States," *Journal for the Scientific Study of Religion* 2 (1990): 19–34. For discussions on "status inconsistency" in the context of Korean American community, see Pyong Gap Min, *Caught in the Middle*; and Hurh and Kim, *Korean Immigrants in America: A Structural Analysis of Ethnic Confinement and Adhesive Adaptation* (Rutherford, N.J.: Fairleigh Dickinson University Press, 1984).

68. Sang Hyun Lee, "Pilgrimage and Home in the Wilderness of Marginality: Symbols and Context in Asian American Theology," *Amerasia Journal* 22 (1996): 149–60.

69. Funded by the Atlanta Prevention Institute, five hundred Korean American families were randomly selected to participate in the survey research during 1992 by the author.

70. Kwang Chun Kim and Shin Kim, "The Ethnic Roles of Korean Immigrant Churches in the U.S.," in *Pilgrims and Missionaries from a Different Shore: Korean Americans and Their Religions*, ed. Ho-Youn Kwon, Kwang Chung Kim, and Stephen Warner (University Park: Pennsylvania State University Press, 2001).

71. Kim and Kim, "Ethnic Roles of Korean Immigrant Churches."

72. The feminization of Korean American Christian faith communities in the United States is well documented in Hurh and Kim, "Religious Participation of Korean Immigrants"; A. R. Kim, *Women Struggling for a New Life*; and J. H. Kim, *Bridge-Makers and Cross-Bearers*.

73. A. R. Kim, *Women Struggling for a New Life*; and J. H. Kim, *Bridge-Makers and Cross-Bearers*.

74. Kim and Kim, "Ethnic Role of Korean Immigrant Churches."

75. The list of the ordained clergywomen was obtained from the Division of the Ordained Ministry of the United Methodist Church denomination headquarters in Nashville, Tennessee. The list was compiled in 1998.

76. Raymond Brady Williams, *Christian Pluralism in the United States* (New York: Cambridge University Press, 1996), 23–25.

77. Huping Ling, *Surviving on the Golden Mountain: A History of Chinese American Women and Their Lives* (Albany: State University of New York, 1998), 102.

78. Ling, *Surviving on the Golden Mountain*, 102.

79. Korean immigrants often use *yokimin* (translated as "reverse immigration") to imply what social scientists call "return migration" or "twice migration."

80. John J. Macionis, *Sociology*, 7th ed. (Upper Saddle River, N.J.: Prentice Hall, 1999), 295.

81. *The Korean Journal*, February 19–25, 1989; and *The Southeast News*, December 18–24, 1988, and October 30–November 4, 1989.

82. This report of the *New York Times* (August 11, 1995) is cited in Kim and Kim, "Ethnic Role of Korean Immigrant Churches."

83. The U.S. Immigration and Naturalization Service counted 35,849 Korean immigrants' entry into the United States in 1987; 34,703 in 1988; 34,222 in 1989; 32,301 in 1990; and 26,516 in 1991. The drastic decline in the number of Korean immigrants is recorded from 1992 to 1995: 19,359 in 1992; 18,026 in 1993; and 10,799 in 1994. The same data are also cited in Min (*Caught in the Middle*) and K. Park (*Korean American Dream*).

84. This estimate is released by "Radio Seoul" (a Korean-language radio station in the United States) and was also printed in *Korea Times Los Angeles*, English edition, May 11, 1992. The same data and a more detailed table of categories of Korean-owned businesses are also documented in Min, *Caught in the Middle*.

85. *Korea Times*, May 11, 1992; and *The Southeast News*, May 19, 1992.

86. The term, *Sa-I-Ku* refers to the L.A. riot/uprising. The literal meaning of *Sa-I-Ku* is "4–2–9" in Korean. It commemorates the significance of April 29 (1992) in the formation of the Korean American consciousness in the United States. Korean Americans' reluctance to name what had happened during April 29 to May 2, 1992, in Los Angeles as a "riot," "uprising," or "rebellion" is significant in and of itself. To them, the date of the historical incident that marked the new consciousness of being Korean American is connoted in the term *Sa-I-Ku*.

87. The U.S. Bureau of the Census, 1990.

88. Timothy P. Fong, *The Contemporary Asian American Experience: Beyond the Model Minority* (Upper Saddle River, N.J.: Prentice Hall, 1998), 41.

89. Vern L. Bengston, "Is the 'Contract across Generations' Changing? Effects of Population Aging on Obligations and Expectations across Age Group," in *The Changing Contract across Generations*, ed. Vern L. Bengston and W. Andrew Achenbaun (New York: Aldine de Gruyter, 1993), 39.

90. Yoo, *New Spiritual Homes*, 11.

91. Bengston, "Is the 'Contract across Generations' Changing?" xvi.

92. Bengston and Achenbaun, *Changing Contract across Generations*. This is an insightful edition that published fourteen articles by scholars whose works addressed issues related to generation, age cohort, generation gap, and generational contract.

93. Bengston, "Is the 'Contract across Generations' Changing?" 9–11.

94. David K. Kim, "Becoming: Korean Americans, Faith, and Identity—Observations on an Emerging Culture" (Master of Divinity thesis, Harvard Divinity School, Cambridge, Massachusetts, 1993); and Anthony W. Alumkal, "Being Korean, Being Christian: Particularism and Universalism in a Second Generation

Congregation," in *Pilgrims and Missionaries from a Different Shore,* ed. Kwon, Kim, and Warner.

95. Minho Song, "Towards the Successful Movement of the English-Speaking Ministry within the Korean Immigrant Churches" (paper presented at Katalyst, March 21–24, 1994); cited in Chai, "Competing for the Second Generation," 295–332; and Helen Lee, "Silent Exodus," *Christianity Today,* August 12, 1996, 51–52.

96. Pyong Gap Min and Dae Young Kim, "Intergenerational Transmission of Religion and Culture: Korean Immigrants in New York" (paper presented at the annual meeting of the Association for the Sociology of Religion, Washington, D.C., August 2000).

97. Chai, "Competing for the Second Generation"; and Chong, "What It Means to Be Christians."

98. In his book, *Christ and Culture* (N.Y.: Harper, 1975), Richard H. Niebuhr talks about several models for describing the relationship between the Church (i.e., religion) and the surrounding society (i.e., culture). "Christ over/against culture" and "Christ in culture" are two of Niebuhr's own models.

99. Chong, "What It Means to Be Christians," 4.

100. Karl Mannheim, "The Problem of Generations," in *Essays on the Sociology of Knowledge by Karl* Mannheim, ed. Paul Keeskemeti (London: Routledge & Kegan, 1928 [1963]), 127.

101. Kim and Yu, *East to America,* 174.

102. R. Stephen Warner, "The Korean Immigrant Church as Case and Model," in *Pilgrims and Missionaries from a Different Shore,* ed Kwon, Kim, and Warner.

103. Williams, *Christian Pluralism in the United States,* 272.

104. Donald C. Goellnicht, "Blurring Boundaries: Asian American Literature as Theory," in *An Interethnic Companion to Asian American Literature,* ed. King-Kok Cheung, 355.

105. T. Minh-ha Trinh, *Women, Native, Other: Writing Postcoloniality and Feminism* (Bloomington: Indiana University Press, 1989), 84.

CHAPTER EIGHT

ASIAN AMERICAN PAN-ETHNIC FORMATION AND CONGREGATIONAL CULTURE

Russell Jeung

Paul would say, "To the Jews I'll be a Jew and to the Greeks I'll be a Greek." So maybe, in order to share the gospel among Asians, you must first understand what does it mean to be Asian. Why is it that you can do outreach to Asian Americans while another Anglo congregation can't? What is it that attracts people to each other?

—Chinese American minister of an Asian American congregation

When China and Japan were at war, Chinese and Japanese churches in the United States organized their members to support homeland movements.[1] During World War II, Chinese Americans wore buttons declaring "I am Chinese" to distinguish themselves from Japanese Americans who were being rounded up for internment camps. As one of the primary social institutions in the community, these congregations served to maintain ethnic ties and to reinforce a specific linguistic/cultural identity.

Two generations later, Chinese and Japanese American congregations are undergoing a significant transformation into pan-ethnic congregations. Groups who were once at war now pray and worship together with common songs, liturgies, and religious understandings. Those who distanced themselves from the other now unite under a single group identity and new subculture. In fact, half of this study's churches in the San Francisco Bay Area now target *Asian* Americans instead of focusing on a single ethnic group. As congregational entrepreneurs, Christian leaders have chose a newly constituted racial group as their spiritual market niche.[2]

Given the traditional enmity between Chinese and Japanese and the historic American congregational pattern of assimilation, an Asian American pan-ethnic church seems an unlikely new form of religious congregation. The minister in the opening quotation asks, "What is it that attracts people to each other?" Similarly, this chapter explores why Asian Americans have formed new pan-ethnic congregations instead of remaining ethnic-specific or assimilating into the American mainstream denominational landscape. *What are the factors that have led Chinese and Japanese American congregations to claim new identities as pan-ethnic Asian American ones?* Furthermore, this minister suggests that we "understand what does it mean to be Asian." If these pan-ethnic congregations are no longer based on a common cultural or linguistic solidarity, *what do ministers mean when they identify their congregations as pan-Asian? What are the congregational cultures that emerge?* This study of forty-four congregations in the San Francisco Bay Area tells the story of the emergence and expressions of Asian American congregations.

I argue that today, Asian American churches that are purposely pan-ethnic have begun to mobilize around racial identities that are not fixed, but fluid. Because the racial experiences of Asian Americans vary by ethnicity, generation, class, and gender,[3] Asian American pan-ethnic identity tends to be more symbolic in nature than grounded in a particular common cultural or linguistic background.[4] Similar to the notion of symbolic ethnicity, a symbolic racial identity deals more with the expressive feeling of connection to a group than actual ethnic cultural commonalties.[5] Yet this subjective connection to pan-ethnic group symbols might be very salient and meaningful so that one's identity does affect both individual and group behavior and patterns. Building solidarity and mobilizing a congregation around this pan-ethnic identity is thus significantly different from organizing around common roots, as previous ethnic congregations have.

Because the group boundaries of Asian American pan-ethnicity are relatively undefined, ministers as cultural entrepreneurs have much say and influence over the construction of this new grouping. This study includes in-depth interviews of forty-four San Francisco Bay Area ministers that identify their Christian churches as Chinese, Japanese, or Asian American Christian congregations.[6] I interviewed the ministers about their views on topics such as the nature of racial and ethnic groups, their theology, and the role of the church within the community. In particular, I examined the ministers' definitions of pan-ethnicity and the ethnic makeup of their congregations.

First, this chapter reviews theories about the development of ethnic congregations. The formation of Asian American pan-ethnic congregations challenges theories in the sociology of race and religion that expect the assimilation of Chinese and Japanese American churches. Second, it discusses the political economy of the San Francisco Bay Area that categorizes groups by race and structures pan-ethnic formation. Third, it details the demographic trends and generational transitions that necessitate organizational changes to ensure the survival and growth of congregations that were originally Chinese or Japanese American. Fourth, it examines the broader institutional contexts that inform ministers of racial discourse and models for church development. Because evangelical and mainline ministers differ in how they define the group, Asian American, their respective congregational cultures differ in worship style, ministry focus, and activities. By comparing mainline Christian with evangelical congregational cultures, this chapter shows how pan-ethnicity remains a fluid, socially constructed grouping.

Theories of Ethnic Church Development

Churches of previous white immigrant groups to America have tended to evolve from ethnic institutions to nonethnic, denominational churches.[7] As members acculturated to such an extent that their ethnicity no longer distinguished them much from other Americans, ethnic churches no longer had to meet particular group needs and could not sustain themselves by serving only one ethnic constituency. Immigrant congregations either died out or moved to the suburbs without retaining ethnic specificity. The building that remained would house a new congregation meeting the needs of the local population.[8] As American-born generations of Chinese and Japanese Americans also become acculturated, move away from ethnic neighborhoods, and out-marry in high percentages, we would expect these groups to assimilate into local congregations.[9]

Not only do individuals acculturate, but ethnic institutions assimilate into the American religious landscape as well. Following a trajectory suggested by H. Richard Niebuhr, Mark Mullins argues that, over time, ethnic churches deethnicize as they adapt to generational differences.[10] Immigrant congregations, preserving the culture for newcomers, maintain language and ethnic traditions. Second-generation congregations are bilingual to serve the linguistic needs of both the older and younger generations. As the older generation dies out, congregations must broaden their target group and create an environment that would be attractive to others. The process of accommodating English-speaking members and incorporating families of mixed marriages leads to the transition from ethnic congregations to multiethnic congregations.

Similarly, R. Stephen Warner and Judith Wittner emphasize the role of the American cultural context in shaping the generational transition of ethnic churches.[11] In the introduction to the anthology, *Gatherings in Diaspora: Religious Communities and the New Immigration*, Warner stresses "the continuity of the immigrant religious experience between the nineteenth century and the present."[12] Although regional, national, and linguistic cultural identities may decline, religious identities eventually win out and survive.

Warner also writes that racial dynamics, although currently opera-tive, are not permanent factors affecting the life cycle of ethnic churches. He believes "the irreducibility of 'race' applies primarily to the African American experience."[13] Furthermore, he suggests that assimilation is a protracted process so that "there is no consensus among us whether de-scendants of the groups we focus on will maintain in the middle of the next century the same racial status that they occupy today."[14]

Contrary to expectations, however, Chinese and Japanese American churches are not dying out or becoming open to all but are adapting by becoming Asian American. Of the forty-four congregations in the San Francisco Bay Area that were surveyed in this study, half now claim a pan-ethnic identity. These findings require new understandings of the re-lationships between race and religion beyond the straight-line assimila-tion paradigm that accounts for the acculturation of Asian Americans but not the structural assimilation of this group.

The Racialization of Asian Americans in the San Francisco Bay Area

Possessing the oldest and one of the largest concentrations of Asians in the United States, the San Francisco Bay Area structures pan-ethnic for-mation through its politics and its economy. Within the Bay Area, Asians make up 31 percent of San Francisco County, 20 percent of Alameda County, and 21 percent of Santa Clara County, according to the 2000 U.S. Census. This presence of Asian Americans has clearly affected the public education system, the regional economy, and, increasingly, local politics. In turn, these institutions have shaped the character and contours of the ethnic and racial identities of Asian Americans.

As Asians receive their education in the San Francisco Bay Area, they become socialized into a system that acknowledges students' ethnic backgrounds and multiculturalism to a limited degree.[15] Almost every school district in the area now has a policy regarding multicultural edu-cation and developing ethnic pride. As an example, Santa Clara Unified School District, with minority students making up 57 percent of the pop-ulation, approved a set of "Community Values and Beliefs" that included fostering a "respect for diversity."

Institutions of higher education in the area also recognize ethnic and racial groupings. At the University of California at Berkeley, where the undergraduate student body in 1998 was 41 percent Asian and 62 percent minority, students must take an "American Cultures" course in which three of five racial groups are covered in a comparative manner. Not only do students learn about different racial groups, but also they divide into these groups socially.[16] On campus, students learn what it means to be Asian American. This racialization, in which race becomes a significant factor in interpreting social patterns, exemplifies how social structures such as the school system legitimate certain groupings.

Upon entering the labor force in the Bay Area, Asian Americans find themselves within a globalized economy where transnational Pacific Rim ties are valued. For example, in Cupertino, a suburb on the San Francisco peninsula, the chamber of commerce targeted a membership drive specifically toward Asian Americans who make up 22 percent of the businesses in the city.[17] As industries and businesses increasingly view Asians and Asian Americans as a viable market, a side result is a growing group consciousness among Asians of their common market identity.

Political activities also structure how Asians view themselves and group together. The increased number of Asian Americans elected to office in the 1990s, especially in the Bay Area, signals an emergence of a possible ethnic voting bloc pursuing its own material interests. Whereas Oakland had only one elected Asian American official in 1990, voters had elected two Asian American city council members, one county supervisor, and one state assembly member in 2001. With the increased attention on immigrant issues recently, large voter registration drives aimed at Asian Americans have been successful.[18]

The San Francisco Bay Area, in sum, acknowledges the ethnic and racial presence of Asian Americans even though they may be an invisible minority throughout the rest of the country or caught between either black or white. Through the educational system, business affairs, local politics, and the media, the Bay Area embraces a form of multiculturalism that accentuates and superficially celebrates ethnic and racial differences while still promoting a common culture based on market forces.[19]

Although churches operate independently from much state intervention, these racial categories also influence the religious world. Ministers are cognizant of the racial categories imposed by government policies and understand that mainstream society views Asian Americans as a monolithic group. An evangelical minister who works with a pan-ethnic network of churches expressed why Asian Americans need to organize across ethnic lines:

> Our vision is that we see when you get to second, third generations, the ethnic lines are very blurred. I think a large part of it is because the way the school system categorizes people. The census categorizes people. That kind of gives Asian ethnic groups a sense of being lumped together. And the Asian American movement grew out of a political agenda, basically for funding and resources are so limited and the struggle for identity and recognition. Since we're lumped together anyway, when we get together, we get more attention.

Within this multiethnic, multiracial context in which almost everyone is a minority and seeks a group identity, ministers build their churches along pan-ethnic lines legitimated by identity politics and consumer marketing.

As Asian Americans have become networked within the Bay Area, pan-ethnic congregations have emerged. The number of pan-ethnic Asian American congregations in the region has risen dramatically over the past decade, from one in 1989 to five in 1993 and twenty-two in 1998. Eight are new pan-ethnic start-up congregations or networks and fourteen were originally ethnic-specific but now have a broader mission focus. Why does this institutional change toward pan-ethnicity occur? The next sections, identifying demographic trends and generational transitions, analyze factors initiating change.

Demographic Trends: The Need for Japanese American Congregations to Expand Their Target Market

Both Chinese and Japanese American churches have existed in the United States for over one hundred years and for five generations.[20] However, they differ in that Japanese American churches now face a shrinking pool of families from which to draw but Chinese American churches have a growing population base. Within the San Francisco Bay Area, the Japanese American population has grown 41.8 percent in the last two decades. The Chinese American population, on the other hand, has seen much more dramatic growth, 193.4 percent in the same time period. Demographers predict that the Chinese American population in California will continue to grow by 38 percent while the Japanese American population will increase by only 7 percent in the next decade.[21]

The age distribution of these two ethnic communities indicates varying potentials for future growth. The Japanese American community is markedly older and has smaller household sizes. Within California, 34.6 percent of the population is under twenty-five years of age but only 26.7 percent of the Japanese American population are this young. While the mean number of children per household in California is 0.72, Japanese Americans only average 0.42 children per household. Chinese American households roughly match the general population's profile. With fewer families and young adults, the Japanese American church community cannot grow through biological growth as much as the Chinese American church can.

Out-marriage rates also portend the market potential for ethnic and pan-ethnic congregations. A recent study of out-marriage rates nationally indicates that 25.6 percent of Japanese Americans marry outside of their ethnicity and 12.1 percent of Chinese Americans marry outside of their ethnicity.[22] However, these out-marriage rates also indicate a greater number of interethnic marriages between Asian ethnic groups. For example, the percent of Japanese Americans marrying other Asians increased from 11.9 percent of all out-marriages in 1980 to 20.3 percent in 1990. The number of Chinese Americans marrying other Asian groups grew from 22.2 percent in 1980 to 32.7 percent in 1990. Increased Asian intermarriage provides a larger pool for pan-ethnic congregations.

Ministers also noted that Japanese Americans no longer reside in ethnic concentrations and have moved out of urban centers. As a result, these churches have less potential members in their neighborhoods. In contrast, Chinese congregations will continue to have large spatial concentrations of Chinese Americans to serve.[23] A Japanese American minister observed the impact of these shifts in out-marriage and residency on his church:

> Our congregation is 85 to 90 percent Japanese American but the direction is Asian American. Two couples in our church who are members have married Caucasians. The majority by far have been with Chinese Americans. Most of them live outside [San Francisco]. That's another difference between the Japanese American community and the Chinese American community. A greater percentage of the third generation have left the City, haven't had the same kind of family unit, family support and reason to stay in the City as the Chinese Americans have. Because of the professions, they've moved out.

These demographic changes have spurred the transition of Japanese American congregations into pan-ethnic ones.

Generational Issues: Causes for Schisms within Chinese American Congregations

As the Japanese American church faces a shrinking target population in the Bay Area, the Chinese American churches now welcome more immigrants joining their congregations. Unfortunately, great numbers of newcomers exacerbate a tension already present between the first generation and the 1.5 and second generations in these congregations.[24] To service the heterogeneous Chinese population, Chinese American churches have to minister to different subgroups of language, age, and culture. This tension between the immigrant and American-born generations has long been the central organizational issue for the Chinese American church. Cultural differences and unequal power relations can lead to sectarian splits that spawn new pan-ethnic congregations.

Cultural differences between generations make up one tension. Just as Niebuhr observed that previous immigrant churches were primarily cultural institutions, the Chinese and Japanese American congregations today play a strong role in preserving cultural traditions and values. One Chinese American minister described the desire of immigrant parents to maintain ethnic customs and practices through the church: "There's a second agenda to say that we also want to maintain Chinese culture. We want the church to reflect the Chinese culture so that it maintains it for the young people and it maintains it for those Chinese that have grown up here that have lost touch with their culture."

The culture that immigrants wish to preserve and transmit contrasts with the upbringing and values of those born here. According to those pastors who are developing Asian American congregations, the Confucian ethic of "saving face" and maintaining formal respect for those with status is a significant cultural orientation that distinguishes the generations. As Asians grow up in the United States, these concerns for keeping quiet, controlling emotions, and avoiding embarrassment lessen. One minister explained the difference between Asian Americans and Chinese immigrants:

> I think I'm realizing that Asian Americans—like a lot of the boomers—value authenticity over formality. In fact I think the older generation, they almost have a reaction if you are too open with them. Or they don't want you to show weakness. In fact they may even have a problem with weakness or problem with emotions. And so they want and expect and desire a leader to be strong, to be impregnable. They don't expect you necessarily to be real close.

According to these ministers, differences in cultural orientation discourage younger Asian Americans from staying in church or joining a church.

Power relations within the church is another issue facing ethnic congregations. As the younger members come of age in the Chinese American church, they conflict with the older members about unequal relations of power. Younger, English-speaking ministers complained of lacking status and resources within bilingual congregations. Furthermore, they felt relegated to doing "youth ministry," which was considered less important by the Chinese-speaking. One minister complained that by controlling church functions, the Chinese-speaking congregation effectively disenfranchised the English-speaking congregation and, as a result, individuals abandoned the church. Not even the strongest ethnic sentiment, one's connection to the community through ethnic food, could keep these Chinese Americans coming:

> There's a luncheon. But it's hardly a joint lunch because it's catered Chinese food and the whole thing has this sense of flavor and environment

of being really Taiwanese. They make announcements without translating, they make Taiwanese jokes without translating. And whenever there's special occasions like a birthday, it's in Chinese and it's not translated. And so basically they're expecting the English to kind of fit in and, "Oh yeah, this is wonderful time of community!"

Due to their lack of autonomy, resources, and status, Chinese American ministers seeking to introduce major changes to worship or ministry focus had to establish new churches.[25] Chinese Americans have started seven of the eight pan-ethnic congregations that were new church-starts. One justified his rationale to create a new church by claiming that a pan-ethnic start-up would not face competing agendas and thus be more effective in accomplishing the spiritual mission of the gospel.

In summary, numerous Chinese and Japanese American congregations now identify as Asian American. Demographic shifts require a change for the institutional survival of Japanese American congregations. With a smaller market niche, these congregations have gradually shifted focus and target. Immigration and generational differences have prompted Chinese American ministers to start new pan-ethnic congregations. Lacking opportunity, resources, and freedom of ministry, they have seceded to begin new congregations.

Mainline Construction of Asian American Pan-Ethnicity: The Institutional Context

Given these congregational issues, where do churches find models for change? Their broader religious worlds, also known as institutional fields, furnish innovative and alternative models for organizing congregations and developing ministries.[26] American Christians fall into two basic groups with mainline, liberal, and progressive Christians within one institutional field and conservatives, evangelicals, charismatics, and fundamentalists within another.[27] This two-party thesis is helpful in understanding the divergent expressions of Asian American pan-ethnic congregations. Not only do the ministers align as either evangelical or mainline in theological orientation, but also they remain organizationally distinct from one another with different institutional fields. From their theological discourse that circulates with their institutional circles, mainline ministers construct a broad definition for Asian Americans.

The Mainline Institutional Field

Mainline church leaders look to their denominations, seminaries, and nonprofit organizations as sources of pan-ethnic understanding. Mainline denominations recognized and established pan-ethnic Asian American professional caucuses and youth camps as early as 1971. Acknowledging a need for Asian American leadership development, representation on boards, and resources for Asian American ministries, these caucuses advocated official recognition within their respective denominations.[28]

When a group in the South Bay wanted to develop a pan-ethnic congregation, it contacted the former associate executive of the regional presbytery who had also come from their same home church. The institutional work of the caucus to increase awareness of minority needs as well as the presence of minorities in presbytery leadership opened up opportunities to establish new pan-ethnic church developments. This minister recounted why his denomination recognized the legitimate need for minorities to have their own congregations because they were not being served:

> If you look at Santa Clara, there's easily half a dozen [Presbyterian churches]. Some of those churches might have 10 percent ethnic. I would say that's true for all denominations. You can probably pick those churches that are genuinely multicultural. They would be the exception to the rule. So the Presbytery said "Fine, go with our blessings. We'll even help with some funding and help secure leadership."

These official denominational activities establish the institutional space need for the development of pan-ethnic church models and the diffusion of its elements to other churches.

Mainline seminaries promote pan-ethnicity as well. The mainline Graduate Theological Seminary (GTU) has trained several Asian American ministers in the Bay Area. As early as 1972, the GTU provided institutional space for the Asian Center for Theologies and Strategies, now called the Pacific Asian Center for Theologies and Strategies (PACTS). PACTS and other schools of the GTU sponsor courses on "Asian American Religions" and employ texts such as *Out of Silence: Emerging Themes in Asian American Churches*.[29] Formal education thus establishes normative pressures to organize along pan-ethnic lines.

The community nonprofit world also furnishes models to the church. Mainline liberal congregations, who tend to be more involved in community issues of race and social justice, work more closely with these nonprofits and view them as peer organizations. Within the San Francisco Bay Area, the Asian American nonprofit sector is especially well established with long-standing organizations such as the Asian Law Caucus, Asian Neighborhood Design, and Asian Health Services. Because these agencies address the same kinds of concerns and work with the same constituencies as their congregations, mainline ministers conceive of their congregations as peers to these organizations.

Institutional structures within denominations, educational curricula that recognize Asian American pan-ethnicity, and nonprofit organizational models shape how ministers think about congregational identity. They establish pan-ethnic congregations with understandings from these institutional bases that circulate a broad definition of the group, Asian Americans.

The Mainline Definition of Pan-Ethnicity

What is this understanding of Asian Americans that mainline ministers hold? Following a politics of identity model, ministers acknowledge the historical, racialized experiences of this group as the primary bond of pan-ethnic identity and solidarity. Two characteristics of mainline liberalism that structure racial understandings are its prophetic morality and its belief in tolerance. In their religious role as being a prophetic voice to the community, mainline churches address concerns of peace and social justice.[30] When examining the Asian American situation through these lenses, ministers identify issues of racial discrimination and community development as major arenas of struggle. In their belief in tolerance, mainline Christians reject the orthodox teaching that Christianity is the only true religion. This relativism allows Asian American ministers to more easily accept and embrace Asian traditions and religious beliefs as part of their identity, faith experience, and congregational practice. Mainline liberals thus see Asian Americans as a marginalized group in need of empowerment, as well as a group that must reconstruct its ethnic identity in order to be whole children of God.

In analyzing the issues of injustice that Asians face in the United States, mainline ministers in this study often named racism, both institutional and individual, as the major cause for the social inequities and marginalization that they and their members experienced.[31] On a broad level, racism creates barriers for Asian Americans in gaining acceptance and power within American corporations and institutions. On an individual level, mainline ministers express that racism affects members' self-esteem and interpersonal relationships. One minister describes the Asian American experience of being categorized and treated as a foreigner or newcomer to this country:

> The Church does a disservice when we don't accept people as they fully are. [Unfortunately, we] first try to put them in some category. For my experience and for many Asians when they come in contact with wider society, when [others] can't tell what your ethnicity is, they try to find out. But they're not always good about coming out and asking what your ethnic background is.
>
> It's more like, "Where are you from?" And you say, "I'm from San Francisco." "No, no, where are you *really* from?!?" they ask.

The mainline ministers interpret this everyday assignation as foreigner as a symbol of the marginalization of Asian Americans. Even though this group has been here for generations, they remain perpetual outsiders to American society who still face discrimination. While Asian Americans are marginalized as a group, they are also pressured to assimilate into Western values, religious traditions, and culture that are deemed superior.

However, the ministers believe that Asian Americans do have vibrant ethnic heritages that their members should embrace and practice. The tolerance of mainline and liberal churches toward other religions and traditions opens up space for the exploration of Asian traditions by Asian American congregations. By embracing both their religious and ethnic/racial identities, mainline churches help Asian Americans be "accepted as they fully are," as the minister quoted previously recommended. Another minister expresses why he places emphasis on Asian cultural practices:

> There's so many things within the Japanese, Chinese, Asian culture that can be affirmed within Christianity if a person studies it in depth. The Euro-Western approach is to say those things are maybe pagan or heathen or primordial or primitive. . . . Not so! There are ancient cultures which are longer than what we have in the West and there are a lot of richness. If we find the contribution we can make towards reality or Christianity that comes out of culture, that'd be great.

These two theological orientations framing Asian American mainline churches result in an understanding of Asian Americans as a racialized grouping that needs to reclaim its ethnic heritage and claim rights as a disenfranchised minority.

Mainline Asian American Congregational Culture

With this definition of Asian American identity, mainline ministers utilize religious resources both from their faith traditions and their ethnic cultures to establish practices regarding what Fumitaka Matsuoka terms "the Asian American faith quest for identity." He suggests, "Asian Americans are caught in a web of assimilation that will not easily let us go. . . . To compound the problem, we Asian Americans find ourselves in a liminal world that is cultural and linguistic, as well as cross-generational in character. A liminal world is the 'place of in-betweenness.'"[32]

The liminality of Asian Americans as culturally and linguistically marginal to Asia and racially marginal to America becomes a dominant spiritual issue for mainline congregations. To address this issue, ministers create Asian American mainline religious practices through the reinterpretation of Christian symbols, the rearticulation of Asian practices, and outreach to communities in a multiracial American setting.

Worship Style

In mainline Asian American congregations, the worship style is more traditional and liturgical than evangelical congregations. Very few Asian or Asian American songs or hymns are sung, but the liturgical rites are the worship practices that ministers have more easily contextualized for the Asian American experience.[33] Festivals, communion, and prayers symbolize and commemorate Asian American group boundaries.

Celebrations of festivals and memorials are the primary symbolic occasions that reinforce the congregation's Asian American group identity. Though the mainline churches usually followed the Christian calendar and employed denominational liturgies, church services would often recognize Asian holidays and particularly held ceremonies to remember ancestors, a Confucian ethic. These ministers did not consider Asian festivals and rituals as pagan, especially since Asian Americans do not celebrate them as ancestor worship. One pastor noted:

> I haven't found the difference and true distinction between when Asian culture says we remember, honor our ancestors and a Christian understanding of we celebrate the saints and we celebrate when we gather around the Lord's Table.
>
> For Asian Americans who grow up here, who are as far from the Christian experience as they are from their traditional ancestral experience, the ones in America are not calling on their ancestors.

Instead, honoring one's ancestors is an Asian value that the congregations attempt to instill. A priest commented:

> Even though the English service is in English, we respect Chinese traditions. For example, at Chinese New Year's, we had a big liturgy. At Chinese New Year's we have a very beautiful bilingual liturgy in Cantonese and English with Chinese and American music. At the end, we do the traditional tribute, ceremonial tribute to the ancestors. We build a shrine and at the conclusion of mass, we pay tribute to the ancestors. That's one way we keep ties to the culture.

Rites that remember one's ancestors, then, are Asian family practices that are legitimated by the church both to reinforce Asian group identity and to introduce Asian rituals into a Christian service.

Along with rearticulating Asian practices, mainline congregations infuse Christian rituals with new meanings. Ministers often alter the form of

Christian rituals to refresh the meaning behind the practice and to make them resonate more closely with Asian Americans. One Asian American congregation served Chinese moon cakes and tea for communion. Round moon cakes (*yuebing*), filled with red bean paste or some other filling, symbolize unity and family. Eaten especially during the Mid-Autumn Festival by Chinese, the roundness of the cakes and the moon represents a family reuniting. When combined with the Christian communion of the saints, this ritual is a poignant act for members who grew up eating moon cakes. For those who did not know about the moon cakes, the ritual is both a reminder of Christian unity and a lesson about Chinese heritage. The pastor summarizes: "For the people, family is very important. To me, that's a chance for people trying to stay connected to that story, to the family story. . . . Asian Americans typically feel, on a gut level, more strongly connected to family than [American] culture in general."

Other churches also modify the form of communion. One employed *bao* (Chinese steamed buns) and tea to illustrate how integral Jesus was to their daily lives. Another used *mochi* (Japanese pastry) and *sake* (rice wine), and yet another pastor called Jesus the "Rice of Life" instead of the "Bread of Life."

These new rituals are distinctly hybridized elements of Asian American Christianity, an emergent subculture with its own symbols and practices that invent and borrow from Asia and America. A minister describes how he tries to integrate the varied ethnic and generational backgrounds of his members in this new expression of faith:

> [One member] writes a song about an Asian American journey, her Asian American journey. It's all about being raised biculturally and how the messages she got caused her considerable personal anguish. She brings that to Jesus and it's now in our songbook. While such a conflicted upbringing is such a big part of her journey, for me it isn't. We're both Asian Americans, she's a second generation, I'm third, but our stories are quite different. Part of the journey is figuring out what do we have in common as Asian Americans.

Programs: Social/Cultural Activities and Community Engagement

Because these churches see their role as to affirm ethnic heritage and to claim rights as minorities, their programs and activities reflect these emphases. Mainline congregations have small groups, Bible studies, and conferences like the evangelical ones, but they are not as popular as the ethnic and social programming of the church. More central to pan-ethnic congregational identity are the efforts to celebrate ethnicity, to build Asian American community, and to minister programs to the neighborhood.

Like ethnic-specific congregations, mainline congregations observe ethnic festivals, bazaars, and holidays in their programming. These events draw the most involvement of the members and attract the most nonmembers. Often, nonactive members return to their congregations with their families to participate in annual bazaars, see old friends, play carnival games, and eat chicken teriyaki or chow mein. Because these events are so popular, one priest said that one of their primary functions was to raise money as well as to introduce their ethnic heritage to Asian Americans: "The bazaar is a major fund-raising effort and also a method of bringing all the members together in a project. To promote fellowship as well as to generate some income. It's a way of introducing the culture to Asian Americans and the white Americans, too. A lot of them come."

Pan-ethnic congregations also host programs to meet the social needs of the community. They primarily seek to provide an environment in which Asian Americans can socialize or gain leadership skills. Social programs that are common are summer day camps, basketball leagues, Boy Scout troupes, and social dance classes for seniors. The large congregational commitment to sponsoring basketball teams, for example, is for the youth to learn teamwork and sportsmanship and to make Asian American friendships.

Church ministries to the traditional ethnic community and the new panethnic community often develop as ecumenical projects and become modern nonprofit organizations. Why they take the form they do—ecumenical and formally organized as service programs—stems from their mainline orientations of public engagement. They seek to be Christ's presence in a community primarily by their acts of love, compassion, and justice. As one Chinese American priest explained:

> Today, our understanding of evangelization is not so much that converts are made, but more that we profess and teach Christian values and to expose people who are coming from a culture where Christianity is not a major religion, to expose them, to teach them, to preach Christian values and see how they complement Chinese traditional values.

With this focus on ministering God's love and with less emphasis on conversion, the mainline churches are willing to work with other institutions, the government, and nonprofit agencies in serving their neighborhoods.[34]

Individual church programs for the community range from direct service to advocacy and organizing. Popular ministries that meet direct needs include English as a second language and citizenship classes, tutoring for low-income and immigrant youth, and activities for the elderly. Participation through denominational caucuses involves congregations in activities and stances geared toward broader social change, such as advo-cacy around affirmative action or organizing against anti-Asian violence. However, a few individual congregations do spearhead such efforts. For example, this minister explained that his congregation expected him to become engaged in politics:

> The [church members] know that I'm involved with politics. To some ex-tent, it is an almost unwritten rule that their pastor is involved with com-munity politics. I got arrested last year. The congregation thought it was a kick. Well, that's not quite why I did it. For the most part, they have un-derstood that part of my calling is to be involved with the community and the politics.

The church activities and programs thus reflect the theological orienta-tion of the mainline in seeking to be an institutional voice within the community.

These ministers' understanding of Asian American pan-ethnicity in-fluences how they develop their church's ministries in serving them. Mainline theology is liberal and tolerant so that Asian cultural and reli-gious practices are accepted and even promoted in Asian American main-line churches. And because the mainline has historically been concerned with social issues of the day, ministers in this study tend to address con-cerns regarding racial injustice and community development.

Evangelical Construction of Asian American Pan-Ethnicity: The Institutional Context

Evangelical ministers work together and learn from each other in an in-stitutional field separate from the mainline and thus have a very different understanding of Asian Americans. Just as mainline ministers receive for-mal training from certain seminaries, evangelicals learn about church growth methodology within their educational institutions. But instead of looking to denominations and the public nonprofit sector for insights on serving Asian Americans, evangelical ministers look more to leading evangelical publications and their professional networks to target and minister to this group. Employing a different theological orientation that gets promoted through these circles, evangelicals construct an under-standing of Asian Americans that is quite distinct from the mainline one.

The Evangelical Institutional Field

Since the 1980s, campus ministries have recognized the growing pres-ence of Asian Americans on campuses and have sought to evangelize students along these groupings.[35] Throughout California and on many elite university campuses in the United States, Asian American Christian Fellowships (AACFs) have been established by the InterVarsity Christian Fellowship (IVCF) and the Japanese Evangelical Missionary Society (JEMS). Once graduated, these students seek similar fellowship and church settings. They leave their ethnic congregations, and Asian American churches have received many of these alumni.

Theological seminaries also promote and legitimate pan-ethnicity by offering courses tailored toward this grouping. The largest seminary in North America, the evangelical Fuller Seminary in Pasadena, California, offers the course, "Multiculturalism Today: Reflections and Response," and the instructors use the text, *Racial Conflict and Healing: An Asian American Theological Perspective*.[36] These courses, texts, and Asian American instructors are official, professional recognition that pan-ethnicity is a valid grouping, field of theological study, and ministerial concern.

Most importantly, the evangelical pastors have professional and ministerial networks that introduce pan-ethnic models of congregational development. Online, Chinese American pastors keep connected on a mailing list called "Chinese American Christians" (CAC). In the San Francisco Bay Area, these official networks include the Bay Area Asian American Youth Fellowship, the Promise Keepers, and the Asian American Bay Area Fellowship.

For example, the Asian American Bay Area Fellowship is made up of about fifty Chinese, Filipino, Japanese, and Korean American evangelical pastors that meet irregularly. Since 1991, they have addressed similar issues as those posted on CAC, including the role of ethnic culture in the church and Asian American racial reconciliation between individual ethnic groups. These professional networks are the "interorganizational contexts" within which the discourse of pan-ethnicity and race become circulated, appropriated, and infused with meaning. Whether pan-ethnic congregations become the premier model for Chinese and Japanese American churches remains a debated conversation between ministers within these networks. These forums, along with seminary training and books on church growth, create the menu of options from which ministers can choose in building their congregations.

With limited options of strategies and rules about church growth circulating within the evangelical field, ministers often follow leaders in the field.[37] Within the local Bay Area Asian American church networks, ministers perceive pan-ethnic congregations as being successful in attracting members and growing them. For example, this pastor felt called to establish a ministry similar to other pan-Asian ones: "Most of the successful churches, either in Southern California or here, they're mostly pan-Asian. They have been very successful, not only in terms of numbers but also spiritual growth. So I thought that this church, that's why God place me here." Pan-ethnic churches emerge as new congregations by intentionally patterning themselves after successful pan-ethnic ones.

Even if the innovations do not prove to be effective in increasing church growth, they are still adopted to demonstrate that the ministers are trying to effect some kind of reform and to meet the demands of what potential members expect. Pan-ethnicity, as a new model for organizing a congregation, enabled ministers to start afresh and rethink every aspect of church. As a sectarian movement, its novelty encouraged a reenvisioning of what church could be. This minister explained how people seek change and want to build something new:

> I think a lot of ministries have a tremendous desire to do something great and different. There's a lot of churches that I know that have great aspirations when they start, finally start up their English ministry. And it's funny because when they start it from their perspective, they always think that they're doing something radical like, "Wow! Let's do an English ministry!" And from their perspective, I'm beginning to see, yeah, that it is.

Another aspect of the perceived success of pan-ethnic churches is that they are new and cutting edge. These churches attract members who want to avoid the cultural baggage of ethnic churches. A minister explained that his new congregation was tailored for those who had left the church: "The original purpose was to be ministry designed for those who had given up on traditional churches, what we call the 'Silent Exodus' where a lot of Asian Americans are leaving their ethnic churches, seeking more of a contemporary worship environment." Asian American evangelical congregations, therefore, become established in order to mimic successful church growth models and to initiate reforms of outdated elements within the ethnic church.

The Evangelical Definition of Pan-Ethnicity

While mainline ministers see Asian Americans mostly as a politically marginalized grouping, evangelicals employ a "church growth" perspective that views Asian Americans as a spiritual target group with a distinctive family upbringing and a professional class status. If they can meet the needs of this target group, then they have a means of attracting unchurched Asian Americans and growing their church. Two theological tenets of American evangelicalism particularly shape this understanding of Asian Americans.[38] First, in their belief that Jesus is one's personal savior, evangelicalism now focuses on the personal, that is, an individual's concerns for self-fulfillment and therapeutic health. Second, in their practice of sharing the faith, evangelicals have developed church-growth strategies that involve target marketing and church specialization. By targeting Asian Americans and developing church community around their individual needs and professional backgrounds, ministers help create a group identity as they try to outreach a particular subpopulation.

Given their focus on the private individual, American evangelical congregations and ministries have responded to Americans' need for expressive individualism by promoting positive new religious experiences and becoming therapeutic.[39] Asian American evangelicals view Asian Americans in this way, as a people with common family dynamics and psychological issues. Despite the range and diversity in Asian American family experience, from low-income refugees in inner cities to fifth-generation professionals growing up in affluent suburbs, Asian American ministers highlight certain family histories as being characteristically definitive. They note that since Asian American parents raise their children with high expectations, their offspring often must deal with issues of self-worth and perfectionism. One explained that "typical" Asians share a family pressure to succeed with little emotional support:

> You look at the typical childhood experience for many of us growing up. I share this at different camps, retreats and it strikes an instant nerve. What was it like when you were a kid? You come home, you got a test and you got a score of 98 percent. You parents shower you with positive affirmation that you did so well? Hardly ever. If anything, they might yell at you for missing the 2 percent!

Seeing Asian Americans as a group with specific identity, psychological, and emotional issues, ministers believe that these distinctions make Asian Americans a viable grouping to serve. Although they teach and stress spiritual development and one's relationship with God, they find that these markers bond Asian Americans together:

> [God's calling us to] building an Asian American church where people of Asian American descent feel comfortable coming. We don't exclude non-Asian Americans, but there are definitely needs, concerns, family issues, relational issues that a lot of Asian Americans face that people from other ethnic cultures or races don't. We want a ministry designed for those Asian Americans.

With their emphasis on evangelism, Asian American pastors regard Asian Americans as a target group and design their churches according to their professional tastes. They follow "biblical principles" for church growth promoted by evangelical megachurch leaders such as Bill Hybels and Rick Warren. One principle is the "homogeneous principle" that suggests that churches grow fastest when members bring friends who are like themselves. When looking at the friends and personal networks of their church members, ministers saw that they were primarily Asian American. The Asian American pan-ethnic congregation, then, developed out of a focus of growing churches around the personal networks and friendship circles of existing members. One pastor explained:

> We draw more towards relationships, relationships that we build. That is what we're focusing on right now. Not trying to minister to all these strangers, but to say, "Who are our natural contacts?" You may find that for Asian Americans, still a lot of our natural contacts still may be Asian. With those personal contacts, we draw them in.

Also, Warren states that a target group such as Asians should be defined culturally, by their "lifestyle and mind-set" and by their "values, interests, hurts and fears."[40] In analyzing their target group, ministers have examined the culture of Asian Americans and saw a group of young, urban professionals. They believe that Asians' work ethic and stress on education have led Asian Americans to share common class backgrounds and class interests. For example, this pastor suggests that this ethic is the common bond of Asian Americans:

> There is a shared experience in terms of being second generation, immigrant drive to success, focus on education. Again I also understand that's also some of the Asian American ethos. What draws the Chinese American or Japanese American together oftentimes is the fact that they come out of this environment which has stressed education, which has stressed success, family and that kind of ties them together in a way that I'm not sure is in Caucasian churches.

Congregations are remarkably similar in their professional status, their upwardly mobile families, and spare-time activities. Indeed, lifestyle affinities characterize these Asian American networks. Evangelicals therefore see Asian Americans as bound by their common upbringing, their individual therapeutic needs, their friendship networks, and their professional lifestyles.

Evangelical Asian American Congregational Culture

From their evangelical viewpoint, ministers strategize about the target group of their congregations and how to best serve it. When planning for their churches, they focus more on the tastes and social needs that arise from the lifestyle choices of Asian Americans. To attract this target group, ministers recommend certain strategies regarding worship style, small-group formats, and practical seminars. The implementation of such strategies targeting a spiritual market group and the weekly work of the churches serve to reinforce the group boundaries of Asian Americans as individuals with professional lifestyle expectations.

Worship Style

Despite their sensitivity to a need for identity and their call to affirm differences, Asian American evangelical congregations have not developed their own distinctive worship style. Instead, they have borrowed from the broader contemporary evangelical style stemming from Calvary Church and the Vineyard Christian Fellowship. The songs, projected on large screens through overheads, come from large Christian music publishing houses and other liturgical elements, such as responsive prayers, weekly communion, or Scripture readings that can be found in mainline churches, have largely been abandoned.

Worship as "a positive experience" and "celebrative encounter with God" corresponds to the therapeutic orientation of contemporary evangelicals who want intimacy with God. To help Asian Americans worship in a more meaningful and heartfelt way, evangelical congregations seek to create a worship experience in which an individual could enter and feel God's presence and respond joyfully to God. One pastor elaborates on employing a worship style that would attract Asian Americans:

> I think basically what we were saying was that we could reach people that were like us. Which is primarily American-born, English-speaking Asian Americans who liked contemporary music and weren't interested in a very liturgical, high church kind of experience. We were very influenced by movements like the Vineyard, Calvary Chapel, Hope Chapel. We were doing their music. Part of it was using their songs, getting their training. A lot of it was their values—the value that worship should foster intimacy with God. That we don't sing about God but we sing to God.

To establish a meaningful worship experience, simple songs are sung repeatedly for twenty to thirty minutes so that people could memorize the words and focus on singing to God. In this adoration of God, people hopefully enter a different mood or disposition that enables them to transcend their immediate circumstances. Likewise, this pastor explains his congregation's shift to a contemporary worship style:

> We do a lot of singing because again, we really feel like we want somebody to come to church and have a real positive experience that we're

worshipping together. Maybe a little bit more experiential. We want to say that when we've come to church, we've actually met with God. He's there in our presence and we feel His joy worshipping Him. We're really focused on that.

Because ministers have seen that a contemporary worship style has drawn in more Asian Americans, they have included it as an integral component of a new, pan-ethnic congregation.

The worship style that works in mediating Asian American evangelicals' experiences with God is clearly a southern California cultural sensibility that is being exported around the world.[41] The fact that Asian Americans seem to respond to it and shy from more traditional forms found in ethnic churches indicates that this cohort has indeed acculturated. Feeling comfortable with contemporary forms of worship with few theological or cultural references, they identify with the broader American evangelical subculture and, hence, the universal church.

Small Groups

Another major aspect of pan-ethnic congregations is the establishment of small groups to meet the fellowship needs of Asian American evangelicals and to promote social belonging. A pastor noted:

I think that the pressing need is definitely in the area of community. And maybe this is part of the Asian American identity—being a part of a community of like-minded people with similar values. And they want that kind of connection. People are willing to drive a distance to come. So it seems to sit well in my mind because they want that kind of connection and they have that need.

To address this need for belonging, all of the pan-ethnic evangelical congregations have some sort of small-group format in which people can get to know others, develop intimate relationships, and develop community. Another pastor explained another principle for cell-group development: "Our young adults, that group is constantly growing because of people coming into the area. They're looking for a place to belong. A cell group reaches out to them. BAM! They've got seven, eight friends. You need seven to ten significant relationships to feel like you belong." This community of friends and personal networks, based on racial, professional, and religious commonalties, becomes what Asian American evangelicals see as the source of group solidarity among Asian Americans.

Most small groups orient themselves around Bible study, prayer, and sharing personal struggles at work or home. Ministers believe that newcomers would be drawn in by the loving welcome, acceptance, and sense of belonging that Christians should offer. Others also offer social activities or "fellowship opportunities" to promote this sense of belonging:

> All the small groups focus around an affinity. Affinity is the key point on how the group is established and founded. There are membership groups that are basically the first step in bringing somebody into the church. So they include our investors group, our Monday Night Football group, stuff like that. There are women now who've been talking about they want to do some weekday workout group.

These affinity groups are much like what Bellah and associates coined as "lifestyle enclaves." Linked most closely to leisure and consumption, a lifestyle enclave "brings together those who are socially, economically, or culturally similar and one of its chief aims is the enjoyment of being with those who 'share one's lifestyle.'"[42] Perhaps the most distinguishing aspect of lifestyle enclaves is that they deal only with individuals' private lives, their lives of personal faith, networks of friends, and lifestyle affinities. As described previously, this focus on the private is also a distinguishing characteristic of American evangelicals.

Asian American churches sanction these lifestyle enclaves because they see them as an opportunity to infiltrate a target group and reach out to the unchurched. Ministers do not promote these lifestyles and aspirations but they do mobilize around the lifestyle affinities that Asian Americans share. A pastor explained why he organized fishing trips and Christmas craft fairs:

> I think the Asian Americans are very, what's the right word? Utilitarian. They will do things that they think will enhance their child, their education, their socialization. They're very alert to that and so you have to put on a fine product which ends up being utilitarian for them to be attracted to it.

By creating regularly meeting small groups made up of primarily Asian Americans, these pan-ethnic congregations create institutional space for the personal networks of their members. By concentrating on members' individual and social needs, these groups reinforce the notion of Asian Americans as a group with lifestyle affinities rather than as a racial minority dealing with broader, structural issues or an ethnic group with traditional cultural commonalties.

Seminars and Conferences
Besides small groups, these churches often sponsor seminars and conferences that tend to promote evangelical understandings of discipleship

and spiritual growth. Biblical principles that are taught are seen to be applicable to all and they are not particularly affirming of specific, ethnic cultural practices. One church encouraged its members to attend two weekend conferences that were only two weeks apart from each other. At the first, six hundred Asian American men joined together for a conference modeled after Promise Keepers conferences. The use of the Promise Keepers format illustrates how pan-ethnic congregations utilize and accept teachings and trends from the broader, American evangelical subculture.

So what made an Asian American men's conference distinct and, for that matter, made pan-ethnic congregations uniquely tailored to serve Asian Americans? The conference's workshop topics provide insight on this matter. Again, this conference was highly therapeutic and oriented toward meeting the emotional and psychological needs of individuals. The workshops, led by Christian psychologists, counselors, and pastors, included "Perfectionism," "How To Keep Your Cool," and "When West Meets East: Connecting with Our Fathers." The coordinator of the men's conference explains:

> There are whole cultural nuances for Asian American men that are different than men in general in the United States. Stuff like self-esteem, how to be a godly husband in an Asian cultural setting where there are more family issues that Asian men have to face. Issues of work—a lot of Asian men feel like they're in a glass ceiling and how do you deal with those kinds of issues—how do you deal with perfectionism, being a workaholic, those kinds of things. Obviously there's a lot of common ground.

The second conference was entitled "Living Free in Christ: A Life Impact Workshop on Resolving Personal and Spiritual Conflicts." A new identity in Christ, according to the speaker, can provide a sense of significance, acceptance, and security that the audience felt they lacked. To experience the freedom that God provides, Christians need to renounce old lies and claim the truths of the gospel. The first step is to "renounce your previous or current involvement with satanically inspired occult practices and false religions." Experiences to renounce include fortune-telling, magic eightball, New Age activities, spirit worship, Buddhism, and the religion of martial arts. The latter three "false religions" are traditional Asian beliefs held by families of members in this particular congregation. Embracing a Christian identity, in this case, entails a renunciation of one's ancestral heritage and, perhaps, the practices of one's immediate family.

Through these kinds of conferences and retreats, Asian American evangelicals adopt the identities and practices that assimilate them into the broader evangelical world and discourage them from maintaining certain traditional ways. One's Asian American background is more of a negative past from which one has to be healed and a culture that needs to be transformed. By categorizing ethnic traditions and values as, at worst, "satanically inspired" and, at best, "unhealthy patterns," Asian American pan-ethnic congregations discard cultural resources and experiences that might make them distinct from other evangelical Christians. How to build an Asian American expression of faith, then, becomes problematic when Asian Americans have become acculturated into a very American evangelical subculture.

Conclusion

In contrast to ethnic-specific Asian congregations, pan-ethnic Asian American congregations mobilize around racial boundaries. Within the San Francisco Bay Area, these congregations organize around pan-ethnic networks that are constructed and legitimated by state and market forces.[43] However, what it means to be Asian American must be understood given the theological and institutional discourses utilized by the ministers themselves. The institutional fields within the Christian church circulate these discourses that frame racial understandings.

Evangelical and mainline ministers hold divergent understandings of Asian American pan-ethnicity because this group identity is permeable and fluid. What it means to be Asian American depends on the symbolic boundaries used to identify who belongs to this population. The former group of ministers draws symbolic boundaries around family upbringing and professional status. On the other hand, the latter group focuses on the racialized experiences of the people and their ethnic heritages. As a result of these different symbolic boundaries, the congregational cultures of these two groups also differ. Evangelicals establish new pan-ethnic congregations that appeal to the sensibilities of young professionals and serve them by meeting their psychological and spiritual needs. Mainline ministers create pan-ethnic churches that integrate Asian cultural resources with Christian rituals and address racial justice issues.

Asian American pan-ethnicity does have its limitations. These Asian American congregations tend to be dominated by one group, either Chinese American or Japanese American. None of these congregations have music or songs that express Asian American themes or cultural styles. And while many ministers claim this identity for their congregations, Asian American church start-ups in the San Francisco Bay Area have not attracted large numbers yet.

Nonetheless, the emergence of pan-ethnic congregations does refute theories that assert that Asian ethnic congregations will assimilate after the first generation. Their presence indicates that race continues to play a significant role in the lives of Asian Americans and their faith development. Ministers note that given the multiplicity of identities that Asian Americans have simultaneously—as ethnic Americans, as racialized Americans, and as religious Americans—a diversity of congregations will emerge to serve them.

Notes

1. Brian Hayashi, *For the Sake of Our Brethren: Assimilation, Nationalism, and Protestantism among the Japanese of Los Angeles, 1895–1942* (Stanford, Calif.: Stanford University Press, 1995); Wesley Woo, "Protestant Work among the Chinese in the San Francisco Bay Area, 1850–1920" (unpublished Ph.D. diss., Graduate Theological Union, Berkeley, California, 1983); Diane Mark, *Seasons of Light: The History of Chinese Christian Churches in Hawaii* (Honolulu: Chinese Christian Association of Hawaii, 1989).

2. The emergence of pan–Asian American congregations has not gone unnoticed by the media. See Tini Tran, "Pan-Asian Churches Emerging," *Los Angeles Times*, March 8, 1999; and De Tran and Ariana Cha, "Congregations at the Crossroads: Asian American Christians Leaving Their Parents' Style of Worship Behind," *San Jose Mercury News*, April 12, 1998.

3. Lisa Lowe, "Heterogeneity, Hybridity, Multiplicity: Marking Asian American Differences," *Diaspora* 1 (1991): 24–44; Yen Le Espiritu, *Asian American Panethnicity* (Philadelphia: Temple University Press, 1992).

4. Pyong Gap Min ("Pan-Ethnic Boundaries among Asian Americans in the United States.") suggests that Chinese, Japanese, and Korean Americans are more likely to maintain close social relations in the forms of friendship and dating at the individual level because they share cultural and physical similarities. Indeed, pan-Asian congregations are more likely to have these three groups while South Asians, Southeast Asians, and Filipinos do not affiliate with pan-ethnic organizations as often. See also Pyong Gap Min, "Ethnicity: Concepts, Theories and Trends," in *Struggle for Ethnic Identity*, ed. Pyong Gap Min and Rose Kim (Walnut Creek, Calif.: AltaMira, 1999); Lavina Dhingra Shankar and Rajimi Srikanth, eds., *A Part, Yet Apart: South Asians in Asian America* (Philadelphia: Temple University Press, 1997). However, I argue that native-born Asian Americans are so acculturated that they do not draw group distinctions based on cultural affinities. Instead, congregations adopt a pan-ethnic identity first and then establish new cultural values and patterns for this emergent subculture. The nonparticipation of other Asian groups in pan-ethnic congregations may be attributable to how symbolic group boundaries are drawn.

5. Herbert Gans, "Symbolic Ethnicity: The Future of Ethnic Groups and Cultures in America," *Ethnic and Racial Studies* 2 (1979): 1–20; Stephen Steinberg, *The Ethnic Myth* (Boston: Beacon, 1981); Mary Waters, *Ethnic Options* (Berkeley: University of California Press, 1990); Richard Alba, *Ethnic Identity: The Transformation of White America* (New Haven, Conn.: Yale University Press, 1990).

6. This study is part of my larger dissertation project. It includes in-depth interviews of forty-four ministers who pastor Chinese, Japanese, or Asian American Christian congregations in the San Francisco Bay Area. From lists of the Northern California Japanese Christian Federation and James Chuck's "An Exploratory Study of the Growth of Protestant Chinese in the San Francisco Bay Area" (1996), I randomly selected a list of English-speaking congregations.

Surprisingly, half of the ministers self-identified their congregations as being Asian American. The meanings of this self-identification varied: Some meant that their congregations targeted all Asian ethnic groups, others suggested that their members included a combination of Asian ethnic groups, and some used the term *Asian American* interchangeably with *Chinese American* or *Japanese American*. I interviewed two ministers of Asian American congregations that were originally Korean American in the later phase of my data collection for comparison purposes. Of these ministers, twenty-seven were Chinese American, eight were Japanese American, five were European American, two Filipino/Chinese American, and two Korean American. The churches were similar in generation, income level, and educational attainment.

7. Will Herberg, *Protestant, Catholic, Jew* (Garden City, N.J.: Anchor Press, 1955); Jay Dolan, *The American Catholic Experience* (Garden City, N.Y.: Doubleday, 1985); James Wind and James Lewis, eds., *American Congregations* (Chicago: University of Chicago Press, 1994).

8 . Paul Douglass, *The Church in the Changing City* (New York: Doran, 1927); James Davis and Robert Wilson, *The Church in the Radically Changing Community* (Nashville, Tenn.: Abingdon, 1966); Nancy Ammerman, *Congregation and Community* (New Brunswick, N.J.: Rutgers University Press, 1998).

9. Richard Alba and Victor Nee, "Rethinking Assimilation Theory for a New Era of Immigration," *International Migration Review* 31 (1997): 826–74.

10. Mark Mullins, "The Life Cycle of Ethnic Churches in Sociological Perspective," *Japanese Journal of Religious Studies* 14 (1987): 321–34.

11. R. Stephen Warner and Judith Wittner, eds., *Gatherings in Diaspora: Religious Communities and the New Immigration* (Philadelphia: Temple University Press, 1998).

12. Warner and Wittner, *Gatherings in Diaspora,* 14

13. Warner and Wittner, *Gatherings in Diaspora.*

14. Warner and Wittner, *Gatherings in Diaspora,* 15

15. Teresa Moore, "Kids and Color: In the Multicultural Bay Area, Young People Learn Early that Differences Are a Way of Life," *San Francisco Chronicle,* September 20, 1998.

16. Asian/Pacific American organizations make up 23 percent of the student organizations registered with the U.C. Berkeley Student Activities and Services office. See Julie Chao, "Teaching the Asian American Experience: More College Students Are Reclaiming a Heritage Many Did Not Know They Had," *San Francisco Examiner,* May 3, 1998.

17. "Cupertino Business Group Formed: New Council Will Try to Expand Involvement of Asian American Community," *San Jose Mercury,* July 30, 1998.

18. Julie Chao, "San Francisco's Sleeping Giant: The City's Significant Asian Population Is Joining the Electoral Process," *San Francisco Examiner,* May 3, 1998;

Sarah Lubman, "Latinos, Asians Gain Influence in Elections," *San Jose Mercury,* April 27, 1998.

19. Nathan Glazer, *We Are All Multiculturalists Now* (Cambridge, Mass.: Harvard University Press, 1997); Robert Bellah, "Is There a Common American Culture?" *Journal of the American Academy of Religion* 66 (1998): 613–26.

20. Lester Suzuki, "Persecution, Alienation, Recognition: History of Japanese Methodist Churches," in *Churches Aflame: Asian Americans and United Methodism,* ed. Artemio Guillermo (Nashville, Tenn.: Abingdon, 1991); Wing Ng Pang, "The Chinese American Ministry," *Yearbook of American and Canadian Churches, 1995,* ed. Kenneth Bedell (Nashville, Tenn.: Abingdon, 1995).

21. Sharon Lee, "Asian Americans: Diverse and Growing," *Population Bulletin* 53 (1998): 2–41.

22. Sharon Lee and Marilyn Fernandez, "Trends in Asian American Racial/Ethnic Intermarriage: A Comparison of 1980 and 1990 Census Data 1998," *Sociological Perspectives* 41 (1998): 323–42.

23. Mark Landberg and Reynolds Farley, "Residential Segregation of Asian Americans in 1980," *Sociology and Social Research* 63 (1985): 71–75.

24. The 1.5 generation includes persons born abroad but raised in the United States.

25. Similarly, generational conflicts in Korean American congregations often result in new congregational forms. See Karen Chai, "Competing for the Second Generation: English-Language Ministry at a Korean Protestant Church," in *Gatherings in Diaspora,* ed. Warner and Wittner.

26. The broader religious world of evangelicals and mainline churches is known as "institutional fields" in sociological literature. See Richard Scott, "Unpacking Institutional Arrangements," in *The New Institutionalism in Organizational Analysis,* ed. Walter Powell and Paul DiMaggio (Chicago: University of Chicago Press, 1991).

27. Martin Marty, *The Public Church: Mainline-Evangelical-Catholic* (New York: Crossroad, 1981), 91–108; Robert Wuthnow, *The Restructuring of American Religion* (Princeton, N.J.: Princeton University Press, 1988); Wade Clark Roof, *A Generation of Seekers* (New York: Harper Collins, 1993).

28. By 1977, denominations had officially recognized national caucuses and offices to deal with Asian American ministries. These include the Asian American Baptist Caucus, the Asian Presbyterian Caucus, the National Federation of Asian American United Methodists, the Pacific American and Asian American Ministries of the UCC, the Episcopal Asian American Strategies Task Force, and the North American Pacific Asian Disciples of Christ.

29. Fumitaka Matsuoka, *Out of Silence: Emerging Themes in Asian American Churches* (Cleveland, Ohio: United Church Press, 1995).

30. Dean Hoge, Benton Johnson, and Donald Luidens, *Vanishing Boundaries: The Religion of Mainline Protestant Baby Boomers* (Louisville, Ky.: Westminster/John Knox, 1994).

31. Asian American mainline theology takes as its starting point the grounded, racially marginalized experiences of Asian Americans. See David Ng, *People on the Way: Asian North Americans Discovering Christ, Culture and Community* (Valley Forge, Pa.: Judson Press, 1996).

32. Matsuoka, *Out of Silence*, 54.

33. The number of Asian American pan-ethnic mainline congregations is not yet large enough to describe a definite type of worship style or church setting. Only two of the mainline congregations were new church developments. However, emerging trends about "racial/ethnic/cultural affirmation" in church setting and worship style can be detected both in ethnic-specific and pan-ethnic congregations.

34. In Oakland, ministers cited the Asian Health Services, the Oakland Asian Cultural Center, and Asian Community Mental Health Services as nonprofit agencies founded by their churches or church members. In San Francisco, Asian mainline congregations helped to create the Career Resources Development Center, the Chinese Hospital, and Cameron House, each now independent, secular organizations. Ecumenical groups such as the Chinese Christian Union and the Northern California Japanese Christian Federation also have undertaken social service efforts, mostly for the elderly.

35. Rudy Busto, "The Gospel According to the Model Minority? Hazarding an Interpretation of Asian American Evangelical Students," in *New Spiritual Homes: Religion and Asian Americans,* ed. David Yoo (Honolulu: University of Hawaii Press, 1999).

36. Andrew Sung Park, *Racial Conflict and Healing: An Asian American Theological Perspective* (Maryknoll, N.Y.: Orbis Books, 1996).

37. The tendency of organizations to mimic those other organizations perceived to be successful is called "mimetic isomorphism." Paul DiMaggio and Walter Powell, "The Iron Cage Revisited: Institutional Isomorphism and Collective Rationality in Organizational Fields," *American Sociological Review* 48 (1983): 147–60.

38. A "subcultural identity of contemporary American evangelicalism" has developed within the last two decades. See Mark Shibley, *Resurgent Evangelicalism in the United States: Mapping Cultural Change since 1970* (Columbia: University of South Carolina Press, 1996); Donald Miller, *Reinventing American Protestantism: Christianity in the New Millennium* (Berkeley: University of California Press, 1997); Christian Smith, *American Evangelicalism: Embattled and Thriving* (Chicago: University of Chicago Press, 1998).

39. Robert Bellah et al., *Habits of the Heart: Individualism and Commitment in American Life* (Berkeley: University of California Press, 1985).

40. Rick Warren, *The Purpose Driven Church* (Grand Rapids, Mich.: Zondervan Publishing, 1995) 165.

41. Shibley, *Resurgent Evangelicalism*; Miller, *Reinventing American Protestantism.*

42. Bellah et al., *Habits of the Heart,* 72.

43. For an examination of state-constructed racial formation, see Michael Omi and Howard Winant, *Racial Formation in the United States,* 2d ed. (New York: Routledge, 1994).

BIBLIOGRAPHY

Abelmann, Nancy, and John Lie. *Blue Dreams: Korean Americans and the Los Angeles Riots*. Cambridge, Mass.: Harvard University Press, 1995.

Ahmed, Nafufer, Gladis Kaufman, and Shamin Naim. "South Asian Families in the United States: Pakistan, Bangladesh, and Indian Muslims." In *Family and Gender among American Muslims*, ed. Barbara C. Aswad and Barbara Bilge. Philadelphia: Temple University Press, 1996.

Alba, Richard. *Ethnic Identity: The Transformation of White America*. New Haven, Conn.: Yale University Press, 1990.

Alba, Richard, and Victor Nee. "Rethinking Assimilation Theory for a New Era of Immigration." *International Migration Review* 31 (1997): 826–74.

Allen, James, and Eugene Turner. *The Ethnic Quilt: Population Diversity in Southern California*. Los Angeles: California State University at Northridge, Center for Geographical Studies, 1997.

Almirol, Edwin. "Church Life among Filipinos in California: Social Ties and Ethnicity." In *Religion and Society in the American West*, ed. Carl Guarneri and David Alvarez. Lanham, Md.: University Press of America, 1987.

Alumkal, Anthony. "Preserving Patriarchy: Assimilation, Gender Norms, and Second-Generation Korean American Evangelicals." *Qualitative Sociology* 22 (1999): 129–40.

———. "Being Korean, Being Christian: Particularism and Universalism in a Second Generation Congregation." In *Korean Americans and Their Religions: Pilgrims and Missionaries from a Different Shore*, ed. Ho-Youn Kwon, Kwang Chung Kim, and Stephen Warner. University Park: Pennsylvania State University Press, 2001.

Ammerman, Nancy. *Congregation and Community*. New Brunswick, N.J.: Rutgers University Press, 1997.

Anderson, Gerald H. , ed.*Studies in Philippine Church History*. Ithaca, N.Y.: Cornell University Press, 1969.

Andezian, S. "Women's Roles in Organizing Symbolic Life: Algerian Female Immigrants in France." In *International Migration: The Female Experience*, ed. R. J. Simon and C. B. Brettel. Totowa, N.J.: Rowman and Allanheld, 1986.

Antonovsky, Aaron. *Unraveling the Mystery of Health*. San Francisco: Jossey-Bass, 1987.

Arnold, Fred, Urmil Minocha, and James Fawcett. "The Changing Face of Asian Immigration to the United States." In *Pacific Bridges: The New Immigration from*

Asia and the Pacific Islands, ed. James Fawcett and Benjamin Carino. Staten Island, N.Y.: Center for Migration Studies, 1987.

Bachu, Parminder. *Twice Migrants: East African Sikh Settlers in Britain*. London: Tavistock, 1985.

Badr, Hoda. "Al-Noor Mosque: Strength through Unity." In *Religion and the New Immigrants*, ed. Helen Rose Ebaugh and Janet Saltzman Chafetz. Walnut Creek, Calif.: AltaMira, 2000.

Baldwin, Beth. *Capturing the Change: The Impact of Indochinese Refugees in Orange County, Challenges and Opportunities*. Santa Ana, Calif.: Immigrant and Refugee Planning Center, 1982.

———. *Patterns of Adjustment: A Second Look at Indochinese Settlement in Orange County*. Orange County, Calif.: Immigrant and Refugee Planning Center, 1984.

Bankston, Carl, III. "Bayou Lotus: Theravada Buddhism in Southwestern Louisiana." *Sociological Spectrum* 38 (1997): 18–37.

———. "Education and Ethnicity: Community and Academic Performance in an Urban Vietnamese Village." In *Beyond Black and White: New Faces and Voices in U.S. Schools*, ed. Lois Weiss and Maxine Seller. New York: State University of New York Press, 1997.

Bankston, Carl, III, and Min Zhou. "The Ethnic Church, Ethnic Identification, and the Social Adjustment of Vietnamese Adolescents." *Review of Religious Research* 38 (1996): 18–37.

———. "Religious Participation, Ethnic Identification, and Adaptation of Vietnamese Adolescents in an Immigrant Community." *Sociological Quarterly* 36 (1995): 523–34.

Barrett, David, ed. *World Christian Encyclopedia*. New York: Oxford University Press, 1982.

Basch, Linda, Nina Glick-Schiller, and Cristina Szanton Blanc, eds. *Nations Unbounded: Transnational Projects, Postcolonial Predicaments, and Deterritorialized Nation-States*. Langhorne, Pa.: Gordon and Breach, 1994.

Batchelor, Stephen. *The Awakening of the West: The Encounter of Buddhism and Western Culture*. Berkeley, Calif.: Parallax Press, 1994.

Bellah, Robert. *Beyond Belief: Essays on Religion in a Post-Traditional World*. New York: Harper & Row, 1976.

———. "Is There a Common American Culture?" *Journal of the American Academy of Religion* 66 (1998): 613–26.

Bellah, Robert, Richard Madsen, William Sullivan, Ann Swidler, and Steve Tipton. *Habits of the Heart: Individualism and Commitment in American Life*. Berkeley: University of California Press, 1985.

Bengston, Vern L. "Is the 'Contract across Generations' Changing? Effects of Population Aging on Obligations and Expectations across Age Group." In *The Changing Contract across Generations*, ed. Vern L. Bengston and W. Andrew Achenbaum. Hawthorne, N.Y.: Aldine de Gruyter, 1993.

Berger, Peter. *The Sacred Canopy: Elements of a Sociological Theory of Religion*. New York: Doubleday, 1969.

Bono, Rick. *Locating Filipino Americans: Ethnicity and Cultural Politics of Space*. Philadelphia: Temple University Press, 2000.

Bousquet, Gisele. *Behind the Bamboo Hedge: The Influence of Homeland Politics in the Parisian Vietnamese Community.* Ann Arbor: University of Michigan Press, 1991.

Brown, Thompson. *Christianity in China,* revised ed. Atlanta: John Knox, 1986.

Bryant, William, ed. *The Church's One Hundred Years in the Japanese American Community.* San Francisco: Christ United Presbyterian Church, 1988.

Bulatao, Jaime. *Split-Level Christianity.* Quezon City, Philippines: Ateneo de Manila University Press, 1966.

Bunson, Maggie. *Faith in Paradise: A Century and a Half of the Roman Catholic Church in Hawaii.* Boston: St. Paul Edition, 1977.

Burghart, Richard. "The Perpetuation of Hinduism in an Alien Cultural Milieu." In *Hinduism in Great Britain: The Perpetuation of Religion in an Alien Cultural Milieu,* ed. Richard Burghart. London: Tavistock, 1987.

Burns, Jeffrey. *The Catholic American Parish: A History from the 1850s to the Present,* vol. 2, ed. Jay Nolan. New York: Paulist, 1987.

Busto, Rudy. "The Gospel According to Model Minority?: Hazarding an Interpretation of Asian American Evangelical College Students." *Amerasia Journal* 22 (1996): 133–48.

Caplan, Nathan, Marcella Choy, and John Whitmore. *Children of the Boat People: A Study of Educational Success.* Ann Arbor: University of Michigan Press, 1989.

Cayton, Horace, and Anne O. Lively. *The Chinese in the United States and the Chinese Christian Church.* New York: Bureau of Research and Survey, National Council of the Churches of Christ in the United States, 1955.

Chai, Karen. "Competing for the Second Generation: English-Language Ministry at a Korean Protestant Church." In *Gatherings in Diaspora,* ed. Stephen Warner and Judith Wittner. Philadelphia: Temple University Press, 1998.

———. "Intra-Ethnic Religious Diversity: Korean Buddhists and Protestants in Greater Boston." In *Pilgrims and Missionaries from a Different Shore,* ed. Ho-Youn Kwon, Kwang Chung Kim, and Stephen Warner. University Park: Pennsylvania State University Press, 2001.

Chan, Sucheng. *Asian Americans: An Interpretive History.* Boston: Twayne, 1991.

———. *Hmong Means Free: Life in Laos and America.* Philadelphia: Temple University Press, 1994.

———, ed. *Entry Denied: Exclusion and the Chinese in America, 1882–1943.* Philadelphia: Temple University Press, 1991.

Chandler, David. *The Tragedy of Cambodian History: Politics, War, and Revolution Since 1945.* New Haven, Conn.: Yale University Press, 1991.

Chandler, Stuart. "Chinese Buddhism in America." In *The Faces of Buddhism in America,* ed. Charles Prebish and Kenneth Tanaka. Berkeley: University of California Press, 1998.

Cheng, Lucie, and Edna Bonacich. *Labor Immigration under Capitalism: Asian Workers in the United States before World War II.* Berkeley: University of California Press, 1984.

Cheng, Lucie, and Philip Yang. "Asians: The 'Model Minority' Deconstructed." In *Ethnic Los Angeles,* ed. Roger Waldinger and Mehdi Bozorgmehr. New York: Russell Sage Foundation, 1996.

Ching, Julia. *Chinese Religions*. Maryknoll, N.Y.: Orbis Books, 1986.

Chinn, Thomas, ed. *A History of the Chinese in California: A Syllabus*. San Francisco: Chinese Historical Society of America, 1969.

Chong, Kelly. "What It Means to Be Christians: The Role of Religion in the Construction of Ethnic Identity and Boundary among Second-Generation Korean-Americans." *Sociology of Religion* 59 (1998): 259–86.

Choy, Bong Yoon. *Koreans in America*. Chicago: Nelson Hall, 1979.

Chuck, James. *An Exploratory Study of the Growth of Chinese Protestant Congregations from 1950 to Mid-1996 in Five Bay Area Counties*. Berkeley, Calif. American Baptist Seminary of the West, 1996.

Clymer, Kenton. *Protestant Missionaries in the Philippines: An Inquiry into the American Colonial Mentality*. Urbana: University of Illinois Press, 1986.

Condit, Ira. *The Chinaman as We See Him and Fifty Years of Work for Him*. Chicago: Missionary Campaign Library, 1900.

Cordova, Fred. *Filipinos: Forgotten Asian Americans, A Pictorial Essay, 1763–1963*. Dubuque, Iowa: Kendall/Hunt, 1983.

Covell, Ralph R. *Confucius, the Buddha, and Christ: A History of the Gospel in Chinese*. Maryknoll, N.Y.: Orbis Books, 1986.

Daly, Mary. *The Church and the Second Sex*. Boston: Beacon, 1985.

Daniels, Roger. *Asian America: Chinese and Japanese in the United States since 1850*. Seattle: University of Washington Press, 1988.

Daniels, Roger, Harry Kitano, and Sandra Taylor, eds. *Japanese Americans: From Relocation to Redress*. Seattle: University of Washington Press, 1976.

Dart, John. "Filipino Services Offer Touch of Home." *Los Angeles Times*, December 25, 1993.

Dasgupta, S. D., and S. Dasgupta. "Public Face, Private Space: Asian Indian Women and Sexuality." In *Bad Girls, Good Girls: Women, Sex and Power in the Nineties*, ed. N. B. Maglin and D. Perry. New Brunswick, N.J.: Rutgers University Press, 1996.

Deats, Richard L. *Nationalism and Christianity in the Philippines*. Dallas: Southern Methodist University Press, 1967.

Diaz-Stevens, Ana Maria. *Oxcart Catholicism on Fifth Avenue: The Impact of the Puerto Rican Migration upon the Archdiocese of New York*. Notre Dame, Ind.: University of Notre Dame Press, 1993.

Dobie, Charles Caldwell. *San Francisco Chinatown*. New York: D. Appleton-Century, 1936.

Doran, Jay. *The American Catholic Experience: History from Colonial Times to the Present*. Garden City, N.J.: Doubleday, 1985.

Douglass, Paul. *The Church in the Changing Community*. New York: Doran, 1927.

Du Bois, W. E. B. *The Philadelphia Negro*. New York: Schocken Books, 1967.

Dunnigan, Timothy, Douglas Olney, Miles McNall, and Marline Spring. "Hmong." In *Case Studies in Diversity: Refugees in America in the 1990s*, ed. David Haines. Westport, Conn.: Praeger, 1997.

Durkheim, Emile. *The Elementary Forms of Religious Life*, trans. J. W. Swain. New York: Free Press, 1965.

Dusenbery, Verne. "A Sikh Diaspora? Contested Identities and Constructed Realities." In *Nation and Migration: The Politics of Space in the South Asian Di-*

aspora, ed. Peter van der Veer. Philadelphia: University of Pennsylvania Press, 1995.

Dvorak, Katharine. *An African-American Exodus: The Segregation of Southern Churches*. Brooklyn, N.Y.: Carson, 1991.

Ebaugh, Helen Rose, and Janet Saltzman Chafetz, eds. *Religion and the New Immigrants: Continuities and Adaptations in Immigrant Congregations*. Walnut Creek, Calif.: AltaMira, 2000.

Ebihara, MayMayko. *Interrelations between Buddhism and Social Systems in Cambodian Peasant Culture*. New Haven, Conn.: Yale University Press, 1966.

Ellison, Christopher, David Gay, Thomas Glass. "Does Religious Commitment Contribute to Individual Life Satisfaction?" *Social Forces* 68 (1989): 100–123.

———. "Religion, the Life Stress Paradigm, and the Study of Depression." In *Religion in Aging and Health*, ed. J. S. Levin. Thousand Oaks, Calif.: Sage, 1994.

Elwood, Douglas. *Churches and Sects in the Philippines: A Descriptive Study of Contemporary Religious Group Movements*. Dumanguete City, Philippines: Silliman University, 1968.

Elwood, Douglas, and Patricia Ling Magdamo. *Christ in the Philippine Context*. Quezon City, Philippines: New Day Publishers, 1971.

Espiritu, Yen. *Asian American Panethncity*. Philadelphia: Temple University Press, 1992.

———. *Asian American Women and Men*. Thousand Oaks, Calif.: Sage, 1997.

Fairbank, John King, ed. *The Missionary Enterprise in China and America*. Cambridge, Mass.: Harvard University Press, 1974.

Fenton, John. *Transplanting Religious Traditions: Asian Indians in America*. New York: Praeger, 1988.

Fink, Roger, and Rodney Stark. *The Churching of America, 1976–1990: Winners and Losers in Our Religious Economy*. New Brunswick, N.J.: Rutgers University Press, 1992.

Folower, Robert Booth. *Religion and Politics in America*. Metuchen, N.J.: Scarecrow, 1985.

Foner, Nancy. "What's New about Transnationalism? New York Immigrants Today and at the Turn of the Century." *Diaspora* 6 (1997): 355–75.

Fong, Ken Uyeda. *Pursuing the Pearl: A Comprehensive Resource for Multi-Asian Ministry*. Valley Forge, Pa.: Judson Press, 1999.

Fong, Timothy. *The Contemporary Asian American Experience: Beyond the Model Minority*. Upper Saddle River, N.J.: Prentice Hall, 1998.

Fukei, Budd. *The Japanese American Story*. Minneapolis, Minn.: Dillon Press, 1976.

Fung, Karl. *The Dragon Pilgrims: A Historical Study of a Chinese-American Church*. San Diego: Providence Price, 1989.

Gans, Herbert. "Symbolic Ethnicity: The Future of Ethnic Groups and Cultures in America." *Ethnic and Racial Studies* 2 (1979): 1–20.

George, Sheba. "Caroling with the Keralites: The Negotiation of Gendered Space in an Indian Immigrant Church." In *Gatherings in Diaspora*, ed. Stephen Warner and Judith Wittner. Philadelphia: Temple University Press, 1998.

Gibson, Margaret. *Accommodation without Assimilation: Sikh Immigrants in an American High School*. Ithaca, N.Y.: Cornell University Press, 1988.

BIBLIOGRAPHY

Giddings, Paula. *When and Where I Enter: The Impact of Black Women on Race and Sex in America.* New York: Morrow, 1984.

Glass, Thomas. "Does Religious Commitment Contribute to Individual Life Satisfaction?" *Social Forces* 68 (1990): 100–123.

Glazer, Nathan. *We Are All Multiculturalists Now.* Cambridge, Mass.: Harvard University Press, 1997.

Glick-Schiller, Nina. "Transmigrants and Nation-States: Something Old and Something New in the U.S. Immigrant Experiences." In *The Handbook of International Migration,* ed. Charles Hirschman, Philip Kasinitz, and Josh Dewind. New York: Russell Sage Publications, 2000.

Gold, Steven *Refugee Communities: A Comparative Field Study.* Newbury Park, Calif.: Sage, 1992.

———. "Religious Agencies, Immigrant Settlement, and Social Justice." *Research in Social Policy* 5 (1997): 47–65.

———. "Transnationalism and Vocabularies of Motive in International Migration: The Case of Israelis in the United States." *Sociological Perspectives* 40 (1997): 409–27.

Goropse, Vitaliano. *Banahaw: Conversations with a Pilgrim to the Power Mountain.* Manila: Bookmark, 1992.

Gowing, G. *Muslim Filipinos—Heritage and Horizon.* Quezon City, Philippines: New Day Publishers, 1979.

Greeley, Andrew. *The Denominational Society: A Sociological Approach to Religion in America.* Glenview, Ill.: Scott Foresman, 1972.

———. *Why Can't They Be Like Us? America's White Ethnic Groups.* New York: E. P. Dutton & Company, 1971.

Guillermo, Artemio. "Gatherings of the Scattered: History of Filipino American United Methodist Churches." In *Churches Aflame: Asian Americans and United Methodism,* ed. Artemio Guillermo. Nashville, Tenn.: Abingdon Press, 1991.

Gupta, Sangeeta R. *Emerging Voices: South Asian American Women Redefine Self, Family, and Community.* Thousand Oaks, Calif.: Sage, 1999.

Hacker, Andrew. *Two Nations: Black and White, Separate, Hostile, Unequal.* New York: Scribner's, 1992.

Haddad, Yvonne, and Adair Lummis. *Islamic Values in the United States: A Comparative Study.* New York: Oxford University Press, 1987.

Hall, D. G. E. *A History of South-East Asia.* London: St. Martin's, 1955.

Hartmann, Edward. *The Movement to Americanize the Immigrant.* New York: Columbia University Press, 1948.

Hayashi, Brian Massaru. *"For the Sake of Our Japanese Brethren": Assimilation, Nationalism, and Protestantism among the Japanese of Los Angeles, 1895–1942.* Stanford, Calif.: Stanford University Press, 1995.

———. "The Untold Story of the Nikkei Baptists in Southern California." *Foundations* 22 (1979): 313–23.

Herberg, Will. *Protestant, Catholic, and Jew: An Essay in American Religious Sociology.* 2d ed. Garden City, N.Y.: Doubleday, 1960.

Hing, Bill Ong. *Making and Remaking Asian America through Immigration Policy.* Stanford, Calif.: Stanford University Press, 1993.

Hoge, Dean, Benton Johnson, and Donald Luidens. *Vanishing Boundaries: The Religion of Mainline Protestant Baby Boomers.* Louisville, Ky.: Westminster/John Knox, 1994.

Hopkins, Mary Carol. *Braving a New World*. Westport, Conn.: Bergin and Garvey, 1996.

Houchins, L., and C. S. Houchins. "The Korean Experiences in America, 1903–1924." In *The Asian American*, ed. N. Hundley. Santa Barbara, Calif.: Clio Press, 1976.

Hunter, Louis. *Buddhism in Hawaii*. Honolulu: University of Hawaii Press, 1971.

Hurh, Won Moo. "How They Fared in American Homes: A Follow-Up Study of Korean-American Children." *International Journal of Sociology of Family* 2 (1972): 10–20.

Hurh, Won Moo, and Kwang Chung Kim. *Korean Immigrants in America: A Structural Analysis of Ethnic Confinement and Adhesive Adaptation*. Rutherford, N.J.: Fairleigh Dickinson University Press, 1985.

———. "Religious Participation of Korean Immigrants in the United States." *Journal of the Scientific Study of Religion* 29 (1990): 19–34.

———. "The 'Success' Image of Asian Americans: Its Validity and Its Practical Implications." *Ethnic and Racial Studies* 12 (1989): 512–38.

Huynb, Thuan. "The Center for Vietnamese Buddhism: Recreating Home." In *Religion and the New Immigrants*, ed. Helen Rose Ebaugh and Janet Chafetz. Walnut Creek, Calif.: AltaMira, 2000.

Ichioka, Yuji. *The Issei: The World of First Generation Japanese Immigrants, 1885–1924*. New York: Free Press, 1988.

Ileto, Reynaldo. *Pasyon and Revolution: Popular Movements in the Philippines, 1840–1910*. Quezon City, Philippines: Ateneo de Manila University Press, 1979.

Iwamura, Jane. "Homage to Ancestors: Exploring the Horizons of Asian American Religious Identity." *Amerasia Journal* 22 (1996): 162–67.

James, Wilson, ed. *Women in American Religion*. Philadelphia: University of Pennsylvania Press, 1980.

Jenkins, S. *Ethnic Associations and Welfare States: Services to Immigrants in Five Countries*. New York: Columbia University Press, 1988.

Jensen, Joan. *Passage from India: Asian Indian Immigrants in North America*. New Haven, Conn.: Yale University Press, 1988.

Johnston, Ronald. *Religion in Society: A Sociology of Religion*. 5th ed. Upper Saddle River, N.J.: Prentice Hall, 1997.

Kanda, Shigeo. "Recovering Cultural Symbols: A Case for Buddhism in the Japanese American Communities." *Journal of the American Academy of Religion* 44 (1978): 445–75.

Kandiyoti, D. "Bargaining with Patriarchy." *Gender and Society* 2 (1988): 274–90.

Kang, Hyun Y. "Remembering Home." In *Dangerous Women: Gender and Korean Nationalism*, ed. Elaine Kim and Chungmoo Choi. New York: Routledge, 1998.

Kashima, Tetsudan. *Buddhism in America: The Social Organization of an Ethnic Religious Institution*. Westport, Conn.: Greenwood, 1977.

Kelley, John. *A Politics of Virtue: Hinduism, Sexuality, and Countercolonial Discourse in Fiji*. Chicago: University of Chicago Press, 1987.

Kibria, Nazli. "College and Notions of 'Asian American': Second Generation Chinese and Korean Americans Negotiate Race and Identity." *Amerasia Journal* 25 (1999): 29–52.

———. "The Construction of 'Asian American': Reflections on Intermarriage and Ethnic Identity among Second-Generation Chinese and Korean Americans." *Ethnic and Racial Studies* 20 (1997): 523–44.

———. "Not Asian, Black or White: Reflections on South Asian Racial Identities." *Amerasia Journal* 22 (1996): 77–88.

Kim, Ai Ra. *Women Struggling for a New Life: The Role of Religion in the Cultural Passage from Korea to America*. Albany: SUNY Press of New York, 1996.

Kim, Bok-Lim. "Casework with Japanese and Korean Wives of Americans." *Social Case Work* 53 (1972): 272–79.

Kim, Elaine. "Korean American Literature." In *An Interethnic Companion to Asian American Literature*, ed. King-Kok Cheung. New York: Cambridge University Press, 1997.

Kim, Elaine, and Eui-Young Yu, eds. *East to America: Korean American Life Stories*. New York: New Press, 1997.

Kim, Illsoo. *New Urban Immigrants: The Korean Community in New York*. Princeton, N.J.: Princeton University Press, 1981.

Kim, Jung Ha. *Bridge-Makers and Cross-Bearers: Korean American Women and the Church*. Atlanta: Scholar's Press, 1997.

———. "The Labor of Compassion: Voices of 'Churched' Korean American Women." *Amerasia Journal* 22 (1996): 93–105.

———. "Sources Outside of Europe." In *Spirituality and the Secular Quest*, ed. Peter van Ness. New York: Cross Road, 1996.

Kim, Kwang Chung, and Shin Kim. "The Ethnic Role of Korean Immigrant Churches in the U.S." In *Korean Americans and Their Religions: Pilgrims and Missionaries from a Different Shore*, ed. Ho-Youn Kwon, Kwang Chung Kim, and Stephen Warner. University Park: Pennsylvania State University Press, 2001.

Kim, Kwang Chung, Stephen Warner, and Ho-Youn Kwon. "Korean-American Religion in Transnational Perspectives." In *Korean Americans and Their Religions: Pilgrims and Missionaries from a Different Shore*, ed. Ho-Youn Kwon, Kwang Chung Kim, and Stephen Warner. University Park: Pennsylvania State University Press, 2001.

Kim, Warren. *Koreans in America*. Seoul, Korea: Po Chin Cha, 1971.

Kitagawa, Daisuke. *Issei and Nisei*. New York: Seabury, 1967.

Kitagawa, Joseph, and Mark Cummings, eds. *Buddhism and Asian History*. New York: Macmillan, 1989.

Kitano, Harry. *Race Relations*. 5th ed. Upper Saddle River, N.J.: Prentice Hall, 1997.

Koga, Sumio, ed. *A Centennial Legacy: History of the Japanese Christian Missions in North America, 1877–1977*. Chicago: Nobart, 1977.

Krivisto, Peter. "Religion and the New Immigrants." In *A Future for Religion*, ed. William H. Swatos Jr. Newbury Park, Calif.: Sage, 1993.

———. "The Transplanted Then and Now." *Ethnic and Racial Studies* 13 (1990): 455–81.

Kuo, Chia-ling. *Social and Political Change in New York's Chinatown*. New York: Praeger, 1977.

Kurien, Prema. "Becoming American by Becoming Hindu: Indian Americans Take Their Place at the Multicultural Table." In *Gatherings in Diaspora*, ed. Stephen Warner and Judith Wittner. Philadelphia: Temple University Press, 1998.

———. "Gendered Ethnicity: Creating a Hindu Indian Identity in the United States." *American Behavioral Scientist* 42 (1999): 648–70.

———. "Religion, Ethnicity and Politics: Hindu and Muslim Indian Immigrants in the United States." *Ethnic and Racial Studies* 24 (2001): 263–93.

Kwon, Ho-Youn, Kwang Chung Kim, and Stephen Warner. *Korean Americans and Their Religions: Pilgrims and Missionaries from a Different Shore.* University Park: Pennsylvania State University Press, 2001.

Kwon, Victoria Hyunchu. *Entrepreneurship and Religion: Korean Immigrants in Houston, Texas.* New York: Garland, 1997.

———. "Houston Korean Ethnic Church: An Ethnic Enclave." In *Religion and the New Immigrants,* ed. Helen Rose Ebaugh and Janet Chafetz. Walnut Creek, Calif.: AltaMira, 2000.

Kwong, Peter. *The New Chinatown.* New York: Hill and Wang, 1987.

La Brack, Bruce. *The Sikhs of Northern California, 1904–1975: A Socio- Historical Study.* New York: AMS Press, 1988.

Laguerre, Michel. *Diasporic Citizenship: Haitian Americans in Transnational America.* New York: St. Martin's, 1998.

Lal, Vinay. "Sikh Kirpans in California Schools: The Social Construction of Symbols, the Cultural Politics of Identity, and the Limits of Multiculturalism." In *New Spiritual Homes,* ed. David Yoo. Honolulu: University of Hawaii Press, 1999.

Landberg, Mark, and Farley Reynolds . "Residential Segregation of Asian Americans in 1980." *Sociology and Social Research* 63 (1985): 71–75.

Lavine, Amy. "Tibetan Buddhism in America: The Development of American Vajrayana." In *The Faces of Buddhism in America,* ed. Charles Prebish and Kenneth Tanaka. Berkeley: University of California Press, 1998.

Law, Gail, ed. *Chinese Churches Handbook.* Hong Kong: Chinese Coordination Center of World Evangelism, 1981.

Layman, Emma M. *Buddhism in America.* Chicago: Nelson Hall, 1976.

Lee, Jung Young. "Marginality: Multi-Ethnic Approach to Theology from an Asian American Perspective." *Asian Journal of Theology* 7 (1993): 244–53.

Lee, Sang Hyun. "Pilgrimage and Home in the Wilderness of Marginality: Symbols and Contexts in Asian American Theology." In *New Spiritual Homes,* ed. David Yoo. Honolulu: University of Hawaii Press, 1998.

Lee, Sharon. "Asian Americans: Diverse and Growing." *Population Bulletin* 53 (1998): 2–41.

Lee, Sharon, and Marilyn Fernandez. "Trends in Asian American Racial/Ethnic Intermarriages: A Comparison of 1980s and 1990 Census Data." *Sociological Perspectives* 41 (1998): 323–42.

Lehman, Edward, Jr. *Women Clergy: Breaking through Gender Barriers.* New Brunswick, N.J.: Transaction, 1985.

Leon, Louis. "Born Again in East LA: The Congregation as Border Space." In *Gatherings in Diaspora,* ed. Stephen Warner and Judith Wittner. Philadelphia: Temple University Press, 1998.

Leonard, Karen I. "Ethnic Identity and Gender: South Asians in the United States." In *Ethnicity, Identity, and Migration: The South Asian Context,* ed. M. Israel and N. K. Wagle. Toronto, Canada: Center for South Asian Studies, University of Toronto, 1993.

———. *Making Ethnic Choices: California's Punjabi Mexican Americans*. Philadelphia: Temple University Press, 1992.

Lessinger, Johanna. *From the Ganges to the Hudson: Indian Immigrants in New York City*. Boston: Allyn & Bacon, 1995.

Lester, Robert. *Theravada Buddhism in Southeast Asia*. Ann Arbor: University of Michigan Press, 1973.

Levitt, Peggy. "Local-Level Global Religion: The Case of U.S.–Dominican Migration." *Journal for the Scientific Study of Religion* 37 (1998): 74–89.

Light, Ivan, and Edna Bonacich. *Immigrant Entrepreneurs: Koreans in Los Angeles, 1965–1982*. Berkeley: University of California Press, 1988.

Lim, Shirley Geok-Lin. "Immigration and Diaspora." In *Interethnic Companion to Asian American Literature*, ed. King-Kok Cheung. New York: Cambridge University Press, 1997.

Lin, Irene. "Journey to the Far West: Chinese Buddhism in America." In *New Spiritual Homes*, ed. David Yoo. Honolulu: University of Hawaii Press, 1999.

Lin, Jan. *Restructuring Chinatown: Ethnic Enclave, Global Change*. Minneapolis: University of Minnesota Press, 1998.

Ling, Huping. *Surviving on the Golden Mountain: A History of Chinese American Women and Their Lives*. Albany: State University of New York, 1998.

Links, R. M. *American Catholicism and European Immigrants*. Staten Island, N.Y.: Center for Migration Studies, 1975.

Liu, William, Maryanne Lamanna, and Alice Murata. *Transition to Nowhere: Vietnamese Refugees in America*. Nashville, Tenn.: Charter House, 1979.

Loewen, James. *The Mississippi Chinese: Between Black and White*. Cambridge, Mass.: Harvard University Press, 1971.

Lyman, Stanford. *Chinese Americans*. New York: Random House, 1974.

Majul, Cesar. *Muslims in the Philippines*. Quezon City: University of the Philippines Press, 1973.

Marty, Martin. *The Public Church: Mainline-Evangelical-Catholic*. New York: Crossroad, 1981.

Mathew, Biju, and Bijay Prashad. "The Protean Forms of Yankee Hindusta." *Racial and Ethnic Studies* 23 (2000): 516–34.

Matsumoto, Valerie. *Farming the Home Place*. Ithaca, N.Y.: Cornell University Press, 1993.

Matsuoka, Fumitaka. *Out of Silence: Emerging Themes in Asian American Churches*. Cleveland: United Church Press, 1995.

McAlister, Elizabeth. "The Madonna of 115th Street Revisited: Vodou and Haitian Catholicism in Age of Transnationalism." In *Gatherings in Diaspora*, ed. Stephen Warner and Judith Wittner. Philadelphia: Temple University Press, 1998.

McDonough, Sheila. "The Impact of Social Change on Muslim Women." In *Gender Genre and Religion*, ed. Morny Joy and Eva K. Neumaier-Dargyay. Waterloo, Ontario: Wilfred Laurier University Press, 1999.

McGuire, Meredith B. *Religion: The Social Context*. 4th ed. Belmont, Calif.: Wadsworth, 1997.

Mearns, David James. *Shiva's Other Children: Religion and Social Identity amongst Overseas Indians*. New Delhi: Sage, 1995.

Miller, Donald. *Reinventing American Protestantism: Christianity in the New Millennium.* Berkeley: University of California Press, 1997.

Mills, C. Wright. *The Sociological Imagination.* New York: Grove Press, 1961.

Min, Pyong Gap. *Changes and Conflicts: Korean Immigrant Families in New York.* Boston: Allyn & Bacon, 1998.

———. "A Comparison of Post-1965 and Turn-of-the-Century Immigrants in Intergenerational Mobility and Cultural Transmission." *Journal of American Ethnic History* 18 (1999): 66–94.

———. "Cultural and Economic Boundaries of Korean Ethnicity: A Comparative Analysis." *Ethnic and Racial Studies* 14 (1991): 224–41.

———. "An Exploratory Study of Kin Ties among Korean Immigrant Family in Atlanta." *Journal of Comparative Family Studies* 15 (1984): 75–86.

———. "Immigrants' Religion and Ethnicity: A Comparison of Indian Hindu and Korean Christian Immigrants in the United States." *Bulletin of the Royal Institute of Inter-Faith Studies* 2 (2000): 122–40.

———. "Korean Americans." In *Asian Americans: Contemporary Trends and Issues,* ed. Pyong Gap Min. Thousand Oaks, Calif.: Sage, 1995.

———. "Korean Immigrants in New York." In *New Immigrants in New York,* 2d ed., ed. Nancy Foner. New York: Columbia University Press, 2001.

———. "Pan-Ethnic Boundaries among Asian Americans in the United States." Paper presented at the annual meeting of the American Sociological Association, Washington, D.C., August 2000.

———. "The Structure and Social Functions of Korean Immigrant Churches in the United States." *International Migration Review* 26 (1992): 1370–94.

———. ed. *Asian Americans: Contemporary Trends and Issues.* Thousand Oaks, Calif.: Sage, 1995.

Min, Pyong Gap, and Rose Kim, eds. "Formation of Ethnic and Racial Identities: Narratives by Young Asian-American Professionals." *Ethnic and Racial Studies* 23 (2000): 735–60.

———. *Struggle for Ethnic Identity: Narratives by Asian American Professionals.* Walnut Creek, Calif.: AltaMira, 1999.

Morales, Royal. *Makibaka 2: The Filipino American Struggle.* Laoan, Philippines: Crown Printers, 1998.

Morikawa, Jitsuo. "Toward an Asian American Theology." *American Baptist Quarterly* 12 (1993): 179–89.

Mukta, Parita. "The Public Face of Hindu Nationalism." *Ethnic and Racial Studies* 23 (2000): 442–66.

Mullins, Mark R. "The Life Cycle of Ethnic Churches in Sociological Perspective." *Japanese Journal of Religious Studies* 14 (1987): 321–34.

———. "The Organizational Dilemmas of Ethnic Churches: A Case Study of Japanese Buddhism in Canada." *Sociological Analysis* 49 (1988): 217–33.

Munekata, Ryo, ed. *Buddhist Churches of America, 75-Year History, 1899–1974.* Chicago: Nobart, 1974.

Nash, Jesse W. *Vietnamese Catholicism.* Harvey, La.: Art Review Press, 1992.

Nee, Victor, and Brett de Bary Nee. *Longtime California: A Documentary Study of an American Chinatown.* Boston: Houghton Mifflin, 1973.

Neitz, Mary. "Inequality and Difference." In *A Future for Religion*, ed. William Swatos Jr. Newbury Park, Calif.: Sage, 1993.

Ng, David. *People on the Way: Asian North Americans Discovering Christ, Culture and Community*. Valley Forge, Pa.: Judson Press, 1996.

Nichols, B. *Religion, Refugee Work, and Foreign Policy*. New York: Oxford University Press, 1988.

Niebuhr, Richard. *Christ and Culture*. New York: Harper, 1975.

Numrich, Paul David. *Old Wisdom in the New World: Americanization in Two Immigrant Theravada Buddhist Temples*. Knoxville: University of Tennessee Press, 1996.

Oberoi, Harjot S. "From Ritual to Counter-Ritual: Rethinking the Hindu Sikh Question, 1884–1915." In *Sikh History and Religion in the Twentieth Century*, ed. Joseph T. O'Connel, Milton Israel, and Willard Gurdon Oxtoby. Toronto: Center for South Asian Studies, 1988.

Okihiro, Gary Y. "Religion and Resistance in America's Concentration Camps." *Phylon* 45 (1984): 220–33.

Olasky, Marvin. *The Tragedy of Compassion*. Washington, D.C.: Regnery Gateway, 1992.

Omni, Michael, and Howard Winant. *Racial Formation in the United States: From the 1960s to the 1990s*. 2d ed. New York: Rutledge, 1994.

O'Neill, Michael. *The Third America: The Emergence of the Non-Profit Sector in the United States*. San Francisco: Jossey-Bass, 1989.

Ostergren, Robert. "The Immigrant Church as a Symbol of Community and Place in the Upper Midwest." *Great Plains Quarterly* 1 (1981): 225–38.

Palinkas, L. A. *Rhetoric and Religious Experience: The Discourse of Immigrant Chinese Churches*. Fairfax, Va.: George Mason University Press, 1989.

Pan, Lynn. *Sons of the Yellow Emperor: A History of the Chinese Diaspora*. New York: Kodansha International, 1994.

Park, Andrew Sung. *Racial Conflict and Healing: An Asian American Theological Perspective*. Maryknoll, N.Y.: Orbis Books, 1996.

Park, Kyeyoung. *The Korean American Dream: Immigrants and Small Business in New York*. Ithaca, N.Y.: Cornell University Press, 1997.

Park, Soyoung. "The Intersection of Religion, Ethnicity and Gender in the Identity Formation of Korean-American Evangelical Women." In *Pilgrims and Missionaries from a Different Shore*, ed. Ho-Youn Kwon, Kwang Chung Kim, and Stephen Warner. University Park: Pennsylvania State University Press, 2001.

Patterson, Wayne. *The Korean Frontier in America: Immigration to Hawaii, 1896–1910*. Honolulu: University of Hawaii Press, 1988.

Phan, Pet, and Jung Young Lee, eds. *Journey at the Margin*. New York: United Press, 1999.

Phelan, John Leddy. *Hispanization of the Philippines: Spanish Aims and Filipino Responses*. Madison: University of Wisconsin Press, 1959.

Pido, Antonio J. A. *The Filipinos in America*. Staten Island, N.Y.: Center for Migration Studies, 1986.

Pitts, Walter F. *Old Ship of Zion: The Afro-Baptist Ritual in the African Diaspora*. New York: Oxford University Press, 1993.

Pollner, Melvin. "Divine Relations, Social Relations, and Well-Being." *Journal of Health and Social Behavior* 30 (1989): 92–104.

Portes, Alejandro, Luis Guarnizo, and Patricia Landolt. "The Study of Transnationalism: Pitfalls and Promise of an Emergent Research Field." *Ethnic and Racial Studies* 22 (1999): 217–37.

Powell, Walter. "The Iron Cage Revisited: Institutional Isomorphism and Collective Rationality in Organizational Fields." *American Sociological Review* 48 (1983): 147–60.

Prebish, Charles. *American Buddhism*. North Scituate, Mass.: Duxbury Press, 1979.

———. Introduction to *The Face of Buddhism in America*, ed. Charles Prebish and Kenneth Tanaka. Berkeley: University of California Press, 1998.

Raboteau, Albert. *A Fire in the Bone: Reflections on African-American Religious History*. Boston: Beacon, 1995.

———. *Slave Religion: The "Invisible" Institution in the Antebellum South*. New York: Oxford University Press, 1978.

Rafael, Vicente. *Contracting Colonialism: Translation and Christian Conversion in Tagalog Society under Early Spanish Rule*. Durham, N.C.: Duke University Press, 1993.

Rajagopal, Arvind. "Hindu Nationalism in the U.S.: Changing Configurations of Political Practice." *Ethnic and Racial Studies* 23 (2000): 467–96.

Reuter, Frank. *Catholic Influence on American Colonial Policies, 1898–1904*. Austin: Texas University Press, 1967.

Roof, Wade Clark. *A Generation of Seekers*. New York: Harper Collins, 1993.

Roots, Maria, ed. *Filipino Americans: Transformation and Identity*. Thousand Oaks, Calif.: Sage, 1997.

Rosenberg, S. *The New Jewish Identity in America*. New York: Hippocrene Books, 1985.

Rumbaut, Rubén. "Vietnamese, Laotian, and Cambodian Americans." In *Asian Americans: Contemporary Trends and Issues*, ed. Pyong Gap Min. Thousand Oaks, Calif.: Sage, 1995.

Rutledge, Paul. *The Role of Religion in Ethnic Self-Identity: A Vietnamese Community*. Lanham, Md.: University Press of America, 1985.

Saida, Edward. "Secular Criticism." In *Critical Theory since 1965*, ed. Hazard Adams and Leroy Searle. Tallahassee: Florida State University, 1986.

San Buenaventura, Steffi. "Filipino Folk Spirituality and Immigration: From Mutual Aid to Religion." *Amerasia Journal* 22 (1996): 1–30.

———. "Hawaii's '1946 Sakada.'" *Social Process in Hawaii* 37 (1996): 81–82.

———. "The Master and Federation: A Filipino-American Social Movement in California and Hawaii." *Social Process in Hawaii* 33 (1991): 169–93.

———. "Nativism and Ethnicity in a Filipino-American Experience." Unpublished Ph.D. diss., University of Hawaii at Manoa, 1990.

———. "Old and New Immigration: Catholic and Protestant Filipinos in Twentieth Century America." Paper presented at the annual meeting of the Western Historical Association, Sacramento, California, October 1997.

Saran, P. *The Asian Indian Experience in the United States*. Cambridge, Mass.: Schenkman, 1985.

Schumacher, John. *The Filipino Clergy and the Nationalist Movement, 1850–1903*. Quezon City, Philippines: Ateneo de Manila University Press, 1981.

———. *The Propaganda Movement, 1880–1895*. Manila: Solidaridad, 1972.

BIBLIOGRAPHY

Scott, Richard. "Unpacking Institutional Arrangements." In *New Institutionalism in Organizational Analysis*, ed. Walter Powell and Paul DiMaggio. Chicago: University of Chicago Press, 1991.

Scott, William Henry. *Cracks in the Parchment Curtain and Other Essays in Philippine History*. Quezon City, Philippines: New Day Publishers, 1982.

Shankar, Lavina Dingra, and Rajini Srikanth, eds. *A Part, But Apart: South Asians in Asian America*. Philadelphia: Temple University Press, 1998.

Shaunessy, Gerald. *Religion in America: Has the Immigrant Kept the Faith?* New York: Arno Press and New York Times, 1969.

Shibley, Mark. *Resurgent Evangelicalism in the United States: Mapping Cultural Change since 1970*. Columbia: University of South Carolina Press, 1996.

Skinner, Kenneth. "Vietnamese in America: Diversity in Adaptation." *California Sociologist* 3 (1980): 103–24.

Smith, Christian. *American Evangelicalism: Embattled and Thriving*. Chicago: University of Chicago Press, 1998.

Smith, Timothy. "Religion and Ethnicity in America." *American Historical Review* 83 (1978): 1155–85.

Southard, Naomi, and Ruth Nakashima Brock. "The Other Half of the Basket: Asian American Women and the Search for a Theological Home." *Journal of Feminist Studies of Religion* 3 (1987): 133–50.

Spickard, Paul. *Japanese Americans: The Formation and Transformations of an Ethnic Group*. New York: Twayne, 1996.

Stark, Steven. "The Effect of Religious Commitment on Suicide: A Cross-National Analysis." *Journal of Mental Health and Social Behavior* 24 (1983): 362–74.

Steinberg, Laurence. *Beyond the Classroom: Why School Reform Has Failed and What Parents Need to Do*. New York: Simon & Schuster, 1996.

Steinberg, Stephen. *The Ethnic Myth: Race, Ethnicity, and Class in America*. Boston: Beacon, 1981.

Strong, Edward. *Japanese in California*. Stanford, Calif.: Stanford University Press, 1933.

Sullivan, Kathleen. "*Iglesia de Dios:* An Extended Family." In *Religion and the New Immigrants*, ed. Helen Rose Ebaugh and Janet Chafetz. Walnut Creek, Calif.: AltaMira, 2000.

Sung, Betty Lee. *Mountain of Gold: The Story of the Chinese in America*. New York: Macmillan, 1967.

Swatos, William, Jr., ed. *Gender and Religion*. New Brunswick, N.J.: Transaction, 1993.

Takagi, Dana. "Post–Civil Rights Politics and Asian-American Identity: Admission and Higher Education." In *Race*, ed. Steven Gregory and Roger Sanjek. New Brunswick, N.J.: Rutgers University Press, 1994.

Takahashi, Jere Kahahashi. *Nisei/Sansei: Shifting Japanese American Identities and Politics*. Philadelphia: Temple University Press, 1997.

Takaki, Ronald. *Strangers from a Different Shore: A History of Asian America*. Boston: Little, Brown, 1989.

Tambiah, Stanley. *Buddhism and the Spirit Cult*. New York: Cambridge University Press, 1976.

———. *The Buddhist Saints of the Forest and the Cult of Amulets: A Study in Charisma, Hagiography, and Millennial Buddhism*. New York: Cambridge University Press, 1984.

Tamura, Eileen. *Americanization, Acculturation, and Ethnic Identity: The Nisei Generation in Hawaii.* Urbana: University of Illinois Press, 1994.

Tang, Joyce. "The Career Attainment of Caucasian and Asian Engineers." *Sociological Quarterly* 34 (1993): 467–96.

Thomas, Dorothy. *The Salvage: Japanese American Evacuation and Resettlement.* Berkeley: University of California Press, 1952.

Tomasi, S. M., and M. H. Engel. *The Italian Experience in the United States.* Staten Island, N.Y.: Center for Migration Studies, 1971.

Tran, De, and Ariana Cha. "Congregations at the Crossroads: Asian American Christians Leaving Their Parents' Style of Worship Behind." *San Jose Mercury News*, April 2, 1998.

Tran, Thanh Van. "Sponsorship and Employment Status among Vietnamese Refugees in the United States." *International Migration Review* 25 (1991): 536–50.

———. "The Vietnamese-American Family." In *Ethnic Families in America 4th edition*, ed. Charles Mindel, Robert Habenstein, and Roosevelt Wright Jr. Upper Saddle River, N.J.: Prentice Hall, 1998.

Tran, Tini. "Pan-Asian Churches Emerging." *Los Angeles Times*, March 8, 1999.

Trinh, Minh-ha. *Women, Native, Other: Writing Postcoloniality and Feminism.* Bloomington: Indiana University Press, 1989.

Tsai, Shih-Shan Henry. *The Chinese Experience in America.* Bloomington: Indiana University Press, 1986.

Tseng, Timothy. "Chinese Protestant Nationalism in the United States, 1870–1927." In *New Spiritual Homes*, ed. David Yoo. Honolulu: University of Hawaii Press, 1998.

———. *Ministry at Arms-Length: Asian Americans in the Radical Ideology of American Mainline Protestants.* Ph.D. diss., Union Theological Seminary, New York, 1995.

Tuan, Mia. *Forever Foreigners or Honorary Whites: The Asian Ethnic Experience Today.* New Brunswick, N.J.: Rutgers University Press, 1999.

Tuck, Donald. *Buddhist Churches of America.* Lewiston, N.Y.: Edwin Mellen Press, 1987.

Tweed, Thomas. *The American Encounter with Buddhism, 1844–1912.* Bloomington: Indiana University Press, 1992.

———. *Our Lady of Exile: Diasporic Religion at a Cuban Catholic Shrine in Miami.* New York: Oxford University Press, 1997.

U.S. Bureau of the Census. *1990 Census of Population, Asian and Pacific Islanders in the United States.* Washington, D.C.: U.S. GPO, 1993.

U.S. Department of the Interior, War Relocation Authority. *The Evacuated People: A Quantitative Description.* Washington, D.C.: U.S. GPO, 1946.

Vertovec, Steven. *Hindu Trinidad: Religion, Ethnicity and Social-Economic Change.* London: Macmillan, 1992.

Wain, Brian. *The Refused: The Agony of the Indochinese Refugees.* New York: Simon & Schuster, 1981.

Wallace, Ruth. "Bringing Women In: Marginality in the Churches." *Sociological Analysis* 36 (1975): 291–303.

Warner, Stephen. "Approaching Religious Diversity: Barriers, Byways, and Beginnings." *Sociology of Religion* 59 (1998): 193–215.

———. "Immigration and Religious Communities in the United States." In *Gatherings in Diaspora*, ed. Stephen Warner and Judith Wittner. Philadelphia: Temple University Press, 1998.

———. "The Korean Immigrant Church as a Case and Model." In *Pilgrims and Missionaries from a Different Shore*, ed. Ho-Youn Kwon, Kwang Chung Kim, and Stephen Warner. University Park: Pennsylvania State University Press, 2001.

———. "The Place of Congregation in the American Religious Configuration." In *American Congregations*. Vol.2, *New Perspectives in the Study of Congregations*, ed. James Wind and James Lewis. Chicago: University of Chicago Press, 1994.

———. "Work in Progress toward a New Paradigm for the Sociological Study of Religion in the United States." *American Journal of Sociology* 94 (1993): 1044–93.

Warner, Stephen, and Judith Wittner, eds. *Gatherings in Diaspora: Religious Communities and the New Immigration*. Philadelphia: Temple University Press, 1998.

Warner, W. L., and Leo Srole. *The Social System of American Ethnic Groups*. New Haven, Conn.: Yale University Press, 1945.

Warren, Rick. *The Purpose Driven Church*. Grand Rapids, Mich.: Zondervan, 1995.

Waters, Mary. *Ethnic Options: Choosing Identities in America*. Berkeley: University of California Press, 1990.

Waters, Mary, and Karl Eschbach. "Immigration and Ethnic and Racial Inequality in the United States." In *Majority and Minority: The Dynamics of Race and Ethnicity in American Life*, 6th ed., ed. Norman Yetman. Needham Heights, Mass.: Allyn & Bacon, 1999.

Weglyn, Michi. *Years of Infamy: The Untold Story of America's Concentration Camps*. New York: William Morrow, 1976.

Weiss, M. S. *Valley City: A Chinese Community in America*. Cambridge, Mass.: Shenkman, 1974.

Welch, Holmes. *The Buddhist Revival in China*. Cambridge, Mass.: Harvard University Press, 1968.

Wellmeier, Nancy. "Santa Euralia's People in Exile: Maya Religion, Culture, and Identity in Los Angeles." In *Gatherings in Diaspora*, ed. Stephen Warner and Judith Wittner. Philadelphia: Temple University Press, 1998.

Whittemore, Lewis Bliss. *Struggle for Freedom: History of the Philippine Independent Church*. Greenwich, Conn.: Seabury, 1961.

Wickberg, Edgar. "An Overseas Chinese Adaptive Organization, Past and Present." In *Reluctant Exiles? Migration from Hong Kong and the New Overseas Chinese*, ed. Ronald Skeldon. Armonk, N.Y.: M. E. Sharpe, 1994.

Williams, Raymond Brady. *Christian Pluralism in the United States: The Indian Immigrant Experience*. New York: Cambridge University Press, 1996.

———. *Religions of Immigrants from India and Pakistan: New Threads in the American Tapestry*. New York: Cambridge University Press, 1988.

Wilson, Robert. *The Church in the Radically Changing Community*. Nashville, Tenn.: Abingdon Press, 1966.

Wilson, William. *When Work Disappears: The World of the New Urban Poor*. New York: Knopf, 1996.

Wind, James, and James Lewis, eds. *American Congregations*. Chicago: University of Chicago Press, 1994.

Witter, Robert, William Stock, Morris Okun, and Marilyn Haring. "Religion and Subjective Well-Being in Adulthood: A Quantitative Synthesis." *Review of Religious Research* 26 (1985): 332–42.

Wong, Bernard. *Chinatown: Economic Adaptation and Ethnic Identity of the Chinese.* New York: Holt, Rinehart and Winston, 1982.

———. "Hong Kong Immigrants in San Francisco." In *Reluctant Exiles? Migration from Hong Kong and the New Overseas Chinese,* ed. Ronald Skeldon. Armonk, N.Y.: M. E. Sharpe, 1994.

Wong, Kevin Scott, and Sucheng Chen, eds. *Claiming America: Constructing Chinese American Identities during the Exclusion Era.* Philadelphia: Temple University Press, 1988.

Woo, Wesley S. "Chinese Protestants in the San Francisco Bay Area." In *Entry Denied,* ed. Sucheng Chan. Philadelphia: Temple University Press, 1991.

———. "Protestant Work among the Chinese in the San Francisco Area, 1850–1920." Unpublished Ph.D. diss., Graduate Theological Union, Berkeley, California, 1983.

Wuthnow, Robert. *After Heaven: Spirituality in America since the 1950s.* Berkeley: University of California Press, 1998.

———. *The Restructuring of American Religion: Society and Faith since World War II.* Princeton, N.J.: Princeton University Press, 1988.

Xenos, Peter, Herbert Barringer, and Michael Levin. *Asian Indians in the United States: A 1980 Census Profile No. 111.* Honolulu: East–West Population Institute, 1989.

Yanagawa, Keiichi, ed. *Japanese Religions in California.* Tokyo: Department of Religious Studies, University of Tokyo, 1983.

Yang, Fenggang. "ABC and XYZ: Religious, Ethnic and Racial Identities of the New Second Generation Chinese in Christian Churches." *Amerasia Journal* 25 (1999): 89– 114.

———. "Chinese American Religions." In *Encyclopedia of Contemporary American Religion,* ed. Wade Clark Roof. New York: Macmillan Reference, 2000.

———. *Chinese Christians in America: Conversion, Assimilation, and Adhesive Identities.* University Park: Pennsylvania State University Press, 1999.

———. "Chinese Conversion to Evangelical Christianity: The Importance of Social and Cultural Contexts." *Sociology of Religion* 59 (1998): 237–57.

———. "Chinese Gospel Church: The Sinicization of Christianity." In *Religion and the New Immigrants,* ed. Helen Rose Ebaugh and Janet Saltzman Chafetz. Walnut Creek, Calif.: AltaMira, 2000.

———. "Tenacious Unity in a Contentious Community: Cultural and Religious Dynamics in a Chinese Christian Church." In *Gatherings in Diaspora,* ed. Stephen Warner and Judith Wittner. Philadelphia: Temple University Press, 1998.

Yang, Fenggang, and Helen Rose Ebaugh. "Religion and Ethnicity among New Immigrants: The Impact of Majority/Minority Status in Home and Host Countries." *Journal for the Scientific Study of Religion* 41 (2001): 369–78.

Yoo, David. "For Those Who Have Eyes to See: Religious Sightings in Asian America." *Amerasia Journal* 22 (1996): xiii–xxii.

———. "Introduction: Reframing the U.S. Religious Landscape." In *New Spiritual Homes,* ed. David Yoo. Honolulu: University of Hawaii Press, 1999.

———, ed. *New Spiritual Homes: Religion and Asian Americans.* Honolulu: University of Hawaii Press, 1999.

Young, Kathrine. "Upholding Norms of Hindu Womenhood: An Analysis Based on Reviews of Hindi Cinema." In *Gender Genre and Religion: Feminist Reflections*, ed. Morny Joy and Eva K. Neumaier-Dargyay. Waterloo, Ontario: Wilfred Laurier University Press, 1999.

Yu, Eui-Young. "The Growth of Korean Buddhism in the United States, with Special Reference to Southern California." *Pacific World* 4 (1988): 82–93.

Yzendoorn, Reginald. *History of the Catholic Mission in the Hawaiian Islands.* Honolulu: Honolulu Star-Bulletin Limited, 1927.

Zafra, Nicolas. *Philippine History through Selected Sources.* Quezon City, Philippines: Alemar-Phoenix, 1967.

Zhou, Min, and Carl Bankston III. *Growing Up American: How Vietnamese Children Adapt to Life in the United States.* New York: Russell Sage Foundation, 1998.

Zhou, Min, and Yoshinori Kamo. "An Analysis of Earnings Patterns for Chinese, Japanese, and Non-Hispanic Whites in the United States." *Sociological Quarterly* 35 (1994): 581–602.

NAME INDEX

SUBJECT INDEX

ABOUT THE EDITORS AND CONTRIBUTORS

Carl L. Bankston III is associate professor of sociology at Tulane University. His areas of research include international migration, Asian American populations, sociology of education, and sociology of religion. He is co-author of *Growing Up American: How Vietnamese Children Adapt to Life in the United States* (with Min Zhou, 1998); and co-author of *A Troubled Dream: The Promise and Failure of School Desegregation in Louisiana* (with Stephen J. Caldas, forthcoming).

Russell Jeung is an assistant professor of sociology at Foothill College teaching race relations and social psychology. His Ph.D. dissertation from the University of California, Berkeley, examined the development of Asian American pan-ethnic congregations. Also a community activist, he has organized Cambodian and Latino tenants to win a landmark housing law case in Oakland, California, where he resides.

Jung Ha Kim was academically trained in religion, theology, and sociology and is a faculty member of the Department of Sociology at Georgia State University. She considers herself as an "organic intellectual" and is a community educator and organizer at the Center for Pan Asian Community Services. She has written many articles on Asian American women and the family, the reappropriation of Asian religions in the United States, and religious experiences of Korean American women. She is the author of *Bridge-makers and Cross-bearers: Korean American Women and the Church* (1996). Currently she is conducting a research on the status of racial-ethnic minority clergywomen in the United Methodist Church and writing a book about Korean/Asian American never-married women's experiences.

Rebecca Y. Kim is a Ph.D. candidate in sociology at the University of California, Los Angeles. Her research interests are in immigration, ethnicity, and religion. She has done work on the educational achievement and adaptation of Vietnamese and Cambodian children in the United States. She is currently working on her dissertation on Asian American evangelicals and their ethnic religious participation.

Prema Kurien is assistant professor of sociology at the University of Southern California. In the 2000–2001 year, she was a fellow at the Center for the Study of Religion, Princeton University. Her work focuses on the reformulation of religion and ethnicity by Indian immigrants of different religious backgrounds, both in India and the United States. She is currently working on two book manuscripts, *The Emergence of American Hinduism* and *From Minority to Majority: The Travails of an Asian Indian American Church*. In addition, she has published several journal articles and book chapters on Indian immigrants' religions, ethnicity, and gender role.

Pyong Gap Min is professor of sociology at Queens College and the Graduate Center of the City University of New York. He is the author of three books, including *Caught in the Middle: Korean Communities in New York and Los Angeles* (1996), the winner of two national book awards, and *Changes and Conflicts: Korean Immigrant Families in New York* (1998). He is the editor of *Asian Americans: Contemporary Trends and Issues* (1995) and *The Second Generation: Ethnic Identity among Asian Americans* (2002) and co-editor of *Struggle for Ethnic Identity: Narratives by Asian American Professionals* (with Rose Kim, 1999).

Steffi San Buenaventura is an ethnohistorian in the faculty of Asian American Studies at the University of California, Davis. She specializes in Filipino Studies and has published in the areas of immigration, religion and social movements, and Filipino American historical relations in the early twentieth century. She received a Ph.D. in American Studies from the University of Hawaii and a postdoctoral fellowship award from the Asian American Studies Center at UCLA. Since moving from Hawaii to California in the early 1990s, she has taught at UCLA, UC Irvine, and UC Riverside. She now teaches Asian American courses and Filipino American history at UC Davis.

Fenggang Yang received his Ph.D. from the Catholic University of America, did postdoctoral research at the University of Houston, and is assistant professor of sociology at the University of Southern Maine. His research has focused on new immigrant religions. He is the author of *Chinese Christians in America* (1999), chapters in various books, and articles in the *Journal for the Scientific Study of Religion, Sociology of Religion, Amerasia Journal, Journal of the Asian American Studies*, and *American Sociological Review.*

David Yoo is associate professor of history at Claremont McKenna College and chairman of the Intercollegiate Department of Asian American Studies at the Claremont Colleges. Since he received his Ph.D. from Yale University in 1994, he has done research mainly on Japanese and Korean American history. He is the author of *Growing Up Nisei* (2000) and the editor of *New Spiritual Homes: Religion and Asian Americans* (1999).

Min Zhou is professor of sociology and Asian American Studies at the University of California, Los Angeles. Her areas of research include immigration and immigrant adaptation, Asian Americans, race/ethnicity, entrepreneurship, and urban sociology. She is author of *Chinatown: The Socioeconomic Potential of an Urban Enclave* (1992), co-author of *Growing up American: How Vietnamese Children Adapt to Life in the United States* (with Carl L. Bankston III, 1998), and co-editor of *Contemporary Asian America* (with James V. Gatewood, 2000).